MODERN HUMANITIES RESEARCH ASSOCIATION

TUDOR & STUART TRANSLATIONS

VOLUME 10

General Editors
ANDREW HADFIELD
NEIL RHODES

JAMES MABBE

THE SPANISH BAWD

JAMES MABBE
THE SPANISH BAWD

Edited by

José María Pérez Fernández

MODERN HUMANITIES RESEARCH ASSOCIATION
2013

Published by
The Modern Humanities Research Association,
1 Carlton House Terrace
London SW1Y 5AF

© The Modern Humanities Research Association, 2013

José María Pérez Fernández has asserted his right under the Copyright, Designs and Patents Act 1988 to be identified as the author of this work.

All rights reserved. No part of this publication may be reproduced, stored in a retrieval system, or transmitted, in any form or by any means, electronic, mechanical, photocopying, recording or otherwise, without the prior permission of the publishers.

First published 2013

ISBN (hardback) 978–1–907322–09–9
ISBN (paperback) 978–1–78188–040–1

Copies may be ordered from www.tudor.mhra.org.uk

MHRA TUDOR AND STUART TRANSLATIONS

GENERAL EDITORS

Andrew Hadfield (University of Sussex)
Neil Rhodes (University of St Andrews)

ASSOCIATE EDITORS

Guyda Armstrong (University of Manchester)
Fred Schurink (University of Northumbria)
Louise Wilson (University of St Andrews)

ADVISORY BOARD

Warren Boutcher (Queen Mary, University of London); Colin Burrow (All Souls College, Oxford); A. E. B. Coldiron (Florida State University); José María Pérez Fernández (University of Granada); Robert S. Miola (Loyola College, Maryland); Alessandra Petrina (University of Padua); Anne Lake Prescott (Barnard College, Columbia University); Quentin Skinner (Queen Mary, London); Alan Stewart (Columbia University)

For details of published and forthcoming volumes please visit our website:

www.tudor.mhra.org.uk

TABLE OF CONTENTS

General Editors' Foreword viii

Acknowledgements ix

Introduction 1

THE SPANISH BAWD 67

Glossary 365

Bibliography 370

Index 396

GENERAL EDITORS' FOREWORD

The aim of the *MHRA Tudor & Stuart Translations* is to create a representative library of works translated into English during the early modern period for the use of scholars, students and the wider public. The series will include both substantial single works and selections of texts from major authors, with the emphasis being on the works that were most familiar to early modern readers. The texts themselves will be newly edited with substantial introductions, notes, and glossaries, and will be published both in print and online.

The series aims to restore to view a major part of English Renaissance literature which has become relatively inaccessible and to present these texts as literary works in their own right. For that reason it will follow the same principle of modernisation adopted by other scholarly editions of canonical literature from the period. The series will have a similar scope to that of the original *Tudor Translations* published early in the last century, and while the great majority of the works presented will be from the sixteenth century, like the original series it will not be rigidly bound by the end-date of 1603. There will, however, be a very different range of texts with new and substantial scholarly apparatus.

The *MHRA Tudor & Stuart Translations* will extend our understanding of the English Renaissance through its representation of the process of cultural transmission from the classical to the early modern world and the process of cultural exchange within the early modern world.

Andrew Hadfield
Neil Rhodes

ACKNOWLEDGEMENTS

There are a number of people and institutions that have been helpful in the completion of this volume. I would like to thank the general editors of the series, Andrew Hadfield and Neil Rhodes, for proposing the project in the first place. I would also like to thank: Edward Wilson-Lee of Sidney Sussex College, Elizabeth Drayson and Elsa Strietman of Murray Edwards College, and Louise Haywood of the Spanish and Portuguese Department, all of whom kindly extended their hospitality to me when I was visiting and research scholar at the University of Cambridge. Without their help I could not have completed the work required for the edition. Andrew Hadfield and Neil Rhodes also read a previous draft and made useful comments that improved the edition. Mandy Green saw me through the final stages of the edition: her careful, and attentive reading, and her valuable suggestions have made this a better book. I alone am of course responsible for any remaining errors. I will always remain grateful to my family for their patience, and for being there to dissipate the dry fumes of academia.

INTRODUCTION

Lo here thy Celestine, that wicked wight,[1]
Who did her tricks upon poor lovers prove;
And in her company, the god of Love.
Lo! Grace, beauty, desire, terror, hope, fright,
Faith, falsehood, hate, love, music, grief, delight,
Sighs, sobs, tears, cares, heats, colds, girdle, glove,
Paintings, Mercury Sublimate,[2] dung of Dove.
Prison, force, fury, craft, scoffs, Art, despite,
Bawds, Ruffians, Harlots, servants false, untrue:
And all th'effects that follow on the same:
As war, strife, loss, death, infamy, and shame.
All which and more, shall come unto thy view.
But if this Book speak not his English plaine,
Excuse him, for he lately came from Spain.[3]

This poem features as an afterword to the 1631 edition of *The Spanish Bawd*, James Mabbe's translation of *La Celestina* into English. The sonnet conveys the combination of moral disgust and fascination which this text had for decades elicited from its readers, and which had turned it into a *succès d'escandale* since it first appeared in late fifteenth-century Castile. Mabbe had translated this poem, which was never part of the Spanish original, from the Italian version by Alfonso Ordóñez, the first among many renderings of *La Celestina* into a foreign language. Published only seven years after its first known Spanish edition, Ordóñez's version of 1506 demonstrates that the fate of *La Celestina* was from the start linked to the processes of translation. Its Italian rendering is still today a fundamental piece of

---

[1] wight] A human being, a person (often implying commiseration, or as is the case here, contempt).
[2] Mercury Sublimate] Spanish 'solimán', a mercury-based cosmetic.
[3] *The Spanish bavvd, represented in Celestina: or, The tragicke-comedy of Calisto and Melibea: Wherein is contained, besides the pleasantnesse and sweetnesse of the stile, many philosophicall sentences, and profitable instructions necessary for the younger sort: shewing the deceits and subtilties housed in the bosomes of false seruants, and cunny-catching bawds* (London: Printed by I[ohn] B[eale] and are to be sold by Robert Allot at the signe of the Beare in Pauls Church-yard, 1631), STC (2nd edn.) 4911. This is the text used for this edition.

evidence in the complex puzzle that is the history of the textual transmission of the Spanish original, and it was also used by many other European translators to produce their own versions. An anonymous French translation first printed in 1527 went through more than ten editions until Jacques de Lavardin authored a new translation in 1578, which was to a considerable extent based on Ordóñez's Italian rendering; besides the Spanish original, Mabbe seems to have consulted both Ordóñez and Lavardin's texts.

'I will not much marvel,' said a prescient Rojas in his introduction to *La Celestina*, 'if this present work shall prove an instrument of war to its readers, putting strife and differences among them, every one giving his verdict and opinion thereupon, according to the humour of his own will' (Prologue, 105–9).[4] And, indeed, after all these years *La Celestina* has not lost its capacity to seduce and scandalize audiences. There are many testimonies of its modernity and continuing relevance. One of the most recent among them has been voiced by the Spanish novelist Juan Goytisolo in his introduction to Peter Bush's translation. Beyond the indisputable literary and historical importance of a unique text that prefigures the picaresque and *Don Quijote*, Goytisolo emphasizes the visionary quality that lies at the origins of Rojas's work: 'Five centuries after its first edition, *Celestina* portrays with disturbing lucidity and precision the fast-approaching universe of chaos and strife that we now endure.'[5] Only a few years before Peter Bush's version for Penguin Classics, John Clifford had also translated and adapted the text for a stage production at the 2004 Edinburgh Festival. This version was produced by Calixto Bieito, an internationally renowned *provocateur* who elicited enthusiastic reviews hand in hand with less favourably inclined opinions. Charles Spenser accused Bieito of inflicting 'grievous bodily harm on yet another helpless masterpiece of dramatic literature.' Ksenija Horvat by contrast described the production as 'Theatre at its best [. . .] gripping, passionate and merciless in its portrayal of the squirming humanity'. In a more academically detached review Dorothy

---

[4] References to *The Spanish Bawd* indicate section and line number (as in this case the prologue) or act and line numbers in the text of the present edition.

[5] Juan Goytisolo, 'Introduction, in Fernando de Rojas, *Celestina*, trans. by Peter Bush (Harmondsworth: Penguin, 2009), pp. vii–xvi (p. x).

INTRODUCTION

Sherman Severin acknowledged both the predictably scandalous production of Bieito and the fact that he did not have to go to great lengths in order to extract sordid and squalid readings from *La Celestina* since most of that material was already there in the first place.[6]

In an age like ours, when the threshold of tolerance for scandal among modern audiences has reached significantly low levels, and when the self-righteous indignation of *fundamentalistes sans frontiers* is frequently stirred up so that it can be turned to the advantage of the culture and entertainment industries, Bieito was at least using a text with an actual potential for non-gratuitous provocation. This is confirmed by the reactions that *La Celestina* elicited from day one of its publication. In the early years of the sixteenth century, Juan Luis Vives, while acknowledging its literary value, referred to it as a *liber pestifer*. Simón Borgoñón, the editor of a new edition published in 1570, reported how some priests in Salamanca refused to give the absolution to readers of *La Celestina*. In one of the opening poems of the first part of *Don Quijote*, Cervantes famously proclaimed that the art of *La Celestina* would be divine if it could have managed to conceal its raw humanity. And, as we have seen, Mabbe's translation of Ordóñez's Italian sonnet conveys what is probably the earliest documented international response to the text when it describes it as brimming over with 'warr, strife, losse, death, infamie, and shame'. *La Celestina* has lost none of its power to elicit catalogues of responses: when attempting to outline the nature of its atmosphere and its plot, readers cannot help listing the range of human passions given expression in this work. In his introduction to the 2011 edition published by the *Real Academia Española*, Francisco Rico praises the extraordinary capacity of the text to articulate in verisimilar and artistically accomplished prose a long list of

---

[6] For Charles Spenser's review ('Edinburgh reports: an arrogant ego-trip', *The Daily Telegraph*, 19 August 2004) see: <http://www.telegraph.co.uk/culture/theatre/drama/3622456/Edinburgh-reports-an-arrogant-ego-trip.html> (accessed on 29 September 2012). For Ksenija Horvat ('Celestina', EdinburghGuide.com, August 2004) see http://www.edinburghguide.com/festival/2004/eif/review.shtml?celestina (accessed on 29 September 2012). Severin's review can be found at <http://lists.umanitoba.ca/pipermail/la-celestina/2004-September/000110.html> (published by Enrique Fernández Sat Sep 18 20:12:44 CDT 2004, accessed on 29 September 2012).

human passions.[7] *Nihil novum sub sole* with Bieito's provocative production, then. But whether its scabrous and squalid aspects attract or repulse, the indisputable artistic merit of *La Celestina* must be actually held accountable for its position at the centre of the Hispanic canon, where it is second only to *Don Quijote*. Its living legacy has furthermore been sanctioned by that unequivocal indicator of cultural relevance: common Spanish usage has adopted the proper name of its protagonist, *Celestina*, to denote a person who acts as a go-between.

The purpose of this edition is to facilitate access to James Mabbe's 1631 translation in a modernized text that also provides a succinct account of how it was received in early modern England, and how both the original and its English translation relate to their respective cultural milieus. To this effect, this introduction will provide a series of snapshots that can first outline the origins and relevance of *La Celestina* within its own Castilian context, and then situate Mabbe and his version as part of intricate international networks of exchange.[8] These networks included cultural agents engaged in the establishment of vernacular canons through the appropriation of literary capital from classical antiquity and from other contemporary European traditions. As they did so, these emerging national traditions were also striving to homogenize their respective linguistic communities,

---

[7] The list is much longer, but it includes 'el egoísmo, la inconstancia, la avaricia, la capacidad de manipular, el cálculo, la ingenuidad, la suficiencia, el desprecio, los complejos, la envidia, el odio, la cautela, la impaciencia, la temeridad, el temor, la cobardía'. Francisco Rico, in Fernando de Rojas (y 'Antiguo Autor'), *La Celestina. Tragicomedia de Calisto y Melibea*, ed. by Francisco J. Lobera y Guillermo Serés, Paloma Díaz-Mas, Carlos Mota e Iñigo Ruiz Arzálluz, y Francisco Rico (Barcelona: Crítica, 2000; 2nd edn, Madrid: Real Academia Española, 2011), pp. ix-x.

[8] The existing scholarship on *La Celestina* is enormous, and does not cease to grow. Those readers interested in further details should consult the second edition (2011, see previous note) of *La Celestina* edited by Francisco J. Lobera *et al*. Hand in hand with a veritable trove of notes on the text with information about, *inter alia*, its textual history, variations, and sources, this volume provides extensive surveys of the most relevant topics around Rojas and his work ('Estudios y anexos', pp. 355–560). It also lists — in more than one hundred pages of small print — the secondary literature published so far (pp. 959–1061). I shall use the 2000 edition of this volume for quotations from the original Spanish text of *La Celestina*, and will also refer to its 2011 edition when necessary.

INTRODUCTION

with a view to the creation of a commonwealth of speakers that could be used for the establishment of a comprehensive polity upon a common body of laws and social norms. These complex processes involved, *inter alia*, foreign language instruction and grammatical standardization, as well as a rearrangement of the international cartographies of languages and disciplines through lexicography and encyclopedism. This was an age where the production of all sorts of translations, dictionaries and early encyclopedias flourished thanks to the development of print and the expansion of a transnational book trade.[9] All of this took place within an international context rife with political and religious controversies, where exile, war or diplomacy provided excellent opportunities for the exchange and appropriation of all sorts of capitals and goods, both tangible and intangible, and where the development of print had facilitated the production of chapbooks, pamphlets, and corantos — those early modern newsletters which reported events from abroad as much as they intensified controversies at home. An unsettling sensation of swift change through a ceaseless process of destruction and creation, an exciting perception of the new, pervade the period. The sophisticated and vigorous thematization of this atmosphere is one of the most remarkable literary skills displayed by Rojas, which then Mabbe deftly conveyed for his English readers at a time when London had already grown into an international metropolis engulfed in identical processes of change and exchange.

The Spanish Bawd appeared in London just eight years after the publication of Shakespeare's *First Folio*, a literary milestone to which Mabbe contributed with a poem: few translators have enjoyed the privilege of being simultaneously involved in such central icons within the two canons with which they were working. James Mabbe was indeed an exceptional agent of cultural exchange who displayed a unique critical acumen in his choice of texts, many of them produced by foundational authors in the Spanish canon of prose fiction: Fernando de Rojas, Mateo

---

[9] For details on some of these European networks, and how they relate to new developments in translation, the book trade, diplomacy and early modern encyclopedism, see José María Pérez Fernández, 'Andrés Laguna: Translation and the Early Modern Idea of Europe', *Translation and Literature*, 21 (2012), 299–318.

Alemán, and Miguel de Cervantes. Immediate editorial success and controversy, as much as literary quality and novelty, all come together in the production of these three writers, whose volumes soon started to circulate in translation.

A translator is a privileged reader with the power to weave a critical response into his text: *La Celestina* and *The Spanish Bawd* consequently illuminate each other, and an examination of their respective milieus will provide a fresh approach to the formation of the early modern European canon. Few texts are as seminal as *La Celestina* when it comes to the creation of early modern networks of literary and cultural exchange. When it appeared in the last decade of the fifteenth century, Fernando de Rojas's *Comedia de Calisto y Melibea* became an immediate domestic and international success. Between 1499 and 1644, printing houses in Spain, Italy, France, the Low Countries and Portugal issued nearly ninety Spanish editions of the work, and it also spawned a series of sequels which grew into the bestselling subgenre of *Celestinesca*.[10] In the century and a half that witnessed its heyday as a domestic and European bestseller, *La Celestina* was translated into Italian, German, French, Dutch, English, Latin and Hebrew. The Italian translation was an editorial success in its own day and, as we saw, is still relevant today for the analysis of the textual transmission of its Spanish original. It was first printed in Rome (1506), followed by two editions in Milan (1514, 1515), and another two in Venice (1515, 1519). The young student Christoph Wirsung read this version during a stay in Italy, which he then translated into his native German in two different versions (1520, 1534). As we have seen the first French translation was issued in 1527. Subsequent translations of *La Celestina* into other languages also used one or several of these early translations in parallel with the Spanish original. Its Dutch

---

[10] For a recent account of the origins and development of *Celestinesca*, see Consolación Baranda Leturio & Ana María Vian Herrero, 'El nacimiento del 'género' celestinesco: historia y perspectivas', in *Orígenes de la novela: Estudios*, ed. by Raquel Gutiérrez Sebastián & Borja Rodríguez Gutiérrez (Santander: Servicio de Publicaciones de la Universidad de Cantabria & Sociedad Menéndez Pelayo, 2007), pp. 407–82. Roberto González Echevarría's *Celestina's Brood: Continuities of the Baroque in Spanish and Latin American Literature* (Durham and London: Duke University Press, 1993) has provided a now classic account of *La Celestina* and its legacy in the world of Hispanic literatures.

translation was issued in Antwerp in 1550, and it was also rendered into Latin in 1624. The fame of *Celestina* in Europe became immediately associated with the hermeneutic processes of translation and the development of print, which facilitated the international circulation of the work for an enormous variety of readers in different linguistic communities. James Mabbe and his milieu constitute excellent case studies that illustrate the nature and the strategies of these early modern networks.[11]

∽

Mabbe has been described as the first English Hispanist,[12] and certainly the fact that the same scholar undertook the translation of texts as relevant as *La Celestina*, *Guzmán de Alfarache*, or the *Novelas Ejemplares*, gives his production an unprecedented dimension, especially if we take into account not just Cervantes's position in the international canon, but also the influence that the Spanish picaresque would exert on the subsequent development of the English novel during the eighteenth century. Mabbe´s most popular and prestigious translation is *The Rogue*, the influential

---

[11] Keith Whinnom has described the status of *La Celestina* as a bestseller among other successful Spanish Golden Age volumes; see 'The problem of the 'bestseller' in Spanish Golden-Age Literature', *Bulletin of Hispanic Studies*, 57 (1980), 189–98. Further details can be found in Guillermo Serés's survey, 'Fortuna editorial' in Lobera *et al.*, eds (2000), pp. lxxxviii–lxxxix. On the now lost Hebrew translation, see D. W. McPheeters's 'Una traducción hebrea de *La Celestina* en el siglo XVI', in *Homenaje a Rodríguez-Moñino. Estudios de erudición que le ofrecen sus amigos o discípulos hispanistas norteamericanos* (Madrid: Castalia, 1966), I, pp. 399–411; see also Michelle M. Hamilton, 'Joseph ben Samuel Ṣarfati's 'Tratado de Melibea y Calisto': A Sephardic Jew's Reading of the *Celestina* in Light of the Medieval Judeo-Spanish Go-between Tradition', *Sefarad* 62 (2002), 329–347. Joseph T. Snow has published a series of three long articles which trace the reception of *La Celestina* between its publication and the early nineteenth century: 'Hacia una historia de la recepción de *La Celestina*: 1499–1822', *Celestinesca* 21 (1997), 115–72; 'Historia de la recepción de *La Celestina*: 1499–1822, II', *Celestinesca* 25 (2001), 199–282; 'Historia de la recepción de *La Celestina*: 1499–1822, III', *Celestinesca* 26 (2002), 53–121. See the bibliography at the end of this volume for a list of modern editions of early translations of *La Celestina*.
[12] P. E. Russell, 'A Stuart Hispanist: James Mabbe', *Bulletin of Hispanic Studies*, 30 (1953), 75–84 (p. 76); see also J. R. Yamamoto-Wilson, 'Mabbe's Maybes: A Stuart Hispanist in Context', *Translation and Literature*, 21 (2012), 3.19–42.

first rendering into English of Mateo Aleman's *Guzmán de Alfarache*, the two parts of which originally appeared, respectively, in Madrid (1599) and Lisbon (1604). Published in 1622 by Edward Blount in a lavish edition, *The Rogue* was reprinted on several occasions.[13] This was also Mabbe's first published translation, followed in 1629 by *Devout Contemplations*, his rendering of a popular collection of sermons authored by Fray Cristóbal de Fonseca (*Discurso para Todos los Evangelios de la Cuaresma*, Madrid 1614).[14] Next came *The Spanish Bawd* in 1631, and only one year later Mabbe also translated Fray Juan de Santa Maria's *República y policía cristiana para reyes y príncipes* (Madrid, 1615), published as *Christian Policie: or, The Christian Commonwealth* (London, 1632).[15] Mabbe's last published translation was a partial rendering of Cervantes's *Novelas ejemplares* (Madrid, 1613), which appeared in London as *Exemplarie Novels; in Sixe Books* in 1640.

Mabbe's early work included a now lost treatise called *The Dyet of Healthe* (1598). He wrote occasional poetry in Latin and Italian, and contributed with an anagram to John Florio's dictionary, *Queen Anna's New World of Words*, published by Edward Blount in 1611. It was also Blount who entrusted Mabbe with the composition of a poem for the preface of Shakespeare's

---

[13] On *The Rogue*, and the picaresque in general, and its relation to the English novel, see Michael McKeon, *The Origins of the English Novel. 1600–1740* (Baltimore & London: The Johns Hopkins University Press, 2002), pp. 96–100. See also J. R. Yamamoto-Wilson, 'James Mabbe's Achievement in his Translation of *Guzmán de Alfarache*', *Translation and Literature*, 8 (1999), 137–156, and Gustav Ungerer's excellent account of the phenomenon of *gusmanry* in his 'English Criminal Biography and Guzmán de Alfarache's Fall from Rogue to Highwayman, Pander and Astrologer', *Bulletin of Hispanic Studies* 76 (1999), 189–197.

[14] Fonseca is one of the candidates for the authorship of the apocryphal second part of *Don Quijote*, the so-called *Quijote de Avellaneda*.

[15] For more detailed information on the editorial avatars of this work, which ended up with the title *Policie Vnveiled, Or Maximes of State* in its fifth, 1650 edition (and which, in spite of being an originally Catholic volume continued to be popular under Cromwell's rule), see James Mabbe, trans., [Fernando de Rojas's] *Celestine or the Tragick-Comedie of Calisto and Melibea* [the Alnwick manuscript], ed. by Guadalupe Martínez Lacalle (London: Tamesis Books, 1972), p. 20. During his final years Mabbe appears to have been working on another translation (*Medicina Hispánica*), which was unfinished at the time of his death: see Yamamoto-Wilson (2012), p. 325, n. 27.

First Folio.¹⁶ His connection with Blount places Mabbe within the literary circles of early seventeenth-century London, which included authors, publishers, scholars and translators with a keen interest in other European vernacular literatures. Ben Jonson famously composed a poem in praise of Mabbe and his *Rogue* for Blount's 1622 edition.¹⁷ Trained as a printer under William Ponsonby, another notorious cultural and literary agent, Blount also published Florio's translation of Montaigne's *Essays*, and Shelton's Englishing of *Don Quijote*.

If these London circles linked Mabbe with literary and publishing networks, Magdalen College in Oxford connected him with another interesting group of linguists, translators and diplomats. Mabbe was from his youth attached to Magdalen, where he matriculated at the age of sixteen in 1588. He became a permanent fellow in 1594, and remained attached to it for the rest of his life. One of these Magdalen linguists was Charles Butler (1560–1647), who obtained his MA in 1587 — just one year before Mabbe matriculated for the first time as an undergraduate

---

¹⁶ On Mabbe, Blount and the First Folio, see A. W. Secord, 'I. M. of the first folio Shakespeare and other Mabbe problems', *Journal of English and Germanic Philology*, 47 (1948), 374–81, (p. 378); see also Gary Taylor's 'The cultural politics of Maybe', in *Theatre and Religion: Lancastrian Shakespeare*, ed. by R. Dutton, A.G. Findlay & R. Wilson (Manchester, UK: Manchester University Press, 2003), pp. 242–258; Taylor has opened up new paths for research on Mabbe and his situation within the political and religious controversies of these years. A more recent account of Mabbe's literary associates, and his possible connection with Shakespeare, can be found in Yamamoto-Wilson (2012). For more information on Edward Blount, see Leah Scragg, 'Edward Blount and the History of Lylian Criticism', *Review of English Studies*, 46 (1995), 1–10, and also 'Edward Blount and the Prefatory Material to the First Folio of Shakespeare, *Bulletin of the John Rylands University Library of Manchester*, 79 (1997), 117–26.

¹⁷ Barbara Fuchs addresses the tropes of imperial appropriation and piracy used to describe translation in this poem in 'Pirating Spain: Jonson's Commendatory Poetry and the Translation of Empire', *Modern Philology*, 99 (2002), 341–356. Recent surveys of Anglo-Spanish political and cultural relations which can be used to contextualize Mabbe and his world during this period include Alexander Samson's '1623 and the politics of translation', in *The Spanish Match: Prince Charles's Journey to Madrid*, ed. by Alexander Samson (London: Ashgate, 2006) pp. 91–106, and also by Samson, '"A Fine Romance": Anglo-Spanish Relations in the Sixteenth Century', *Journal of Medieval and Early Modern Studies*, 39 (2009), 65–94 (the latter was part of a special issue of the *Journal of Medieval and Early Modern Studies* devoted to the subject, under the general title *Intricate Alliances: Early Modern Spain and England*).

in 1588. Since it was usual for senior students to lecture the younger members of their college, Mabbe may have studied under Butler, whose most successful publication was a handbook entitled *Rhetoricae libri duo*. First published in 1597, it went through seven editions, and was published again in 1629 in the same volume with Butler's new *Oratoriae libri duo*. Victor W. Cook has described Butler's *Rhetorica* as 'a pared-down version of the *Rhetorica* of Talaeus [. . .] a colleague of and collaborator with Ramus'.[18] Mabbe appears in the volume as the author of a blurb of sorts, praising Butler's handbook through a quotation that he culls from another contemporary manual, John Brinsley's *Ludus Literarius: or, The Grammar Schole* (1612).[19] Butler's interest in Ramus and Talaeus, and the fact that his *Rhetoricae libri duo* became a popular textbook — which contributed to spreading the ideas of Petrus Ramus in a non-controversial manner — illustrate the background of Mabbe's linguistic and rhetorical education in Oxford.[20] Butler also proposed a spelling reform with his *English grammar, or, The institution of letters, syllables, and words in the English tongue, whereunto is annexed an index of words like and unlike* (1633, with a second edition only one year later). This situates him within a well-established European tradition of scholars who sought to homogenize spelling and language use in their respective vernaculars — about which more below.

---

[18] Butler 'was highly instrumental in spreading the ideas of Pierre de la Ramée and Ramus's collaborator, Talaeus, in Britain by means of his preparatory texbooks.' (Victor W. Cook, 'Charles Butler (ca. 1560–29 March 1647)', in *British Rhetoricians and Logicians, 1500, 1660. Dictionary of Literary Biography*. First series, vol. ccxxxvi, ed. by Edward A. Malone. (London: Buccoli Clark Layman, 2001), pp. 81–90 (pp. 81–2).

[19] Mabbe appears to have come on board first as the author of the blurb in the 1618 edition of Butler's handbook, and then again at least in two subsequent editions (1621, 1629). Mabbe quotes Brinsley as declaring that: 'In stead of Talaeus, you may use Mr Butlers Rhetoricke of Magdalens in Oxford; being far more easie to bee learned of Schollars, and also supplying very many things wanting in Talaeus: yea the use and benefit will be found to be farre aboue all, that euer haue beene written to the same'. The edition cited is *Rhetoricae libri duo* (London: William Stanby, 1621), [A3ᵛ].

[20] For some more details on the sort of linguistic and rhetorical education that was at the time provided in Oxford, see J. M. Fletcher's 'The Faculty of Arts', in *The History of the University of Oxford* (gen. ed., T. H. Aston), *The Collegiate University*, ed. J. McConica (Oxford: Clarendon Press, 1986), III, pp. 157–98 (pp. 174–75, *et passim*).

INTRODUCTION

Part of Mabbe's Magdalen background was the legacy of another scholar from a previous generation. Laurence Humphrey (1527–1589) spent some years abroad as one of the Marian exiles in Basel, and translated three dialogues attributed to Origen which were published in 1571 by Oporinus as part of his edition of *Origensis opera*. He also produced a volume on the reading and interpretation of Greek literature, with a focus on Homer, the *Epistola de Graecis litteris et Homeri lectione et imitatione* (Basel: Oporinus, 1558). According to Andrew Taylor, Humphrey's 'recondite synthesis of classical and biblical wisdom' served to legitimize a certain branch of early modern political thought: his translation of Philo's *De nobilitate* influenced Sir Thomas Smith's *De republica anglorum*. But Humphrey is of particular interest to us as the author of an exceptional treatise on translation, the *Interpretatio linguarum: seu de ratione convertendi et explicandi autores tam sacros quam prophanos* (Basel, 1559), whose third book amounts to a proposal for an early modern canon of eminent English translators.[21] Humphrey returned to Oxford in 1560, where he succeeded Peter Martyr as the Regius chair in divinity, and was elected president of Magdalen College (1561). Although they belonged to different generations, Humphrey and Mabbe shared an interest in translation, political theory and religious doctrine.

Diplomatic activity facilitated Mabbe's first documented contact with Spain, which he visited in 1611 as member of an English legation led by Sir John Digby (1580–1653). Ambassador Digby, later first Earl of Bristol, was also a fellow of Magdalen. He would become a diplomatic and political agent of the first order in the controversial years leading to the Civil War. As a member of the Dorset aristocracy, Digby also appears closely associated with Sir John Strangways, who was the dedicatee of several of Mabbe's translations. We know next to nothing about Mabbe's activities in Spain, except for the fact that through the mediation of Leonard Digges he sent to Oxford a copy of the 1613 edition of Lope de Vega's *Rimas* for their common friend

---

[21] See Andrew W. Taylor, 'Humanist Philology and Reformation Controversy: John Christopherson's Latin Translations of Philo Judaeus and Eusebius of Caesarea', in *Tudor Translation*, ed. by F. Schurink (London: Palgrave, 2011), pp. 79–100 (pp. 85–87, *et passim*) for further details on Humphrey's connections.

Will Baker.[22] Sixteen years younger than Mabbe, Leonard Digges (1588–1635) was a well travelled and internationally educated scholar with important Spanish connections. A translator too, Digges rendered Gonzalo de Céspedes y Meneses' *Poema trágico del español Gerardo, y desengaño del amor lascivo* into English as *Gerardo the Vnfortunate Spaniard, Or a Patterne for lasciuious louers*, published by Edward Blount in 1622. Like Mabbe, Digges composed a poem for Shakespeare's *First Folio* of 1623. John Sanford was another Magdalen fellow who travelled with Mabbe on Digby's diplomatic mission to Madrid in 1611. That very year Sanford also published a short handbook entitled *Propylaion, or An entrance to the Spanish tongue* — copies of which he distributed among the members of the embassy. Sanford became famous as a neo-Latin poet, translated unmistakably Catholic works, and produced other practical dictionaries, grammars, and phrase-books, in French, Latin and Italian.[23]

Mabbe's presence in Digby's embassy must have acquainted him with the networks of international diplomacy, and the political situation at the Spanish court; also with the busy world of letters in Madrid, its *corrales de comedias*, and its literary associations, such as the *Academia de Madrid*, where the popular and controversial Lope de Vega had read his *Arte nuevo de hacer comedias* around 1607–1608.[24] His education in rhetoric, his acquaintance with modern languages both in Oxford and London, and with the tradition of sixteenth-century English translations and translators listed by Humphrey in book III of his *Interpretatio* must have spurred Mabbe's interest in these disciplines. And although there is no doubt that his involvement

---

[22] Martínez Lacalle ed., p. 9. This edition of Lope's *Rimas* also included his recent and controversial *Arte nuevo de hacer comedias*. For Mabbe's manifold affairs during these years, see José María Pérez Fernández, 'Translation, Diplomacy and Espionage: New Insights into James Mabbe's Career' (forthcoming in *Translation and Literature*).

[23] John W. Stoye, *English Travellers Abroad, 1604–1667*, 2nd edn (New Haven & London: Yale University Press, 1989), p. 254, and 'John Sanford', *DNB*, C. Fell-Smith, rev. by E. Haresnape.

[24] For the sort of urban literary scene that Mabbe found in Madrid see José María Díez Borque, *Sociedad y teatro en la España de Lope de Vega* (Barcelona: Bosch, 1978) and Enrique García Santo-Tomás, *Espacio urbano y creación literaria en el Madrid de Felipe IV* (Frankfurt & Madrid: Vervuet & Iberoamericana, 2004).

in diplomacy must have facilitated his contact with literary circles in Madrid, his interest in Spanish literature certainly predates his presence in the country as a member of Digby's embassy in 1611. For Mabbe's first documented translation is a manuscript rendering of *La Celestina* that dates from the very early years of the seventeenth century.

This manuscript, now in the archives of the Duke of Northumberland at Alnwick Castle, preceded the printed version of *The Spanish Bawd* and remained unpublished until the edition of Guadalupe Martínez Lacalle (1972), who dates it *c.* 1603–1611.[25] Mabbe dedicated the manuscript '*To the rig[h]t worthie and my most honored frende I[ohn] St[rangeways] Esqr*'. Martínez Lacalle uses this evidence to establish 1611 as the *terminus ante quem* for her dating of the manuscript, since that year Strangways had just matriculated at the Middle Temple, and in the records there he is listed as a knight. However, more recent information provided by Thomas G. Olsen in his edition of John Strangway's commonplace book establishes that the dedicatee of Mabbe's manuscript had been knighted already by June 1608, and consequently this could constitute the new *terminus ante quem*.[26] Martínez Lacalle establishes the *terminus post quem* in 1603 based on Mabbe's sonnet at the end of the manuscript, which he dedicates '*To the Right worshippfull and right worthie Knight G[eorge] Tr[enchard] the Younger*', knighted in June 1603. However, in his epistle dedicatory Mabbe refers to John Strangways's brother, Nicholas, as if he were still alive. And Martínez Lacalle mentions that a 1602 volume with an anonymous translation of Giovanni Botero's *Obseruations vpon the liues of Alexander, Caesar, Scipio. Newly Englished* (STC (2nd ed.) 3397) was dedicated to Nicholas Strangways, Squire — and addresses him, again, as if he were still alive. Both references, Mabbe's and that of the anonymous translator of Botero's text, coincide in praising Nicholas Strangways's skill in languages — in this case, Spanish and Italian. Mabbe actually describes him in his introduction to the manuscript as a mentor of sorts, to

---

[25] Martínez Lacalle, ed., p. 34.
[26] *The Commonplace Book of Sir John Strangways (1645–1666)*, ed. by Thomas G. Olsen (Tempe, AZ: Arizona Center for Medieval and Renaissance Studies & Renaissance English Text Society, 2004), p. 33. Olsen also describes Strangways as a sophisticated and highly educated reader, knowledgeable in ancient Latin authors, legal literature and political theory (*ibid.*).

whose authority and skills in Spanish he entrusts the emendation of his errors in the translation. According to Olsen (2004, p. 2), by 1603 'Strangways had already inherited a considerable part of the family estate (his elder brother dying of the plague)'. This would mean that the Alnwick manuscript could be dated somewhat more precisely to 1602–1603. Or it could also be the case that the dedicatory epistle was composed earlier, and that the dedication of the final sonnet to Trenchard was composed after 1603, when he had already been knighted.[27] Whatever the case, this new information narrows down the dating of the manuscript, and above all it confirms that Mabbe's activities as a translator of Spanish literature had started well before his trip to Madrid in 1611.

There is also an entry in the Stationers' Register on 5 October 1598 that reads: 'Wm aspley Entred for his copie vnder the handes. of Mr Samuell Harsnett, and both the wardens, a booke intituled. *The tragick Comedye of Celestina. / wherein are discoursed in most pleasant stile manye Philosophicall sentences and advertisementes verye necessarye for Younge gentlemen Discoveringe the sleightes of treacherous servantes and the subtile cariages of filthye bawdes*'. The similarities between this item and the Spanish title of the 1501 Sevillian edition of *La Celestina* (*Comedia de Calisto y Melibea — la qual contiene además de su agradable y dulce estilo muchas sentencias filosofales e avisos muy necesarios para mancebos, mostrandoles los engaños que están encerrados en sirvientes y alcahuetas*) suggest that this 1598 volume could be a translation.[28] Although the Alnwick manuscript has many features in common with the 1631 edition of the *Spanish Bawd*, Martínez Lacalle holds that it cannot be its direct source 'since the latter is a complete, though revised, version and the earlier manuscript is incomplete and altogether more

---

[27] Olsen, ed. (2004), pp. 2–3.
[28] Dorothy Sherman Severin suggests that this text corresponds to the Alnwick manuscript, which she dates *c.* 1598 too: 'In the year 1631 James Mabbe [. . .] published in London his translation of *The Spanish Bawd* [. . .] It was his second translation of the work. His first of *ca.* 1598 exists only in a single manuscript', i.e. the Alnwick Manuscript; see Fernando de Rojas, *Celestina*, ed. by Dorothy Sherman Severin, with the translation of James Mabbe [1631] (Warminster: Aris & Phillips, 1987), p. xiv. See also Dale B. J. Randall, *The Golden Tapestry: A Critical Survey of Non-chivalric Fiction in English Translation* (Durham, NC: Duke University Press, 1963), p. 169; Martínez Lacalle (ed.), p. 6.

literal'.²⁹ She concludes that the Alnwick manuscript and *The Spanish Bawd* derive from a different common source, which she suggests might be this book registered by William Aspley in 1598. Whatever the case, it is true — as some of the footnotes in my edition illustrate — that the Alnwick manuscript was a more literal rendering than the printed version, in particular as regards sexually explicit sections, the impact of which the 1631 edition strives to tone down or eliminate. Mabbe naturally appeared as a much bolder translator in his early years in a manuscript meant for private circulation than he did about three decades later, when he finally decided to publish his translation.

There has also been some speculation as to which of the Spanish editions Mabbe may have used.³⁰ After a careful survey of the data on this subject, Patrizia Botta and Elizabetta Vaccaro focus on a Plantinian edition published in Antwerp in 1599. A copy of this particular edition, now in the *Biblioteca Nacional* in Madrid, contains manuscript annotations in early modern English which Botta and Vaccaro claim are in Mabbe's hand.³¹ Botta establishes an interesting genealogy between the Alnwick manuscript, the annotations in the Plantinian 1599 edition, and the printed translation of 1631. She also suggests the existence of a now lost second manuscript, between the Alnwick text and the

---

²⁹ Martínez Lacalle (ed.), pp. 45, 52.

³⁰ For more information and details on the sources of Mabbe's translation see *Celestina, or the Tragicke-Comedy of Calisto and Melibea. Englished from the Spanish of Fernando de Rojas by James Mabbe, anno. 1631*, ed. by James Fitzmaurice-Kelly (London: David Nutt, 1894), p. xxxiv; also *Celestina, or the Tragi-Comedy of Calisto and Melibea*, ed. by H. W. Allen (London: George Routledge and Sons, 1908), pp. lxxxiii-lxxxiv; Russell 1953, pp. 81–82; Randall, 1963, p. 171, n. 22; Martínez Lacalle (1972), p. 24.

³¹ See Patrizia Botta and Elizabetta Vaccaro, 'Un esemplare annotato della *Celestina* e la traduzione inglese di Mabbe', *Cultura Neolatina*, 52 (1992), 353–419 (pp. 357, 365). They list the similarities between Mabbe's text and the Plantinian editions in pp. 365–369 of their article; see also pp. 370–373. For further details on published secondary literature on Mabbe's sources, and above all for a great wealth of detailed information about the 1599 Plantinian edition as the text used and annotated by Mabbe for his translation, see the online material provided by Elizabetta Vaccaro at <http://rmcisadu.let.uni roma1.it/celestina/traduzioni_ing/mabbe/> (accessed on 23 September 2012). This includes a transcription of the annotations in this particular copy, and a detailed table that compares the Spanish original in the Plantinian text, its English annotations, and the corresponding texts in the two existing versions of Mabbe's translation, i.e. the Alnwick manuscript and the 1631 edition.

printed edition of 1631.[32] The Alnwick manuscript also records Mabbe's response to certain aspects of the plot through his own notes in the margins. These normally take the form of moralizing reproaches to the most controversial developments of the story, such as Celestina's deceitfully persuasive manipulation of Scripture, or Calisto's heretical remarks about Melibea as his only goddess.[33] In general, the 1631 edition is more cautious about these potentially controversial aspects of *La Celestina*. The Alnwick manuscript is also considerably shorter than the 1631 *Spanish Bawd*. Martínez Lacalle attributed the numerous omissions and its shortened format to its possible use as the script for a staged performance, or perhaps for a public reading. The title of the Alnwick manuscript, *Celestine or the Tragick-Comedie of Calisto and Melibea*, is also significantly closer to the original title of Rojas's work. In the light of all this information, it is rather revealing that, after almost three decades in the making, and subsequent to all these textual avatars, Mabbe could finally proclaim, in his introduction to the 1631 edition, that *La Celestina* had been 'put into English cloathes' as *The Spanish Bawd*.

Unlike *The Rogue*, and in spite of its remarkable prose, *The Spanish Bawd* was not a publishing success. In an attempt to market them more easily, its unsold copies were bound with the second edition of *The Rogue* in 1634. And it would not be reprinted again until 1894 in James Fitzmaurice-Kelly's edition, as part of the first Tudor Translations series. In this eclipse of more than two centuries, the fortunes of *The Spanish Bawd* in print ran parallel to those of the original *Celestina*, which disappeared from view around the middle of the seventeenth century, when it was first censured (twice, in 1640 and 1667) and then explicitly banned by the Spanish Inquisition a century later (1773). It did not regain the place it now enjoys in the Spanish canon until the last decade of the nineteenth and the early years

---

[32] Botta and Vaccaro (1992), pp. 375–377, pp. 382–84.

[33] Calisto's adoration of Melibea was among the most scandalous parts of *La Celestina*, which earned unanimous condemnation by all its translators and commentators: Cristóbal de Fonseca, whose *Discurso para Todos los Evangelios de la Cuaresma* Mabbe translated in 1629, also condemned this part of *La Celestina*. For details on this and other readerly reactions to *La Celestina*, see Maxime Chevalier 'La Celestina según sus lectores', in *Estudios sobre 'La Celestina'*, ed. by Santiago López Ríos (Madrid: Istmo, 2001), pp. 601–621.

of the twentieth centuries. After Fitzmaurice-Kelly's edition, Mabbe's text has been reprinted on several occasions. The most recent is D.S. Severin's useful bilingual edition (Warminster: Aris & Phillips, 1987, rpt. 1992), which synthetically records the variations between the Alnwick Manuscript and the 1631 edition, as well as Mabbe's additions and omissions with respect to the original. My edition stands on the shoulders of all these scholars, and follows the new paths that they opened up in *Celestina* and Mabbe studies.[34]

∽

The missing pages in the only remaining copy of the first known edition of *La Celestina* (Burgos, 1499) have left us with 16 acts without a title. A new edition, now entitled *Comedia de Calisto y Melibea*, appeared first in Toledo (1500) and then Seville (1501). This edition already contained prefatory material that was missing in the Burgos volume: a *Carta del auctor a un su amigo* ('A letter from the author to a friend of his'), some verses entitled *Coplas: el autor excusándose*, and a final poem by the humanist Alonso de Proaza.[35] A few years later Proaza also supervised a new edition (Valencia, 1514) that included significant changes: it added five more acts to the sixteen of the earlier editions and changed its title from *Comedia* to *Tragicomedia de Calisto y Melibea*. The new edition also sought to smooth off the rough edges of the plot in the first version, for instance, in the sexually explicit scene leading to Calisto's death. Circumstantial evidence also suggests the publication of a now missing edition between the 1501 Seville edition and the 1514 Valencia edition: Ordóñez's

---

[34] In 1954 and 1969 Mabbe's rendering was used for a BBC adaptation of Rojas's work, and also for a performance in London in 1958 (for further details, and other versions dating from these decades, see Martínez Lacalle, ed., p. 2 n. 3) Literature Online (Chadwyck-Healey, 1997) has published an electronic transcription of the 1631 edition. (See the bibliography at the end of this volume for further details, and other modern editions.)

[35] For a brief survey of the latest developments on the controversial issue of the first version of *La Celestina*, see Snow (2008), p. 293; see also the sections included among the 'Estudios y anexos' in Lobera *et al.*, eds (2011). There is a recent edition of the sixteen-act version, i.e. the *Comedia de Calisto y Melibea* ed. by José Luis Canet Vallés (Valencia: Publicaciones de la Universidad de Valencia, 2011).

Italian translation of *La Celestina* (Rome, 1506) was already entitled *Tragicocomedia*, and also featured the new five acts which were absent in the previous Burgos, Toledo and Seville editions. The different layers of paratexts, the changes in the text itself, the material evolution of these early editions, and the controversy that surrounded *La Celestina* over the course of the sixteenth and the first half of the seventeenth centuries, evince the variety of readerly and critical reactions that it provoked.

In the *Carta del auctor a un su amigo* Rojas claims to have chanced upon a previously existing first act penned by an unknown hand. Seeing that it was a profitable and enjoyable text, Rojas decided to continue the story himself, and added his own fifteen acts to complete the first version of the *Comedia*. Absent from the anonymous first 1499 edition, early reactions to the text might have moved the author and his editors to include this introductory letter in subsequent editions, together with a poem in which the author's name, Fernando de Rojas, appears in acrostics.[36] This poetic encryption of the author's identity betrays a reluctance on the part of Rojas to take responsibility for the text, as it also invites a closer reading beyond a merely literal interpretation. The need to delve deep into its different layers is one of the leitmotifs in the author's introductory letter. The other founding principle that features in its preface, immediately following the letter and the acrostic, is the Heraclitean *omnia secundum litem fiunt* principle, that is, the *strife* that Mabbe lists in his sonnet as one of *La Celestina's* main ingredients:

> It is the saying of that great and wise philosopher Heraclitus, that all things are created in manner of a contention or battle. His words are these: *omnia secundum litem fiunt*. A sentence in my opinion worthy perpetual memory, and, for that most certain it is, that every word of a wise man is pregnant and full, of this it may be said, that through too much fulness it is ready to burst, shooting forth such spreading and well-grown boughs and leaves that out of the smallest sucker or least sprig thereof,

---

[36] The question of the early Spanish editions of *La Celestina* constitutes a fascinating but intricate story, and to this day it continues to pose problems, many of which remain unsolved. For a recent survey see Rico and Lobera's 'El problema textual' in Lobera *et al.*, eds (2011), pp. 538–49.

fruit enough may be gathered by men of discretion and judgment. (Prologue, 1–10)

Rojas's brief experience with his recently published text appears to have made him prescient of how a text which was indeed 'ready to burst' from 'too much fulness', and which had been intricately woven from threads and 'well-grown boughs' culled from other authors, had the potential to 'shoot forth' abundant new branches and leaves once it had been set in circulation through the growing networks of reading communities facilitated by print and translation. Rojas's prologue evinces his awareness of a new communicative context dominated by the inexhaustible fluidity, change and spirit of competition that a tradition coming down from Heraclitus, Epicurus, Lucretius, and Petrarch had already identified as the creative drive behind all the forces of nature and human endeavours:

> This sentence did I find to be strengthened by that great orator and poet laureate Francisco Petrarca, who tells us, *sine lite atque offensione nihil genuit natura parens*: that nature, who is the mother of all things, engendered nothing without strife and contention. [. . .] The stars encounter one another in the whirling firmament of heaven, your contrary elements wage war each with other, the earth, that trembles and quakes as if it were at odds with itself, the sea, that swells and rages, breaking its billows one against another, the air, that darts arrows of lightning and is moved this way and that way, the flames, they crack and sparkle forth their fury, the winds are at perpetual enmity with themselves, times with times do contend, one thing against another, and all against us. (Prologue, 15–33)[37]

Like the cosmos, human societies are also continually engaged in a process of destruction and reconstruction. Its artefacts, including printed volumes and their interpretation, are also

---

[37] The classic account of Petrarch's influence upon Rojas is Allan D. Deyermond's *The Petrarchan Sources of 'La Celestina'* (Oxford: Clarendon Press, 1961). On the subject of strife and contention as inherent in all natural processes, and one of the underlying principles in *La Celestina*, see also the monograph by Consolación Baranda Letura, La Celestina *y el mundo como conflicto* (Salamanca: Ediciones Universidad de Salamanca, 2004).

subject to controversy, competition and strife. The prologue gives away Rojas's anxiety — tempered with a certain ironic distance — at the fact that, once a text has been launched into the public arena, its author can hardly control the responses it will elicit, or their consequences. And in fact — for reasons about which scholarship can only speculate — Rojas never penned or published anything again, and his voice was never heard after he vanished from the literary scene following the publication of his *Tragicomedia*. However, *La Celestina* was from 1499, and for many years to come, a domestic and an international bestseller as much as a *succès de scandale*. As its own author proclaims, everybody found some fault with it, and its different European translators also engaged in an interpretation of the text that sought to eliminate, modify or tone down its most controversial aspects.

This keen awareness of change and strife as part of the new realities of life also features as one of the driving leitmotifs in the plot of *La Celestina*. When Melibea's parents, Pleberio and Alisa, discuss their daughter's marriage, Pleberio suggests they consult her on their choice of husband, since 'in this particular, the laws allow both men and women, though they be under paternal power, for to make their own choice' (16.15–33). Alisa retorts with alarm that consulting their daughter about her marriage is a 'grande novedad' or 'strange news' in Mabbe's rendering. In the opinion of some scholars, this sense of novelty appears hand in hand with the awareness of the passage of time, the cycle of creation and destruction which is inherent to life and the cosmos, and it responds to a new concept of history.[38] These ideas, explicitly laid out as we have seen in Rojas's introduction, also crop up in the rest of the text. They are even voiced by Sempronio, one of Calisto's servants, who records the fast and futile pace of news and events as the best index and measure to this situation:

---

[38] Stephen Gilman, 'A generation of *conversos*', *Romance Philology*, 33 (1979), 87–101 (p. 100); for changes and 'strange news' in the realms of society and legal thought at the University of Salamanca during this period, see Consolación Baranda Letura, 'Cambio social en *La Celestina* y las ideas jurídico-políticas en la Universidad de Salamanca' in *El mundo social y cultural de* La Celestina, ed. by I. Arellano & J.M. Usunárriz (Madrid & Frankfurt: Iberoamericana & Vervuert, 2003), pp. 9–25. On the perception of time see Corinne Mencé-Caste, 'Temporalité et éthique dans *La Celestine*', *Celestinesca* 32 (2008), 209–29.

INTRODUCTION

Ill and good, prosperity and adversity, glory and grief, all these with time lose the force and strength of their rash and hasty beginning; whereas matters of admiration, and things earnestly desired, once obtained, have no sooner been come, than forgotten, no sooner purchased but relinquished. Every day we see new and strange accidents, we hear as many, and we pass them over; leave those, and hearken after others; them also doth time lessen and make contingible, as things of common course. And I pray, what wonder would you think it, if some should come and tell you: 'there was such an earthquake in such a place', or some such other things; tell me, would you not straight forget it? As also, if one should say unto you, 'such a river is frozen', 'such a blind man hath recovered his sight', 'thy father is dead', 'such a thunderbolt fell in such a place', 'Granada is taken, the king enters it this day', 'the Turk hath received an overthrow', 'tomorrow you shall have a great eclipse', 'such a bridge is carried away with the flood', 'such a one is now made a noble man', 'Peter is robbed' 'Innes hath hanged herself'. Now in such cases, what wilt thou say, save only this? That some three days past, or upon a second view thereof, there will be no wonder made of it. All things are thus; they all pass after this manner; all is forgotten and thrown behind us, as if they had never been. (3.42–64)

Some might object that this element of chaos and disorder was already present in certain medieval traditions. This argument could be illustrated with some passages from Juan de Mena's *Laberinto de Fortuna*, where the poet contrasts the order and system of the cosmos against the chaotic workings of Fortune. Composed *c.* 1444, Mena's *Laberinto* was first printed in Salamanca in 1481, during the years when Rojas was a law student at its university.[39] The fundamental difference is that whereas in Mena this disorder is exceptional and depends on the irregular whims of Fortune against the permanent background of an otherwise stable and hierarchic cosmos, in Rojas this disorder is systemic and *natural*. A certain sense of novelty and

---

[39] See 'Disputa con la Fortuna' in Juan de Mena (1411–1456), *Laberinto de Fortuna*, ed. by John G. Cummings, 6th edn (Madrid: Cátedra, 2008), p. 58. Several scholars have also detected certain echoes from Mena in Rojas's text too; see e.g. *et al.*, eds (2000), p. 333, n. 38; p. 339, n. 22; and p. 340, n. 29.

change was not uncommon in the decades that followed the publication of *La Celestina* and manifested itself in a variety of ways that ranged from the moderate proposals of the commonsensical humanism of Vives and Erasmus, to Lutheran reformers, through the more radical postulates of the millennarian Anabaptists. But the existential hopelessness and the melancholy-inducing sentiments that emanate from certain passages of *La Celestina* were quite exceptional. With Pleberio's final monologue before the corpse of his daughter, *La Celestina* concludes in a most pessimistic tone imbued with the nihilistic acknowledgment that systemic change, strife and contention — not order and reason — do indeed preside over life and nature. And Love, far from being the nourishing principle of the Neoplatonists, is a force not for creation, but destruction:

> Oh world, world! much have men spoken of thee, much have men writ concerning thy deceits; and much have I heard myself [. . .] I thought in my more tender years, that both thou and thy actions were governed by order, and ruled by reason. But now I see [. . .] there is no certainty in thy calmes: thou seemest now unto me to be a labyrinth of errors [. . .] (21.72–90)

> [. . .]

> What did enforce my daughter to die, but only the strong force of love? (21.164–65)

> [. . .]

> Some led with I know not what error have not sticked to call thee a god, but I would have such fools as these to consider with themselves, it savours not of a deity to murder or destroy those that serve and follow him. Oh thou enemy to all reason! [. . .] Thou art an enemy to thy friends, and a friend to thy enemies, and all this is because thou dost not govern thyself according to order and reason. (21.203–12)

> [. . .]

> I complain me of the world because I was bred up in it; for had not the world given me life, I had not therein begot

INTRODUCTION

Melibea; not being begot, she had not been borne; not being borne, I had not loved her; and not loving her, I should not have mourned, as now I do, in this my latter and uncomfortable old age! (21.230–35)

This underlying existential pessimism may have been far more disturbing for some readers of *La Celestina* than the indecency of its sexual innuendoes, or its scandalous heresies, were for others.

Beyond its author's introduction, anxious appeals to readers on how to properly interpret the text are a constant feature in the paratexts provided by its editors and translators — and, as we shall see, Mabbe was no exception. Readers and reading were also structurally ingrained in the plot of *La Celestina* and in the narrative tradition upon which it was founded. *La Celestina* emerged as part of a late fifteenth-century Castilian vogue for romance fiction; some of the most important and popular works included Diego de San Pedro's *Cárcel de amor* (1492) and Juan de Flores's *Grimalte y Gradissa* (*c.* 1485). The 1490s were also the years when internationally successful romances like Boccaccio's *Fiammetta*, or Piccolomini's *Historia de duobus amantibus* made their debut in the Castilian book market. The *Estoria de dos amantes*, an anonymous Spanish rendering of Piccolomini's work, was first printed in 1496, and 1497 saw the publication of a Castilian translation of *Fiammetta*. Both volumes were issued in Salamanca. These were all prose narratives that constructed their central characters as readers. Like Calisto and Melibea, the protagonists in Boccacio's *Fiammetta*, or Juan de Flores's *Grimalte & Gradissa*, are defined by the books they read and the way they internalize their emotional rhetoric. Severin has argued persuasively in favour of interpreting Calisto as a parody of Leriano, the protagonist of *Cárcel de Amor*. And Calisto does indeed fashion his amorous rhetoric after this sort of literature, as much as his paramour Melibea justifies her illicit love affair by alleging the examples of ancient ladies and goddesses who also trespassed the boundaries of conventional sexuality, in the tradition of Ovid's *Heroides*. Severin has also proved that some of Melibea's remarks stem from popular songs and ballads, as much as from her reading of *Fiammetta* and *Cárcel de amor*.[40]

---

[40] Dorothy Sherman Severin, *Tragicomedy and Novelistic Discourse in 'Celestina'* (Cambridge: Cambridge University Press, 1989), pp. 97–98.

In his introduction to *The Spanish Bawd* Mabbe praises what he calls the sententious, 'stoic' style of Rojas, and he emphasizes that *La Celestina* is not affected by the 'guildings of *Rhetorick*'. Its plain but elegant style emerges in particular when contrasted with the elaborate prose of the allegorical *Cárcel de amor*, and the florid rhetoric of its aristocratically heroic lover. Mabbe is using here the term *rhetorick* as synonymous with a profusely ornamented style, such as the prose of Spanish romance or the endless *copia* of euphuism. This *rhetorick* has nothing to do with the classical rhetorical and stylistic ideals that correspond with what Ben Jonson described as a 'strict and succinct style [. . .] where you can take away nothing without loss, and that loss to be manifest.'[41] Mabbe's excellence as a translator must be attributed to his skilful English rendering of the balanced and elegant prose of Rojas's monologues, which he did by simultaneously putting into practice the doctrines that Jonson was compiling at the time: a good measure of this can be ascertained by comparing the euphuism of Mabbe's introduction with the self-possessed style that pervades the passages quoted here so far, or his translation of Melibea and Pleberio's final monologues. They prove how, in spite of his apologetic claims to the contrary in his dedicatory epistle (154), Rojas's 'concisely significant' prose style did inform Mabbe's English rendering.

In his Epistle Dedicatory, and hand in hand with a variety of opinions and insights on the task of the translator, Mabbe also strikes two of the central ideas which Rojas mentions in his introduction to *La Celestina*: that readers should look beyond the obscene surface of the text and the plot. In Mabbe's words: 'Her [Celestina's] life is foul, but her precepts fair; her example naught, but her doctrine good' (Epistle Dedicatory, 10–12), for it is 'written reprehensively, and not instructively' (*ibid.*, 49–50). The

---

[41] Ben Jonson, *Discoveries*, ed. by Lorna Hutson in *The Cambridge Edition of the Works of Ben Jonson*, ed. by D. Bevington, M. Butler and I. Donaldson, 7 vols, *1641 Bibliography* (Cambridge University Press, 2012), VII, p. 565, ll. 1396–97. Hutson's splendid new edition demonstrates that Jonson translated much of his stylistic doctrine from authors like Juan Luis Vives, or Justus Lipsius, who in turn reflected the classical ideals of Quintilian and Cicero. These included the conversational epistolary style, which informed the models followed by Rojas's prose (e.g. Piccolomini's stylistic doctrine and prose fiction). For further details see Enea Silvio Piccolomini, *Estoria muy verdadera de dos amantes*, ed. by Ines Ravasini (Roma: Bagatto Libri, 2003).

nature of the text mutates with the subjective moral disposition of its readers:

> [. . .] the reading of *Celestina*, to those that are profane, is as poison to their hearts; but to the chaste, and honest mind, a preservative against such inconveniences as occur in the world. (*ibid.*, 79–81)

La Celestina requires a discerning reader, since 'he that reads all things alike, and equally entertaines them in his thought, that Reader shall easily shew himselfe obnoxious to many vices' (*ibid.*, 110–12). In the thought of humanism, literature — and in particular, the epic — had as one of its main functions the role of *speculum animi*, a mirror for the soul that amounted to a secular equivalent of Scripture. But the new world of letters that *La Celestina* foreshadowed, with its polished but plain prose style and with the realism of its social landscape, pointed to the picaresque and the early modern novel. This is the 'concisely significant' style of Rojas, his pregnant 'sense' as opposed to the *copia* of 'words': *superfluous, superabundant, affected, undiscreet*, as Mabbe euphuistically describes it. The text has such density and potential that Rojas's terse style and his pithy sentences will appeal to a wide range of readers, from 'lascivious *Clodius*, or effeminate *Sardanapalus*' to 'the gravest *Cato*, or severest Stoick' (Epistle Dedicatory, 43–44). Like *Doctor Faustus*, that other early modern *succès d'escandale*, *La Celestina* did not preach to its readers. It rather sought to offer its audiences — to paraphrase the opening chorus of Marlowe's play — the fluctuating fortunes of life in early modern cities, and the ethos of early modern life, whether *good or bad*. Some aspects of Mabbe's prologue underline this moral neutrality when it advises the contemplation of the *art* more than the *matter* being treated. The author, Mabbe holds, is just a *workeman* who flaunts his *art* and *skill*, like painters who frequently represent 'those actions that are absurd', such as '*Medea* killing her children' or '*Orestes* murdering his mother'. And he concludes that 'when we read the filthy actions of whores, their wicked conditions, and beastly behaviour, we are neither to approve them as good, nor to embrace them as honest, but to commend the Authors judgement in *expressing his Argument so fit and pat to their dispositions.*' (Epistle Dedicatory, 82–95; my italics). The translator is just a 'poor parrot', who simply reproduces what the author has said. But Mabbe incurs here in a contradiction of sorts. As the conveyor of the morals of the story, he disingenuously claims to be an innocent 'parrot', when he has actually either modified or removed potentially scandalous portions from the text. When he talks as a translator that needs to display the skills of a prose stylist, he adopts an apologetic tone and declares to have shown more boldness than judgment, because the style he has deployed in the English version falls short of the original, which is 'concisely significant'. As Rojas acknowledged in his own preface to *La Celestina*, Mabbe has no choice but to submit his text to the reader's 'favourable interpretation'. In Mabbe's case, what is at stake here is not simply the text itself, but the intentions and the artistic skills of the translator, possibly his moral and religious principles, too. The translator knows that, like the author, he is also bound to be translated, i.e. interpreted. Once they are set in circulation within the public spheres of domestic and international readers, the original and the translation are lost to their originators. In the case of the translator, this anxiety is compounded by the impossibility of an exact, spotless, reproduction in the translation of the style and the artistic quality of the original:

> But to leave *Celestina* to a favourable censure, I must now come to entreat some favour for myself, who am so far from pleading my excuse, that I must wholy submit myself to your favourable interpretation;[42] for I must ingeniously confess, that I have in the undergoing of this translation, shown more boldness than judgement. For though I do speake like *Celestina*, yet come I short of her; for she is so concisely significant, and indeed so differing is the idiom of the Spanish from the English, that I may imitate it, but not come near it. Yet have I made it as natural, as our language will give leave, and have more beaten my brains about it in some places, then a man would beat a flint to get fire; and, with much ado, have forced those sparks, which increasing to a greater flame, gave light to my dark understanding. (Epistle Dedicatory, 152–64)

---

[42] Instead of 'favourable interpretation', the Alnwick Manuscript reads 'gracious pardon' (Martínez Lacalle, ed., p. 108).

INTRODUCTION

Mabbe encourages a critical and discerning reader. More than just a good scholar, this is someone with the moral disposition to draw the right lessons from negative examples like those provided by Calisto and Melibea, both of whom are destroyed by their untempered approach to poetic fiction. In presenting the ill fortunes of two lovers whose tragic outcome stems from their subjective appropriation of some of the most popular literature of the period as a textual mirror for their eventually lost souls, *La Celestina* appears as a sophisticated handbook for readers.

Whether chivalric or sentimental (or a combination of both) the popularity of romance prose fiction and of its translations was enormous, and it contributed to the creation of a widespread network of influences, as well as to the generation of new characters that would determine the future of the European novel. The inventory of Rojas's library shows that he owned many of these volumes.[43] *La Celestina* was a sophisticated and immediate response to this type of literature, in itself a literary response to an essentially literary question which ran parallel to the more explicit and mundane responses of its moralizing critics. It flowed first into the picaresque — which would appear just a few decades later — and also anticipated some essential aspects of Cervantes's fiction in its literary thematization of the reader gone astray as the centre of its narrative concerns.[44]

---

[43] They included *Cárcel de amor*, a considerable amount of chivalric fiction (including three volumes of the *Amadis* series), and also Spanish translations of Ovid's *Metamorphoses*, Boccaccio's *De claris mulieribus*, Aesop's *Fables*, and of Apuleius's *Asinus Aureus*. For more details on Rojas's interesting library, see Victor Infantes, 'Los libros "traydos y viejos y algunos rotos" que tuvo el Bachiller Fernando de Rojas, nombrado autor de la obra llamada *Celestina*', *Bulletin Hispanique*, 100 (1998), 7–51. For a most useful account of the international success of this type of literature, see A. Deyermond's excellent preface to Diego de San Pedro, *Cárcel de amor*, ed. by Carmen Parrilla, (Barcelona: Crítica, 1995), in particular pp. xxxii–xxxiii. On *La Celestina* as a parody of sentimental romance see Yolanda Iglesias, *Una nueva mirada a la parodia de la novela sentimental en 'La Celestina'* (Madrid & Frankfurt: Iberoamericana & Vervuert, 2009).

[44] Severin concludes that *La Celestina* 'is a generic hybrid: neither humanistic comedy nor sentimental romance, it creates its own new dialogic and novelistic

But *La Celestina* also responded to other important concerns embedded in the cultural milieu of late fifteenth-century Spain, which had for some time been exposed to the influence of Italian humanism. *La Celestina* shows that language and its rhetorical operations, far from informing a virtuous self and providing cohesion to social life, could be put to spurious ends. In this Rojas significantly departs from the humanist ideal of a civic self articulated upon the rhetorical principles of classical stoicism and Christian doctrine. The systemic pessimism of *La Celestina* leaves very little room for that aspect of humanism which is founded, in the words of Charles Trinkaus, on the 'orator and the lawyer who work to compose the quarrels of the town and bring decency and civilization to all mankind'.[45] Celestina is an immoral and self-serving Protagoras who exposes the underside of this civic rhetorical ideal. She is a humanist's nightmare: she transgresses sexual and family morals, turns to witchcraft instead of socially acceptable religious practices, and uses eloquence for all the wrong purposes. As a skilled restorer of cracked maidenheads, her trade also responded to a demand that resulted from the internal logic of the market. As a procuress, she trades in desire. In other words, Celestina and her associates reproduced within the sphere of the urban underworld they inhabited the same strategies that the new bureaucratic and mercantile classes used in the social, legal and discursive spaces that they were negotiating. *La Celestina* exposed the contradictions between the tenets of the Christian-Stoic *ratio* and the actual drift of the new socio-economic drives. Like the cohort of prostitutes and servants over which she presides, Celestina needed to negotiate her way through the social fabric by means of her own illicit version of these

---

genre which prefigures the world of both *Lazarillo* and *Don Quijote*' (1989, p. 2 and p. 5). Francisco Rico has also provided an eloquent account of the relevance of *La Celestina* for current readers, and of its complex relation with the evolution of the picaresque and early modern prose fiction in general; see Rico, 'Estudio preliminar' in Lobera *et al.*, eds (2000), pp. xv-xlvii, in particular pp. xxxiii–xxxv). For a survey of the controversies regarding its generic ascription, see I. Ruiz Arzálluz's 'Género y fuentes' in Lobera *et al.*, eds (2011), pp. 402–434.

[45] Charles Trinkaus, *The Poet as Philosopher. Petrarch and the Formation of Renaissance Consciousness* (New Haven and London: Yale University Press, 1979), pp. 49–50.

mechanisms of profit and self-interest. The humanist programme that proclaimed the primacy of individual will, and subjectivity as a form of knowledge, and sought their ideal co-efficiency within the superior framework of divine providence, does not hold at all within the moral universe of *La Celestina*.

This unmediated depiction of human passions and hedonistic self-interest runs parallel in *La Celestina* with its generic indeterminacy, its moral neutrality and the multiplicity of readings that it could unleash. Juan Goytisolo confirms this interpretation when he claims that Rojas 'created a unique, unrepeatable narrative, beyond concepts of model or genre' which proceeds to question 'existing social and literary hierarchies and subvert their meaning'.[46] Peter Bush's translation and John Clifford's adaptation prove the versatility of a text which lends itself simultaneously to a typographic rendition that reads like a novel and to a stage production that can elicit contradictory responses from its audiences. This discursive diversity goes hand in hand with its inherent dialogism and a new type of linguistic verisimilitude that overrides the orthodoxies of contemporary literary decorum, which classified and assigned registers and styles to each of the characters according to their social extraction. The language and the dialogues are not, as in other humanistic comedies and interludes across Europe, mere vehicles for humanist indoctrination. Its first, highly moralizing adaptation into English — the early Tudor interlude *Calisto and Melebea*, c. 1525 — precisely defused *La Celestina* by turning it into one of these closet dramas.[47] Rojas's dialogues respond instead to

---

[46] Goytisolo (2009), p. ix.

[47] Of uncertain authorship, but stemming from the circles around Thomas More and John Rastell, the first English adaptation of *La Celestina* evinces the influence of the moralising attitude to the literary canon and the role that it should play in the education of women defended by Juan Luis Vives, a close acquaintance of More, who was in England at the time the interlude was composed. Here Melibea is never seduced, Celestina is duly punished, and Pleberio sees his daughter repent and submit to his authority after a dream reveals to her the evil nature of the bawd. The interlude has a happy ending and concludes with a paean to the values of a proper education that could prepare women for their socially acceptable roles within the boundaries of matrimony. For further details, see my introduction to the interlude in the *EEBO Introductions Series*, gen. ed. Edward Wilson-Lee: <http://eebo.chadwyck.com/intros/htxview?template=basic.htx&content=calisto.htm> (accessed on 23 September 2012).

his deft combination of realistic communicative contexts with the ends pursued by equally verisimilar speakers: this is what Mabbe in his dedicatory epistle described as Rojas's skill 'in expressing his argument so fit and pat' to his characters' 'dispositions'. Once more, by transferring this particular feature of Rojas's style into his own text, Mabbe was putting into practice one of the rhetorical postulates that his contemporary Ben Jonson was also proposing, and which the latter had in turn found in Juan Luis Vives: 'Words [. . .] are to be chosen according to the persons we make speak, or the things we speak of. Some are of the camp, some of the council-board, some of the shop, some of the sheepcote, some of the pulpit, some of the bar, etc'.[48] Working in different periods, both Rojas and his English translator were actually implementing stylistic principles stemming from common classical sources, such as Cicero or Quintilian, or from more recent authors like Petrarch or Piccolomini, all of whom the humanism of Vives or Erasmus first, and then the neostoic ideal of Justus Lipsius, had systematically updated and developed for their respective contexts. This is one of the reasons why *La Celestina* and its English translation, hand in hand with the milieus from which they emerged, constitute excellent case studies that exemplify the evolution that this sort of humanism underwent in the sixteenth and the early seventeenth centuries.

The dialogues and the narrative structure of *La Celestina* display the mechanisms for sociolinguistic exchange described by humanists like Giovanni Pontano in his *De sermone* (1509). These involved the common linguistic skills and strategies that were circumscribed by everyday communication, and which thus proved to be an essential component for civic cohesion. Pontano distinguished the elevated oratory of social leaders from the common language in which regular citizens go about their daily affairs, that is, those who weave the social networks of a harmonious commonwealth:

> But in this regard I am not referring at all to what is called the power, the skill, or the art of oratory, but only to the common language in which men conduct themselves above all in addressing their friends, going about their affairs, in everyday

---
[48] Hutson, ed., p. 562, ll. 1339–43.

conversations, in meetings, assemblies, and the accustomed reunions both private and public.[49]

Pontano goes on to defend urbanity and politeness as virtues that facilitate social exchange and can be used to assuage difficult situations in the conduct of everyday business, or to overcome obstacles in the middle of negotiations. Celestina proves that these communicative skills can be perverted to serve ends other than the common, public good. And when characters like Calisto do not abide by these rules, it can lead to situations that range from social irrelevance to personal demise. Calisto's erotic ravings are discursive anomalies that do not respond to healthy, common norms of linguistic exchange. The nature of Calisto's emotional and social dissonance is embodied in his Ovidian rants, which contrast with the commonsensical advice of his servant Sempronio. This contrast reveals the different spheres of discourse that both inhabit, hence the servant's advice that Calisto use 'el lenguaje que a todos es común':

> Good sir, leave off these circumlocutions; leave off these poetical fictions: for that speech is not comely which is not common unto all, which all men partake not of as well as yourself, of which few do but understand. (8.345–48)

Sempronio's role here, as the commonsensical servant of a deranged master whose madness originates in the exuberant rhetoric of the volumes he reads, prefigures the relation between Sancho Panza and Don Quijote. Among Alonso Quijano's favourite volumes are Feliciano de Silva's best-selling romances, some of which belonged in the *celestinesca* sub-genre. In the

---

[49] 'Sed nos hac in parte de ea quae oratoria siue uis facultasque siue ars dicitur nihil omnino loquimur, uerum de oratione tantum ipsa communi quaque homines adeundis amicis, communicandis negociis in quotidianis praecipue utuntur sermonibus, in conuentibus, consessionibus, congressionibus familiaribusque ac ciuilibus consuetudinibus.' Giovanni Giovano Pontano, *De Sermone* [1509], ed. by Florence Bistagne (Paris: Honoré Champion, 2008), I.iii.1–2, in my own translation. Compare this with Jonson, over one hundred years later, who claimed that speech (i.e. *sermo*, which can also be translated as *conversation*) 'is the instrument of society' (Hutson, ed., p. 561, l. 1334; see also her footnote, which confirms that Jonson translated this idea from Juan Luis Vives's *De ratione dicendi*).

opening pages of *Don Quijote*, the narrator describes the process that led to his protagonist's madness, and shows him in his library, obsessed with his books:

[. . .] and among them all, none pleased him better then those, which famous *Felician of Silua* composed. For the smoothnesse of his prose, which now and then some intricate sentence meddled, seemed to him peerslesse; and principally when he did reade the courtings of letters of challenge, and Knights sent to Ladies, or one to another; where, in many places he found written 'the reason of the unreasonablenesse, which against my reason is wrought, doth so weaken my reason, as with all reason I doe iustly complaine on your beauty'. And also when he read 'the high Heauens, which with your divinity doe fortifie your diuinely with the starres, and make you deseruresse of the deserts that your Greatnesse deserues', &c. With these and other such passages the poore Gentleman grew distracted, and was breaking his braines day and night, to vnderstand and vnbowell their senses.[50]

Mabbe's translation of 'dejá esas poesías' as 'leave off these poetical fictions' is particularly perceptive of the implications that lurk within the servant's reply, and constitutes one of the most eloquent pieces of evidence that prove Mabbe as a critically acute reader and interpreter. *La Celestina* exposes the shortcomings of the new linguistic habits that humanists in the tradition of Pontano were proposing to regulate social relations, trade, and moral standards. It does so by having Celestina and her associates appear before readers as verisimilar characters moved by naked self-interest, without the legitimation of the rhetorical, legal, or moral veneers provided by humanist thought.

As a forerunner of the picaresque, *La Celestina* is a realistic account of the dissolution of the social and moral orders detected in communicative disharmony. This is an important feature that *La Celestina* shares with *Guzmán de Alfarache*. Mateo Alemán's subtitle for his novel was 'atalaya de la vida humana', that is, 'a watch tower of human existence', and its leitmotiv is an adage that expresses the ultimate fragmentation of sociolinguistic

---

[50] *The History of Don-Quichote. The First Parte*, trans. by Thomas Shelton [London]: Printed [by William Stansby] for Ed: Blounte, [1620?] (1620), pp. 2–3.

credit: 'todos mienten' — 'everybody lies'. A century before Guzmán, *La Celestina* displayed in its plot an early case of what Thomas Pavel has described as the breakdown of the links of fidelity among humans.[51] As they do in *Guzmán de Alfarache*, fidelity, credit and trust, all appear broken in *La Celestina*, but they do so in a dialogic narrative devoid of the moralizing comments provided by the autobiographical narrator of Alemán's novel. As Mabbe acknowledges in the introduction of his *Spanish Bawd*, Rojas's prose is concise and full of proverbial wisdom, 'not so full of words as sense; each other line being a sentence' (Epistle Dedicatory, 26–27). The problem was that these 'sentences' which combine popular refrains with authoritative *sententiae* taken from Seneca, Aristotle, or Petrarch, tend to appear woven into Celestina's deceitful orations, or in other contexts where they acquire originally unintended ironic, or even sarcastic, overtones. It took a most sophisticated and discerning reader indeed to disentangle the moral conundrums posed by a dialogic story devoid of an explicit third voice to guide her through the plot.

Lidia de Malkiel and Francisco Rico coincide in their analysis of *La Celestina* as a text that goes well beyond the boundaries of humanist comedy by distancing itself from the postulates of literary decorum in order to adjust its language and style to the principle of truth to individual experience. The characters who best embody this verisimilar use of language are the commonsensically cynical servants and Celestina's wenches. They proclaim with unashamed eloquence the right to pursue their own self-interest as the only legitimate motivation for their actions, beyond any other moral or social consideration, such as fidelity to their social superiors. Areusa, one of Celestina's wenches, defends her freedom and her right to trade with sex in order to gain personal autonomy:

> For I could never endure to be called by any other name, than mine own; especially by these ladies we have nowadays [...]

---

[51] On the relation between the picaresque, the breakdown of moral order and the fragmentation of social bonds, see Thomas Pavel, *Representar la existencia. El pensamiento de la novela*, [*La pensée du roman*, 2003], trans. by D. Roas Deus (Barcelona: Crítica, 2005), pp. 93–95. Pavel distinguishes between the moralizing picaro (like Guzmán) and the cynic picaro who accepts and embraces his condition (such as the protagonist of *Lazarillo de Tormes*).

And this, mother, is the reason why I have rather desired to live free from controlment, and to be mistress in a poor little house of mine own, than to live a slave, and at command in the richest palace of the proudest lady of them all. (9.366–433, my emphasis)

'Que jamás me precié de llamarme de otrie sino mía' ('I never accepted to be addressed as if I belonged to anyone but myself' my translation; an alternative translation of 'llamarme' here could be 'regard myself'). In the Alnwick manuscript Mabbe does not translate this sentence. *The Spanish Bawd* does translate it, and like Rojas, Mabbe here also identifies the mode of address as an index to the personal status of Areusa, whether she is free or subject to a mistress. But at the same time Mabbe subtly alters the original in a way that tones down its more radically libertarian overtones, 'For I could never endure to be called by any other name, than mine own'. This defence of freedom in the words of a marginal character like Areusa finds a parallel in Melibea's defence of her own personal autonomy; both girls, the aristocratic Melibea and the social outcast Areusa, have learned the exercise of their freedom under Celestina's mentorship. In one of Celestina's most remarkable orations, peppered with *adagia* and proverbial wisdom, the old bawd eloquently encourages her wench to make a mercenary living by enjoying the company of several male friends (7.513–58). This reckless and cynical pursuit of self-interest goes hand in hand with the emphasis on particulars, the contingent nature of subjective experience, and the systemic strife that pervades nature. And in narrative terms it runs parallel with the different points of view that Rojas uses to represent the same situation, first through direct dialogue, and then as this is reported by a character. With this Rojas affords his readers a panorama of perspectives without the explicitly unifying voice of a single narrator. As a complement to these dialogues, monologues contribute additional psychological depth to the characters.[52] This monological self-fashioning, through which characters persuade themselves of their own vision of reality as they show the reader how this subjective process is taking place, is not reserved for the most aristocratic or socially relevant characters: it is used across different social

---

[52] Mota, in Lobera *et al.*, eds (2011), pp. 446–448.

groups, and consequently those in the lower classes appear as complex psyches on an equal literary and ontological footing with their social superiors.[53] The final result of all these combined techniques is a verisimilar fresco of public and private situations which ranges from details of psychological depth in individual characters to a collection of more panoramic samples of the social and civic landscape across which they move.

Although *La Celestina* eventually witnesses their destruction, it also enfranchises the servants, the wenches and the old bawd by turning them into skilled — albeit marginal — players within the sociolinguistic mechanisms of civic life. Beyond traditional doctrines of decorum, *La Celestina* thematizes poverty through the construction of complex characters that stem from the lowest rungs of society, instead of its centre.[54] Patent proof of this is that soon after its publication, the title *Comedia* or *Tragicomedia de Calisto y Melibea* — which followed other romances in entitling the story after the names of the aristocratic lovers — was immediately refashioned after the name of its true protagonist: *La Celestina*. As mentioned above, these characters subsist through tricks and deceits that mirror the rhetorical and economic strategies used by their social superiors. After an inexperienced but honest Parmeno proclaims his obligation to remain faithful to Calisto, Celestina immediately retorts by describing how the traditional bonds of mutual fidelity founded upon service and reward have vanished. There is not a whit of nostalgia for the times past in Celestina, and far from censoring this selfish conduct, she proclaims that this is precisely what the times call for, concluding that, since these new masters now only pursue their own ends, their servants must follow them in this too:

---

[53] See Rico, "Estudio preliminar" in Lobera *et al.*, eds (2000), p. xxxv.

[54] The thematization of poverty in *La Celestina* and the picaresque is the topic of Juan Carlos Rodríguez's *La literatura del pobre* (Granada: Comares, 1994). See also Anne J. Cruz's *Discourses of Poverty: Social Reform and the Picaresque Novel in Early Modern Spain* (Toronto: University of Toronto Press, 1999). For a description of society in the period, see Jose Antonio Maravall, *El mundo social de 'La Celestina'* (Madrid: Gredos, 1972); Miguel Ángel Ladero Quesada, 'Aristócratas y marginales: aspectos de la sociedad castellana en *La Celestina*', *Espacio, Tiempo y Forma: Revista de la Facultad de Geografía e Historia*, 3 (1990), 95–120; or the more recent, *El mundo social y cultural de* La Celestina, ed. by I. Arellano and J. M. Usunárriz (Madrid & Frankfurt: Iberoamericana & Vervuert, 2003).

The masters of these times love more themselves than their servants. Neither in so doing do they do amiss. The like love ought servants to bear unto themselves. Liberality was lost long ago; rewards are growne out of date; magnificence is fled the country, and with her, all nobleness. Every one of them is wholly now for himself, and makes the best he can of his servants' service, serving his turn, as he finds it may stand with his private interest and profit. And therefore they ought to do no less, seeing that they are less than they in substance, but to live after their law, and to do as they do. (1.1118–28)

When Parmeno wavers again in his fidelity to Celestina's cause, she encourages him once more in his pursuit of self-interest through a mutually beneficial alliance with Sempronio, as the only strategy to gain personal autonomy from servitude and enjoy a life of leisure and repose (7.87–100).

When Calisto's servants contemplate in amazement Celestina's eloquence, Sempronio wonders how she has acquired those skills. Parmeno's answer is revealing: 'necessity, poverty, and hunger', he says, are Celestina's mentors, since 'there are no better tutors in the world, no better quickeners, and revivers of the wit'. Even animals can learn through necessity: 'Who taught your [mag]pies and your parrots to imitate our proper language, and tone, with their slit tongues, save only necessity?' (9.56–62). Parmeno's response constitutes a disenchanted account that contradicts the humanist myth of eloquence as the bedrock of civilization, law and harmonious commonwealths. It also implicitly undermines the humanist definition of man as *homo sermocinalis*, as immanently linguistic and communicative, by setting him on a par with 'your pies and your parrots'.

Taking as its starting points the generic conventions of humanistic comedy and the principles of the humanist philosophy of language, *La Celestina* skilfully drives them to their ultimate consequences and ends up with a fresh variety of literary discourse that displays an unprecedented type of social and psychological verisimilitude. Francisco Rico has called attention to the contrast between the deliberate choice of the familiar *tu* mode of address in *La Celestina* for all its characters irrespective of social extraction, and the existing varieties in modes of address during this period, each of which bestowed their respective discursive and communicative contexts with connotations based on social class and power-relations.⁵⁵ Rico attributes its use to a well-documented humanist effort to reproduce in the vernacular the stylistic traits and modes of address in classical Latin prose from Cicero's epistles to Terence's urban comedies. According to this interpretation, the use of *tu* was meant to provide the text with a sort of classical universalism. The Spanish rhetorician and lexicographer Elio Antonio de Nebrija — a contemporary of Rojas, and professor of rhetoric at Salamanca, where Rojas studied — also defended this use of *tu* on the grounds of what we might call linguistic rationalism. It was absurd, he claimed, to use *vos* — with its accompanying verb also in the plural — to address a single individual. This linguistic doctrine had potentially far-reaching epistemological consequences, since it responded to the uses and laws of Nature and Reason.⁵⁶ In the opening paragraphs of his *Introduciones Latinas* of 1488 (a Castilian translation of his successful *Introductiones Latinae*, Salamanca, 1481), Nebrija proposed to use Latin as the model for Castilian usage, among other reasons because it is:

[. . .] la lengua en la que está no solamente fundada nuestra religion i república christiana, mas aun el derecho civil i canónico, por el qual los hombres biven igualmente en esta gran compañía que llamamos ciudad.⁵⁷

In this, Nebrija followed first the Italian humanist Lorenzo Valla, who in turn followed Quintilian, in their defence of an 'habla derecha y natural' ('right and natural speech'). This was

---

⁵⁵ Rico, 'Estudio preliminar', in Lobera *et al.*, eds (2000), pp. xxxiii, pp. xlii–xliii.
⁵⁶ Rico, *ibid.* pp. xliii-xliv. On Nebrija and his polemical writings against more traditional grammarians, see Francisco Rico, *Nebrija frente a los bárbaros: El canon de gramáticos nefastos en las polémicas del humanismo*. (Salamanca: Universidad de Salamanca, 1978). For a recent useful and comprehensive survey of Nebrija's project (including a collection of his most relevant Latin texts), see Antonio de Nebrija. *Gramática sobre la lengua castellana. Paginae Nebrissenses*, ed. by Carmen Lozano and Felipe González Vega (Madrid: Real Academia Española, 2011).
⁵⁷ Latin is 'the language that constitutes the foundation not just of our Christian religion and republic, but also of the civil and canon laws, by virtue of which men live equally in this great company we call the city' (*Introduciones latinas*, Salamanca, 1488, f. a2, quoted by Lozano and González Vega, eds pp.367–68, n. 76, who also trace this idea back to Quintilian, *Institutio oratoria*, proem 5).

of course the discursive counterpart of *right Reason* and the *law of Nature*, concepts which were part of the common stock of humanist thought in the late fifteenth and early sixteenth centuries; see, for instance, Juan Luis Vives, who in his rhetoric described the best type of language as the 'flow of reason'.[58] Hence Nebrija's intention to homogenize and reform Castilian speech along the lines established by 'artificio y razón', through 'art and reason', or in other words, through a combination of human-created conventions and rules (art), on the one hand, and the dictates of transcendental *ratio* (nature) on the other.

This notion of the *natural language*, whose remote origins hailed from the poetic doctrines of Horace and from Quintilian's rhetoric, is of a piece with Pontano's *urbanitas*. Horace proposes the use of a poetic style which is sophisticated and imaginative, but also natural and firmly rooted in common usage, an idiom that resorts to poetic licence for the creation of new vocabulary as it avoids the excess of raving poets. In the same passage where Horace acknowledges the decline and the constantly changing nature of language — a fact of which humanists were quite aware, and one of the axes of their debates on language — he also promotes common usage, natural, everyday speech, as the proper norm. This is what he calls 'nomen [. . .] signatum praesente nota', that is, words stamped with the mint-mark of the day.[59] The comparison of the linguistic sign with a piece of currency, bestowed with the contingent value of public exchange, constitutes an image rich in socio-economic overtones that can take us far in a cultural materialist analysis of the idea of common language as a social and marketable commodity. This was a trope that Ben Jonson would take up again in his *Discoveries*: 'Custom is the most certain mistress of language, as the public stamp makes the current money'.[60] For both the currency

---

[58] Juan Luis Vives, *De ratione dicendi. Del arte de hablar*, ed. and trans. by J. M. Rodríguez Peregrina (Granada: Servicio de Publicaciones de la Universidad de Granada, 2000), book I, p. 8.
[59] Horace, *Ars Poetica*, 59 from *Satires, Epistles and Ars Poetica* (Cambridge, Mass. & London: Harvard University Press & William Heinemann Ltd., 1978) ed. and trans. by H. R. Fairclough, p. 455. A few lines later, Horace refers to 'usus / quem penes arbitrium est et ius et norma loquendi' (*ibid.*, 71–72), that is, 'usage [. . .] in whose hands lies the judgment, the right, and the rule of speech'.
[60] Hutson, ed. (2012), p. 563, ll. 1365–66.

INTRODUCTION

system and language to function effectively, they need to rely on the principles of consensual truthfulness and fidelity. It is quite revealing that in his *Ars poetica*, hand in hand with proposals for the use of current language, and with his trope of *verba* as currency, Horace also proposes the use of *publica materies* when it comes to *res*. An accomplished author must use current language, as well as subjects and plots that constitute common currency and concerns. The discursive and stylistic strategies that sustain Rojas's prose and plot take this ideal as their starting point, and they also chime in, many decades later, with Ben Jonson's poetry and poetics, the latter of which were an important part of Mabbe's age of exchange.[61] The trope that construes linguistic processes in terms of common currency, trade and exchange could not be more apposite for this period, when translators all over Europe were busy appropriating the literary, cultural, religious and political capitals that they found in the texts of classical antiquity and of the new thriving vernaculars.

The language, and the plot, of *La Celestina* resulted to a large extent from one of these processes of literary and stylistic appropriation, since it follows in the steps of works like Piccolomini's *Historia de duobus amantibus*, as it enhances its atmosphere of urban verisimilitude. It does so by transforming the emotional realism of Piccolomini's epistles, circumscribed to rhetorical exchanges between its two lovers, into the more verisimilar dialogues between Rojas's characters, which now deploy a much larger social palette. Piccolomini's epistolary account is indeed peppered with the conventions of a rhetorical education and a reading background in Terentian and Plautian comedy as well as romance prose fiction. Piccolomini's *Historia* also features a group of servants and go-betweens who provide a sort of moderately saucy social backdrop for its two main protagonists, the

---

[61] On the concept of 'right and natural speech' in Quintilian, Valla and Nebrija, see Rico, 'Estudio preliminar' in Lobera *et al.*, eds (2000), p. xliv. On Horace's *Ars poetica* in relation to translation, see Stuart Gillespie, *English Translation and Classical Reception: Towards a New Literary History* (Oxford: Wiley-Blackwell, 2011), who claims that Horace 'sanctions the use of the common stock of cultural material' (pp. 45–46). See also Neil Rhodes, *Shakespeare and the Origins of English* (Oxford: Oxford University Press, 2004), who points out that in this period the 'figuring of language as saleable goods was quite common' (p. 74)

lovers Eurialo and Lucretia.[62] In *La Celestina* this background grows and evolves into a great fresco that engages itself with the realistic depiction of the underworld of servants and prostitutes in which Celestina acts as some sort of demi-monde Venus. In the following paragraph, Calisto proclaims his wonder at Celestina's ability to persuade Melibea to love him, and compares her role to that of Venus in the *Aeneid*, when the goddess managed to make Dido fall in love with the hero of Virgil's epic:

> Oh admirable craft! Oh rare woman in thy art! Oh cunning creature! Oh speedy remedy! Oh discreet deliverer of a message! What humane understanding is able to reach unto so high a means of helpe? And I verily persuade myself, that if our age might purchase those years past, wherein *Æneas* and *Dido* lived, *Venus* would not have taken so much pains, for to attract the love of *Elisa* to his son, causing *Cupid* to assume the form of *Ascanius*, the better to deceive her: but would (to make short work of the business) have made choice of thee to mediate the matter: and therefore do I hold my death happily employed, since that I have put it into such hands, and I shall evermore be of this mind, that if my desire obtain not its wished effect, yet know I not what could be done more, according to nature, for my good and welfare. (6.298–311)

Unlike the nourishing *Eros* of neoplatonists, who stood as the principle that sustained the hierarchies of Nature and gave them continuity, Celestina appears as a barren Aphrodite whose reckless pursuit of self-interest wrecks her own life and those of her creatures. In Rojas the benevolent goddess of Neoplatonic beauty has degenerated into an urban old bawd who reeks of wine and thrives on the lust and greed of others. Parmeno, who appears first as an honest and faithful servant to Calisto, is

---

[62] Ines Ravasini provides an excellent introduction to Piccolomini's work and its European influence in the preface to her edition of the first anonymous Spanish translation of the *Historia de duobus amantibus*. Her introduction also includes an insightful analysis of Piccolomini's influence upon Rojas (Ravasini, ed., 2003). On Rojas and Piccolomini, see also Ottavio Di Camillo 'When and where was the first act of *La Celestina* composed? A reconsideration' in '*De ninguna cosa es alegre posesión sin compañía*'. *Estudios celestinescos y medievales en honor del profesor Joseph Thomas Snow*, coord. by D. Paolini (New York: Hispanic Seminar of Medieval Studies, 2010), pp. 91–157 (pp. 141–44).

INTRODUCTION

eventually won to Celestina's cause when she procures for him sexual intercourse with Areusa. But before that final blow, she starts to soften his initial reticence with a persuasive combination of Senecan proverbs and fragments from Aristotle's *Ethics*, a fact which cannot have escaped the attention of the university audiences that were among Rojas's first readers (1.1087–145, *passim*). Celestinas's main sources on the question of friendship and mutually beneficial associations in this and in other exchanges included Pedro Díaz de Toledo's *Proverbios de Séneca* — published in 1495, in Seville, just a few years before the appearance of *La Celestina* — and fragments from book VIII of Aristotle's *Ethics* which circulated thanks to the *Auctoritates Aristotelis*, a late medieval anthology much used in university circles. With his portrayal of this host of self-serving characters from the urban underclasses whose only alternatives to a thankless life of servitude are prostitution and trickery Rojas does indeed prefigure the picaresque by parodying and perverting the *topoi* and narrative conventions of well-established genres like epic and romance, as much as the Senecan and Aristotelian foundations of humanist moral philosophy.[63]

Celestina also plays her persuasive skills on the inexperienced lovers and the sentimental patterns they had obtained from their readings in the romance literature in circulation at the time. Frequently overshadowed by the overwhelming character of the old bawd, one of Rojas's most remarkable achievements is the creation with Melibea of a complex female character whose emotions have been moulded by her readings. As he did with Piccolomini's *Historia de duobus amantibus*, here Rojas is developing a trend that he had already found in Boccaccio's *Fiammetta* and the sort of romance prose fiction that both works had so successfully spawned in late fifteenth-century Spain. Celestina combines witchcraft with persuasion to beguile Melibea into embarking on an affair with Calisto.[64] But important as witchcraft can be within the plot to justify an unexpected

---

[63] For this intellectual background, see Íñigo Ruiz Arzallus, 'El mundo intelectual del 'antiguo autor': las *Auctoritates Aristotelis* en la *Celestina* primitiva', *Boletín de la Real Academia Española* 76 (1996), 265–84.

[64] On witchcraft in *La Celestina* see D. S. Severin, *Female Empowerment and Witchcraft in 'Celestina'* (London: Department of Hispanic Studies, Queen Mary and Westfield College, 1995), and also her 'Witchcraft in *Celestina*: A Bibliographical Update since 1995', *La Corónica* 36 (2007), 237–346.

change of heart in an otherwise obedient daughter and common-sensical young woman — as she appears in act I during her first encounter with Calisto in her garden — it soon vanishes towards the end of the story to let Melibea's emotions, her amorous rhetoric, and her eventual self-assertiveness, take control of her character. Melibea declares Celestina to have been her mentor ('astuta maestra') in this process:

> I was wooed and sued unto, and captivated by Calisto's good deserts; being thereunto solicited by that subtle and cunning mistress in her art, dame Celestina, who adventured herself in many a dangerous visit, before that ever I would yield myself true prisoner to his love. (16.116–21)[65]

In the Alnwick manuscript James Mabbe omits the lines where Melibea admits that she has been 'persuaded by such a subtle mentor as Celestina'. Rojas plays here with the double meaning of 'maestra': as a person skilled in some art, but also a *magister*, one whose skills precisely turn her into a role model and an authoritative source of knowledge. Elsewhere, Melibea addresses the old bawd as 'amiga Celestina, mujer bien sabia y maestra grande', which Mabbe translates as 'Friend, *Celestina*, Thou wife Matrone, and great Mistress in thy Art' (10.107–08).[66] But if Melibea appears vulnerable to Celestina, and also prey to the idealisation of love that destroyed Fiammetta, she also reveals herself as a strong-willed character that grows in stature when it comes to her eloquent justification of the course she has finally taken. Melibea singles out standard *exempla* of reprehensible behaviour and uses them to diminish by contrast the severity of her own faults. But as she does so she champions far more than her right to choose a husband. She proclaims the liberty she enjoys in her choice of a sexual partner out of wedlock (16.76–39). She also starts to follow a similar pattern when she justifies before her father the suicide she is about to commit in the final act. The Alnwick manuscript omits the following passage, but the 1631 edition

---

[65] Mabbe here expands the text of the Alnwick manuscript, and subtly manipulates the original, to turn Melibea into a prisoner of Calisto's love (the original reads 'concediese por entero en su amor', whereas 1631 renders this as 'yield myself true prisoner to his love').
[66] Lobera *et al.*, eds (2000), p. 223.

renders it in balanced periods - with Mabbe's typical reduplications but free from the excesses of euphuistic *copia* —which turns it into an excellent example of Mabbe's prose:

> I would fain speak some words of comfort unto you, before this gladsome and well-pleasing end, gathered and collected out of those ancient books, which for the bettering of my wit and understanding, you willed me to read, were it not that my memory fails me, being troubled and disquieted with the loss and death of my love, as also because I see your ill-endured tears trickle so fast down your wrinckled cheeks. (20.225–32)

Melibea here reveals that her father encouraged the reading habits that have turned her into such a skilful orator, in particular when it comes to quoting from the classics. In this she appears more accomplished than Calisto, and indeed far more eloquent and dignified. Pleberio in turn comes across as a loving and enlightened father, concerned with her daughter's education and with her personal happiness and even freedom, including the 'strange news' of her right to have a say in her own marriage. All of which adds an even more poignant background to the devastating disappointment of his final lament.

Unique among all the characters of *La Celestina*, Melibea manages to keep to a high moral ground. Next to the tragic final monologue by Pleberio, the only character that somehow manages to rise with dignity above a narrative deprived of an explicit moral undertow is the Melibea we contemplate through the oration she pronounces before her suicide. She may have been bewitched and deluded by Celestina's tricks, but once she has committed herself to an honest devotion to Calisto, she carries what she contemplates as an emotional, even a moral, imperative to its ultimate consequences. She stands in sharp contrast with Calisto, who sets off as a foolish brat full of bombastic amorous rhetoric only to reveal himself as a rough, sex-obsessed lover in the scene before his absurd and bathetic demise. Melibea's dignified idealism also contrasts with the murderous greed of the servants who slaughter Celestina when she refuses to share the profits with them. Melibea may end up paying with her own life and enduring eternal perdition, but at least she does so in coherent pursuit of a sincere sentimental attachment to the person she has come to love.

The mixed response that *La Celestina* met with in Spain over the decades that followed its publication can be illustrated by Simón Borgoñón's dedicatory epistle to his 1570 Salamanca edition. Borgoñón is also relevant here because his case prefigures both the milieu into which Mabbe's English translation was launched, and the kind of reactions it elicited. It also exemplifies the evolution that the conditions for the production and reception of literary texts had undergone both in Spain and in England between the very end of the fifteenth and the early years of the seventeenth centuries. These two topics, and the way in which an approach to them shows how *La Celestina* and *The Spanish Bawd* illuminate each other, will be the subjects of the last part of this introduction.

Borgoñón defends the *Tragicomedia* from its detractors by voicing two of the most common critical assessments that *La Celestina* has traditionally elicited from its defenders. The first of them is its realism: Borgoñón says that comedies and tragedies are nothing but mirrors of real life ('un espejo de lo que pasa en la vida'), and that the plot of *La Celestina* displays nothing but current events. In this he prefigures Mateo Alemán's description of his *Guzmán de Alfarache* as a 'watch tower of human existence' ('atalaya de la vida humana'). Borgoñón's second claim is that only those who follow the bad examples are corrupted by works like this, whereas the truly discerning reader can benefit both from its good examples, and from the warnings offered by the sinful, immoral types that such works depicted.[67]

Borgoñón was one of the most important publishers serving the university of Salamanca, and played an important role in the establishment of another central text in the Spanish canon with his edition of Garcilaso de la Vega's poetry — which so far had only appeared in joint editions with the works of Juan Boscán — in 1569, just one year before his *Celestina*. In other words, Borgoñón was an important agent in the crystallization of an early modern Hispanic canon. He produced a new polished and corrected edition based upon the 1514 text of the *Tragicomedy*

---

[67] Simón Borgoñón, [Dedicatoria], in Fernando de Rojas, *La Celestina. Tragicomedia de Calisto y Melibea* [Salamanca 1570] ed. by Emilio de Miguel (Madrid: Ediciones de la Fundación José Antonio de Castro, 2006), pp. 7–8.

under the supervision of a team of 'doctos', a new generation of rhetoricians and humanists from within the circles of the university of Salamanca, the same milieu where Nebrija had published his dictionaries and grammars, and which had also generated *La Celestina* some eight decades before. The years that elapsed between the author's introduction to the Valencia edition of *La Celestina* in 1514 —ushered in by another 'docto', the humanist Alonso de Proaza — and Borgoñón's new text had witnessed important changes in the conditions of literary production and book distribution. The numbers of readers had risen in parallel with the growth of the printing industry and the expansion of the book market in response to the new demand. The changes in the conditions for the circulation of literary discourse also included the development of commercial theatre in large cities and the emergence of a new kind of reading public — mass consumers of affordable volumes and chapbooks — referred to as 'the vulgar'. In parallel with the urban stage markets, new massive and socially diverse audiences also came into existence for affordable books, pamphlets and chapbooks. The well-known and long-lasting debate between light entertainment and ponderous education was exacerbated by the growing book market, in combination with the responses of moralists, humanists and the reading public to the large variety of texts that were being issued. As Rojas had experienced a few decades before, and Borgoñón now declared, the diversity of demand called for a tempering of the contents, the style and the tenor of a text so it could suit different tastes and inclinations. In order to reach a large audience a truly tempered text must provide private entertainment while establishing a pattern for civic and moral conduct.

This ambivalence also pervaded the international responses that *La Celestina* elicited, including its reception in England and, as we have seen, James Mabbe's introduction to his own *Spanish Bawd*. After the moralizing adaptation of the text into the interlude of *Calisto and Melibea* in the 1520s, the earliest testimonies we have of *La Celestina* in England towards the end of the sixteenth century also demonstrate how the text was being introduced into a milieu that closely resembled the context into which Borgoñón had launched his own edition. In London there was a teeming literary life in which publishers, scholars and hacks, both domestic and international, absorbed, translated and issued new foreign texts as they also produced their own original materials.

And the dilemma between a literature for the educated elites and the new thriving market for popular chapbooks and plays stirred similar concerns.

Although the *Interlude of Calisto and Melibea* translated certain passages from *La Celestina*, the final result was a very free adaptation that shortened the original and modified the tragic outcome of Rojas's plot, turning it into a moralizing interlude, one of those vehicles for humanist indoctrination mentioned above. Its authorship has not been firmly established, but we do know that *Calisto and Melebea* was printed by John Rastell, Thomas More's brother-in-law. The quite radical modifications that *La Celestina* underwent here reflected the educational and moral philosophy of the circle of humanists around Henry VIII's chancellor. This circle included Juan Luis Vives, a personal friend of More, and the author of a handbook for the education of young women (*De institutione foeminae christianae*, 1523), which recommended a list of books for the proper education of girls, but also banned certain other volumes as unsuitable. The latter of these two lists included *La Celestina*, which Vives described as a *liber pestifer*.[68] This interlude was thus produced by an intellectual elite that used their plays to spread humanist doctrine and foster debate among restricted audiences within and around the court. As the sixteenth century progressed, and the literary milieu changed both in Spain and in England, the audiences that gained access to texts like *La Celestina* grew in direct proportion to the anxiety of moralists at the potentially evil effects of this type of recreational prose.

A century elapsed between the first printed adaptation of *La Celestina* (1525) in England and the publication of Mabbe's *The Spanish Bawd* (1631). Both the original, and its English versions shared a certain set of common doctrinal sources in ancient rhetoricians and early modern humanists, among them Quintilian, Petrarch or, later, Vives. But of course the different ways in which these common sources were appropriated and readapted responded to the evolution that this common tradition

---

[68] Vives's handbook was translated into English in 1529 by Richard Hyrde, another member of More's circle. See Juan Luis Vives, *The Instruction of a Christen Woman* [*De institutione foeminae christianae*], trans. Richard Hyrde [*c.* 1529], ed. by V. W. Beauchamp, E. H. Hageman & M. Mikesell (Urbana & Chicago: University of Illinois Press, 2002), p. 9; also Book 1, chapter 5: 'What bokes be to be redde, and what nat. The .v. Chapter', p. 24.

had undergone as much as to the differences between the contexts that determined their appearance, and the responses that they elicited. Mabbe's text was first printed in 1631 by John Beale for Robert Allot, although, as we have seen, the first version of the translation was probably penned about three decades before. In sharp contrast with the changes foisted by the early Tudor interlude upon Rojas's original, Mabbe's is a reasonably faithful version.[69] No other translation or adaptation — if it ever existed — that may have been published or staged between *Calisto and Melebea* and *The Spanish Bawd* has reached us. But there are certain traces of Rojas's work in England, some of which suggest the likelihood of a play based on *La Celestina*, a new edition of the *Interlude of Calisto and Melibea*, or even a new translation.[70]

The earliest of these testimonies originates in the 1566 inventory of Sir Thomas Smith's library at Hill Hall, which contained a volume with the title *Comoedia Celestina*.[71] *Celestina* appears catalogued here under the heading *Grammatica et Poetica* and in the company of works like Piccolomini's *Epistles*, Erasmus's *Adagia*, several other grammars and dictionaries, and volumes by Petrus Ramus and Joachim du Bellay. A near-contemporary of John Rastell and Juan Luis Vives, and a mentor to the English humanist Gabriel Harvey, Sir Thomas Smith (1513–1577) is a good example of the milieu that mediated between the contexts which generated the *Interlude of Calisto and Melibea* and Mabbe's *Spanish Bawd*. Smith graduated in 1530 and was one of the most prominent humanists in Cambridge, where he became regius professor of civil law in 1540. Also a politician, he became

---

[69] John Beale and Robert Allot also issued, in 1631, Ben Jonson's *Bartholomew Fair, The Devil is an Ass* and *The Staple of News*. John G. Ardila has provided an interesting survey and analysis of some relevant changes introduced by Mabbe in his rendering of *La Celestina*: 'Una traducción 'políticamente correcta': *Celestina* en la Inglaterra puritana' *Celestinesca*, 22 (1998), 33–48. Nicholas G. Round has provided an overall evaluation of Mabbe's skills and relevance as a translator: 'What made Mabbe so good?' *Bulletin of Hispanic Studies*, 78 (2001), 145–166.

[70] For further details, see Martínez Lacalle, ed., p. 5; Gustav Ungerer, *Anglo-Spanish Relations in Tudor Literature* (Bern: Francke Verlag, 1956), and Gerard G. Brault, 'English Translations of *La Celestina* in the Sixteenth Century', *Hispanic Review*, 28 (1960), 301–312.

[71] John Strype, *The Life of the Learned Sir Thomas Smith* (Oxford: Clarendon Press, 1820), appendix, p. 280. Gustav Ungerer (1956, p. 34) was the first to note the presence of *La Celestina* in Smith's inventory.

part the household of Edward Seymour, Duke of Somerset and Lord Protector, and reached the office of secretary of state in 1548, a position in which he supervised important political, financial and economic developments. He also involved himself in a controversial campaign to institute a college in Cambridge for the study of civil law. In addition, he illustrates the close relations between the impulse for legal and linguistic normalization, a joint effort which postulated the use of empirical and philological methods for the homogenization and regulation of linguistic usage, as much as for the interpretation of legal texts and the establishment of common judicial standards. John Rastell himself had also published numerous legal texts, including, *inter alia*, the statute books of Edward V and Richard III, the *Expositione terminorum legum Anglorum* (1527) or *La grande abbregement de la ley* (1514–16) by Anthony Fitzherbert, an encyclopaedic compilation of over 13,000 legal cases from the year-books. As Mabbe's Magdalen colleague Charles Butler would do some decades later, Sir Thomas Smith also published his own proposal for a spelling reform, his *De recta & emendata linguae anglicae scriptione, dialogus* (Paris, 1565). His interest in economic and financial affairs also coincides with the mentality and the activities of the dedicatee of the first English translation of *Lazarillo*, Sir Thomas Gresham (*c.*1518–1579), an international merchant, royal agent, financier, founder of the Royal Exchange and of Gresham College.[72] Smith's *Discourse of the commonweal*, written around 1549 but not published until 1581, has been described as 'the most impressive piece of economic analysis produced in the sixteenth century' (I. W. Archer, *DNB*). In that volume, and in sharp contrast with those who thought that society had to be regulated solely by moral principles, Smith acknowledged that the pursuit of self-interest was an unavoidably intrinsic feature in human nature which could not be eliminated or ignored, and should instead be redirected so that it could be mustered for the good of the commonwealth.[73] He was thus

---

[72] The most recent Spanish edition of the original is *Lazarillo de Tormes*, ed. Francisco Rico (Madrid: Real Academia Española, 2011). For a modern edition of Rowland's translation see *The Life of Lazarillo de Tormes*, trans. by David Rowland, ed. by K. Whitlock (Warminster: Aris & Phillips, Ltd., 2003).
[73] I. W. Archer, *DNB*. For further details see also A. N. McLaren, *Political Culture in the Reign of Elizabeth I. Queen and Commonwealth 1558–1585* (Cambridge: Cambridge University Press, 1999), pp. 80–90. For more details

concerned, from a very pragmatic stance, with a socially constructive reorientation of desire. *La Celestina*, as we have seen, engages in its plot with situations that involved the commodification of desire and its socially pernicious outcome, as it also shows how a certain moral disease can be detected in language use. That was the case of Calisto's noxious *poetical fictions*, so far from the standardized and hence socially productive speech *which is common unto all*, and which — in Nebrija's appropriation of Quintilian — constitutes the foundation of civil and canon laws and therefore makes it possible for individuals to live 'igualmente en esta gran compañía que llamamos ciudad'('equally in this great company we call the city').

Other references to *La Celestina* in England towards the end of the sixteenth century demonstrate that the concerns displayed in its original paratexts had not gone away in its transit to other languages.[74] Anthony Munday's *Second and Third Blast of Retrait from Plaies and Theaters* (1580) established a parallelism between the seduction of Melibea by Celestina and the seduction of English audiences by comedies, and described how the London stage absorbed plots and characters from foreign literature. The distress about the new popular audiences appears in Munday's reference to the 'ignorant multitude':

> The nature of their comedies are [. . .] like the tragical Comedie of *Calistus*; where the bawdresse *Scelestina* inflamed the maiden *Melibeia* with her sorceries [. . .] The examples whereof stirre vp the ignorant multitude to seeke by such vnlawful meanes the loue, & goodwill of others.[75]

---

on Smith's political thought in the context of Renaissance republicanism, and the literature of the period see Andrew Hadfield, *Shakespeare and Republicanism* (Cambridge: Cambridge University Press, 2005), pp. 19–22.
[74] Ungerer (1956, pp. 222–23) has also demonstrated that there was a copy of a Spanish edition of *La Celestina* in the library of Sir William Cecil, who also owned many other books in Spanish (Ungerer, 1956 pp. 228–29). Richard Stonley, Queen Elizabeth's teller of the exchequer, had a copy of one of the French translations in his library; see L. Hotson, 'The Library of Elizabeth's Embezzling Teller', *Studies in Bibliography*, 2 (1949/1950), 49–61. I am grateful to Jason Scott-Warren for sharing this information with me.
[75] Munday (1580), pp. 99–101.

The *ignorant multitude* was a source of much concern in Spain too, as proven by the frequent controversies about the *vulgo*, and the contradictory references to the value of its opinions and actual influence, notably in Lope de Vega's *Arte arte nuevo de hacer comedias*.[76] Stephen Gosson's well known *Playes Confuted in fiue Actions* (1582), provides one more reference to bawdy foreign literature used as a quarry for plots subsequently represented on the English stage. The robust demand for plays in the dynamic theatrical market of late sixteenth-century London lent a decisive impulse to the culling of plots from foreign works, which facilitated the distribution and absorption of European literary trends not just among the educated, but also among the popular classes. This contributed in turn to a literary education of sorts, and to the construction of a common idea of other European countries and cultures in the collective imaginary.

Munday's condemnation was not the last appearance of *La Celestina* in an English black list. Frances Meres's *Palladis Tamia* (London: P. Short, 1598) groups *La Celestina* with Machiavelli and a series of popular titles of chivalric fiction as part of a chapter entitled 'A choice is to be had in reading of bookes' (268^r–268^v). Here Francis Meres recommends a reading strategy similar to Mabbe's proposal in his introduction to *The Spanish Bawd*, which also echoes Borgoñón's strategy in his edition of *La Celestina*, and Rojas's injunctions in his own introduction to the Spanish original: '[. . .] all thinges are not to be looked for out of one authour, but we must take that out of each one which is most profitable [. . .] out of obscene and wicked fables some profit may be extracted' (267^v). Edward Topsell took a harder line against this type of popular books in his *Times Lamentation: or An exposition to the prophet Joel, in sundry Sermons or Meditations* (London: Edmund Bollifant, 1599). Topsell talks about 'Italian follies, Spanish inuentions, or French-fayned-wanton-volumes', works which are then 'taught to speak English' for their plots and plays by many 'histrionicall plaiers, whereby many good soules are endangered'. (pp. 63–64). We also have an indirect but potentially revealing reference in a title that appeared in 1591, *The*

---

[76] For a useful survey of references to the *vulgo* in Spanish Golden Age literature, see Aubrey F. G. Bell, *El renacimiento español*, trans. and ed. by Eduardo Julia Martínez (Málaga: Servicio de Publicaciones de la Universidad, 2004), pp. 113–117.

INTRODUCTION

Delightful History of Celestina the Faire. But far from being a translation of Rojas's work, this text is just a pirated version of Book II of *Palmerín de Oliva*, that is, *Primaleón*, probably translated from the French by William Barley. The use of the name *Celestina* in the title invites speculation on whether it was the printer or the translator's intention to boost the sales of the book by trying to associate its contents with those of Rojas's work.[77]

Henry Reynolds's *Mythomystes* of 1632 provides a more revealing, albeit ambivalent, reference to *La Celestina*. In the following passage, Reynolds, a well-read connoisseur of ancient and contemporary European literature, is decrying the degenerate state of contemporary poetry in contrast with the excellence of ancient authors. The passage is part of his introduction to a survey of the current state of poetry in Europe. He starts with Spanish letters, and in the following lines he couples *La Celestina* with other works of prose fiction:

> [. . .] from the multitude, I say, of the common rimers in these our moderne times and moderne tongues, I will exempt some few, as of a better ranke and condition than the rest. And first to beginne with Spaine, I will say it may iustly boast to haue afforded (but many Ages since) excellent Poets, as Seneca the Tragedian, Lucan and Martiall the Epigrammatist, with others; and in these latter times, as diuerse in Prose, some good Theologians also in Rime; but for other Poesies in their now spoken tongue, of any great name (not to extoll their trifling though extolled Celestina, nor the second part of their Diana de Monte Major, better much then the first, and these but poeticke prosers neither), I cannot say it affords many, if at all: The inclination of that people being to spend much more wit, and more happily, in those prose Romances they abound in, such as their Lazarillo, Don Quixote, Guzman, and those kind of Cuenta's of their Picaro's and Gitanillas, then in Rime.[78]

---

[77] See Brault (1960), p. 306; also Randall (1963), pp. 240–242. Ungerer (1956, p. 36) also points out that *La Celestina* was known to John Florio, 'who excerpted the book for his Italian-English dictionary called *Queen Anna's New World of Words* (1611).'

[78] Henry Reynolds, *Mythomystes*, in *Critical Essays of the Seventeenth Century*, ed. by J. E. Spingarn, 3 vols, 2nd edn (Bloomington: Indiana University Press, 1957), I, *1605–1650*, p. 146.

He tentatively groups *La Celestina* with romances ('Poesies') like *Diana*, and samples of prose fiction — which he distinguishes from the former as 'prose Romances' — like *Don Quixote, Lazarillo* and other *pícaros*, upon which Spaniards bestow 'much more wit, and more happily [...] than in Rime'. But though reticent about its true value, and insecure as to the generic ascription of *La Celestina*, Reynolds records the notoriety that Rojas's work — and above all certain types of contemporary Spanish prose fiction —enjoyed in England, and elsewhere. Note that all of the works he mentions had already been translated into English (*Lazarillo, Don Quixote, Diana*), some of them by Mabbe (like *Guzmán* and *Celestina*). Mabbe's activities as a translator, hand in hand with fellow Hispanists like Thomas Shelton or Bartholomew Yong, appear to be already exerting a certain influence on English perceptions of the Spanish canon in 1632, when Mabbe was still active.

Beyond England, there is no doubt that the Spanish canon was perceived as excelling in picaresque prose fiction, as is easily demonstrated by its abundant European translations. Like Venice, Basel, and other important publishing powerhouses, Antwerp and its printing industry played a central role in the international book trade and consequently in the establishment of an early modern European canon. It was also an important centre for the distribution of Spanish literature. Spanish books printed in Antwerp included *Celestina, Lazarillo de Tormes*, and the *Cancionero de romances*. The market for these books was abundant and varied: it comprehended export to Spain and the New World, but it also catered for the Spanish business community in the Netherlands, and for the Spanish troops that arrived there with the Duke of Alba in 1567.[79] John Wolfe probably had the Spanish Netherlands as his target for the volumes he published in that language, since English demand constituted just a fraction of this market. Both in England and in Spain the abundance and relevance of translations had not ceased to grow over the course of the sixteenth century. The following are tentative figures, and it is to be expected that they will soon be updated thanks to the recent creation of new databases and

---

[79] See *Celestina. An annotated edition of the first Dutch translation (Antwerp, 1550)*, ed. by Lieve Behiels and Kathleen V. Kish (Louvain: Louvain University Press, 2005), pp. 13–14.

INTRODUCTION

electronic records, but it has been estimated that during Elizabeth's reign, about twenty per cent of the total output of the book industry in England consisted of translations. And according to Victor Infantes, around thirty-five per cent of the prose fiction published in Spanish between 1489 and 1550 was translated from other languages.[80]

The last years of the sixteenth and the early decades of the seventeenth centuries, i.e. the period during which Mabbe was active as a translator, coincide with important English translations of other foreign works of prose fiction that were somehow close to Rojas's masterpiece. To name just a few in a much longer list, they included the first English version of *Lazarillo de Tormes* (1576, 2nd edn., 1586); David Rowland, the translator, describes it as full of 'strange and mery reports, very recreative and pleasant', and also as 'a true description of the nature and disposition of sundrie Spaniards' (Aii$_r$).[81] Rowland addresses his dedicatee, Sir Thomas Gresham, as someone particularly endowed with the capacity to discern the veracity of these reports, thanks to his 'travail, daily conference with diverse nations, and knowledge in all foreign matters' (Aii$_v$). Bartholomew Yong published his translation of Boccacio's *The Elegy of the Lady Fiammetta* in 1587, following the success of his English version of the Spanish pastoral romance *Diana*, by Jorge de Montemayor (*c*. 1582–83), a translation which he dedicated to Penelope Rich. In 1586 Yong also published a translation of Book IV — the rest of the volume having been rendered by George Pettie — of the influential Italian treatise on manners and sociolinguistic norms, *The Civile Conversation of M. Stephen Guazzo*. The title page of this volume describes its contents as

---

[80] H. S. Bennet, *English Books & Readers 1558–1603: Being a Study of the Book Trade in the Reign of Elizabeth I* (Cambridge: Cambridge University Press, 1965), pp. 102–104; Victor Infantes, 'La prosa de ficción renacentista: Entre los géneros literarios y el género editorial', *Journal of Hispanic Philology*, 13 (1989), 115–23. These new databases include the *Renaissance Cultural Crossroads* project, at the University of Warwick, led by Prof. Brenda Hosington <http://www2.warwick.ac.uk/fac/arts/ren/projects/culturalcrossroads/>, and the *Universal Short Title Catalogue* hosted by the University of St Andrews, directed by Prof. Andrew Pettegree http://www.ustc.ac.uk/ [both accessed on 23 September 2012].

[81] The Spanish original of *Lazarillo* also appeared under the guise of a true report, and Rico suggests that before appearing in print, it may have circulated in manuscript as a newsletter (Rico, ed., 2011, p. 95).

providing rules on 'the manner of conversation meete for all persons, which shall come in any company, out of their own houses, & then of the particular points which ought to be observed'. These were also the years when Robert Greene and his school were producing and translating chivalric and romance fiction in euphuistic prose, the years of Anthony Munday's translations of the Spanish *Amadis* series, and of the proliferation of beggar books like Greene and Thomas Dekker's rogue pamphlets. Thomas Nashe published *The Unfortunate Traveller* — generally acknowledged as the first English picaresque novel — in 1594.[82] Important agents in the English literary and scholarly scene evinced a revealing familiarity with Spanish picaresque and its nature. The last two pages of Gabriel Harvey's personal copy of John Thorius's translation of Antonio del Corro's 1590 *Spanish Grammar* (now at the Huntington Library) features a short manuscript list of Spanish authors and their works.[83] Next to *La Vida de Lazarillo de Tormes y de Fortunas y Adversidades*, the full Spanish title of *Lazarillo*, Harvey noted in his own hand, and in Spanish, 'Todos *(sic)* es nada' ('all is nothing'). This invites speculation on whether Harvey had accurately detected the disenchanted cynicism that pervaded the picaresque, or whether he simply set no value on these volumes. Twelve years before, around 1578, Harvey had grouped *Lazarillo* with *Howleglasse* — a 1565 English translation of the popular German chapbook *Till Eulenspiegel* — and John Scogan's English jestbooks in the same category, and referred to them as 'foolish Bookes'.[84]

Mabbe produced his first version of *La Celestina*, the Alnwick manuscript, in the context of this most dynamic world of letters,

---

[82] For a comparison between the Spanish picaresque and the sort of prose fiction produced in England during this period see Anne J. Cruz's 'Sonnes of the Rogue: Picaresque relations in England and Spain' in *The Picaresque: Tradition and Displacement* ed. by Giancarlo Mariorino (Minneapolis, MN: University of Minnesota Press, 1996), pp. 248–72.

[83] For further details, see C. N. Bourland, 'Gabriel Harvey and the Modern Languages', *Huntington Library Quarterly* 4 (1940), 85–106.

[84] This manuscript note features in Harvey's copy of Murner's *Holwleglas*. See Virginia F. Stern's *Gabriel Harvey. A Study of his Life, Marginalia, and Library* (Oxford: Oxford University Press, 1979), p. 49; see also Alan Paterson's 'Translation in the formation of genre: Edmund Spenser and Gabriel Harvey testify' in *Remapping the Rise of the European Novel*, ed. by Jenny Mander, *Studies on Voltaire and the Eighteenth Century* (Oxford: Voltaire Foundation, 2007), X, pp. 139–44 (pp. 140–43).

when England, and its metropolis, were fully immersed in international disputes, the religious and political controversies that gripped Europe during the last decades of the sixteenth and the early years of the seventeenth century. As London and its citizens engaged in an increasing number of domestic and international controversies, so did the pace of exchange through the publication of all sorts of materials. In the dedicatory introduction of the 1631 version to Sir Thomas Richardson — at the time Chief Justice of the King's Bench — Mabbe configures the figure of the old pander as a literal pleader whom the translator somewhat reluctantly introduces to his dedicatee. She may have been 'put into English clothes', yet 'she is a stranger', for whom Mabbe begs a 'friendly welcome'. He then rushes to declare that he would never 'accompany her with my letters of recommendation' (Epistle Dedicatory, 4–9). Mabbe admits the controversial nature of the text, and compares it with pamphlets, those printed instruments for dispute whose numbers had not ceased to grow, and had flooded the public sphere with religious, political and literary debate couched frequently in bitter terms. This definition of *The Spanish Bawd* by default as *not* a pamphlet testifies to the variety of texts in circulation at the time, their natures and functions. It also helps put Mabbe's rendering of Rojas, and in general his entire production as a translator, in a very interesting perspective under which it appears as a privileged vehicle for public debate amongst the diversity of printed matter and other media — such as the public stage, or preaching — for the circulation and exchange of ideas. *La Celestina* may be controversial, Mabbe admits, but in contrast with these pamphlets, it also provides profitable doctrine in a most pleasant style: 'It is not as many of your Pamphlets be [. . .] prickles without a Rose'. Mabbe's observation situates *The Spanish Bawd* firmly within the public sphere as it also detaches it from the more aggressive types of exchange, and elevates it to the category of that most aesthetic of objects, a rose. This is Mabbe's contribution to the literary dignification of prose fiction, to a rearrangement, as it were, of the hierarchies within the canon. *The Spanish Bawd* does enter the fray of public debate through its sententious austerity, and in doing so it could begin to aspire to stand on a par with the epic, the genre that had traditionally been privileged as the poetic mode of education *par excellence*. After decades of moralizing rejection of this sort of prose fiction, Mabbe appears as one of the champions of its literary and doctrinal relevance. *La Celestina*,

Mabbe concludes, achieves the right proportion of ornament, entertainment, doctrine and controversy. It is a truly tempered text and can thus appeal to a diversity of audiences. It is neither shallow nor vacuous delight — *luxurious* and *superfluous* — nor merely aggressive controversy — 'prickles without a Rose' (Epistle Dedicatory, 36). The kernel of the wisdom contained in *The Spanish Bawd* can be found in its 'sentences', seamlessly woven into its dialogues and its plot, very frequently in complex, paradoxical relation with the context in which they appear, and jarring with the tenor of the communicative situation in which they are put to a new use, quite different from the context in which they originated. Hence stems the complexity and the artistry of the text, and the need for a truly tempered and discerning reader that can separate the wheat from the chaff.

If the intense domestic and international controversies of these years facilitated fragmentation and dispute, there were also other tendencies, running parallel with the former, towards the establishment of common norms and links amidst the linguistic and cultural mosaic that was Europe. The influence of the Spanish translation of *Fiammetta* upon Rojas runs parallel in Spain, about one hundred years later, with Yong's translation into English of Boccaccio's work first and then Mabbe's version of *La Celestina*. As we have seen, each of them in their respective milieus and periods, Rojas and Mabbe were both part of academic and cultural circles involved in the publication of grammars and dictionaries, in the construction and / or reorganization of canons as they also normalized their linguistic communities, and in the translation of texts to furnish their respective national traditions. Educated in Italy under the influence of the linguistic humanism of scholars like Lorenzo Valla, back in Salamanca, Elio Antonio de Nebrija had published his *Gramática castellana* in 1492, and his *Vocabulario Español-Latino* three years later. The Castilian translations of the *Historia de duobus amantibus* and *Fiammetta* mentioned above probably came off the same presses that produced Nebrija's volumes in Salamanca during the 1490s.[85] Mabbe penned a Latin epigram

---

[85] The printer of Nebrija's 1492 *Gramática castellana* has been identified as Juan de Porras. For more details, and a survey of the controversies surrounding the identification of Nebrija's printer, as well as the sort of volumes produced by his workshop, see Julián Martín Abad's 'Noticia Bibliográfica' in Lozano and González Vega, eds, pp. 453–70.

for Florio's 1611 bilingual dictionary *Queen Anna's New World of Words*, and another one for Shakespeare's *First Folio*. Another of the contributors to the preliminary poems in Florio's dictionary was John Thorius. A translator like Mabbe, Thorius had in 1590 rendered into English Antonio del Corro's *Reglas gramaticales para aprender la lengua española y francesa* (Paris [really Oxford], 1586) as *The Spanish grammer: vvith certeine rules teaching both the Spanish and French tongues*.[86] This was the same grammar mentioned above, in which Gabriel Harvey had briefly sketched his reading list of Spanish titles. Thorius's English translation of Del Corro's *Reglas Gramaticales* was issued by John Wolfe, the maverick London publisher with an international dimension, well known for his editions of books in English, Italian, and Spanish.[87]

These circles were engaged in the normalization of linguistic usage in domestic terms and also with a view to the establishment of equivalents between different languages. Frequently their volumes presented bilingual dialogues that reproduced the same communicative situation. After educating their readers in its more formal aspects, they proceeded to inform them about the rules of courtesy and language use that were required in specific situations. These dialogues were introduced by a description of the speakers, their power relations with regard to each other, the topics for discussion, and the end pursued in their conversations. In short, they taught how to operate in a foreign language. This is the pragmatic foundation for an urban transnational 'language which is common to all', as postulated by Giovanni Pontano's *De sermone*, or by Sempronio, Calisto's commonsensical servant. Hence also the close connection of these dictionaries, grammars, phrasebooks, conversation and courtesy handbooks with prose fiction and its dialogues: all of them presented readers with realistic conversations that could and did occur in everyday

---

[86] See *A Catalogue of Hispanic Manuscripts and Books before 1700 from the Bodleian Library and Oxford College Libraries exhibited at the Taylor Institution 6–11 September [1962]* (Oxford: Clarendon Press, 1962), p. 19.

[87] Wolfe issued numerous translations, and also editions of works in languages other than English, not a few of them under false imprints. Many of the Spanish volumes that he produced are listed in the *Catalogue of Hispanic Manuscripts and Books* mentioned above. For further details on John Wolfe's career and publications, see C .C. Huffman, *Elizabethan Impressions. John Wolfe and his Press* (New York: AMS Press, 1988).

situations. They were all verbal mirrors of what goes on in real life, watch towers of human existence.

This ideal of a polished and polite, but nevertheless plain and common style bears an interesting relation to Rojas's combination of popular *refranes* with *adagia* taken from sources like Seneca, Aristotle, or Petrarch, and to the role played by translation as an essential mechanism for the international implementation of this stylistic norm. For there is another dimension of linguistic usage that branches out towards folk wisdom and the legitimacy stemming from the common linguistic usage of popular refrains, as opposed to the elevated wisdom and style of more authoritative *adagia*. The combination of both sources of legitimacy into a tempered and natural style resulted in a linguistic register that evinced a mind ruled by *discreción*, the linguistically productive power in the mind of the discerning reader. Local compilations of refrains and adagia (frequently collected by grammarians, rhetoricians and lexicographers) found their way into the international market of linguistic exchange through the conversation handbooks that circulated abundantly in sixteenth-century Europe, and more significantly for my purposes, also through the use of translated prose fiction as a tool for second language acquisition.

Piccolomini's Latin reflected the linguistic ideal of a civic register commonly shared by an elite of educated citizens. This style in turn rested upon the natural elegance which resulted from the imitation of the best classical authors. A university educated lawyer, Fernando de Rojas adopted and translated multiple devices from the prose patterns provided by Piccolomini's fiction and from Petrarch's stoic wisdom. But Rojas also frequently resorted to the popular register of Castilian *refranes*. This corpus of folk wisdom had already been incorporated into the Castilian canon when the poet Íñigo López de Mendoza had compiled his *Refranes que dicen las viejas tras el fuego* in the middle of the fifteenth century. Rojas combined in his prose the two main principles for the linguistic standardization of vernaculars, that is, the two normative models that competed for supremacy in the period: that of Valla, Piccolomini and Nebrija, founded on the usage of the best authors in the canon, on the one hand, and, on the other, that of Juan de Valdés (1509–1541) and those paremiologists that followed him in his defence of the linguistic and epistemological legitimacy of popular *refranes*.

INTRODUCTION

In his *Diálogo de la lengua* (composed in the 1530s) Juan de Valdés distinguished the learned origin of Erasmus's collection of *Adagia* by Greek and Latin authors from the Castilian *refranes*. The former come from well-established authoritative sources, the latter, by contrast, originate in the *vulgo*.[88] The connotations of the word *vulgo* and its cognates display the values that were bestowed upon this term, and above all how they establish connections with translation and the use of plain style. In the middle of the fifteenth century, Juan de Mena (1411–1456) had already used the verb *vulgarizar* to describe the process of rendering Homer's *Iliad* from a Latin version into a *vulgar* (romance or vernacular) language like Castilian (Juan de Mena, *La Yliada en romance*).[89] This use of the verb *vulgarizar* is parallel to the use of *romançar* (to translate into *romançe* or vernacular) in Juan de Valdés, and in others before him. *Vulgarizar* in Mena connotes making the text available to new audiences whose access to it had been precluded because it was enclosed in the arcana of Greek and Latin. For Valdés the popular origin of *refranes* in the common knowledge of the *vulgo* turns them into living proof of natural and spontaneous wisdom expressed through the purity of the Castilian language, distilled from the common usage and the refined experience of generations.

Other sixteenth-century Spanish humanists with an interest in popular paremiology followed in the wake of Santillana and Valdés. They included one of Nebrija's disciples, Hernán Núñez (also known as *Pincianus*), and Juan de Mal Lara (1524–71). Hernán Núñez (1475–1553) was like Nebrija a professor of Greek and Rhetoric in Salamanca. His *Refranes, o proverbios en romance* (Salamanca: Juan de Cánova, 1555) features a prologue by his fellow Hellenist León de Castro, who declares that their popular origin turns *refranes* into a source of universal wisdom, acknowledged by all because God had bestowed the light of understanding on all human beings. This common knowledge, according to Juan de Mal Lara's preamble to his *Philosophia vulgar* (Seville, 1568) contains the same elevated wisdom that we can find in Aristotle. Philosophy, he claims, can be articulated in

---

[88] Juan de Valdés, *Diálogo de la lengua*, ed. by J. E. Laplana (Barcelona: Crítica, 2010), pp. 125–26.
[89] On the origins of this term, see G. Folena's *Volgarizzare e tradurre* (Torino: Enaudi, 1991; first published in Trieste in 1973).

two different ways: one goes by way of its 'secret mysteries' (which Aristotle saved for his disciple Alexander the Great), whereas the other one relies on the received wisdom of the *vulgo*, obtained from their accumulated experience and expressed in 'the language which is common to all'.[90] A few years before the *Philosophia vulgar*, Ambrosio de Morales (1513–1591) had promoted in his *Discurso sobre la lengua castellana* (1546): 'el hablar ordinario que todos entienden, y todos se siruen del para manifestar lo que sienten, gozando assimismo todo lo que en el se les comunica'.[91] A few years after Lara, Dámaso de Frías continued to defend common usage as the norm for proper and decorous language in his *Diálogo de la discreción* (composed *ca.* 1579).[92] This treatise belongs in the tradition of the arts of conversation, and takes as its starting points Castiglione's *Il Cortegiano* and Giovanni Della Casa's *Il Galateo* (1558). *Il Galateo* was adapted into Spanish by Lucas Gracián Dantisco (1543–1587), and published in 1582 with the title *Galateo español*. Dantisco's admonitions on the use of language echo the same ideas to be found in Sempronio's rebuke to Calisto, and thus he bids his readers not to stray from 'común uso,' and always choose plainness over artifice ('procurando antes llaneza que no artificio').[93] The *Diálogo de la discreción* is also a near contemporary of another important handbook on the art of conversation, Stephano Guazzo's *La civil conversazione* (1574). The art of conversation, in the opinion of de Frías, rests upon the pillars of moderation and decorum. Conversation must always adapt itself to the communicative context in which it takes place, following the *discreción* of each of the interlocutors. The adaptation of speech to communicative context through the application of the speakers' *discreción* results in 'un gentil y acertado discurso de

---

[90] 'Preámbulos' to *Philosophia vulgar*, in Juan de Mal Lara's *Obras Completas*, ed. Manuel Bernal Rodríguez, 3 vols (Madrid: Fundación José Antonio de Castro, 1996) I, p. 30.
[91] Quoted in José Mondéjar Cumpián, *Castellano y Español. Dos nombres para una lengua, en su marco literario, ideológico y político* (Granada: Universidad de Granada & Editorial Comares, 2002), p. 62.
[92] This manuscript dialogue was only published in the early twentieth century by Justo García Soriano, ed., *Diálogos de diferentes materias*. Colección de Escritores Castellanos Críticos. Tomo 161 (Madrid: Imp. de G. Hernández y Galo Sáez, 1929).
[93] Lucas Gracián Dantisco, *Galateo español* ed. by Margherita Morreale (Madrid: *CSIC*, 1968), p. 164.

raçon' (a gentle and proper discourse of reason). De Frías defines *discreción* as the eminently practical application of a natural and common gift in human nature.

The concept of *discreción* is fundamental here as the tempering agent between the extremes of elitist wisdom (*i.e.*, the secret and exclusive mysteries that Aristotle communicated to Alexander the Great), and the potential populist drift of the *vulgo*, understood as the urban masses of poorly educated consumers that increasingly came to determine the commercial success of books and above all of plays on the public stage. *Discreción* is an inherent capacity that is not related to social extraction and displays itself in language. Cervantes proclaims in the second part of *Don Quijote* that: 'The language is pure, proper, and elegant, (indeed) only in your discreet Courtiers, let them be borne where they will: discreet I say, because many are otherwise, and discretion is the Grammar of good language, which is accompanied with practice'.[94] There is thus an inherent potential in all individuals that can turn, for instance, a humble artisan into a discerning reader, and therefore become enfranchised to hold one of those discreet conversations described by Dámaso de Frías. When these men of *entendimiento* (understanding) and *discreción* engage in conversation they create the virtual circles of the court of taste. The discreet reader displays a double capacity, first to draw the right moral lessons, and then to appreciate the aesthetic qualities of good literature.

What conversation signifies within a civic or courtly context, translation facilitated at the international level. Translation wove a rich and complex conversation among persons of understanding made possible by the currency of language and its exchange value, which circulated with the aid of dictionaries and handbooks for language-learning. To this effect, the sixteenth century

---

[94] *The Second Part of the History of the Valorous and Witty Knight-Errant, Don Quixote de la Mançha*, trans. by Thomas Shelton (London: Edward Blount, 1620), pp. 122–23. The sort of evolution that these concepts underwent can be illustrated by Tobias Smollett's translation of the same passage in 1755: '[. . .] purity, propriety, elegance and perspicuity are to be found among *polite people of sense*, tho' they be natives of Majalahonda: I say people of sense, because so great a number of people are not so, and *sense is the foundation of good language*, assisted by *custom and use*.' From *The History and Adventures of the Renowned Don Quixote* [1755] trans. by Tobias Smollett (New York: The Modern Library, 2004), p. 71 (my italics).

witnessed the publication of a series of books devoted to the task of weaving a common European polyglot canon. It was indeed frequent during this period for translations, dictionaries, and language-teaching handbooks to appear alongside each other as part of the same volume. Many of these books also contained collections of refrains, and conversational models in the language being taught, for students to translate and imitate. Some of them became *de facto* anthologies with samples of contemporary literature from the alien linguistic community. Many popular pieces of Castilian sentimental prose fiction were appropriated for the teaching not just of Spanish but also other vernaculars, as second languages.

John Minsheu's *Pleasant and Delightful Dialogues in Spanish*, bound in the same volume with Percyvall's *Spanish Grammar* in 1599 is a case in point.[95] One of the dialogues is introduced with the following description: 'The second Dialogue, wherin is handled to buie and sell iewels and other things, betweene a gentleman called Thomas and his wife Margaret, and a Merchant, and a goldsmith' (Minsheu, p. 10). Another one describes a situation among social peers not altogether dissimilar to some of the situations found in *La Celestina*: 'The fift Dialogue betweene three pages, called the one of them Iohn, the other Frances, the other Guzman, wherein are conteined the ordinarie speeches which pages are wont to haue one with the other' (*ibid.*, p. 38). Although samples of prose fiction that could serve this purpose had circulated for decades, shrewd publishers did not miss a new opportunity now to target simultaneously two of the most profitable niches in the market: readers of recreational prose fiction, and those who wanted to learn a foreign language.

Diego de San Pedro's *Tratado de Amores de Arnalte y Lucenda* (1491), another popular piece of Spanish romance prose fiction, was translated into English from a previous Italian version in a bilingual edition by Claudius Hollyband in 1575 with the title

---

[95] Minsheu was a self-educated polyglot who acquired his expertise through extensive foreign travel. One of the great lexicographers of his age, he was instrumental in the promotion of foreign languages in early modern England. His *Pleasant and Delightful Dialogues in Spanish* were only the prelude to a *Vocabularium Hispanicolatinum et Anglicum*, published as an appendix to his impressive *Ductor in linguas: the Guide into Tongues* (London: W. Stanby, 1617), STC (2nd edn), 17944), a multilingual English dictionary with translations into ten different languages.

INTRODUCTION

The Pretie and wittie Historie of Arnalt & Lucenda: with certen Rules and Dialogues set foorth for the learner of th'Italian tong (later reprinted in 1591).[96] Another different edition of this text, issued in 1583, reprinted in 1597 and 1608, changed its title to *The Italian Schoole-maister: Contayning Rules for the perfect pronouncing of th'italian tongue: With familiar speeches: and certain Phrases taken out of the best Italian Authors. And a fine Tuscan historie called Arnalt & Lucenda*. The fate of Juan de Flores's sentimental romance *Grisalte y Mirabella* is also very revealing. It was first published in the last years of the fifteenth century, and went through at least four Spanish editions in the sixteenth century (Toledo 1526, Seville, 1524, 1529 and 1533). The Italian translation (Milan 1521), which changed its title and went through five Venetian reprints (1526, 1529, 1533, 1543, 1548), was in turn used for both the French translation by Gil Corrozet (*Le juguement damour auquel est racomptee l'hystoire de Isabel fille du roy Descoce, translatee de Espaignol en Francoys*, 1530), and also for a new quadrilingual version published by J. Stelsius in Antwerp in 1556 (*Histoire de Aurelio, et Isabelle [. . .] nouuellement traduict en [quatre] langues, italien, espaignol, françois, & anglois*). Juan Reyne printed another bilingual edition in Antwerp in 1556 (*Historia de Aurelio y Isabela [. . .] puesta en Español y Frances para los que quisieren deprender una lengua de otra*). Some other European translations of *La Celestina* may have also been used for foreign students of Spanish: this is the case of the anonymous 1633 French translation, the third one produced in that language.[97]

Besides the dialogues mentioned above, John Minsheu's *Spanish Grammar* contains samples for the study of Spanish culled from *Lazarillo de Tormes*, Montemayor's *Diana* and *La Celestina* itself.[98] Minsheu's *Dictionarie* was preceded nine years

---

[96] For further details, see Joyce Boro, 'Multilingualism, Romance, and Language Pedagogy; or Why Were So Many Sentimental Romances Printed as Polyglot Texts? in *Tudor Translation*, ed. by F. Schurink (London: Palgrave, 2011), pp. 18–38.

[97] Homer J. Herriott, *Towards a Critical Edition of 'La Celestina'* (Madison, Wisconsin: University of Wisconsin Press, 1964), p. 334.

[98] For his samples from *La Celestina*, Minsheu used one of its international editions (Antwerp: Plantin, 1595). For further details on Minsheu, and a full list of Anglo-Spanish primers, grammars, dictionaries and dialogues printed in Elizabethan England, see Ungerer, ed., (1956), pp. 201–09.

before by Percyvall's *Bibliotheca Hispanica*. And Percyvall in turn had used Nebrija's dictionaries alongside Thomas Doyley's unpublished *Spanish Grammar*, as he declares in his introduction:

> The Dictionarie hath coste me greatest paynes; for after that I had collected it into Spanish and English out of *Christoval de las Casas*, and *Nebrissensis*; casting in some small pittaunce of mine owne, amounting well neere 2000 wordes; which neither of them had [...] In very good time, I chaunced to be acquainted with the learned Gentleman, Master *Thomas Doyley* doctor in Phisicke; who had begunne a Dictionary in Spanish, English, and Latine; and seeing mee to bee more forewards to the presse then himselfe; very friendly gaue his consent to the publishing of mine; wishing me to adde the Latine to it as hee had begunne in his; which I performed, being not a little furthered therein by his aduise and conference.[99]

Doyley's book was never published, as Percyvall himself declares. It has only survived as an entry in the Stationers' Register, entered by none other than John Wolfe on 19 October 1590, with the following title: *A Spanish Grammer conformed to our Englishe Accydence. With a large Dictionarye conteyninge Spanish, Latyn, and Englishe wordes, with a multitude of Spanishe wordes more then are conteyned in the Calapine of x: languages or Neobrecensis Dictionare. Set forth by Thomas D'Oyley, Doctor in phisick, with the co[n]firence of Natyve Spaniardes* (Helen Moore, *DNB*). Like Percyvall, Doyle had also used Nebrija (the *Neobrecensis* of his title) as one of his sources. Nebrija's own *Introductiones Latinae* of 1481 were later adapted and translated by the English Catholic John Hawkins in 1631, thus coinciding with the publication of *The Spanish Bawd*.[100] Hawkins dedicated his adaptation, entitled *A briefe introduction to syntax* to Sir Kenelm Digby, Ben Jonson's patron, and one of the 'tribe of

---

[99] Richard Percyvall, 'To the reader', in *Bibliotheca Hispanica* (London: Richard Watkins, 1591), A3r.
[100] *A briefe introduction to syntax: Compendiously shewing the true vse, grounds, and reason of Latin construction. Collected for the most part out of Nabrissa his Spanish copie. With the concordance supplyed, by I. H. [John Hawkins] med. doct. Together with the more difficult assertions, proued by the vse of the learned languages* (London: Printed by Thomas Harper, for G. Edmondson, 1631), STC (2nd edn) 688.

INTRODUCTION

Ben'. He was also cousin of John Digby, first Earl of Bristol, ambassador to Spain, and Mabbe's patron.

Like Mabbe, Thomas Doyley was a fellow of Magdalen College. He is one of the links that bring together Mabbe's education in Oxford and his interest in modern languages, towards the end of the sixteenth century, with the rhetorical and grammatical texts and with the stylistic doctrines, which were being implemented in Castile under the influence of Italian humanism and its appropriation by Nebrija, towards the end of the fifteenth century. It was then, as we have seen, that Rojas composed *La Celestina*, a text that embodied many of these doctrines, yet, at the same time, subjected them to a sophisticated literary critique.

Although separated by more than a hundred years, a comparison between these two milieus illustrates one of the manifold ways in which *La Celestina* and *The Spanish Bawd* shed light upon each other, and also upon the evolution that their respective intellectual and historical contexts underwent over the decades that mediated between the original and its English translation. Without any doubt a more detailed and comprehensive description of these networks, their agents, and the implications that arise from their mutual interaction is a *desideratum* not just in the field of Anglo-Spanish relations, but as regards the study and analysis of the processes that led to the construction of the early modern European canon. In turn, the growth and expansion of these networks, well beyond the boundaries of literature and into more interdisciplinary realms, facilitated the transition towards the transnational conglomerate that is generally referred to as the Republic of Letters of the late seventeenth, and the eighteenth centuries.

The preceding pages illustrate how the demand for translations and language-learning material naturally increased alongside the linguistic and literary development of European vernaculars, their close attachment to foundational projects of national identity, and the formation of their respective literary canons. All these phenomena were made possible by the growth of reading audiences facilitated by the revolution of print and they also went hand in hand with the important expansion of trade and the creation of profit-oriented markets for cultural products and public entertainment. *La Celestina* was first published at an early stage in the development of these phenomena, and it grew out of the linguistic concerns of humanist thought, and the more traditional patterns of sentimental romance. Thanks to print and translation it became a widespread international phenomenon that exemplifies the formation of an early modern European canon. In Mabbe's *Spanish Bawd* current readers can find a representative example of the intersection of all these phenomena, a case that illustrates the complex series of exchanges that took place through the coming together of two important moments in the Spanish and the English literary canons and the cultures that sustained them.

THE SPANISH BAWD

JOSÉ MARÍA PÉREZ FERNÁNDEZ

THE | SPANISH BAWD | *REPRESENTED* | *IN* CELESTINA, | OR | The Tragicke-Comedy of |CALISTO and MELIBEA | *Wherein is contained, besides the pleasantnesse and sweetenesse* | of the stile, many Philosophical Sentences, and profitable | Instructions necessary for the younger sort | *Shewing the deceits and subtilties housed in the bosomes of false servants* | and cunny-catching bawds | [printer's device] | LONDON | Printed by J.B. And are to be sold by | ROBERT ALLOT *at the Signe of the Beare*| in Pauls Church-yard. 1631[101]

---

[101] This is a transcription of the copy-text title-page.

The Epistle Dedicatory

To my worthy and much esteemed friend, Sir Thomas Richardson, Knight.[102]

Sir, I now send you your long since promised *Celestina*, put into English clothes. I shall entreat you to give her a friendly welcome, because she is a stranger and come purposely out of Spain into these parts, to see you, and kiss your hands. I would not accompany her with my letters of recommendation, whereby she might find the better reception. For, I must ingeniously confess, that this your Celestina is not *sine scelere*; yet must I tell you withal,
10 that she cannot be harboured with you, *sine vtilitate*.[103] Her life is foul, but her precepts are fair; her example naught, but her doctrine good; her coat ragged, but her mind enriched with many a golden sentence. And therefore take her not as she seems, but as she is; and the rather, because black sheep have as good carcasses as white. You shall find this book to be like a court-jack,°[104] which though it be black, yet holds as good liquor as your fairest flagon of silver or like the rod that Brutus offered to Apollo, which was rough and knotty without, but within, all of furbished gold.[105] The bark is bad, but the tree good.

20 Vouchsafe then (gentle Sir) to take a little of this coarse and sour bread; it may be your stomach being glutted with more delicate cates, may take some pleasure to restore your appetite with this homely, though not altogether unsavoury food. It is

---

[102] Sir Thomas Richardson (*bap.* 1569, *d.* 1635) was a Norfolk judge, and speaker of the House of Commons in the Parliament of 1621. In October of 1631, the year *The Spanish Bawd* was published, he was appointed Chief Justice of the King's Bench.

[103] The Spanish lexicographer Sebastián de Covarrubias established a false etymology in his *Tesoro de la Lengua Castellana o Española* (1611) for Celestina's name as derived from the Latin noun *scelus, -eris* (a wicked or accursed act). Hence Mabbe's quip on the contrast between *scelere* and *vtilitate* (utility or profit). In the same entry, Covarrubias also established etymologies for the names of the two lovers, Calisto and Melibea. See Sebastián de Covarrubias Orozco, *Tesoro de la lengua castellana o española* [1611]. ed. by Felipe C.R. Maldonado & Manuel Camarero (Madrid: Castalia, 1995), p. 294.

[104] See Glossary.

[105] According to the Roman historian Livy, Brutus took to Delphi an offering to Apollo, consisting of a rod of gold encased in a wooden tube (Livy 1.56.9) as an allegory of his rough appearance in contrast with his golden spirit.

good plain household-bread, honest maslin;[106] there is a great deal of rye in it, but the most part of it is pure wheat.

Our author is but short, yet pithy: not so full of words as sense, each other line being a sentence; unlike to many of your other writers, who either with the luxury of their phrases, or superfluity of figures, or superabundance of ornaments, or other affected guildings of rhetoric, like indiscreet cooks, make their meats either too sweet, or too tart, too salt, or too full of pepper; whence it happens, that like greedy husbandmen, by enlarging their hand in sowing, they make the harvest thin and barren. It is not as many of your pamphlets be, like a tree without sap; a bough without fruit; a nut without a kernel; flesh without bones; bones without marrow; prickles without a rose; wax without honey; straw without wheat; sulfure without gold; or shells without pearl. But you shall find sentences worthy to be written, not in fragile paper, but in cedar, or lasting cypress, not with the quill of a goose, but the feather of a phoenix; not with ink, but balsamum;[107] not with letters of a black tincture, but with characters of gold and azure; and deserving to be read, not only of a lascivious Clodius, or effeminate Sardanapalus, but of the gravest Cato, or severest Stoic.[108]

All which, though I know to be true, yet doubt I not, but it will meet with some detractors, who like dogs that bark by custom, will exclaim against the whole work, because some part of it seems somewhat more obscene, than may suit with a civil style, which I do not deny. Consequently, since it is written reprehensively, and not instructively, I see no reason why they should more abstain from reading a great deal of good, because they must pick it out of that which is bad, than they should refuse pearl, because it is fished for in a frothy sea; or condemn gold, because it is drawn from a dirty mine; or hate honey, because it is hived in straw; or loath silk, because it is lapped° in soultage.°

---

[106] maslin] a mixture of various grains.
[107] balsamum] i.e. balsam, an aromatic vegetable juice, frequently used in medicine for healing wounds or soothing pain.
[108] Publius Clodius Pulcher (born *c.* 92 BC) was an example of political and moral corruption. He has gone down in history as one of Cicero's most notorious political enemies. In contrast with Clodius, Cato (Marcus Porcius Cato, 95–46 BC) stood as an example of Roman republican virtues (for Cato's reputation in the English Renaissance, see Hadfield, 2005, pp. 71–2). Sardanapalus was king of Assyria, and an epitome of decadent Eastern sensuality.

Which kind of man I can liken to none better than those of whom Plutarch complains, who are of so nice a delicacy, that they will not drink a wholesome potion, unless it be given them in a golden cup, nor wear a winter garment unless it be woven of Athenian wool.

The Lacedaemonians,[109] who were strict livers and as great lovers of virtue as any nation whatsoever, would make benefit even out of vices. But these critical companions, being of a depraved disposition and apt in themselves to be evil, I can compare to nothing better, than the scarab, who overflying the most fragrant flowers, chooses rather to settle in a cow-shard, than to light upon a rose, or Noah's crow, which flew forth of the Ark, and preying upon carrion, returned no more. Howsoever therefore these rigid reprehenders will not stick to say of Celestina that she is like a crow amongst so many swans, like a grasshopper amongst so many nightingales, or like a paper-blurrer amongst so many famous writers. Yet they that are learned in her language, have esteemed it (in comparison of others) as gold amongst metals; as the carbuncle amongst stones; as the rose amongst flowers; as the palm amongst trees; as the eagle amongst birds; and as the sun amongst inferior lights. In a word, as the choicest and chiefest. But as the light of that great planet does hurt sore eyes, and comfort those that are sound of sight, so the reading of Celestina, to those that are profane, is as poison to their hearts; but to the chaste and honest mind, a preservative against such inconveniences as occur in the world.

And for my own part, I am of opinion that writers may as well be borne withal as painters who now and then paint those actions that are absurd. As Timomachus painted Medea killing her children; Orestes, murdering his mother Theo;[110] and Parrhasius, Ulysses counterfeited madness; and Cherephanes, the immodest embracements of women with men.[111] Which the spectators

---

[109] Lacedaemonians] i.e. the Spartans, well-known for their military virtues and strict education.

[110] Theo] an exceptional variant; Clytemnestra was the mother of Orestes.

[111] Timomachus and Parrhasius were Greek painters, made famous by Pliny's references to them in his *Natural History* (35.36–40), where they are praised for the vivid realism of their works. Like Rojas did with his *Celestina*, in their paintings they represented morally reprehensible acts, or even crimes against nature, yet this did not affect their reputation as great artists.

beholding, do not *laudare rem, sed artem*, not commend the matter which is expressed in the imitation, but the art and skill of the workman who has so lively represented what it proposed. In like sort, when we read the filthy actions of whores, their wicked conditions, and beastly behaviour, we are neither to approve them as good, nor to embrace them as honest, but to commend the author's judgement in expressing his argument so fit and pat to their dispositions.

Nor do I see any more reason why a man should prove a villain by reading of other mens' villainies than a man should grow hard-favoured by looking Thersites in the face, or a fool for viewing Will Summers picture, but might rather grow as the Lacedaemonians did by their slaves' drunkenness to a destestation of so foul a sin.[112] When therefore you shall read of Celestina as of a notorious bawd, of Sempronio and Parmeno as of false servants, of Elicia and Areusa as of cunning queans° and professed whores; of Centurio as of a swaggering ruffian and common whoremaster; of Calisto and Melibea as of indiscreet and foolish lovers. And so in the rest, learn thereby to distinguish between good and bad, and praise the author though not the practice; for these things are written more for reprehension than imitation. And the mind that comes so instructed can never take harm, for it will take the best and leave the worst. But he that reads all things alike, and equally entertains them in his thought, that reader shall easily show himself obnoxious to many vices. And it shall happen unto him, as it did unto those who imitated Plato's crookedness, or Demosthenes' stammering. But when a reader shall light upon unworthy lines, I would have him cry out as a philosopher advises on the like occasion: *male hoc, et inconuenienter*.[113] But when he meets with good, *recte hoc et decore*.[114] As the bee feeds upon flowers, and the goat on the tops of herbs, so would I have him that reads Celestina graze like a horse on that which is sweet and wholesome grass, and not like a hungry dog, which snatches and bites at everything that comes in his way. Socrates, when he saw a dishonest woman, would either

---

[112] Homer (*Il.* 2.212 ff.) describes Thersites as the ugliest among all the Trojan heroes. Will Summers (also spelled Somers, or Sommers) was Henry VIII's court jester.
[113] *male hoc, et inconuenienter*] 'evil and unbecoming'.
[114] *recte hoc et decore*] 'right and seemly'.

turn his head aside, or cover his eyes with his cloak, taking whores to be like coals, which either black or burn. Indeed, it was the wisest way for Socrates, for though he were a philosopher, yet withal he was a wanton: and therefore, for such as cannot look, but must offend in viewing of the looser lines, I would have them imitate the lightning, which vanishes before it scarce appears; or your abortive,° which die before they be born. But, as for those that are truly honest and of that perfect temper of goodness that nothing can make them decline from the rule of virtue, I would wish them to do with some pieces in this book (yet to read all, and where they find anything unseemly) as the priests of old were wont to do, who in their sacrifices unto Juno, took forth the garbage of their beasts, and threw it behind the altar. If any phrase savour of immodesty, blame not me, but Celestina. If any sentence deserve commendation, praise not the translator, but the author; for I am no more to be reprehended or commended than the poor parrot, who accents but other folks' words, and not his own.

If there be any that is either a Parmeno, or a Sempronio, an Elicia, or an Areusa, a Celestina, or a Centurio, I would have them to behold themselves in this glass; not doubting but that as Narcissus viewing himselfe in that pure clear fountain wherein he saw his own most beautifull image died overcome with a φιλαυτία, or self-love; so these men will either die, or their vices in them, through an αυτομισια, or hate of themselves; at least make other mens' miserable ends serve as so many seamarks, that they may not run themselves upon the like rocks in the sea of this life, wherein all they are miserably drowned, who strike against them.

But to leave Celestina to a favourable censure, I must now come to entreat some favour for myself, who am so far from pleading my excuse that I must wholly submit myself to your favourable interpretation; for I must ingeniously confess that I have in the undergoing of this translation shown more boldness than judgement. For though I do speak like Celestina, yet come I short of her, for she is so concisely significant, and indeed so differing is the idiom of the Spanish from the English, that I may imitate it, but not come near it. Yet have I made it as natural as our language will give leave, and have more beaten my brains about it in some places than a man would beat a flint to get fire; and, with much ado, have forced those sparks, which increasing to a greater flame, gave light to my dark understanding. Wherein if I have been wanting to give it its true life, I wish my industry herein may awake some better wit and judgement to perfect my imperfections, which as I shall always be willing to acknowledge, so I desire to have them mended by some better hand. Nor am I any whit ashamed that any work of mine should not be absolutely perfect. For it is the statute and decree of heaven, that every composition here beneath, as well framed by the hand of art as fashioned by the help of nature, should sustain some imperfection. For glass has its lead, gold its dross, corn its chaff, Helen her mole, the moon her spots, and the sun its shade.[115] My expression is but like a picture drawn with a coal, wanting those lively colours, which others more skilful might give it, and might better it as much if they would undergo the pains, as bad faces are bettered by painting, and unsavory meats mended by their sauces. But I am too saucy in my desire. Howsoever, I will notwithstanding show myself a good Christian, that though my works do not merit any reward, yet my faith and assurance is such in you that I make no question but my works shall be well accepted by you. In requital whereof, I will ever love you, and rest

Your friend and servant,

Don Diego Puede-ser

---

[115] According to some traditions, Helen of Troy had a facial mole — or a scar, in other versions of this story. Like other cases listed by Mabbe here, this imperfection enhanced her beauty. Mabbe could find echoes of this story in late sixteenth-century authors like Robert Greene, John Lyly, or Francis Meres. For further details see Laurie Maguire's *Helen of Troy: From Homer to Hollywood* (London: Wiley-Blackwell, 2009), pp. 59–61.

JAMES MABBE, THE SPANISH BAWD

The Prologue

It is the saying of that great and wise philosopher Heraclitus, that all things are created in manner of a contention or battle. His words are these: *omnia secundum litem fiunt*. A sentence in my opinion worthy [of] perpetual memory, and, for that most certain it is, that every word of a wise man is pregnant and full, of this it may be said, that through too much fulness it is ready to burst, shooting forth such spreading and well-grown boughs and leaves that out of the smallest sucker° or least sprig thereof, fruit enough may be gathered by men of discretion and
10 judgment. But because my poor understanding is not able to do any more than to nibble on the dry bark and rugged rind of the wise sayings of those who for the clearness and excellency of their wits deserved to be approved, with that little which I shall pluck from thence, I will satisfy the intent and purpose of this short prologue. This sentence did I find to be strengthened by that great orator and poet laureate Francisco Petrarca, who tells us, *sine lite atque offensione nihil genuit natura parens*:[116] that nature, who is the mother of all things, engendered nothing without strife and contention. Furthermore saying, *sic est enim,*
20 *et sic propemodum universa testantur, rapido stellae obuiant firmamento, contraria inuicen elementa confligunt, terrae tremunt, maria fluctuant, aer quatitur, crepant flammae, bellum immortale venti gerunt, tempora temporibus concertant, secum, singula, nobiscum omnia.*[117] Which is as much to say: indeed so it is, and so all things almost in the world do witness as such. The stars

---

[116] Petrarch's preface to Book II of his *De remediis*. Rojas must have used Johan Amerbach's Basel edition of Petrarch's *Opera latina*, which had just been published in 1496. He translated and adapted some of the *topoi* in the *Praefatio* and also many of the *proverbia* he found in the alphabetical index at the end of that volume, not just in the introduction, but also ascribing them to his characters as part of their dialogues, and in particular skilfully weaving them into Celestina's persuasive orations (see for instance, my notes to 5.125 and 7.34 below). For further details see Deyermond 1961 and José Guillermo García Valdecasas, *La adulteración de 'La Celestina'* (Madrid: Castalia, 2000), 234–35. The use of indexes to relate topics and establish connections between different texts was a well-established method: on how Ben Jonson made use of indexes and classifications, see Hutson, ed. 2012, 'Introduction' p. 488.

[117] Also from Petrarch's preface to Book II of *De remediis*. The Latin text is immediately followed by its translation.

encounter one another in the whirling firmament of heaven, your contrary elements wage war each with other, the earth, that trembles and quakes as if it were at odds with itself, the sea, that swells and rages, breaking its billows one against another, the air, that darts arrows of lightning and is moved this way and that way, the flames, they crack and sparkle forth their fury, the winds are at perpetual enmity with themselves, times with times do contend, one thing against another, and all against us. We see that the summer makes us complain of too much heat, and the winter of cold and sharpness of weather. So that this, which seems unto us a temporal revolution, this, by which we are bred up and nourished, and live, if it once begins to pass above its proportion, and to grow to a greater height than usual, it is no better than open war. And how much it ought to be feared is manifested by those great earthquakes and whirlwinds, by those shipwrecks and fires, as well in the air as the earth, by the source of water-courses, and violence of inundations, by those courses, and recourses,° those rackings to and fro of the clouds, of whose open motions to know the secret cause from whence they proceed, no less is the dissension of the philosophers in the schools, than of the waves of the sea. Besides, among your brute beasts, there is not any of them that wants his war; be they fishes, birds, beasts, or serpents; whereof, every kind persecutes and pursues one another. The lion, he pursues the wolf, the wolf the kid, the dog the hare. And if it might not be thought a fable, or old wives' tale sitting by the fireside, I should more fully enlarge this theme. The elephant, that is so powerful and strong a beast, is afraid and flies from the sight of a poor silly mouse, and no sooner hears him coming but he quakes and trembles for fear. Among serpents, nature created the basilisk, so venomous and poisonous, and gave him such a predominant power over all the rest, that only with his hissing, he doth affright them; with his coming, put them to flight, and disperses some one way, some another, and with his fight, kills and murders them. The viper, a crawling creature and venomous serpent, at the time of engendering, the male puts his head into the mouth of the female and she through the great delight and sweetness of her pleasure strains him so hard that she kills him. And concerning her young, the eldest or first of her brood breaks the bars of his mother's belly, eats out his way through her bowels, at which place all the rest issue forth, whereof she dies; he doing this as a revenger of his father's death.[118] What greater conflict, what greater contention or war can there be, than to conceive that in her body which shall eat out her entrails? Again, no less natural dissension can we suppose to be among fishes; for most certain it is, that the sea does contain as many several sorts of fishes as the earth and air do nourish birds and beasts, and much more. Aristotle and Pliny do recount wonders of a little fish called Aecheneis, how apt his nature is and how prone his property for diverse kinds of contentions, especially this one: that if he clings to a ship or carrack, he will detain and stop her in her course, though she have the wind in the poop of her, and cut the seas with never so swift a gale. Whereof Lucan makes mention, saying

Non puppim retinens, Euro tendente rudentes,
In mediis Aechenis aquis.[119]

Nor Aechenis, whose strength, though Eurus rise,
Can stay the course of ships

Oh natural contention! Worthy of admiration that a little fish should be able to do more than a great ship with all the force and strength of the winds. Moreover, if we will discourse of birds and of their frequent enmities, we may truly affirm that all things are created in a kind of contention. Your greater live off rapine, as eagles and hawks; and your craven kites press upon our pullen°, insulting° over them even in our own houses, and offering° to take them even from under the hen's wings. Of a bird called roc, which is bred in the East Indian sea, it is said to be of an incredible greatness, that the like has never been heard of; and that with her beak, she will hoist up into the air, not only one man, or ten, but a whole ship laden with men and merchandise; and how that these miserable passengers, hanging thus in suspension in the air till her wings wax weary, she lets them fall, and so they receive their deaths. But what shall we say of men, to whom all the aforesaid creatures are subject? Who can express their wars, their jars°,

---

[118] All these cases, including the striking story of the viper and its offspring, are directly taken from Petrarch's *De remediis* II, *Praefatio* (see Lobera *et al.*, eds, 2000, pp. 17–18, n. 24).

[119] The echeneis is the remora, or sucking-fish. The Latin verses are from Lucan, *De bello civili* 6.674–75.

their enmities, their envies, their heats, their broils, their brawls, and their discontentments? That change and alteration of fashions in their apparel? That pulling down and building up of houses? And many other sundry effects and varieties; all of them proceeding from the feeble and weak condition of man's variable nature? And because it is an old and ancient complaint, and used heretofore time out of mind, I will not much marvel, if this present work shall prove an instrument of war to its readers, putting strife and differences among them, every one giving his verdict and opinion thereupon, according to the humour of his own will. Some perhaps may say that it is too long, some too short, others to be sweet and pleasant; and other some to be dark and obscure. So that to cut it out to the measure of so many and such different dispositions is only appropriate to God. Especially since that it, together with all other things whatsoever are in this world, march under the standard of his noble sentence. For even the very life of men, if we consider them from their first and tender age till they grow grey-headed, is nothing else but a battle. Children with their sports, boys with their books, young men with their pleasures, old men with a thousand sorts of infirmities, skirmish and war continually. And these papers, with all ages. The first blots and tears them; the second knows not well how to read them; the third (which is the cheerful livelihood of youth, and set all upon jollity) does utterly dislike of them. Some gnaw only the bones, but do not pick out the marrow, saying there is no goodness in it; that it is a history, huddled, I know not how, together, a kind of hodgepodge, or gallimaufry;[120] not profiting themselves out of the particularities, accounting it a fable, or old wives' tale, fitting for nothing, save only for to pass away the time upon the way. Others call out the witty conceits, and common proverbs, highly commending them, but flighting° and neglecting

---

[120] a kind of hodgepodge, or gallimaufry] There is no equivalent for this expression in Rojas's original text. I am grateful to Andrew Hadfield for pointing out the existence of an identical expression in Spenser's *Shepheardes Calender*, where E.K.'s letter to Gabriel Harvey complains against those who have defiled English with 'peces & rags of other languages, borrowing here of the french, there of the Italian, euery where of the Latine, not weighing how il, those tongues accorde with themselues, but much worse with ours: So now they haue made our English tongue, a gallimaufray or hodgepodge of al other speches'. See Spenser, *The Shepheardes Calender* (London: Hugh Singleton, 1579), ¶iiv; STC (2nd edn) 23089.

130   that which makes more to the purpose and their profit. But they for whose true pleasure it is wholly framed reject the story itself as a vain and idle subject, and gather out the pith and marrow of the matter for their own good and benefit, and laugh at those things that savour only of wit and pleasant conceit, storing up in their memory the sentences and saying of philosophers that they may transpose them into such fit places as may make upon occasion for their own use and purpose.[121] So that when ten men shall meet together to hear this comedy, in whom perhaps shall happen this difference of dispositions, as it usually falleth out,
140   who will deny but that there is a contention in that thing which is so diversely understood? The printers, they likewise have bestowed their puncture,[122] putting titles, and adding arguments to the beginning of every act; delivering in brief what is more largely contained therein, a thing very excusable, in former times being much used, and in great request with your ancient writers; others have contended about the name, saying that it ought not to be called a comedy, because it ends in sorrow and mourning, but rather termed a tragedy. The author himself would have it take its denomination from its beginning, which treats of
150   pleasure, and therefore called it a comedy. So that I seeing these differences, between their extremes have parted this quarrel by dividing it in the midst, and call it a tragicomedy. So that observing these contentions, these disagreements, these dissonant and

---

[121] Rojas here acknowledges the variety of the text, which combines 'common proverbs' with 'the sayings and sentences of philosophers' (see introduction). This variety accounts for the diversity of responses that it elicited, and these, in turn, prompted Rojas's instructions on how it should be read by those 'for whose true pleasure it is wholly framed'.

[122] puncture] Mabbe's translation of 'punturas', defined by the *Diccionario de la Real Academia Española* (henceforth *DRAE*) as 'Cada una de las dos puntas de hierro afirmadas en los dos costados del tímpano de una prensa de imprimir, o fijas en la superficie del cilindro de las máquinas sencillas, en las cuales se clava y sujeta el pliego que ha de tirarse', i.e. the pins or nails that were used to fix the sheet of paper to the press during the printing process. Rojas explicitly denies here authorship of the moralizing arguments, which were never part of his original plans. This is both a testimony to the sort of controversy the original text must have caused, and of the changes introduced after these initial reactions, which included a redefinition of its genre, from comedy to tragicomedy, and the addition of five new acts. It also illustrates the role played by printers in the final formatting of a text — and its eventual reception by its readership.

various judgements, I had an eye to mark whither the major part inclined, and found that they were all desirous that I should enlarge myself in the pursuit of the delight of these lovers; whereunto I have been earnestly importuned; insomuch, that I have consented (though against my will) to put now the second time my pen to this so strange a task, and so far estranged from my faculty, stealing some hours from my principal studies, together with others alloted to my recreation, though I know, I shall not want new detractors for my new edition.

JAMES MABBE, THE SPANISH BAWD

THE ACTORS
IN THIS TRAGICOMEDY

CALISTO, a young enamoured gentleman
MELIBEA, daughter to Pleberio
PLEBERIO, father to Melibea
ALISA, mother to Melibea
CELESTINA, an old Bawd
PARMENO, servant to Calisto
SEMPRONIO, servant to Calisto
TRISTAN, servant to Calisto
SOSIA, servant to Calisto
CRITO, a whoremaster
LUCRECIA, maid to Pleberio
ELICIA, whore
AREUSA, whore
CENTURIO, a pander, or ruffian

JOSÉ MARÍA PÉREZ FERNÁNDEZ

A
Comedy
or
Tragicomedy of
Calisto and Melibea

The Argument

Calisto, who was of lineage noble, of wit singular, of disposition gentle, of behaviour sweet, with many graceful qualities richly endowed, and of a competent estate,[123] fell in love with Melibea, of years young, of blood noble, of estate great, and only daughter and heir to her father Pleberio and to her mother Alisa, of both exceedingly beloved. Whose chaste purpose conquered by the hot pursuit of amorous Calisto, Celestina[124] interposing herself in the business, a wicked and crafty woman and, together with her, two deluded servants of subdued Calisto, and by her wrought to be
10 disloyal, their fidelity being taken with the hook of covetousness and pleasure. Those lovers came, and those that served them, to a wretched and unfortunate end. For entrance whereupon, adverse fortune afforded a fit and opportune place, where, to the presence of Calisto, the desired Melibea presented herself.

---

[123] 'Estado mediano' in the original (i.e. middling state), described by Lobera *et al.*, eds, (2000), p. 23, n. 6, as his social position. This information about the social extraction of the two lovers contradicts what Sempronio says about them in 9.204, where Calisto is described as a *caballero*, i.e. an aristocrat (arguably of a *median income*, i.e. somewhat impoverished), whereas Melibea is described as the daughter of an *hidalgo* family (i.e. a member of the lower aristocracy), rendered by Mabbe as 'Calisto is a noble gentleman, Melibea the daughter of honourable parents'. Melibea's father, however, describes himself as a wealthy entrepreneur in his final lament.

[124] *Celestine* in the 1631 edition. I have regularized the few occasions in which this spelling is used into the far more frequent, and common *Celestina*.

JAMES MABBE, THE SPANISH BAWD

Actus I
The Argument

Calisto entering into a garden after his usual manner, met there with Melibea, with whose love being caught, he began to court her. By whom being sharply checked and dismissed, he gets him home, being much troubled and grieved. He consults his servant Sempronio, who after much intercourse of talk, and debating of the business, advised him to entertain an old woman, named Celestina, in whose house his said servant kept a wench to whom he made love, called Elicia, who, Sempronio coming to Celestina's house about his master's business, had at that time another sweetheart in her company called *Crito*, whom they hid out of sight. In the interim that Sempronio was negotiating with Celestina, Calisto falls in talk with another of his servants, named Parmeno, which discourse continues till Sempronio and Celestina arrive at Calisto's house. Parmeno was known by Celestina, who tells him of the good acquaintance which she had of his mother, and many matters that had passed between them; inducing him in the end to love and concord with Sempronio.

INTERLOCUTORS
Calisto, Melibea, Parmeno, Sempronio, Celestina, Elicia, Crito

Calisto. In this, Melibea, I see heaven's greatness, and goodness.
Melibea. In what, Calisto?
Calisto. Greatness, in giving such power to nature, as to endow thee with so perfect a beauty, goodness, in affording me so great a favour as thy fair presence, and a place so convenient to unsheathe my secret grief; a grace undoubtedly so incomparable, and by many degrees far greater than any service I have performed can merit from above. What inhabitant here below ever saw a more glorious creature than I behold. Certainly, if sublunary bodies can give a celestial reflection or resemblance, I contemplate and find it in thy divine beauty: had it perpetuity, what happiness beyond it?[125] Yet wretch that I am, I must

---

[125] The pre-Copernican cosmos consisted of a series of concentric spheres, with the earth as its centre. The most immediate sphere was that of the moon, followed by the planets in a scale of increasing perfection. Sublunary bodies

live like another Tantalus; see what I may not enjoy, not touch; and my comfort must be the thinking of thy disdain, thy pleasing coyness, and the torment which thy absence will inflict upon me.

Melibea. Holdest thou this, Calisto, so great a reward?[126]

Calisto. So great, that if you should give me the greatest good upon earth, I should not hold it so great a happiness.

Melibea. I shall give thee a reward answerable to thy deserts, if thou persevere and go on in this manner.

Calisto. Oh fortunate ears! Which are (though unworthily) admitted to hear so gracious a word, such great and comfortable tidings.

Melibea. But unfortunate, by that time thou hast heard thy doom. For thy payment shall be as foul as thy presumption was foolish, and thy entertainment as small, as thy intrusion was great. How durst such a one as thou hazard thy self on the virtue of such a one as I? Go wretch, be gone out of my sight, for my patience cannot endure that so much as a thought should enter into any man's heart, to communicate his mind unto me in illicit love.

Calisto. I go, but as one who am the only unhappy mark against whom adverse fortune aims the extremity of her hate. Sempronio, Sempronio, why, Sempronio, I say, where is this accursed varlet?

Sempronio. I am here sir, about your horses.

Calisto. My horses, you knave, how haps it then that thou comst out of the hall?

Sempronio. The grey-falcon° bated,[127] and I came in to set him on the perch.

Calisto. Is't e'en so? Now the devil take thee; misfortune wait on thy heels to thy destruction; mischief light upon thee, let some

---

were all those dwelling under the moon — the realm of mortality and decay. Calisto sees in Melibea a celestial reflection of the superior beauty of the higher spheres.

[126] In the original, both lovers use the familiar *tu* mode of address, as do all the characters in the rest of the text (see the introduction). There is a considerable degree of inconsistency in Mabbe's use of *thou / you* and its derivatives, which can hardly be interpreted as significant stylistic choices.

[127] bated] bate, v. to beat with the wings, flutter; here it translates the Spanish *abatirse*, i.e. when applied to a bird of prey, to hurl itself down, usually in search of a prey (for a different, but related meaning, see note to 12.402 below).

perpetual intolerable torment seize upon thee in so high a degree, that it may be beyond all comparison, till it bring thee (which shortly I hope to see) to a most painful, miserable, and disastrous death. Go, thou unlucky rogue, go I say, and open the chamber door, and make ready my bed.

Sempronio. Presently sir, the bed is ready for you.

Calisto. Shut the windows, and leave darkness to accompany him, whose sad thoughts deserve no light. Oh death! How welcome art thou, to those who out-live their happiness? How welcome, wouldst thou but come when thou art called? Oh that Hippocrates and Galen, those learned physicians were now living, and both here, and felt my pain! Oh heaven, if yee have any pity in you, inspire that Pleberian[128] heart therewith, lest that my soul, helpless of hope, should fall into the like misfortune with Pyramus and Thisbe.

Sempronio. What a thing is this? What's the matter with you?

Calisto. Away, be thee gone, do not speak to me, unless thou wilt, that these my hands, before thy time be come, cut off thy days by speedy death.

Sempronio. Since you will lament all alone, and have none to share with you in your sorrows, I will be gone, sir.

Calisto. Now the devil go with thee.

Sempronio. With me, sir? There is no reason that he should go with me, who stays with you. (Oh unfortunate, oh sudden and unexpected ill; what contrarious accident, what squint-eyed star is it that has robbed this gentleman of his wonted mirth? And not of that alone, but of it which is worse, his wits. Shall I leave him all alone? Or shall I go in to him? If I leave him alone, he will kill himself. If I go in, he will kill me. Let him bide alone, and bite upon the bit, come what will. Come I care not. Better it is that he die whose life is hateful unto him, than that I die when life is pleasing unto me, and say that I should not desire to live, save only to see my Elicia, that alone is motive enough to make me look to myself, and guard my person from dangers. But admit he should kill himself without any witness, then must I be bound to give account of his life. Well, I will in for that, but put case when I come in, he will take

---

[128] Pleberian heart] Melibea's heart (since she was Pleberio's daughter). Hippocrates and Galen were famous physicians from classical antiquity, the two greatest authorities in medieval and renaissance medicine.

neither comfort nor counsel. Marry his case is desperate, for it is a shrewd sign of death, not to be willing to be cured. Well, I will let him alone a while, and give his humour leave to work out itself. I will forbear, till his angry fit be over-past, and that his hat be come again to his colour. For I have heard say that it is dangerous to lance or crush an impostume° before it be ripe, for then it will fester the more. Let him alone awhile, let us suffer him to weep who suffers to sorrow, for tears and sighs do ease the heart that is surcharged with grief. But then again, if he see me in sight, I shall see him more incensed against me. For there the sun scorches most, where he reflects most. The sight which has no object set before it, waxes weary and dull, and having its object, is as quick. And therefore I think it my best play, to play least in sight, and to stay a little longer. But if in the mean while he should kill himself, then farewell he. Perhaps I may get more by it than every man is aware of, and cast my skin, changing rags for robes, and penury for plenty. But it is an old saying: he that looks after dead-men's shoes, may chance to go barefoot. Perhaps also the devil has deceived me, and so his death may be my death, and then all the fat is in the fire,[129] the rope will go after the bucket, and one loss follow another.[130] On the other side, your wise men say that it is a great ease to a grieved soul or one that is afflicted to have a companion to whom he may communicate his sorrow. Besides it is generally received that the wound which bleeds inward is ever the more dangerous. Why then in these two extremes hang I in suspense what I were best to do? Sure, the safest is to enter. And better it is that I should endure his anger, than for fear of his displeasure to forbear to comfort him. For, if it be possible to cure without art, and without things ready at hand, far easier is it to cure by art, and wanting nothing that is necessary.)

Calisto. Sempronio?

---

[129] the fat is in the fire] The *OED* defines this expression (*fat*), in its early use, as 'expressing that a design has irremediably failed'. It somewhat freely translates the original 'y si muere, matarme han'.

[130] Mabbe translates thus the general idea that underlies the Spanish proverbial phrase 'irán allá la soga y el calderón' (about which see Lobera *et al.*, eds (2000), p. 31, n. 70): Mabbe clarifies the original meaning of these two proverbs with his 'one loss follow another'.

Sempronio. Sir.
Calisto. Reach me that lute.
Sempronio. Sir, here it is.
Calisto.
> Tell me what grief so great can be
> As to equal my misery

120 *Sempronio.* This lute, sir, is out of tune.
Calisto. How shall he tune it, who himself is out of tune? Or how canst thou hear harmony from him who is at such discord with himself? Or how can he do anything well, whose will is not obedient to reason, who harbours in his breast needles, peace, war, truce, love, hate, injuries and suspicions, and all these at once, and from one and the same cause? Do thou therefore take this lute unto thee, and sing me the most doleful ditty thou canst devise.
Sempronio.

130
> Nero, from Tarpey, does behold
> How Rome does burne all on a flame;[131]
> He hears the cries of young and old,
> Yet is not grieved at the same.

Calisto. My fire is far greater, and less her pity whom now I speak of.
Sempronio. (I was not deceived when I said my master had lost his wits.)
Calisto. What's that, Sempronio, thou mutterest to thyself?[132]
Sempronio. Nothing, sir, not I.
140 *Calisto.* Tell me what thou saidst: be not afraid.

---

[131] Nero is described here contemplating Rome from the Tarpeian rock, a promontory in the Capitolium used for the execution of criminals and traitors. The original that Mabbe translates here was a Castillian *romance* (i.e. a popular type of narrative lyric or ballad, usually anonymous, written in rhyming octosyllables) on the burning of Rome. It circulated orally in the 15th century — *La Celestina* provides its first documented appearance — and it was afterwards frequently distributed in chapbooks and poetic anthologies during the sixteenth and the seventeenth centuries. For further details, see Lobera *et al.*, eds (2000), p. 33, n. 79, and their long notes, p. 530.

[132] This is one of the few instances in which the use of *you / thou* carries significant connotations. Sempronio in his asides uses *thou* to address Calisto, whereas in his direct addresses to his master he resorts to the more respectful *you*.

Sempronio. Marry I said, how can that fire be greater which but torments one living man than that which burnt such a city as that was, and such a multitude of men?

Calisto. How? I shall tell thee. Greater is that flame which lasts fourscore years than that which endures but one day. And greater that fire which burns one soul than that which burns a hundred thousand bodies. See what difference there is betwixt appearance and existence, betwixt painted shadows and lively substances, betwixt that which is counterfeit and that which is real. So great a difference is there betwixt that fire which thou speakest of, and that which burns me.

Sempronio. (I see I did not mistake my bias, which, for aught I perceive, runs worse and worse. Is it not enough to show thyself a fool, but thou must also speak profanely?)

Calisto. Did I not tell thee, when thou speakest, that thou shouldest speak aloud? Tell me what's that thou mumblest to thyself.[133]

Sempronio. Only I doubted of what religion your lovers are.

Calisto. I am a Melibean, I adore Melibea, I believe in Melibea, and I love Melibea.

Sempronio. (My master is all Melibea: who now but Melibea, whose heart able to contain her, like a boiling vessel venting its heat goes bubbling her name in his mouth.) Well I have now as much as I desire: I know on which foot you halt, I shall now heal you.

Calisto. Thou speakest of matters beyond the moon. It is impossible.

Sempronio. Oh sir, exceeding easy, for the first recovery of sickness is the discovery of the disease.

Calisto. What counsel can order that which in itself has neither counsel nor order?

Sempronio. (Ha, ha, ha, Calisto's fire, these his intolerable pains. As if love had bent his bow, shot all his arrows only against

---

[133] Mabbe here omits a significant passage in the original, which contains some of Calisto's heretical remarks: 'si el del purgatorio es tal, más querría que mi espíritu fuese con los de los brutos animales que por medio de aquél ir a la gloria de los santos' (Lobera *et al.*, eds, 2000, p. 34), i.e. if the purifying fire of purgatory is similar to the love that now burns his soul, Calisto proclaims he would rather share the fate of animals — i.e. the death of his own spirit — rather than eventually reach heaven through so much pain.

him. Oh Cupid, how high and unsearchable are thy mysteries? What reward hast thou ordained for love, since that so necessary a tribulation attends on lovers? Thou hast set his bounds as marks for men to wonder at: lovers ever deeming, that they only are cast behind; and that others still out-strip them; that all men break through but themselves like your light-footed bulls, which being let loose in the place, and galled with darts, take over the bars as soon as they feel themselves pricked.)

Calisto. Sempronio.

Sempronio. Sir.

Calisto. Do not you go away.[134]

Sempronio. (This pipe sounds in another tune.)

Calisto. What dost thou think of my malady?

Sempronio. That you love Melibea.

Calisto. And nothing else?

Sempronio. It is misery enough to have a man's will captivated and chained to one place only.

Calisto. Thou wot'st[135] not what constancy is.

Sempronio. Perseverance in ill is not constancy, but obstinacy, or pertinacy. So they call it in my country, however it please you philosophers of Cupid to phrase it.

Calisto. It is a foul fault for a man to belie that which he teaches to others: for thou thyself takest pleasure in praising thy Elicia.

Sempronio. Do you that good which I say, but not that ill which I do.

Calisto. Why dost thou reprove me?

Sempronio. Because thou dost subject the dignity and worthiness of a man to the imperfection and weakness of a frail woman.

Calisto. A woman? O thou blockhead, she's a goddess.

Sempronio. Are you in earnest, or do you but jest?

Calisto. Jest? I verily believe she is a goddess.

Sempronio. As goddesses were of old, that is, to fall below mortality, and then you would hope to have a share in their deity.[136]

---

[134] Here Calisto uses *you* to address Sempronio, but in the next line he returns to *thou*.

[135] wot'st] know.

[136] Mabbe omits another irreverent passage here: Calisto declares that Melibea is his only goddess, and that he does not acknowledge any other sovereign in heaven, since his lady inhabits the world: 'Por Dios la creo, por Dios la confieso,

Calisto. A pox on thee for a fool, thou makest me laugh, which I thought not to do today.
210 *Sempronio.* What, would you weep all the days of your life?
Calisto. Yes.
Sempronio. And why?
Calisto. Because I love her, before whom I find myself so unworthy that I have no hope to obtain her.
Sempronio. Oh coward, baser than the son of a whore: why, Alexander the Great did not only think himself worthy the dominion of one only but of many worlds.
Calisto. I did not well hear what thou saidst, say it again: repeat it again before thou proceed any further.
220 *Sempronio.* I said, sir, should you, whose heart is greater than Alexander's, despair of obtaining a woman? Wherefore many, having been seated in highest estate, have basely prostituted themselves to the embracements of muleteers and stable grooms, suffering them to breathe in their faces, with their unsavoury breaths and to embosom them between their breasts. And other some not ashamed to have companied° with brute beasts. Have you not heard of Pasiphae, who played the wanton with a bull? And of Minerva, how she dallied with a dog?
Calisto: Tush, I believe it not, they are but fables.
230 *Sempronio.* And that of your grandmother and her ape, that's a fable too? Witness your grandfather's knife, that killed the villain that did cuckhold him.[137]

---

y no creo que hay otro soberano en el cielo aunque entre nosotros mora'. Sempronio retorts that Calisto's sin is much worse than those committed in Sodom (*Genesis* 19:1–8), where men pursued abominable intercourse with strange angels ('procuraron abominable uso con los ángeles no conocidos'), whereas Calisto aspires to do so with someone he calls his God ('y tú con el que confiesas ser Dios', Lobera *et al.*, eds, 2000, p. 37). This is the very irreverent joke which provokes Calisto's laughter: as a result of its omission, the young lover's hilarity does not make much sense in Mabbe's rendering. In spite of this, Mabbe skilfully interweaves his modification within the context of the ensuing references to those 'goddesses of old' who fell 'below mortality': i.e. Pasiphae, daughter of the sun-god Helios, and mother of the Minotaur, which she conceived after intercourse with a bull , and Minerva, who, as Mabbe puts it 'dallied with a dog' (although no such episode has been documented in the case of Minerva, see Lobera *et al.*, eds, 2000, p. 39, and their long note, pp. 535–36).

[137] This bizarre reference to Calisto's grandmother, and the rumour about her dalliance with an ape (which was subsequently murdered by his grandfather)

Calisto. A pox on this coxcomb[138], what girds[139] he gives.

Sempronio. Have I nettled you, sir? Read your histories, study your philosophers, examine your poets, and you shall find how full their books are of their vile and wicked examples, and of the ruins and destructions whereunto they have run who held them in that high esteem as you do. Consult with Seneca, and you shall see how vilely he reckons of them. Hearken unto Aristotle, and you shall find that all of them to this agree.[140] But whatsoever I have, or shall hereafter speak in them, mistake me not, I pray you, but consider them as words, commonly and generally spoken. For many of them have been and are holy, virtuous and noble, whose glorious and resplendent crowns blot out this general reproach. But touching the other, who can recount unto you their falsehoods, their tricks, their tradings, their truckings, their exchanging commodities, their lightness, their tears, their mutabilities, and their boldness and impudencies. For whatsoever they conceit, they dare to execute without any deliberation or advisement in the world; their dissemblings, their talkativeness, their deceits, their forgetfulness, their unkindness, their ingratitude, their inconstancy, their fickleness, their saying and gainsaying, and all in a breath; their windings and turnings, their presumption, their vainglory, their baseness, their foolishness, their disdainfulness, their coyness, their pride, their haughtiness, their base submissions, their prattlings, their gluttony, their luxury, their sluttishness, their timorousness, their witcheries, their cheatings, their jibings, their slanderings, and their bawdry. Now consider with yourself, what idle giddy-headed brains are under those large and fine cobweb veils; what wicked thoughts under those gay gorgets;[141]

---

remains obscure to this day (see Lobera *et al.*, eds, 2000, p. 39, and their long notes, pp. 536–37).

[138] coxcomb] fool.

[139] girds] biting remarks.

[140] Mabbe omits Rojas's reference to Solomon ('Oye a Salomón do dice que las mujeres y el vino hacen a los hombres renegar', Lobera *et al.*, eds, 2000, p. 39), which he takes from Ecclesiasticus 19:2. In general, Mabbe shortens the list of authorities on the evil nature of women, and the cases that illustrate them. Rojas's two main sources are Boccaccio's *De casibus virorum illustribus* and above all Alfonso Martínez de Toledo's misogynist *Corbacho* (whose manuscript was composed in 1438, and first published in 1498).

[141] gorgets] collars, or ornaments for the neck.

what pride and arrogance under those their long, rich and stately robes; what mad toys under their painted temples.[142]

Calisto. Tell me, I pray, this Alexander, this Seneca, this Aristotle, this Virgil, these whom thou tell'st me of, did not they subject themselves unto them? Am I greater than these?

Sempronio. I would you should follow those that did subdue them; not those that were subdued by them. Fly from their deceits. Know you, sir, what they do? They do things that are too hard for any man to understand. They observe no mean, they have no reason, nor do they take any heed in what they do. They are the first themselves that cause a man to love: and themselves are the first that begin to loathe. They will privately pleasure him whom afterwards they will openly wrong, and draw him secretly in at their windows whom in the streets they will publicly rail at. They will give you roast-meat, and beat you with the spit.[143] They will invite you unto them, and presently send you packing with a flea in your ear; call you, and yet exclude you; seal you her love, and yet proclaim hate; quickly be won, and quickly be lost; soon pleased as soon displeased; and (which is the true humour of a woman) whatsoever her will divines, that must be effected. Her apprehensions admit no delays, and be they impossible to be attained to, yet not effecting them, she straightaway censures its want of wit or affection, if not both. Oh what a plague? What a hell? Nay, what a loathsome thing is it for a man to have to do with them any longer than in that short prick of time that he holds them in his arms, when they are prepared for pleasure.

Calisto. Thou seest the more thou tell'st me, and the more inconveniences thou settest before me, the more I love her. I know not how, nor what it is, but sure I am, that so it is.

Sempronio. This is no fit counsel I see for young men who know not how to submit themselves to reason, nor to be governed by

---

[142] For further details on Rojas's abundant antifeminist sources, see Lobera *et al.*, eds (2000), pp. 39–41, and their long notes, pp. 537–42.

[143] To beat with the spit] 'to treat with unexpected harshness (following upon kindly usage or hospitality)' (*OED*). This is part of Mabbe's fairly free translation of Sempronio's misogynistic tirade. There is no exact equivalent to this English proverb in the original text.

discretion; it is a miserable thing, to think that he should be a
master, who was never a scholar.[144]

Calisto. And you sir, that are so wise, who I pray taught you all
this?

Sempronio. Who? Why, they themselves, who no sooner discover
their shame, but they lose it. For all this, and much more than
I have told you, they themselves will manifest unto men.
Balance thyself then aright in the true scale of thine honour,
giue thy reputation its due proportion, its just measure, and
think yourself to be more worthy than in your own esteem you
repute yourself. For (believe me) worse is that extreme,
whereby a man suffers himself to fall from his own worth, than
that which makes a man overvalue himself, and seat himself in
higher place than beseems him.

Calisto. Now, what of all this? What am I the better for it?

Sempronio. What? Why this: first of all, you are a man; then, of
an excellent and singular wit; to this, endued with those better
sort of blessings wherewith nature has endowed you, to wit,
wisdom, favour, feature, largeness of limbs, force, agility, and
abilities of body. And to these, fortune has in so good a
measure shared what is hers with thee, that these thy inward
graces, are by thy outward the more beautified. For, without
these outward goods, whereof fortune is chief mistress, no man
in this life comes to be happy. Lastly, the stars were so propitious at thy birth, and thyself borne under so good a planet,
that thou art beloved of all.

Calisto. But not of Melibea. And in all that, wherein thou dost
so glorify my gifts, I tell thee (Sempronio) compared with
Melibea's, they are but as stars to the Sun, or dross compared
to gold. Do but consider the nobleness of her blood, the
ancientness of her house, the great estate she is born unto, the
excellency of her wit, the splendour of her virtues, her stately,
yet comely carriage, her ineffable gracefulness in all that she
does; and lastly, her divine beauty, whereof (I pray thee) give
me leave to discourse a little, for the refreshing of my soul. And
that which I shall tell thee, shall be only of what I have discovered, and lies open to the eye: for if I could discourse of that

---

[144] 'Miserable cosa es pensar ser maestro el que nunca fue discípulo'. The source
of this proverb is the *Auctoritates Aristotelis* (XXVI.7–8). See the introduction,
and also Lobera *et al.*, eds (2000), p. 42, n. 171, and their long note, p. 542.

which is concealed, this contestation would be needless, neither should we argue thereupon so earnestly as now we do.

Sempronio. (What lies and fooleries will my captived master now tell me?)

Calisto. What's that?

Sempronio. I said, I would have you tell me: for I shall take great pleasure in hearing it. (So fortune befriend you sir, as this speech of yours shall be pleasing unto me).[145]

Calisto. What sayst thou?

Sempronio. That fortune would so befriend me, as I shall take pleasure to hear you.

Calisto. Since then, that it is so pleasing unto thee, I will figure forth unto thee every part in her, even in the fullest manner that I can devise.

Sempronio. (Here's a deal of do indeed: This is that I looked for, though more than I desired, it will be a tedious piece of business, but I must give him the hearing.)

Calisto. I will begin first with her hairs; hast thou seen those skeins of fine twisted gold which are spun in Arabia? Her hairs are more fine, and shine no less than they; the length of them is to the lowest pitch of her heel, besides, they are daintily combed, and dressed, and knit up in knots with curious fine ribanding, as she herself pleases to adorn and set them forth, being of power themselves, without any other help, to transform men into stones.

Sempronio. (Into asses, rather.)

Calisto. What sayst thou?

Sempronio. I say that these could not be asses' hairs.

Calisto. See what a beastly and base comparison this fool makes!

Sempronio. It is well, sir, that you are so wise.

Calisto. Her eyes are quick, clear and full; the hairs to those lids rather long than short; her eyebrows thinnish, not thick of hair, and so prettily arched, that by their bent they are much the more beautiful; her nose of such a middling size as may not be mended; her mouth little; her teeth small and white; her lips red and plump; the form of her face rather long than round; her breasts placed in a fitting height, but their rising roundness,

---

[145] Sempronio's sarcastic aside is: '¡Así te medre Dios como me será agradable ese sermón!' (Lobera *et al.*, eds, 2000, p. 43). As is his wont, Mabbe attenuates the profanity of the original.

and the pretty pleasing fashion of her little tender nipples, who is able to figure forth unto thee? So distracted is the eye of man when he does behold them. Her skin as smooth, soft, and sleek as satin, and her whole body so white that the snow seems darkness unto it; her colour so mingled and of so singular a temper, as if she had chosen it herself.

Sempronio. (This fool is fallen into his thirteens.[146] Oh how he overreaches!)

Calisto. Her hands little, and in a measurable manner and fit proportion accompanied with her sweet flesh; her fingers long; her nails large and well coloured, seeming rubies intermixt with pearls. The proportion of those other parts which I could not eye, undoubtedly (judging things unseen by the seen) must of force be incomparably far better than that which Paris gave his judgment of in the difference between the three goddesses.[147]

Sempronio. Have you done, sir?

Calisto. As briefly as I could.

Sempronio. Suppose all this you say were true, yet in that you are a man, I still say, you are more worthy than she.

Calisto. In what?

Sempronio. In that she is imperfect: out of which defect she lusts and longs after yourself or someone less worthy. Did you never read that of the Philosopher, where he tells you that as the matter desires the form, so woman desires man?[148]

Calisto. Oh wretch that I am, when shall I see this between me and Melibea?

Sempronio. It is possible that you may; and as possible that you may one day hate her as much as now you love her, when you shall come to the full enjoying of her, and to looking on her with other eyes, free from that error which now blinds your judgment.

Calisto. With what eyes?

Sempronio. With clear eyes.

---

[146] This is a literal translation of the original 'En sus trece está este necio', referring to Calisto's foolish obduracy. The *OED* does not list this idiomatic use.

[147] See note 350 to 6.565 below.

[148] the Philosopher] i.e. Aristotle. Lobera *et al.*, eds (2000, p. 46, n. 298, and longer note, p. 547) trace the origin of this proverb to the *Auctoritates Aristotelis* II.32.

Calisto. And with what, I pray, do I see now?

Sempronio. With false eyes, like some kind of spectacles which make little things seem great, and great little. Do not you despair, myself will take this business in hand, not doubting but to accomplish your desire.

Calisto. Jove grant thou maiest, howsoever, I am proud to hear thee, though hopeless of ever obtaining it.

Sempronio. Nay, I will assure it you.

Calisto. Heaven be thy good speed; my cloth of gold doublet, which I wore yesterday, it is thine, Sempronio. Take it to thee.

Sempronio. I thank you for this. (And for many more which you shall give me. My jesting has turned to my good. I hitherto have the better of it. And if my master clap such spurs to my sides, and give me such good encouragements, I doubt not, but I shall bring her to his bed. This which my master has given me is a good wheel° to bring the business about, for without reward, it is impossible to go well thorough with anything.[149])

Calisto. See you be not negligent now.

Sempronio. Nay, be not you negligent. For it is impossible that a careless master should make a diligent servant.[150]

Calisto. But tell me, how doth thou think to purchase her pity?[151]

Sempronio. I shall tell you. It is not a good while ago, since at the lower end of this street, I fell acquainted with an old bearded woman, called Celestina; a witch, subtle as the devil, and well practised in all the rogueries and villanies that the world can afford; one who, in my conscience, has marred and made up again a hundred thousand maidenheads in this city. Such a power and such authority she has, what by her persuasions and other her cunning devices, that none can escape her: she will

---

[149] *Auctoritates Aristotelis* XIV.9.

[150] *Auctoritates Aristotelis* XIV.13. Note that this and the previous borrowing from the *Auctoritates* are almost consecutive (XIV.9 and 13). When borrowing from Amerbach's edition of Petrarch *Opera latina*, Rojas frequently used within the same passage *adagia* that appeared consecutively in its alphabetical index (see notes to Prologue 17, 5.126, 8.117).

[151] To attenuate the profanity of the original remark — '¿Cómo has pensado de hacer esta piedad?', in which Sempronio's mission is described as a good work which is done out of piety — Mabbe resorts to a verb that denotes the mercantilization of love. Compare, for instance, the use of the verb *purchase* here with the list of verbs that describe the behaviour of women in Sempronio's misogynistic tirade above.

move hard rocks, if she list, and at her pleasure provoke them to luxury.

Calisto. Oh that I might but speak with her!

Sempronio. I will bring her hither unto you; and therefore prepare yourself for it, and when she comes, in any case use her kindly, be frank and liberal with her; and while I go my way, do you study and devise with yourself, to express your pains, as well as I know she is able to give you remedy.

Calisto. Oh but thou stayest too long.

Sempronio. I am gone, sir.

Calisto. And good luck with thee. You happy powers that predominate human actions, assist and be propitious to my desires, second my intentions, prosper Sempronio's proceedings, and his success in bringing me such an advocatrix as shall, according to his promise, not only negotiate, but absolute compass and bring to a wished period the preconceived hopes of an incomparable pleasure.[152]

Celestina. Elicia, what will you give me for my good news? Sempronio is come.

Elicia. Oh hush, peace, peace.

Celestina. Why? What's the matter?

Elicia. Peace, I say, for here is Crito.

Celestina. Put him in the little chamber where the besoms° be. Quickly, quickly, I say, and tell him a cousin of yours, and a friend of mine is come to see you.

Elicia. Crito, come hither, come hither, quickly. Oh, my cousin is come, my cousin is beneath. What shall I do? Come quickly, I am undone else.

Crito. With all my heart: do not vex yourself.

---

[152] In the original, Calisto invokes God's assistance, with references to the star of Bethlehem, and he establishes a parallelism between the guidance God provided for the three Wise Men, and the guidance he is now beseeching for Sempronio in his search for Celestina's help: '¡Oh todopoderoso, perdurable Dios, tú que guías los perdidos y los reyes orientales por el estrella precedente a Betlén trujiste y en su patria los redujiste, humíldemente te ruego que guíes a mi Sempronio [. . .]' (Lobera *et al.*, eds, 2000, p. 48).

Sempronio. Oh my dear mother, what a longing have I had to come unto you! I thank my fate, that has given me leave to see you.

Celestina. My son, my king, thou hast ravished me with thy presence, I am so overjoyed, that I cannot speak to thee. Turn thee about unto me, and embrace me once more in thine arms. What? Three whole days? So long away together, and never see us? Elicia, Elicia, wot you who is here?

Elicia. Who, mother?

Celestina. Sempronio, daughter.

Elicia. Out, alas! Oh, how my heart rises! How it leaps and beats in my body! How it throbs within me! And what of him?

Celestina. Look here, do you see him? I will embrace him, you shall not.

Elicia. Out, thou accursed traitor; impostumes, pocks, plagues and botches° consume and kill thee. Die thou by the hands of thine enemies, and that for some notorious crime, worthy cruel death, thou mayst see thyself fall into the rigorous hands of justice.[153] Ay, ay me!

Sempronio. He, he, he! Why, how now my Elicia? What is it that troubles you?

Elicia. What? Three days? Three whole days away? And in all that time not so much as once come and see me? Not once look upon me? Fortune never look on thee, never comfort thee, nor visit thee. Woe to that woman, wretched as she is, who in thee places her hope and the end of all her happiness.

Sempronio. No more, dear love. Thinkest thou, sweet heart, that distance of place can divorce my inward and embowelled affection from thee? Or dead but the least spark of that true fire which I bear in my bosom? Wherever I go, thou goest with me, where I am, there art thou. Thou hast not felt more affliction and torment for me than I have suffered and endured for thee. But soft, methinks I hear somebody's feet move above. Who is it?

Elicia. Who is it? One of my sweethearts.

Sempronio. Nay, like enough, I easily believe it.

Elicia. Nay, it is true: go up and see else.

Sempronio. I go.

---

[153] Elicia's feigned curse will prove to be prophetic of Sempronio's fate.

500 *Celestina.* Come hither, my son, come along with me, let this fool alone, for she is idle-headed, and almost out of her little wits: such thought has she taken for thy absence. Regard not what she says, for she will tell you a thousand flimflam tales. Come, come with me, and let us talk. Let us not spend the time thus in idlements.[154]

Sempronio. But I pray, who is that above?

Celestina. Would you know who?

Sempronio. I would.

Celestina. A wench recommended unto me by a friar.

510 *Sempronio.* What friar?

Celestina. Oh, by no means.

Sempronio. Now, as you love me, good mother, tell me what friar is it?

Celestina. Lord, how earnest you be! You would die now, if you should not know him. Well, to save your longing, it is that fat friar's wench: I need say no more.

Sempronio. Alack, poor wench, what a heavy load is she to bear!

Celestina. You see, we women must bear all, and it were greater, we must endure it: you have seen but few murders committed
520 upon a woman in private.[155]

Sempronio. Murders? No, but many great swellings, besides bunches, blaines, boils, kernels, and pocks, what not?

Celestina. Now fie upon you, how you talk. You do but jest, I am sure.

Sempronio. If I do but jest, then let me see her.

Elicia. Oh wicked wretch, doest thou long to see her? Let thy eyes start out of thy head, and drop down at thy feet, for I see that

---

[154] idlement] idle or profitless occupation, idling; the *OED* cites only two examples, both of them from Mabbe's translations: this one, and another sample in *The Rogue*.

[155] Mabbe uses *murder* here as synonymous with 'torment [. . .] severe injury or damage'. It translates the Spanish noun 'mataduras'. In the Spanish original, Celestina responds to Sempronio's comment on the heavy burden this wench will have to bear with a reference to the fact that all women must bear similar burdens. She then proceeds to compare the plight of women with that of beasts of burden: 'Todo lo llevamos', she retorts, 'pocas mataduras has tú visto en la barriga'. Lobera *et al.* (2000, p. 50, n. 243) gloss this Spanish term as: 'llagas que les producen a los animales los aparejos (arneses, yugos, etc.)', i.e. the wounds and sores produced in these animals by yokes, saddles or such implements.

it is not one wench that can serve your turn. I pray go your ways, go up and see her, but see you come at me no more.

Sempronio. Be patient, my dear, thou that art the only idol of my devotion. Is this the gall that wrings you? This your grief? Nay, if this make you so angry, I will neither see her, nor any other woman in the world. I will only speak a word or two with my mother, and so bid you adieu.

Elicia. Go, go, begone, ungrateful, unthankful as thou art, and stay away three years more if thou wilt, ere ever thou see me.

Sempronio. Mother, you may rely upon what I have told you, and assure yourself, that of all the women in the world, I would not jest or dissemble with you. Put on your mantle then, and let us go and by the way I will tell you all. For if I should stay here dilating upon the business and protract the time in delivering my mind, it would turn much to both our hurts, and hinder thy profit and mine.

Celestina. Let us go then. Elicia, fare well; make fast the door. Farewell, walls.[156]

Sempronio. So law. Now, mother, laying all other things apart, listen unto me, be attentive to that which I shall tell you; let not your ears go wool-gathering, nor scatter your thoughts, nor divide them into many parts, for he that is everywhere is nowhere, and cannot (unless it be by chance) certainly determine anything. I will that you know that of me, which as yet you never heard. Besides, I could never since the time that I first entered into league with thee, and had plighted my faith unto thee, desire that good, wherein thou mightest not share with me.

Celestina. And Jove,[157] my good son, share his good blessings with thee, which — if so it please him — he shall not do without cause. Because thou takest pity of this poor wicked old woman. Say on therefore, make no longer delay, for that friendship which betwixt thee and me has taken such deep

---

[156] 'Farewell walls' translates the original 'Adios paredes', which at face value might be interpreted as Celestina's indirect way of informing Crito, the concealed lover, that they are leaving and that he can now come out of the broom-closet. Lobera *et al.*, however, while acknowledging the deliberate ambiguity of the expression, rephrase it as as 'Parad, quedad con Dios' (i.e. 'May God remain with you').

[157] Jove] 'Dios', i.e. God, in the original.

rooting needs no preambles, no circumlocutions, no preparations or insinuation to win affection. Be brief therefore and come to the point. For it is idle to utter that in many words that may be understood in a few.

Sempronio. It is true, and therefore thus: Calisto is hot in love with Melibea, he stands in need of thine and my help. And because he needs our joint furtherance, let us join together to make some purchase of him. For to know a man's time, to make use of opportunity, and to take occasion by the foretop,[158] and to work upon a man while his humour serves him, why it is the only round by which many have climbed up to prosperity.

Celestina. Well hast thou said. I perceive thy drift. The winking, or beckoning of the eye is enough for me, for as old as I am, I can see day at a little hole. I tell thee, Sempronio, I am as glad of this thy news as surgeons of broken-heads. And as they at the first go festering the wounds, the more to endear the cure, so do I mean to deal with Calisto: for I will still go prolonging the certainty of his recovering of Melibea, and delay still the remedy. For (as it is in the proverb) delayed hope afflicts the heart. And the farther he is off from obtaining, the fairer will he promise to have it effected. Understand you me?

Sempronio. Hush. No more. We are now at the gate, and walls, they say, have ears.

Celestina. Knock.

Sempronio. Tha, tha, tha.

Calisto. Parmeno!

Parmeno. Sir.

Calisto. What a pocks,[159] art thou deaf? Canst thou not hear?

Parmeno. What would you, sir?

Calisto. Somebody knocks at the gate. Run.

Parmeno. Who's there?

Sempronio. Open the door for this matronly dame and me.

Parmeno. Sir, wot you who they are that knock so loud? It is Sempronio, and an old bawd he has brought along with him. Oh how she is bedaubed with painting!

---

[158] foretop] forelock.
[159] An expression of annoyance, a short form for *a pox on you*. The *OED* lists it under *pock*, 2.c, and takes one of its samples from Mabbe's 1631 text: (J. Mabbe tr. F. de Rojas *Spanish Bawd* I. 23 'A pocks on you for a rogue').

Calisto. Peace, peace, you villain. She is my aunt. Run, run, you rascal, and open the door. Well, it is an old saying, and I perceive as true, the fish leaps out of the pan and falls into the fire. And a man thinking to shun one danger, runs into another worse than the former. For I thinking to keep close this matter from Parmeno, on whose neck, either out of love, faithfulness, or feare, reason has laid her reins, I have fallen into the displeasure of this woman, who hath no less power over my life, than Jove himself.[160]

Parmeno. Sir why do you vex yourself? Why grieve you? Do you think that in the ears of this woman the name by which I now call her, does any way sound reproachfully? Believe it not. Assure yourself, she glories as much in this name, as oft as she hears it, as you do when you hear some voice Calisto to be a gallant gentleman. Besides, by this is she commonly called, and by this title is she of all men generally known. If she passes along the streets among a hundred women, and someone perhaps blurts out: 'see, where's the old bawd', without any impatience, or any the least distemper, she presently turns herself about, nods the head, and answers them with a smiling countenance and cheerful look. At your solemn banquets, your great feasts, your weddings, your gossippings°, your merry meetings, your funerals, and all other assemblies whatsoever where there is any resort of people, thither does she repair, and there they make pastime with her. And if she pass by where there be any dogs, they straightaway bark out this name; if she come amongst birds, they have no other note but this; if she light upon a flock of sheep, their bleatings proclaim no less; if she meet with beasts, they bellow forth the same; the frogs that lie in ditches croak no other tune. Come she amongst your smiths, your carpenters, your armourers, your farriers, your braziers, your joiners, why, their hammers beat all upon this word. In a word, all sorts of tools and instruments return no other echo in the air. Your shoemakers sing this song, your combmakers join with them, your gardeners, your ploughmen, your reapers, your vine-keepers pass away the painfulness of their labours in making her the subject of their discourse. Your

---

[160] Mabbe translates again the original 'Dios' as *Jove*.

table-players,[161] and all other gamesters never lose but they peal forth her praises. To be short, be she wheresoever she be, all things, whatsoever are in this world, repeat no other name but this: oh what a devourer of roasted eggs was her husband?[162] What would you more? Not one stone that strikes against another, but presently noises out: "old whore!".

Calisto. How canst thou tell? Dost thou know her?

Parmeno. I shall tell you, sir, how I know her. It is a great while ago since my mother dwelt in her parish, who, being entreated by this Celestina, gave me unto her to wait upon her, though now she know me not, grown out perhaps of her remembrance, as well by reason of the short time I abode with her, as also through the alteration which age has wrought upon me.

Calisto. What service didst thou do her?

Parmeno. I went into the market place, and fetched her victuals. I waited on her in the streets, and supplied her wants in other the like services, as far as my poor sufficiency, and slender strength was able to perform. So that though I continued but a little while with her, yet I remember everything as fresh as if it were but yesterday, in so much that old age has not been able to wear it out. This good honest whore, this grave matron, forsooth, had at the very end of the city, there where your tanners dwell, close by the waterside, a lone house, somewhat far from neighbours, half of it fallen down, ill contrived and worse furnished. Now, for to get her living, you must understand, she had six several trades: she was a laundress, a perfumeress, a former of faces,[163] a mender of cracked maidenheads, a bawd, and had some smatch[164] of a witch. Her first trade was a cloak to all the rest, under colour whereof being

---

[161] 'Table players' translates 'al perder en los tableros', referring to 'juegos de tablero', i.e. table games (see Lobera *et al.*, eds, 2000, p. 53, n. 276). *Tables* (*sic*, in plural) is described by the *OED* as the game of backgammon, or any other game played with dice. The *OED* uses this passage from Mabbe to illustrate the meaning of *table-player* as a player of tables, in the former sense.

[162] This is a literal translation of the original, which runs: '¡Oh qué comendador de huevos asados era su marido!', implying that Celestina's husband was a cuckold —since it was common opinion that by invoking a cuckold when roasting eggs, they would not crack (see Lobera *et al.*, eds, 2000, p. 54, n. 280).

[163] Mabbe's translation of 'maestra de hacer afeites', i.e. Celestina also produced make-up.

[164] smatch] smack.

withal a piece of a seamstress, many young wenches that were of your ordinary sorts of servants, came to her house to work: some on smocks, some on gorgets and many other things. But not one of them that came thither but brought with her either bacon, or wheat, flour, or a jar of wine, or some other the like provision which they could conveniently steal from their mistresses, and some other thefts of greater quality, making her house (for she was the receiver, and kept all things close) the rendezvous of all their roguery. She was a great friend to your students, noblemen's caterers and pages. To these she sold that innocent blood of these poor miserable souls, who did easily adventure their virginity, drawn on by fair promises, and the restitution and reparation which she would make them of their lost maidenheads. Nay, she proceeded so far, that by cunning means, she had access and communication with your very Vestals, and never left them till she had brought her purpose to pass. And what time do you think she chose when she would deal with any of these? At the time of their chiefest ceremonies, as when they kept their most mysterious celebration of the feasts of their Vesta, nay, and that most strictly solemnized day of *Bona Dea*, where it is death to admit men.[165] Even then, by unheard of disguises, she had her plots and projects effectually working upon them, to the utter abolition of their vows and virginity. Now, what think you, were the trades and merchandise wherein she dealt? She professed herself a kind of physician, and fained that she had good skill in curing of little children. She would go and fetch flax from one house, and put it forth to spinning to another, that she

---

[165] Mabbe paganizes the text again to obliterate an irreverent passage. In the original, Celestina used late-night Christian rituals and celebrations — when both men and women could walk the streets without arousing suspicion — as a cover for her illicit dealings. Rojas describes this strategy with irreverent sarcasm, all of which Mabbe turns into the ceremonies associated with the worship of the Roman goddess Vesta: '[. . .] por medio de aquéllas comunicaba con las más encerradas, hasta traer a ejecución su propósito, y aquéstas, en tiempo honesto, como estaciones, procesiones de noche, misas del gallo, misas del alba, y otras secretas devociones, muchas encubiertas vi entrar en su casa. Tras ellas hombres descalzos, contritos, y rebozados, destacados, que entraban allí a llorar sus pecados' (Lobera *et al.*, eds, 2000, p. 55). On Mabbe's paganization of *La Celestina*, see Helen P. Houck, 'Mabbe's Paganization of the *Celestina*', *PMLA* 54 (1939), 422–31.

might thereby have pretence for the freer access unto all. One would cry 'here, mother', and another 'there, mother'; 'look', says the third, 'where the old woman comes: yonder comes that beldam[166] so well known of all'. Yet notwithstanding all these her cares, troubles, and trottings to and fro, being never out of action, she would never miss any great meeting, any religious processions, any nuptials, love-ties, balls, masks or games whatsoever. They were the only markets where she made all her bargains. And at home in her own house she made perfumes, false and counterfeit storax°, benjamin,[167] gum, anime°, amber, civet, powders, musk and *mosqueta*:[168] She had a chamber full of limbecks,° little vials, pots, some of earth, some of glass, some brass, and some tin, formed in a thousand fashions. She made sublimated Mercury, boiled confections for to clarify the skin, waters to make the face glister, paintings, some white, some vermillion, lipsalves, scarlet-dyed clothes fitted purposely for women to rub their faces therewith, ointments for to make the face smooth, lustrifications,[169] clarifications, pargetings, fardings°, waters for the morphews,[170] and a thousand other slibber-slabbers:[171] Some made of the lees of wine, some of daffodils, some of the barks and rinds of trees, some of scare-wolf,[172] otherwise called cittibush or trifolium,[173] some of tarragon, some of centaury,[174] some of

---

[166] beldam] loathsome old woman, hag.

[167] benjamin] a resinuous substance used in medicine and perfumery (see note to 1.705 below).

[168] mosqueta] a Spanish term, which refers to a type of wild rose from which oil is extracted for medicinal and cosmetic use.

[169] lustrification] making lustrous; this is the only entry listed in the *OED*.

[170] morphews] a skin disease, consisting of its discoloration.

[171] slibber-slabber] slibber-sauce, i.e. a compound or concoction of a messy, repulsive, or nauseous character, used esp. for medicinal and cosmetic purposes (*OED*). The *OED* quotes from Mabbe's *The Spanish Bawd* and his *Rogue*, from Florio's Montaigne, and L'Estrange's translations of Quevedo's *Visions*, to illustrate the meaning of this expression.

[172] scare-wolf] a literal translation of 'corteza de espantalobos' (i.e. scare-wolf bark), a bush whose bark was employed to produce cosmetics. See Lobera *et al.*, eds (2000), p. 57, n. 321.

[173] cittibush] not listed in the *OED*: Mabbe lists it as synonymous with *trifolium*, i.e. clover or trefoils, described as 'a large genus of leguminous plants, with trifoliate leaves'.

[174] centaury] a plant whose medicinal properties were said to have been discovered by Chiron the centaur.

sour grapes, some of must, or new wine taken from the press, first distilled, and afterwards sweetened with sugar. She had a trick to supple and refine the skin with the juice of lemons, with turpentine, with the marrow of deer, and of heron-shawes,[175] and a thousand the like confections. She distilled sweet-waters,° of roses, of flowers, of oranges, of jasmine, of three-leafed grass,[176] of woodbine, of gillyflowers, incorporated with musk and civet, and sprinkled with wine. She made likewise lees for to make the hair turn yellow, or of the colour of gold; and this she composed of the sprigs of the vine, of holm,° of rye, of horehound[177] intermixt with saltpetre, with alum, milfoil,[178] which some call yarrow or nosebleed, together with diverse other things. The oils, the butters, and the greases which she used, it is loathsome to tell you, and would turn your stomach: as of kine, bears, horses, camels, snakes, coneys, whales, herons, bitterns, bucks, cats of the mountains,[179] badgers, squirrels, hedgehogs, and others. For her preparatives for bathings, it is a wonderful thing to acquaint you with all the herbs and roots which were ready gathered and hung high in the roof of her house: as camomile, rosemary, marsh mallows, maidenhair, bluebottle,° flowers of elder°, and of mustard, spike° and white laurel, buds of roses, rosecakes,° gramonilla,[180] wild-savory,[181] green figs, picodorae, and folia-tinct.[182] The oils which she extracted for the face it is incredible

---

[175] heron-shawes] Mabbe probably refers here to the long legs of the heron as the 'heron-stalks': *shaw* is defined, by the *OED* as 'The stalks and leaves of certain plants, esp. potatoes and turnips.' This would be as close as Mabbe could get to a translation of the original, which refers to 'tuétano de ciervo y de garza', i.e. the marrow of deers and herons.

[176] three-leafed grass] i.e. shamrock, or another variety of *trifolium* (see above).

[177] horehound] a labiate herb, *Marrubium vulgare*.

[178] milfoil] yarrow, *Achillea millefolium*.

[179] cats of the mountains] a literal translation of the Spanish 'gato montés' (Lobera *et al.*, eds, 2000, p. 59), i.e. the wildcat (*felis silvestris*).

[180] gramonilla] taken literally from the original text. Lobera *et al.* (2000, p. 59, n. 358) could not document this word in Spanish.

[181] savory] not listed as a plant in the *OED*, which however records a use of this word as part of a list of plants in Shakespeare's *Winter's Tale* (1623) II.iv.104: "Here's flowres for you: Hot Lauender, Mints, Sauory, mariorum."

[182] picodorae] folia-tinct] Mabbe's literal translation of the Spanish 'pico de oro y hojatinta'. Lobera *et al.* (2000, p. 60, n. 360) have been unable to document the names of these plants in other Spanish texts or glossaries.

to recount, of storax[183] and of jasmine, of lemons, of apple-kernels, of violets, of benivy,[184] of fistic° nuts, of pineapple kernels, of grapestones, of jujube,[185] of axenuz[186] or melanthion, of lupins, of peas, of carilla,[187] and pajarera;[188] and a small quantity of balsamum she had in a little vial, wherewith she cured that scotch[189] given her overthwart° her nose. For the mending of lost maidenheads, some she helped with little bladders, and other some she stitched up with the needle. She had in a little cabinet, or painted workbox, certain fine small needles, such as your glovers sow withal, and threads of the slenderest and smallest silk, rubbed over with wax. She had also roots hanging there of folia-plasme,[190] fuste-sanguinio,[191] squill[192] or sea-onion and ground thistle. With these she did work wonders; and when the French ambassador came thither, she made sale of one of her wenches, three several times for a virgin.

Calisto. So she might a hundred as well.

---

[183] storax] the aromatic resin of the tree, *Styrnax officinalis*.
[184] benivy] Mabbe's translation of the Spanish 'menjuí' (also spelled *benjuí*) whose definition in the *DRAE* coincides with the *OED* definition of *benjamin* (see note to 1.669 above).
[185] jujube] a berry, the fruit of various species of *Zizphus*.
[186] axenuz] not in the *OED*. Probably a transliteration of the Spanish *axenuz*, or *ajenuz*, also called *arañuela*. The equivalent in the Spanish original is *neguilla*, according to the *DRAE*, a synonym of *arañuela*, i.e. *nigella sativa*, which in English is called *cumin, nutmeg, peppergrass*, or *Roman coriander*, and, as Mabbe himself declares, *melanthion*, i.e. black cumin.
[187] carilla] transliteration of the Spanish 'carillas', also called *judía de careta*, a type of bean, probably the pinto bean (*Phaseolus vulgaris*).
[188] pajarera] transliteration of the Spanish 'pajarera' or 'paxarera' (probably *stellaria media*), also known in English as *stellaria*, or *chickweed*. According to Lobera *et al.* (2000) this plant produces thousands of seeds, which are frequently used as food by birds, hence que equivalent nouns of *pajarera* and *chickweed* in Spanish and English.
[189] scotch] a cut, or gash.
[190] folia-plasme] Mabbe's translation of the Spanish 'hojaplasma', 'todabuena, androseno, castellar' (apparently *androsaemum officinale* or *hypericum androsaemum*), a variety of the species St. John's wort.
[191] fuste-sanguinio] Mabbe's transliteration of 'fuste sanguino', unidentified by Lobera *et al.* (2000, p. 61, n. 374).
[192] squill] the root, or bulb, of the sea-onion (*Urginea maritime*), or the plant itself (as in this case).

Parmeno. Believe me, sir, it is true as I tell you. Besides, out of charity forsooth, she relieved many orphans, and many straggling wenches, which recommended themselves unto her. In another partition, she had her knacks for to help those that were love-sick, and to make them to be beloved again, and obtain their desires. And for this purpose, she had the bones that are bred in a stag's heart, the tongue of a viper, the heads of quails, the brains of an ass, the cauls of young colts when they are new foaled, the bearing cloth of a new-born babe, barbary beans,[193] a sea-compass,[194] a horn-fish,° the halter of a man that has been hanged, ivy berries, the prickles of a hedgehog, the foot of a badger, fern-seed,[195] the stone of an eagle's nest,[196] and a thousand other things. Many both men and women came unto her. Of some she would demand a piece of that bread where they had bit it, of others some part of their apparel, of some she would crave to have of their hair; others, she would draw characters in the palms of their hands with saffron; with othersome she would do the same with a kind of colour, which you call vermillion; to others she would give hearts made of wax and stuck full of broken needles; and many other the like things made in clay, and some in lead, very feareful and ghastly to behold. She would draw circles, portrait forth figures, and mumble many strange words to herself, having her eyes still fixed on the ground. But who is able to deliver unto you those things that she has done? And all these were mere mockeries and lies.

Calisto. Parmeno, hold thy hand; thou hast said enough. What remains, leave it till some fitter opportunity. I am sufficiently instructed by thee, and I thank thee for it. Let us now delay them no longer, for necessity cuts off slackness. Know thou, that she comes hither requested, and we make her stay longer than stands with good manners. Come, let us go, lest she be

---

[193] barbary beans] 'Habas moriscas' in the original. Lobera *et al.* (2000) suggest that these are probably common beans.

[194] sea-compass] Sea-compass translates Rojas's 'guija marina', i.e. lodestone.

[195] Fern and its seeds were esteemed as good contraceptives, and they were also used to provoke abortions (Lobera *et al.*, eds, 2000, p. 62, n. 390).

[196] eagle's nest] according to Lobera *et al.* (2000, *ibid.*): 'la piedra del nido del águila' was thought to facilitate delivery; it might have also been used as a female aphrodisiac.

offended, and take it ill. I fear, and fear makes me more and more think upon her, quickens my memory, and awakens in me a more provident carefulness how I communicate myself unto her. Well, let us go, and arm ourselves as well as we can against all inconveniences. But I pray thee Parmeno, let me entreat thee, that the envy thou bearest unto Sempronio, who is to serve and pleasure me in this business, be not an impediment to that remedy, whereon no less than the safety of my life relies. And if I had a doublet for him, thou shalt not want a mandillion.[197] Neither think thou, but that I esteem as much of thy counsel and advice as of his labour and pains; and as brute beasts (we see) do labour more bodily than men, for which they are well respected of us, and carefully looked unto, but yet for all this, we hold them not in the nature of friends, nor affect them with the like love: the like difference do I make between thee and Sempronio. And laying aside all power and dominion in myself, under the privy-seal of my secret love, sign myself unto thee for such a friend.

Parmeno. Sir, it grieves me not a little that you should seem doubtful of my fidelity and faithful service, which these your fair promises and demonstrations of your good affection cannot but call into question and jealousy. When, sir, did you ever see my envy prove hurtful to you? Or when for any interest of mine own, or dislike, did I ever show myself cross, to cross your good, or to hinder what might make for your profit?

Calisto. Take it not offensively, nor misconstrue my meaning: for assure thyself, thy good behaviour towards me, and thy fair carriage and gentle disposition, makes thee more gracious in mine eyes than any, nay, than all the rest of my servants. But because in a case so difficult and hard as this, not only all my good, but even my life also wholly depends, it is needful that I should in all that I am able, provide for myself. And therefore seek to arm myself in this sort as thou see'st against all such casualties, as may endanger my desire; howsoever, persuade thyself that thy good qualities as far excel every natural good, as every natural good excels the artificial from whom it has its beginning. But of this, for this time, no more. But let us now go and see her, who must work our welfare.

---

[197] mandillion] loose coat or cassock.

Celestina. (Soft: methinks I hear somebody on the stairs; they are now coming down. Sempronio, make as though you did not hear them. Stand close, and listen what they say, and let me alone speak for us both. And thou shalt see how handsomely I will handle the matter, both for thee and me.[198]

Sempronio. Do so then. Speak thou.)

Celestina. Trouble me no more, I say, leave importuning me, for to overcharge one who is heavy enough already laden with pain and anguish were to spur a sick beast. Alas, poor soul, methinks thou art so possessed with thy master's pain and so affected with his affliction, that Sempronio seems to be Calisto, and Calisto to be Sempronio; and that both your torments are both but in one and the same subject. Besides, I would have you think that I came not hither to leave this controversy undecided, but will die rather in the demand and pursuit of this my purpose, than not see his desire accomplished.

Calisto. (Parmeno, stay, stay awhile, make no noise. Stand still, I pray thee, and listen a little what they say. So, hush, that we may see in what state we live; what we are like to trust to, and how the world is like to go with us. Oh notable woman! Oh worldly goods, unworthy to be possessed by so high a spirit! Oh faithful and trusty Sempronio! Hast thou well observed him, my Parmeno? Hast thou heard him? Hast thou noted his earnestness? Tell me, have I not reason to respect him? What sayst thou, man? Thou that art the closet of my secrets, the cabinet of my counsel, and the counsel of my soul?

Parmeno. Protesting first my innocence for your former suspicion, and complying with my fidelity, since you have given me such free liberty of speech, I will truly deliver unto you what I think. Hear me therefore, and let not your affection make you deaf, nor hope of your pleasure blind you. Have a little patience, and be not too hasty, for many through too much eagerness to hit the pin,° have shot far beside the white.° And albeit I am but young, yet have I seen somewhat in my days. Besides, the observation and sight of many things does teach a man much experience. Wherefore, assure yourself, and thereon I dare pawn my life, that they overheard what we said, as also our coming down the stairs, and have of set purpose

---

[198] Celestina uses here both *you* and *thou* to address Sempronio.

fallen into this false and feigned expression of their great love and care, wherein you now place the end of your desire.)
Sempronio. (Believe me, Celestina, Parmeno aims unhappily.
870 *Celestina.* Be silent. For I swear by my halidom,[199] that wither comes the ass, thither also shall come the fardle.[200] Let me alone to deal with Parmeno, and you shall see, I will so temper him e'r I have done with him that I will make him wholly ours. And see what we gain, he shall share with us: for goods that are not common, are not goods. It is communication that makes combination in love: and therefore let us gain, let us all divide the spoil, and let us laugh and be merry all alike. I will make the slave so tame and so gentle that I will bring him like a bird to pick bread from my fist. And so we will be two to two,
880 and all three join to cozen the fourth. Thou and I will join together, Parmeno shall make a third, and all of us cheat Calisto.)
Calisto. Sempronio?
Sempronio. Sir?
Calisto. What art thou doing, thou that art the key of my life? Open the door. Oh Parmeno! Now that I see her I feel myself well. Methinks, I am now alive again. See what a reverent matron it is. What a presence she bears, worthy respect! A man may now see how for the most part the face is the index of the
890 mind. Oh virtuous old age! Oh enaged[201] virtue! Oh glorious hope of my desired end! Oh head, the allayer[202] of my passion! Oh reliever of my torment, and vivification of my life, resurrection from my death! I desire to draw near unto thee, my lips long to kiss those hands, wherein consists the fullness of my recovery. But the unworthiness of my person debars me of so great a favour. Wherefore I here adore the ground whereon

---

[199] haliodom] a holy object, or relic, frequently used (as it is here) in oaths and adjurations.
[200] 'Wither comes the ass, thither also shall come the fardle' is a literal translation of the Spanish proverb 'do vino el asno vendrá el albarda' ('albarda' being the main piece in the saddle used for beasts of burden, hence my correction of the original *faddle* — apparently a misspelling of *fardle*). Lobera *et al.* (2000, p. 65, n. 425) document the proverb in Núñez and Correas.
[201] enaged] grown old, inveterate (*OED* includes only four quotations to exemplify its use, one of which is this phrase in *The Spanish Bawd*).
[202] allayer] He who or that which allays, modifies, or restrains (*OED*, one of the three examples used to illustrate its use is this phrase in *The Spanish Bawd*).

thou treadest, and in reverence of thee, bow down my body to kiss it.

Celestina. (Sempronio, can fair words make me the fatter? Can I live by this? Those bones which I have already gnawed, does this fool thy master think to feed me therewith? Sure the man dreams. When he comes to fry his eggs, he will then find what is wanting.[203] Bid him shut his mouth, and open his purse. I misdoubt his words, much more his works. Holla, I say; are you so ticklish? I will curry you for this geare, you lame ass.[204] You must rise a little more early if you mean to go beyond me.)

Parmeno. (Woe to these ears of mine, that ever they should hear such words as these. I now see, that he is a lost man, who goes after one that is lost. Oh unhappy Calisto, dejected wretch, blind in thy folly, and kneeling on the ground to adore the oldest and the rottennest piece of whorish earth that ever rubbed her shoulders in the stews. He is undone, he is overthrown horse and foot, he is fallen into a trap whence he will never get out. He is not capable of any redemption, counsel or courage.)

Calisto. What said my mother? It seemed unto me, that she thinks I offer words for to excuse my reward.

Sempronio. You have hit the nail on the head, sir.

Calisto. Come then with me, bring the keys with you, and thou shalt see, I will quickly put her out of that doubt.[205]

Sempronio. In so doing, you shall do well, sir. Let us go presently: for it is not good to suffer weeds to grow amongst corn, nor suspicion in the hearts of our friends, but to root it out straight with the weed-hook of good works.

Calisto. Wittily spoken. Come, let us go, let us slack no time.

---

[203] This proverbial phrase is a partial translation of the original 'al freír lo verá', i.e. when he realizes the true nature of the situation it will be far too late to do anything about it (Lobera *et al.*, eds, 2000, p. 66, n. 438). The origin of this expression was a popular late-medieval tale.

[204] Another proverbial phrase, or idiomatic expression, almost literally translated from the original: '¡So, que te estriego, asna coja!' Lobera *et al.* (2000, p. 66, n. 441) document a similar proverb in Covarrubias. They interpret it as an exclamation which expresses Celestina's irritation at the verbosity displayed by Calisto.

[205] Another inconsistent use of *thou / you*.

Celestina. Believe me, Parmeno, I am very glad that we have lighted on so fit an opportunity wherein I may manifest and make known unto thee the singular love wherewithal I affect thee, and what great interest (though undeservedly) thou hast in me. I say undeservedly in regard of that which I have heard thee speak against me, wherof I make no more reckoning, but am content to let it pass. For virtue teaches us to suffer temptations, and not to render evil for evil, and especially when we are tempted by young men, such as want experience and are not acquainted with the courses of the world, who out of an ignorant and foolish kind of loyalty undo both themselves and their masters, as thou thyself dost Calisto. I heard you well enough, not a word you said that escaped mine ear. Nor do you think that with these my other outward senses, old age hath made me lose my hearing. For not only that which I see, hear, and know, but even the very inward secrets of thy heart and thoughts I search into, and pierce to the full with these my intellectual eyes, these eyes of my understanding. I would have thee to know, Parmeno, that Calisto is love-sick, sick even to the death. Nor art thou for this to censure him to be a weak and foolish man: for irresistible love subdues all things. Besides, I would have thee to know, if thou knowst it not already, that there are these two conclusions that are evermore infallibly true. The first is, that every man must of force love a woman, and every woman love a man. The second is, that he who truly loves, must of necessity be much troubled and moved with the sweetness of that superexcellent delight, which was ordained by him that made all things for the perpetuating of mankind, without which it must needs perish. And not only in human kind, but also in fishes, birds, beasts, and all creatures that creep and crawl upon the earth. Likewise in your souls vegetative, some plants have the same inclination and disposition, that without the interposition of any other thing, they be planted in some little distance one of another, and it is determined and agreed upon by the general consent of your gardeners, and husbandmen, to be male and female. How can you answer this, Parmeno? Now my pretty little fool, you mad wag,° my soul's sweet genius, my pearl, my jewel, my honest poor silly lad, my pretty little monkey-face, come hither you little whoreson. Alack, how I pity thy simplicity! Thou knowst nothing of the world, nor of its delight. Let me run mad, and die in that fit, if I suffer thee to come near me, as old as I am. Thou hast a harsh and ill favoured hoarse voice, by thy bristled beard,[206] it is easily guessed what manner of man you are.[207] Tell me, is all quiet beneath? No motions at all in Venus's court?

Parmeno: Oh! As quiet as the tail of a scorpion!

Celestina. It were well, and it were no worse.

Parmeno. Ha, ha, he.

Celestina. Laugh'st thou, thou pocky rogue?

Parmeno. Nay, mother, be quiet. Hold your peace, I pray. Do not blame me, and do not hold me, though I am but young, for a fool. I love Calisto, tied thereunto out of that true and honest fidelity which every servant owes unto his master; for the breeding that he hath given me, for the benefit which I receive from him, as also because I am well respected, and kindly treated by him, which is the strongest chain, that links the love of the servant to the service of his master, as the contrary is the breaking of it. I see he is out of the right way, and has wholly lost himself, and nothing can befall a man worse in this world, than to hunt after his desire, without hope of a good and happy end; especially, he thinking to recover his game (which himself holds so hard and difficult a pursuit) by the vain advice, and foolish reasons of that beast Sempronio, which is all one as if he should go about with the broad end of a spade to dig little worms ouf of a man's hand.[208] I hate it. I abhor it. It is abominable, and with grief I speak it, I do much lament it.

Celestina. Knowst thou not, Parmeno, that it is an absolute folly, or mere simplicity to bewail that, which by wailing cannot be helped?

Parmeno. And therefore do I wail, because it cannot be helped. For if by wailing and weeping, it were possible to work some remedy for my master, so great would the contentment of that

---

[206] 'Bristled beard' here carries a sexual innuendo that attempts to translate a similar pun in the Spanish original: 'las barbas te apuntan, mal sosegadilla debes tener la punta de la barriga' (Lobera *et al.*, eds, 2000, p. 69). Mabbe translates quite freely the second part of this sentence, in spite of which he manages to convey Celestina's references to Parmeno's budding puberty.

[207] Another inconsistent use of *you / thou*.

[208] A somewhat free translation (*ex sensu*) from the original 'sacar aradores a pala de azadón', 'to extract scabies with the broad end of a spade', i.e. to be rough with a task that requires a more subtle approach.

hope be, that for very joy, I should not have the power to weep. But because I see all hope thereof to be utterly lost, with it have I lost all my joy, and for this cause do I weep.

Celestina. Thou weepest in vain for that, which cannot by weeping be avoided; thou canst not turn the stream of this violent passion, and therefore mayst truly presume that he is past all cure. Tell me, Parmeno, has not the like happened to others, as well as to him?

Parmeno. Yes. But I would not have my master through mourning and grieving languish and grow sick.

Celestina. Thy master is well enough. He is not sick, and were he never so sick, never so much pained and grieved, I myself am able to cure him. I have the power to do it.

Parmeno. I regard not what thou sayst. For in good things, better is the act than the power. And in bad things, better the power than the act. So that, it is better to be well, than on the way to be well. And better is the possibility of being sick, than to be sick indeed, and therefore, power in ill is better than the act.[209]

Celestina. Oh thou wicked villain! How idly dost thou talk, as if thou didst not understand thyself. It seems thou dost not know his disease. What hast thou hitherto said? What wouldst thou have? What is it that grieves you, sir? Why lamentest thou? Be you disposed to jest, and make yourself merry? Or are you in good earnest, and wouldst fain face out truth with falsehood? Believe you what you list,[210] I am sure he is sick, and that in act, and that the power to make him whole lies wholly in the hands of this weak old woman.

Parmeno. Nay rather, of this weak old whore.

Celestina. Now the hangman be thy ghostly father,[211] my little rascal, my pretty villain. How dar'st thou be so bold with me?

Parmeno. How, as though I did not know thee?

Celestina. And who art thou?

Parmeno. Who? Marry, I am Parmeno, son to Alberto thy gossip, who lived some little while with thee, for my mother recommended me unto thee, when thou dwelt close by the river's side in tanners' row.

---

[209] Lobera *et al.* (2000, p. 70, n. 477) identify the *Auctoritates Aristotelis* I.230–231 as the source for this passage.
[210] list] please.
[211] the hangman be thy ghostly father] i.e. may the hangman be your confessor.

Celestina. Good Lord, and art thou Parmeno, Claudina's son?
Parmeno. The very same.
Celestina. Now the fire of the pocks consume thy bones, for thy mother was an old whore, as myself. Why dost thou persecute me, Parmeno? It is he in good truth, it is he. Come hither unto me, come I say. Many a good jerk, and many a cuff on the ear have I given thee in my days, and as many kisses too. Ah, you little rogue, dost thou remember, sirrhah, when thou lay'st at my bed's feet?
Parmeno. Passing well, and sometimes also, though I was then but a little apish boy, how you would take me up to your pillow, and there lie hugging of me in your arms. And because you savoured somewhat of old age, I remember how I would fling and fly from you.
Celestina. A pox on you for a rogue. Out, impudent, art thou not ashamed to talk thus? But to leave off all jesting, and to come to plain earnest, hear me now, my child, and hearken what I shall say unto thee. For though I am called hither for one end, I am come for another. And albeit I have made my self a stranger unto thee, and as though I knew thee not, yet thou wast the only cause that drew me hither. My son, I am sure thou art not ignorant, how that your mother gave you unto me, your father being then alive, who, after you went from me, died of no other grief save only that she suffered for the uncertainty of thy life and person. For whose absence in those latter years of her elder age she led a most painful, pensive and careful life. And when the time came, that she was to leave this world, she sent for me, and in secret recommended thee unto me, and told me (no other witness being by, but heaven the witness to all our works, our thoughts, our hearts, whom she alone interposed between her and me) that of all loves I should do so much for her, as to make inquiry after thee, and when I had found thee, to bring thee up, and foster thee as mine own; and that as soon as thou shouldst come to man's estate, and were able to know how to govern thyself, and to live in some good manner and fashion, that then I should discover unto thee a certain place, where, under many a lock and key, she has left thee more store of gold and silver than all the revenues come to that thy master Calisto has in his possession. And because I solemnly vowed and bound myself by promise unto her that I would see her desire as far forth as lay in me, to be

well and truly performed, she peacefully departed this mortal life. And though a man's faith ought to be inviolably observed both to the living and the dead, yet more especially to the dead; for they are not able to do anything of themselves, they cannot come to me and prosecute their right here upon earth. I have spent much time and money in inquiring and searching after thee, and could never till now hear what was become of thee: and it is not above three days since, that I first heard of your being, and where you abode. Verily, it has much grieved me, that thou hast gone travelling and wandering throughout the world, as thou hast done from place to place, losing thy time, without either gain of profit, or of friends. For (as Seneca says), travellers have many ends, and few friends. For, in so short a time they can never fasten friendship with any: and he that is everywhere, is said to be nowhere. Again, that meat cannot benefit the body, which is no sooner eaten, than ejected. Neither does anything more hinder its health, than your diversities and changes of meats. Nor does that wound come to be healed which has daily change of tents and never plasters. Nor doth that tree never prove,° which is often transplanted and removed from one ground to another. Nor is there anything so profitable, which at the first sight brings profit with it.[212] Therefore, my good son, leave off these violences of youth, and following the doctrine and rule of thy ancestors, return unto reason, settle thyself in some one place or other. And where better, than where I shall advise thee, taking me, and my counsel along with thee, to whom thou art recommended both by thy father and mother? And I, as if I were thine own true mother, say unto thee, upon those curses and maledictions, which thy parents have laid upon thee, if thou should'st be disobedient unto me, that yet awhile thou continue here, and serve this thy master which thou hast gotten thee, till thou hearest further from me, but not with that foolish loyalty, and ignorant honesty, as hitherto thou hast done; thinking to find firmness upon a false foundation, as most of these masters nowadays are. But do thou gain friends, which is a durable and lasting commodity; stick closely and constantly unto them; do

---

[212] The actual source of this passage (ll. 1033–43, starting with the sentence attributed to Seneca), is once more the *Auctoritates Aristotelis* (XXI.4–5, 7–9); see Lobera *et al.*, eds (2000), p. 72, n. 507, and their long note, pp. 578–79.

not thou live upon hopes, relying on the vain promises of
masters, who suck away the substance of their servants with
hollow-hearted and idle promises, as the horse-leeches suck
blood; and in the end fall off from them, wrong them, grow
forgetful of their good services, and deny them any recompense
or reward at all. Woe be unto him that grows old in court. The
masters of these times love more themselves than their
servants. Neither in so doing do they do amiss. The like love
ought servants to bear unto themselves. Liberality was lost
long ago; rewards are grown out of date; magnificence is fled
the country, and with her, all nobleness. Every one of them is
wholly now for himself, and makes the best he can of his
servants' service, serving his turn, as he finds it may stand with
his private interest and profit. And therefore they ought to do
no less, seeing that they are less than they in substance, but to
live after their law, and to do as they do.[213] My son Parmeno,
I the rather tell this, because thy master (as I am informed) is
(as it seems likewise unto me) a *rompenecios*,[214] one that
befools his servants, and wears them out to the very stumps,
looks for much service at their hands, and makes them small,
or no recompense. He will look to be served of all, but will part
with nothing at all. Weigh well my words, and persuade
thyself, that what I have said is true. Get thee some friends in
his house, which is the greatest, and preciousest jewel in the
world. For, with him thou must not think to fasten friendship:
a thing seldom seen where there is such difference of estate and
condition as is between you two. Opportunity, thou seest, now
offers herself unto us, on whose foretop, if we will but take
hold, we shall all of us be great gainers, and thou shalt
presently have something wherewithal to help thyself. As for

---

[213] Celestina suggests here that servants should do as their masters do, i.e. 'vivir a su ley', i.e. live according to their own law (a Senecan source has been suggested for this idea, *Epistles* XX.2, 'ad legem suam quisque vivat', 'let everyone live according to his own law'). To that effect, Celestina recommends the establishment of mutually beneficial communication with friends, instead of loyal service to a master in expectation of a hypothetical reward that may never be forthcoming. Besides Seneca, the main sources for her admonitions in this respect are Aristotle's *Ethics* and Cicero's *De amicitia* and *De finibus* (Lobera *et al.*, eds, 2000, p. 73, n. 521 and their long notes, pp. 579–80).

[214] rompenecios] *sic* in Spanish, meaning a selfish and ungrateful person: Mabbe himself explains the meaning of the expression in the comments that follow.

that which I told you of, it shall be well and safely kept, when time shall serve. In the meanwhile, it shall be much for thy profit, that thou make Sempronio thy friend.

Parmeno. Celestina, my hair stands on end to hear thee, I tremble at thy words. I know not what I should do, I am in a great perplexity. One while I hold thee for my mother, another while Calisto for my master. I desire riches, but would not get them wrongfully. For he that rises by unlawful means, falls with greater speed than he got up. I would not for all the world thrive by ill-gotten gain.

Celestina. Marry, sir, but so would I: right, or wrong, so as my house be raised high enough, I care not.

Parmeno. Well, we two are of contrary minds. For, I should never live contented with ill-gotten goods. For I hold cheerful poverty to be an honest thing. Besides, I must tell you, that they are not poor that have little, but they that desire much. And therefore say all you can, though never so much, you shall never persuade me in this to be of your belief. I would fain pass over this life of mine without envy. I would pass through solitary woods and wilderness without fear. I would take my sleep without startings.° I would avoid injuries with gentle answers, endure violence without reviling, and brook oppression by a resolute resistance.

Celestina. Oh my son! It is a true saying, that wisdom cannot be but only in aged persons. And thou art but young.[215]

Parmeno. True, but contented poverty is safe and secure.

Celestina. But tell me, I pray thee, whom doth fortune more advance, than those that be bold and venturous? Besides, who is he that comes to anything in a common-wealth, who hath resolved with himself to live without friends? But (heaven be thanked) thou hast wealth enough of thine own, yet thou knowest not what need thou mayst have of friends for the better keeping of them. Nor do thou think that this thy inwardness° with thy master can any way secure thee. For the greater a man's fortune is, the less secure it is; and then most ticklish,° when most prosperous. And therefore, to be armed against

---

[215] To Parmeno's argument that 'they are not poor that have little, but they that desire much', which originates again in *Auctoritates Aristotelis* (XXI.10–11), Celestina skilfully responds with another proverb from the same source, i.e. 'wisdom cannot be but only in aged persons' (XV. 123).

misfortunes, we must arm ourselves with friends. And where canst thou get a fitter, nearer, and better companion in this kind, than where those three kind of friendships do concur in one? To wit, goodness, profit, and pleasure. For goodness, behold the good will of Sempronio, how agreeable, and conformable it is to thine; and with it, the great similiancy[216] and suitableness which both of you have in virtue. For profit, that lies in this hand of mine, if you two can but agree together. For pleasure, that likewise is very likely. For now you are both in the prime of your years, young and lusty, and fit for all kind of sports and pleasures whatsoever, wherein young men more than old folks do join and link together: as in gaming, in wearing good clothes, in jesting, in eating, in drinking and wenching together. Oh Parmeno, if thou thyself wouldst, what a life might we lead? Even as merry as the day is long. Sempronio, he loves Elicia, kinswoman to Areusa.

Parmeno. To Areusa?
Celestina. Ay, to Areusa.
Parmeno. To Areusa, the daughter of Eliso?
Celestina. To Areusa, the daughter of Eliso.
Parmeno. Is this certain?
Celestina. Most certain.
Parmeno. It is marvellous strange.
Celestina. But tell me man, dost thou like her?
Parmeno. Nothing in the world more.
Celestina. Well, now I know thy mind, let me alone. Here's my hand; I will give her thee. Thou shalt have her, man, she is thine own, as sure as a club.[217]
Parmeno. Nay, soft, mother, you shall give me leave not to believe you. I trust nobody with my faith.
Celestina. He is unwise that will believe all men, and he is in an error that will believe no man.
Parmeno. I said that I believe thee, but I dare not be so bold. And therefore let me alone.

---

[216] similiancy] similarity, likeness; the *OED* only lists two quotations, one from *The Rogue*, and this one. The *Auctoritates* is also the source for the subsequent adagia on the virtues and uses of friendship.

[217] The *OED* only documents one quotation with this expression: 1584 R. Scot *Discouerie Witchcraft* iv.ix.84, 'Hir prophesie fell out as sure as a club'.

Celestina. Alas, poor silly wretch. Faint-hearted is he that dares not venture for his good. Jove[218] gives nuts to them that have no teeth to crack them, and beans to those that have no jaws to chew them.[219] Simple as thou art, thou mayst truly say, fools have fortune. For it is commonly seen, that they who have least wisdom have most wealth, and that they who have the most discretion have the least means.[220]

Parmeno. Oh, Celestina, I have heard old men say that one example of luxury or covetousness does much hurt. And that a man should converse with those that may make him better, and to forsake the fellowship of those whom he thinks to make better. As for Sempronio, neither by his example shall I be won to be virtuous, nor he by my company be withdrawn from being vicious. And suppose that I should incline to that which thou sayst, I would fain know this one thing of thee, how by example faults may be concealed. And though a man overcome by pleasure may go against virtue, yet notwithstanding, let him take heed how he spot his honesty.

Celestina. There is no wisdom in thy words. For without company there is no pleasure in the possession of anything. Do not thou then draw back, do not thou torment and vex thyself. For nature shuns whatsoever savours of sadness, and desires that which is pleasant and delightsome. And delight is with friends in things that are sensual, but especially in recounting matters of love, and communicating them the one to the other: 'this did I do myself', 'thus such a one told me', 'such a jest did we break', 'in this sort did I win her', 'thus often did I kiss her', 'thus often did she bite me', 'thus I embraced her', 'thus came we nearer and nearer', 'oh what speech, what grace, what sport, what kisses!' 'Let us goe thither', 'let us return thither', 'let us have music', 'let us paint mottoes', 'let us sing songs', 'let us invent some pretty devices', 'let us tilt it', 'what shall be

---

[218] Again, Mabbe translates 'Dios' as 'Jove'.

[219] Mabbe here duplicates the refrains to emphasize the main idea, expressed in the original by 'Da Dios habas a quien no tiene quijadas' (Lobera *et al.*, eds, 2000, p. 76). Mabbe's addition is a translation of a common Spanish refrain, still in use today: 'Dios da nueces (o pan) a quien no tiene dientes'.

[220] Another proverb from the *Auctoritates Aristotelis* (XIII.2–3). This and the previous passages, as well as the rest of Celestina's interventions in this act, are peppered with indirect quotations from this collection of *adagia*.

the impress? what the letter to it?', 'tomorrow she will walk abroad, let us round her street', 'read this her letter', 'let us go by night', 'hold thou the ladder, guard well the gate', 'how did she escape thee?', 'look, where the cuckold her husband goes', 'I left her all alone', 'let us give another turn', let us go back again thither' . . . And is there any delight, Parmeno, in all this without company? By my fay,° by my fay, they that have trial° can tell you, that this is the delight, this is the only pleasure. As for that other thing you wot of, your asses have a better, and can do better than you, or the best of you all.[221]

Parmeno. I would not, mother, that you should draw me on by your pleasing persuasions to follow your advice, as those have done, who wanting a good foundation to build their opinion have invited and drawn men to drink of their heresies, sugaring their cup with some sweet kind of poison, for to catch and captivate the wills of weak-minded men and to blind the eyes of their reason, with the powder of some sweet-pleasing affection.[222]

Celestina. What is reason, you fool? What is affection, you ass? Discretion (which thou hast not) must determine that. And discretion gives the upper hand to prudence, and prudence cannot be had without experience, and experience cannot be found but in old folks and such as are well stricken in years. And therefore we are called fathers, and mothers. And good parents do always give their children good counsel, as I more especially now do thee, whose life and credit I prefer before mine own. And when, or how, canst thou be able to requite this my kindness? For parents and tutors can never receive any recompense that may equal their desert.

Parmeno. I am very jealous and suspicious of receiving this doubtful counsel. I am afraid to venture upon it.

Celestina. Wilt thou not entertain it? Well, I will then tell thee, he that wilfully refuses counsel shall suddenly come to

---

[221] A rather blunt remark, which translates an equally crude conclusion in the original: 'Éste es el deleite, que lo ál mejor lo hacen los asnos en el prado', i.e. true delight lies in this conversational communication of the details of one's love affairs with friends, for the physical act itself is incomparably better performed by any ass in a meadow. In other words, communication humanizes sex.

[222] Here Parmeno switches to *you*, whereas in former remarks, he has used *thou* to address Celestina.

destruction. And so, Parmeno, I rid myself of thee, as also of this business.

Parmeno. (My mother, I see, is angry, and what I were best to do I know not. I am doubtful of following her counsel. It is as great an error to believe nothing as it is to believe everything.[223] The more humane and civil course is to have affiance° and confidence in her. Especially in that where besides the present benefit, both profit and pleasure is proposed. I have heard tell that a man should believe his betters and those whose years carry authority with them. Now, what is it she advises me unto? To be at peace with Sempronio, and to peace no man ought to be opposite. For blessed are the peaceful. Love and charity towards our brethren, that is not to be shunned and avoided by us, and few are they that will forgo their profit. I will therefore seek to please her, and hearken unto her.) Mother, a master ought not to be offended with his scholar's ignorance, at least very seldom in matters of depth and knowledge. For though knowledge in its own nature be communicable unto all, yet it is infused but into few. And therefore I pray pardon me, and speak anew unto me. For I will not only hear and believe thee,[224] but receive thy counsel as a singular kindness and a token of thy great favour and especial love towards me. Nor yet would I that you should thank me for this, because the praise and thanks for every action ought rather to be attributed to the giver than to the receiver. Command me, therefore, for to your commandments shall I ever be willing, that my consent submit itself.

Celestina. It is proper to a man to err, but to a beast to persevere in an error. It does much glad me, Parmeno, that thou hast cleared those thick clouds which darkened thy eyesight, and hast answered me according to the wisdom, discretion, and sharp wit of thy father, whose person, now representing itself fresh to my remembrance doth make my tender eyes to melt

---

[223] Parmeno echoes here Celestina's adage, just when he is about to switch from the fidelity he owes to Calisto, to the confidence ('the more humane and civil course') he is about to bestow upon Celestina for the sake of both profit and pleasure. Parmeno has been persuaded, and having internalized Celestina's arguments, he reproduces them in this monological aside from his own subjective standpoint.

[224] Parmeno switches to *thee / thou* and immediately afterwards uses *you* again.

into tears, which thou seest in such abundance to trickle down my cheeks. He sometimes would maintain hard and strange propositions, but would presently (such was the goodness of his nature) see his error, and embrace the truth. I swear unto thee, that in thus seeing thee to thwart the truth, and then suddenly upon it, laying down all contradiction, and to be conformable to that which was reason, methinks I do as lively now behold thy father as if he now were living and present here before me. Oh what a man he was, how proper in his person, how able in his actions, what a part did he bear and what a veneral[225] and reverent countenance did he carry! But hush, I hear Calisto coming, and thy new friend, Sempronio, whose reconcilement with him, I refer to some fitter opportunity. For two living in one heart are more powerful both for action, and understanding.

Calisto. Dear mother, I did much doubt, considering my misfortunes, to find you alive. But marvel more, considering my desire, that myself come alive unto you. Receive this poor gift of him, who with it offers thee his life.
Celestina. As in your finest gold, that is wrought by the hand of your most cunning and curious artificer, the workmanship oftentimes doth far surpass the matter, so the fashion of your fair liberality doth much exceed the greatness of your gift. And questionless,° a kindness that is quickly conferred redoubles its effect; for he that slacks that which he promises seems in a manner to deny it, and to repent himself of his promised favour.
Parmeno. (Sempronio, what has he given her?
Sempronio. A hundred crowns in good gold.
Parmeno. Ha, ha, ha.
Sempronio. Hath my mother talked with thee?
Parmeno. Peace, she hath.
Sempronio. How is it then with us?
Parmeno. As thou wilt thyself. Yet for all this, methinks I am still afraid.

---

[225] veneral] venerable, but also venereal; with the former meaning, the *OED* only lists Mabbe's use in *The Spanish Bawd*; Mabbe has here created a pun in English that did not exist in the original.

Sempronio. No more. Be silent. I fear me, I shall make thee twice as much afraid, e'r I have done with thee.

Parmeno. Now fie upon it. I perceive there can be no greater plague, nor no greater enemy to a man, than those of his own house.)

Calisto. Now mother, go your ways, get you home and cheer up your own house, and when you have done that, I pray hasten hither, and cheer upon ours.

Celestina. Good chance attend you.

Calisto. And you too, and so farewell.

Actus II
The Argument

Celestina being departed from Calisto and gone home to her own house, Calisto continues talking with Sempronio his servant; who like one that is put in some good hope, thinking all speed to flow, sends away Sempronio to Celestina, to solicit her for the quicker dispatch of his conceived business; Calisto and Parmeno in the meanwhile reasoning together.

INTERLOCUTORS
Calisto, Sempronio, Parmeno

Calisto: Tell me, my masters, the hundred crowns which I gave yonder beldame, are they well bestowed, or no?

Sempronio. Yes, sir, exceedingly well. For, besides the saving of your life, you have gained much honour by it. And for what end is fortune favourable and prosperous, but to be a handmaid to our honour, and to wait thereon, which of all worldly goods is the greatest? For honour is the reward and recompense of virtue; and for this cause we give it unto the Divine Essence, because we have not anything greater to give him.[226] The best part whereof consists in liberality and bounty; and this close-fistedness, and uncommunicated treasure, doth eclipse and darken, whereas magnificence and liberality doth gain, and highly extol it. What good is it for a man to keep that to himself, which in the keeping of it, does himself no good?[227]

---

[226] 'Dios' in the original becomes *Divine Essence* in Mabbe.

[227] In the original Sempronio enjoins Calisto to share the 'tesoros comunicables' (See Lobera *et al.*, eds, 2000, p. 83, n. 9). Note that both in the original and the translated text, communication creates friendship, and society, both as conversational exchange, but also in the sharing of business interests, self-profit, as well as counsel. When she was persuading Parmeno towards the end of Act I, Celestina used a similar argument. These different aspects of the verb 'comunicar' feature in Covarrubias's definition, 'comunicar alguno es tratarle y conversarle' and 'comunicarle algún negocio, consultarle y darle parte dél' (*Tesoro de la Lengua Castellana o Española* [1611], 1995, p. 341). As Sempronio says immediately, the horizontal creation of value through the communication of goods and useful information, and through the establishment of bonds for the pursuit of mutual self-interest is far better than the vertical and linear

I tell you, sir, and what I speak is truth: better is the use of riches, than the possessing of them. Oh, how glorious a thing is it to give? And how miserable to receive? See, how much better action is than passion: so much more noble is the giver, than the receiver. Amongst the elements, the fire, because it is more active, is the more noble: and therefore placed in the spheres, in the noblest place. And some say, that nobleness is a praise proceeding from the merit and antiquity of our ancestors. But I am of opinion that another man's light can never make you shine, unless you have some of your own. And therefore do not glory in the nobleness of your father, who was so magnificent a gentleman, but in your own. Shine not out of his, but your own light, and so shall you get yourself honour, which is man's greatest outward good. Wherefore not the bad, but the good, (such as yourself) are worthy to partake of so perfect a virtue. And besides, I must tell you, that perfect virtue doth not suppose that honour hath its fellow: and therefore rejoice with yourself, that you have been so magnificent, and so bountiful. And thus, sir, having told you my mind, let me now advice you that you would be pleased to return back to your chamber, and there take some rest, sithence that[228] your business is deposited in such hands; assuring yourself that the beginning being so good, the end will be much better: and so let us go presently to your chamber, where I shall treat more at large with you concerning this business.

Calisto. Methinks, Sempronio, it is no good counsel that I should rest here accompanied, and that she should go all alone, who seeks to cure my ill: it were better that thou shouldst go along with her, and hasten thereon, since thou knowst, that on her diligence dependeth my welfare; on her slowness my painfulness, on her neglect, my despair. Thou art wise, I know thee to be faithful, I hold thee a good servant. And therefore so handle the matter, that she shall no sooner see thee, but that she may judge of that pain which I feel, and of that fire which tormenteth me, whose extreme heat will not give me leave to

---

descent of value from the mere 'antiquity of our ancestors'. Most of Sempronio's ideas in this paragraph proceed, once more, from the *Auctoritates Aristotelis* (see Lobera *et al.*, eds, 2000, pp. 83–85). See also the note to 8.325 below.

[228] sithence that] seeing that.

50   lay open unto her the third part of my secret sickness. So did it tie my tongue, and took such hold of my senses, that they were not only busied, but in a manner wasted and consumed; which thou, as one that is free from the like passion, mayst more largely deliver, letting thy words run with a looser rein.

Sempronio. Sir, I would fain go to fulfil your command. And I would fain stay, to ease you of your care, your fear puts spurs to my sides, and your solitariness, like a bridle, pulls me back. But I will obey and follow your counsel, which is to go and labour° the old woman. But how shall I go? For, if I leave you
60   thus all alone, you will talk idly, like one that is distracted, do nothing but sigh, weep, and take on, shutting yourself up in darkness, desiring solitude, and seeking new means of thoughtful torment; wherein if you still persevered, you cannot escape either death or madness. For the avoiding whereof, get some good company about you, that may minister unto you occasion of mirth, by recounting of witty conceits, by entertaining you with music, and singing merry songs, by relating stories, by devising mottoes, by telling tales, by playing at cards, jesting, sporting. In a word, by inventing any other kind
70   of sweet and delightful recreation for to pass away the time, that you may not further your thoughts to run still wandering on in that cruel error, whereinto they were put by that your lady and mistress, upon the first trance and encounter of your love.

Calisto. How like a silly fool thou talkest! Know'st thou not, that it easeth the pain to bewail its cause? Oh how sweet is it to the sorrowful to unsheath their griefs? What ease do broken sighs bring with them? Oh what a diminishing and refreshing to tearful complaints is the unfolding of a man's woes, and bitter
80   passions? As many as ever writ of comfort, and consolation, do all of them jump° in this.

Sempronio. Read a little farther, and but turn over the leaf, and you shall find they say thus: that to trust in things temporal, and to seek after matter of sorrow is a kind of foolishness, if not madness. And that Macias,[229] the idol of lovers, forgetful

---

[229] Macías] a fashionable Galician poet who became the epitome of the doleful lover in fifteenth-century Castile (see Lobera *et al.*, eds, 2000, p. 87, n. 36). Unlike Mabbe, the Spanish text does not attribute the subsequent sentences to this legendary poet. Note also that Sempronio has immediately identified

of himself, because his mistress did forget him, and careless of his welfare, because she cared nothing for him, complains himself thus: that the punishment of love consists in the contemplation thereof, and that the best remedy against love is not to think on thy love. The ease lies in forgetting it. Kick not therefore against the prick,[230] feign thyself to be merry, pluck up your spirits and be of good cheer, and all, you shall see, shall be well. For oftentimes, opinion brings things whither it listeth:[231] not that it should cause us to swerve from the truth, but for to teach us to moderate our sense, and to govern our judgment.

Calisto. Sempronio, my friend (for so thy love makes me style thee) since it so grieves thee that I should be alone, call Parmeno hither, and he shall stay with me, and henceforth be thou (as thou hast ever been) faithful and loyal unto me. For, in the service of the servant consisteth the master's remuneration. Oh Parmeno!

Parmeno. Here, sir.

Calisto. Oh I think not, for I cannot see thee. Leave her not, Sempronio. Ply her hard, follow her at an inch. Forget me not, I pray thee. Now Parmeno, what thinkest thou of that which hath passed today? My pain is great, Melibea stately, Celestina wise, she is her craft's master and we cannot do amiss. Thou hast mainly opposed thyself against her, and to draw me to a detestation of her thou hast painted her forth to the purpose, and set her out in her colours: and I believe thee. For such and so great is the force of truth, that it commands even the tongues of our enemies.[232] But be she such, as thou hast described her to be, yet had I rather give her a hundred crowns, than give another five.

Parmeno. (Is the wind in that door? Do you begin to complain already? Have you now better bethought yourself? We shall

---

Calisto's arguments as something he has read in a book, and retorts by enjoining him to 'read farther' and 'turn over the leaf'.

[230] 'Huye de tirar coces al aguijón'. Lobera *et al.* (2000, p. 87, n. 37) trace the origin of this expression to Acts of the Apostles 24.14 ('[it is] hard for thee to kick against the pricks', in the Authorized Version, King James Bible). It was frequent in classical and medieval Hispanic texts.

[231] listeth] pleases.

[232] Petrarch, *De remediis* I.13.

shortly complain too at home, for I fear me, we shall fast for this frankness.°)
120　*Calisto*. It is thy opinion, Parmeno, that I ask. Gratify me therein. Hold, dost thou look? Why hang'st thou down thy head, when thou shouldest answer me? But I perceive, that as envy is sad, and sadness without a tongue, thine own will can do more with thee than fear of my displeasure. What is that thou grumblest at? What didst thou mutter to thyself, as though thou wert angry?

Parmeno. I say, sir, that it had been better you had employed your liberality on some present or the like services upon Melibea herself, than to cast away your money upon this old
130　bawd: I know well enough what she is. And which is worse, on such a one as minds to make you her slave.

Calisto. How, you fool, her slave?

Parmeno. Ay, her slave. For to whom thou tellest thy secret, to him doest thou give thy liberty.

Calisto. It is something that the fool hath said. But I would fain know this of thee: whether or no, when as there is a great distance betwixt the entreater and the entreated, the suitor and the party sued unto, either out of authority of obedience, or greatness of estate and dignity, or nobleness of descent of
140　blood, as there is between my mistress and myself; whether or no, I pray, it be not necessary to have an intercessor, or mediator for me, who may every foot go to and fro with my messages, until they arrive at her ears, of whom, to have a second audience, I hold it impossible. And if it be thus with me, tell me, whether thou approvest of what I have done, or no?

Parmeno. (The devil approve it for me.)

Calisto. What sayst thou?

Parmeno. Marry, I say sir, that never any error came yet unac-
150　companied; and that one inconvenience is the cause of another and the door that opens unto many.

Calisto. Thy saying I approve, but understand not thy purpose.

Parmeno. Then thus, sir, your losing of your hawk the other day was the cause of your entering into the garden where Melibea was, to look if she[233] were there; your entering, the cause that

---

[233] she] i.e. the hawk.

you both saw her and talked with her; your talk engendered love; your love brought forth your pain; and your pain will be the cause of your growing careless and wretchless° both of your body, soul, and goods. And that which grieves me most is that you must fall into the hands of that same trot-up-and-down;[234] that maidenhead-monger, that same gadding° to and fro bawd, who for her villanies and rogueries in that kind hath been three several times emplumed.

Calisto: Is't e'n so, Parmeno? Is this all the comfort thou canst give me? Tell me rather something that may please me, and give me better content than this can. And know withal, that the more thou dost dispraise, the better do I like her. Let her comply with me, and effect my business, and let them emplume her the fourth time too, if they will, I care not. Thou hast thy wits about thee; thou speak'st not having any sense of pain; thou art not heart-sick, as I am, Parmeno, nor is thy mind touched with that sense of sorrow as mine is.

Parmeno. I had rather, sir, that you should be angry with me, and reprehend me out of your choler, for crossing your opinion, than out of your after-repentance, to condemn me for not counselling you to the contrary. For I should but dissemble with you, if I should not tell you, that then you lost your liberty, when you did first captivate and imprison your will.

Calisto. This villain would be well cudgelled. Tell me, thou unmannerly rascal, why dost thou blaspheme that which I adore? And you, sir, who would seem to be so wise, what wot'st thou of honour? Tell me, what is love? Show me wherein civility consisteth, or what belongs to good manners? Thou wouldst fain be accounted discreet, and wouldst that I should think so, and yet dost not consider with thyself, that the first round in folly's ladder is for a man to think himself wise. If thou didst but feel the pain that I do, with other water wouldst thou bathe that burning, and wash that raging wound, which the cruel shaft of Cupid hath made in my heart. See, what remedy Sempronio brings unto me with his feet, the same dost thou put away with thy tongue, with thy vain and

---

[234] trot-up-and-down] Mabbe's translation of *trotaconventos*, i.e. a go-between, a pander. The original Spanish term has anticlerical connotations, since it denotes a woman who *trots*, or goes from convent to convent, procuring sexual intercourse for their inmates.

uncomfortable words. And feigning thyself, forsooth, to be faithful, thou art in reality of truth, nothing else but a mere clot and lump of earth, a box filled with nothing but the very dregs and ground of malice, the very inn and house that gives open entertainment to envy; not caring so as thou mayst defame, and discredit this old woman, be it by right or by wrong, how thou puttest a disaffiance[235] in my affection; thou knowing that this my pain and overflowing grief, is not ruled by reason, nor will admit advice, but is incapable of counsel, which as if one should tell me; that that which is bred in the bone, may be fetched out of the flesh: or that which is glued to the very heart and entrails of a man, may be unloosed without renting° the soul from the body. Sempronio did fear his going, and thy staying: it was mine own seeking; I would needs have it so; and therefore worthily suffer the trouble of his absence and thy presence: and better it is for a man to be alone, than ill accompanied.

Parmeno. Sir, it is a weak fidelity which fear of punishment can turn to flattery; more especially, with such a master, whom sorrow and affliction deprive of reason, and make him a stranger to his natural judgment. Take but away this same veil of blindness, and these momentary fires will quickly vanish; and then shall you know, that these my sharp words are better to kill this strong canker, and to stifle these violent flames, than the soft smoothings of soothing Sempronio, which feed your humour, quicken up your love, kindle afresh your flames, and join the brands to brands, which shall never leave burning, till they have quite consumed you, and brought you to your grave.

Calisto. Peace, peace, you varlet. I am in pain and anguish, and thou readest philosophy unto me. But I expect no better at thy hands; I have not the patience to hear thee any longer. Go, be gone. Get forth my horse. See he be well and clean dressed; girt° him well. For I must pass by the house of Melibea, or rather of my goddess.

---

[235] disaffiance] lack of affiance, trust, or confidence; also used as a verb in 10.7, i.e. to put out of affiance, trust, or confidence; the *OED* lists only the latter example in *The Spanish Bawd* to illustrate the meaning of this verb.

Parmeno. Holla, boys, where be you? Not a boy about the house. I must be fain to do it myself; and I am glad it is no worse: for I fear me ere it be long, we shall come to a worse office than to be boys of the spur, and to lackey it at the stirrup. Well, let the world slide, and things be as they may be, when they cannot be as they should be.[236] My gossips (I see it as in the proverb) are angry with me for speaking the truth. Why, how now you jade?° Are you neighing too? Is not one jealous lover enough in a house? Or dost thou wind Melibea?[237]

Calisto. When comes this horse? Why, Parmeno, what dost thou mean? Why bringst thou him not away?

Parmeno. Here he is: Sosia was not within.

Calisto. Hold the stirrup. Open the gate a little wider. If Sempronio chance to come in the mean while, and the old woman with him, will them to stay, for I will return presently.

Parmeno. (Go, never to return, and the devil go with thee. Let a man tell these fools all that he can for their own good, they will never see it; and I, for my part believe, that if I should now at this instant give him a blow on the heel, I should beat more brain out of his heel than his head. Go whither thou wilt for me: for I dare pawn my life that Celestina and Sempronio will fleece you ere they have done with you, and not leave you so much as one master-feather[238] to maintain your flight. Oh unfortunate that I am, that I should suffer hatred for my truth, and receive harm for my faithful service! Others thrive by their knavery, and I lose by my honesty. The world is now grown to that pass, that it is good to be bad, and bad to be good; and therefore I will follow the fashion of the times, and do as other men do: since that traitors are accounted wise and discreet, and faithful men are deemed silly honest fools. Had I credited Celestina, with her six dozen of years about her, and followed

---

[236] 'Well let the world [...] as they should be' is Mabbe's translation of Parmeno's resigned exclamation '¡Andar, pase!' (Lobera *et al.*, eds, 2000, p. 91), i.e. it is better to let things be as they are.

[237] wind] To get the wind of; to perceive (an animal, a person, or thing) by the scent conveyed by the wind (*OED*). It translates the Spanish 'barruntar', probably with a sexual innuendo, or denoting that Melibea portends such trouble that even the horse (a symbol of irrational passion) gets wind of her ominous presence.

[238] master-feather] 'a primary flight feather' (*OED* only lists three examples, one of which is this phrase in *The Spanish Bawd*)

her counsel, I had not been thus ill treated by Calisto. But this shall be a warning unto me ever hereafter, to say as he says. If he shall say, 'come, let us eat, and be merry', I will say so too. If, 'let us throw down the house', I also will approve it. If he will burn all his goods, I will help to fetch the fire. Let him destroy, hang, drown, burn himself, and give all that he hath (if he will) to bawds; I for my part will hold my peace, and help to divide the spoil.[239] Besides, it is an ancient and true received rule, that it is best fishing in troubled waters. Wherefore I will never any more be a dog in a mill, to be beaten for my barking.)[240]

---

[239] 'Let him destroy...'] Lobera *et al.* (2000, p. 93, n. 90) trace the origins of this *topos* to several comedies by Terence.

[240] Mabbe's somewhat free translation of the proverbial '¡Nunca más perro a molino!'. Lobera *et al.* (2000, p. 93, n. 92) trace and document this proverb in several works and collections of refrains.

Actus III
The Argument

Sempronio goes to Celestina's house. He reprehends her for her slackness. They consult what course they shall take in Calisto's business concerning Melibea. At last comes Elicia. Celestina hies° her to the house of Pleberio. In the mean while, Sempronio remains in the house with Elicia.

INTERLOCUTORS
Sempronio, Celestina, Elicia

Sempronio: Look what leisure the old bearded bawd takes. How softly she goes. How one leg comes drawing after another! Now she has her money, her arms are broken.[241] Well overtaken, mother, I perceive you will not hurt yourself by too much haste.

Celestina. How now, son? What news with you?

Sempronio. Why, this our sick patient knows not well himself what he would have. Nothing will content him. He will have his cake baked before it be dough, and his meat roasted before it be spitted.[242] He fears thy negligence, and curseth his own covetousness. He is angry with this close fistedness, and offended that he gave thee no more.

Celestina. There is nothing more proper to lovers than impatience. Every small tarriance° is to them a great torment,[243] the least delay breeds dislike. In a moment, what they imagine must be fully effected, nay concluded before begun; especially these new lovers, who against any luring whatsoever fly out to check,[244] they care not whither, without any advisement in the

---

[241] Mabbe's literal translation of the proverb 'A dineros pagados, brazos quebrados'. Lobera *et al.* document it in Santillana's *Proverbios*, and also in Correas.

[242] Mabbe reduplicates the original 'no se le cuece el pan', to emphasize Calisto's impatience (according to some, with a sexual innuendo in the original phrase, see Lobera *et al.*, eds, 2000, p. 95, n. 5, and their long note, p. 598).

[243] 'Omnis mora torquet amantem' (Petrarch, *Bucolicum carmen* V.32). See Lobera *et al.*, eds, 2000, p. 95, n. 6.

[244] Mabbe's translation of 'contra cualquiera señuelo vuelan sin deliberación', a falconry metaphor; 'check' here refers to the pursuit of the wrong 'game' (i.e.

world, or once thinking on the harm which the meat of their desire may (by overgorging) occasion unto them, intermingled amidst the affairs and businesses concerning their own persons and their servants.

Sempronio. What sayst thou of servants? Thinkest thou, that any danger is like to come unto us by labouring in this business? Or, that we shall be burned with those sparkles which scatteringly fly forth of Calisto's fire? I had rather see him and all his love go to the devil, upon the first discovery therefore of any danger (if things chance to go cross) I will eat no more of his bread, I will not stay with him, no not an hour. For it is better to lose his service than my life in serving him. But time will tell me what I shall do. For, before his downfall, he will (like a house that is ready to fall) give some token himself of his own ruin. And therefore, mother, let us in any case keep our persons from peril; let us do what may be done; if it be possible, let us work her for him this year: if not this, the next; if not the next, when we may; if never, the worse luck his: though there is not any thing so hard to suffer in its beginning, which time doth not soften and reduce to a gentle sufferance. And there is no wound so painful which in time doth not slaken much of its torment. Nor was there ever any pleasure so delightful, which hath not by long continuance been much diminished and lessened. Ill and good, prosperity and adversity, glory and grief, all these with time lose the force and strength of their rash and hasty beginning; whereas matters of admiration, and things earnestly desired, once obtained, have no sooner been come, than forgotten, no sooner purchased but relinquished. Every day we see new and strange accidents, we hear as many, and we pass them over; leave those, and hearken after others; them also doth time lessen and make contingible,[245] as things of common course. And I pray, what wonder would you think it, if some should come and tell you: 'there was such an earthquake in such a place', or some such other things; tell me, would you not straight forget it? As also, if one should say unto

---

in hunting or falconry the animal being pursued); its use as a verb derives from the meaning of *check* as a noun, i.e. 'a false stoop, when a hawk forsakes her proper game, and pursues some baser game that crosses her flight' (*OED*).
[245] contingible] contingent; not in the *OED*, only documented in *The Spanish Bawd*.

you, 'such a river is frozen', 'such a blind man hath recovered his sight','thy father is dead','such a thunderbolt fell in such a place','Granada is taken, the king enters it this day','the Turk hath received an overthrow','tomorrow you shall have a great eclypse','such a bridge is carried away with the flood','such a one is now made a noble man', 'Peter is robbed', 'Innes hath hanged herself'. Now in such cases, what wilt thou say, save only this? That some three days past, or upon a second view thereof, there will be no wonder made of it. All things are thus; they all pass after this manner; all is forgotten and thrown behind us, as if they had never been. Just so it will be with this my master's love; the farther it goes on, the more it will slacken: for long custom doth allay sorrow, weakeneth and subdueth our delights, and lesseneth wonders. Let us make our profit of him, whilst this plea is depending;[246] and if we may with a dry foot[247] do him good, the easier the better; if not, by little and little we will solder up this flaw, and make all whole by Melibea's holding him in scorn and contempt. And if this will do no good upon him, better it is, that the master be pained, than his man perilled.

Celestina. Well hast thou said, I hold with thee, and jump° in thy opinion; thy words have well pleased me, we cannot err. Yet notwithstanding, my son, it is necessary that a good proctor should follow his client's cause diligently and painfully; that he colour his plea with some feigned show of reason; that he press some quillet or quirk of law, to go and come into open court, though he be checked, and receive some harsh words from the judge's mouth, to the end that they who are present, may both see and say, that though he did not prevail, yet he both spake and laboured hard for his fee. So shall not he want clients, nor Celestina suitors in cases of love.

Sempronio. Do as thou thinkst good. Frame it to thine own liking. This is not the first business thou hast taken in hand.

Celestina. The first, my son? Few virgins (I thank fortune for it) hast thou seen in this city, which have opened their shops, and

---

[246] depend] To be in suspense or undetermined, be waiting for settlement (as an action at law, *OED*). The use of this term is of a piece with other legal terms that feature in this exchange.

[247] Mabbe's translation of 'a pie enjuto' (Lobera *et al.*, eds, 2000, p. 98, n. 33), i.e. without getting too involved in the affair, and thus avoiding trouble.

traded for themselves, to whom I have not been a broker to their first spun thread, and helped them to vent their wares;[248] there was not that wench borne in the world, but I writ her down in my register, and kept a catalogue of all their names, to the intent that I might know how many escaped my net. Why, what didst thou think of me, Parmeno? Can I live by the air? Can I feed myself with wind? Do I inherit any other land? Have I any other house or vineyard? Knowest thou of any other substance of mine, besides this office? By what do I eat and drink? By what do I find clothes to my back, and shoes to my feet? In this city was I born, in it was I bred; living (though I say it) in good credit and estimation,[249] as all the world knows. And dost thou think then, that I can go unknown? He that knows not both my name, and my house, thou mayst hold him a mere stranger.

Sempronio. Tell me, mother, what passed between you and my fellow Parmeno, when I went up with Calisto for the crowns?

Celestina. I told him his dream, and the interpretation thereof,[250] and how that he should gain more by our company, and joining in friendship with us, than with all his gay glozings,[251] and embroidered works which he uttered to his master; how he would always live poor and in want, and be made a scoff and laughing-stock unless he would turn over a new leaf, and alter his opinion; that he should not make himself a saint, and play the hypocrite before such an old beaten bitch as myself. I did put him in mind of his own mother relating unto him what a one she was, to the end that he might not set my office at nought, herself having been of the same trade, for should he but offer to speak ill of me, he must needs stumble first on her.

Sempronio. Is it long, mother, since you first knew her?

---

[248] All this vocabulary related to trade and exchange is a close translation of the original. Lobera *et al.* (2000, p. 99, n. 40) document how in the original Celestina simply reproduces here the actual slang employed by pimps and prostitutes.

[249] Credit and estimation reduplicate the original 'honra' (honour).

[250] Celestina does not refer to the interpretation of an actual dream. The original proverbial expression, 'díjele el sueño y la soltura', signifies that Celestina frankly provided a clear resolution to Parmeno's doubts (Lobera *et al.*, eds, 2000, p. 99, n. 46).

[251] glozing] flattery, cajolery.

Celestina. This Celestina, which is here now with thee, was the woman that saw her born, and helped to breed her up. Why, I tell thee, man, his mother and I were nail and flesh, buckle and thong.[252] Of her I learned the better part of my trade. We did both eat, both sleep, both enjoy our pleasures, our counsels, and our bargains, intermutably[253] one with another; we lived together like two sisters both at home and abroad: there was not a farthing which either of us gained, but was faithfully and truly divided between us. Had she lived, I should never have lived to be deceived. But it was not my fortune to be so happy, she died too soon for me. Oh death, death, how many doest thou discomfort with thy unwelcome and troublesome visitation? For one that thou eatest being ripe, thou croppest a thousand that are green; for were she alive, these my steps should not have been unaccompanied, not driven (as now I am) to walk the streets alone. I have good cause to remember her; for to me she was a faithful friend, and a good companion. And whilst she was with me, she would never suffer me to trouble my body, or my brains about anything: if I brought bread, she would bring meat; if I did spread the cloth, she would lay the napkins. She was not foolish, nor fantastical, nor proud, as most of your women nowadays are. And by my fay,° I swear unto thee, she would go barefaced from one end of the city to the other, with her fan in her hand, and not one, all the way that she went, would give her any worse word than mistress Claudina. And I dare be bold to say it, that there was not a woman of a better palate for wine in the world, nor better skilled in any kind of merchandise whatsoever. And when you have thought that she had been scarce out of doors, with a whip-Sir John,[254] e'r you could scarce say this, she was here again. Everyone would invite and feast her, so great was the affection which they bore unto her. And she never came home,

---

[252] 'Nail and flesh' is a literal translation of 'uña y carne', an idiomatic phrase, still in current use, that expresses very close emotional proximity. As he does elsewhere, Mabbe reduplicates the idea in the translation to make sure that he conveys the original meaning.
[253] Intermutably] intermutually, reciprocally; not in the *OED*.
[254] with a whip Sir John] 'before you can say Jack Robinson', i.e. in a very short time, very quickly and suddenly. The *OED* only lists this phrase from *The Spanish Bawd* to illustrate this expression.

till she had taken a taste of some eight or ten sorts of wine, bearing one pottle in her jar, and the other in her belly. And her credit was so good, that they would have trusted her for a rundlet° or two upon her bare word, as if she had pawned unto them a piece of plate. Why, her word was as current as gold in all the inns and taverns in the town. If we walked the streets, whensoever we found ourselves thirsty, we entered straight the next tavern that was at hand, and called presently for a quart of wine for to moisten our mouths withal, though we had not a penny to pay for it. Nor would they (as from others) take our veils and our coifs[255] from off our heads, till we had discharged the reckoning, but score it up, and so let us go on our way. O, Sempronio, were it but cat after kind,[256] and that such were the son, as was the mother, assure thyself that thy master should remain without a feather, and we without any further care. But if I live, I will bring this iron to my fashion;[257] I will work him like wax, and reckon him in the number of mine own.

Sempronio. How doest thou think to make him thine? He is a crafty subtle fox; he will hardly be drawn in. He is a shrewd fellow to deal withal.[258]

Celestina. For such a crafty knave, we must have a knave and a half, and entertain two traitors for the taking of one.[259] I will bring him to have Areusa, so and make him cock-sure ours; and he shall give us leave without any let, to pitch our nets, for the catching of Calisto's coin.

Sempronio. But dost thou think thou canst do any good upon Melibea? Hast thou any good bough to hang by?[260]

---

[255] coif] a close-fitting cap covering the top, back, and sides of the head.

[256] The *OED* only documents one use of this proverbial expression: '1546 J. Heywood *Dialogue Prouerbes Eng. Tonguei.* xi. sig. Diii, Cat after kynd good mouse hunt'.

[257] 'Yo le haré de mi hierro' (Lobera *et al.*, eds, 2000, p. 101), i.e. I will brand him with the iron as one of my own. As is his wont, Mabbe translates almost literally, and then adds a paraphrase of his own ('I will work him like wax, and reckon him in the number of mine own') to clarify the meaning of the original.

[258] 'He is a crafty [. . .] withal' is an extended translation of Sempronio's 'es un traidor'.

[259] entertain two traitors for the taking of one] translates 'A ese tal, dos alevosos', which echoes the proverb 'a un traidor, dos alevosos', meaning that those who are traitors do not deserve better treatment than they afford. Lobera *et al.* (2000, p. 102, n. 70) document the proverb in Santillana and Correas.

[260] Hast thou any good bough to hang by?] Mabbe's translation of the original

Celestina. There is not that surgeon that can at the first dressing give a true judgment of his patient's wound. But what I see, and think for the present, I will plainly deliver unto thee. Melibea is fair, Calisto fond and frank, he cares not to spare his purse, nor I my pains; he is willing to spend, and I to speed him in his business. Let his money be stirring, and let the suit hang as long as it will. Money can do anything, it splitteth hard rocks, it passeth over rivers dry-footed; there is not any place so high whereunto an ass laden with gold will not get up; his unadvisedness° and ferventness° of affection is sufficient to marr him and to make us. This I have thought upon; this I have searched into; this is all I know concerning him and her; and this is that which must make most for our profit. Well, now must I go to Pleberio's house. Sempronio, farewell. For though Melibea brave it, and stands so high upon her pantofles,[261] yet is not she the first that I have made to stoop, and leave her cackling; they are all of them ticklish, and skittish; the whole generation of them is given to winching° and flinging: but after they are well weighed, they prove good highway jades,° and travel quietly; you may kill them, but never tire them. If they journey by night, they wish it may never be morning. They curse the cocks, because they proclaim it is day; the clocks, because they go too fast; they lie prostrate, as if they looked after the Pleiades and the North Star, making themselves astronomers and star-gazers. But when they see the morning star arise, they sigh for sorrow, and are ready to forsake their bodies. And the clearing of the day, is the clouding of their joy. And above all, it is worth the while to note how quickly they change copy, and turn the cat in the pan;[262] they entreat him,

---

'¿Hay algún buen ramo?' This reference to a bough can be interpreted in different ways. Lovers used to adorn the windows and balconies of their paramours with boughs and flowers; but boughs were also hung from the doors of taverns (which frequently doubled up as brothels) to denote that they were open for business. See Lobera *et al.*, eds (2000), p. 102, n. 74, and their long note, p. 603.

[261] stands so high upon her pantofles] to stand (also walk etc) upon (one's) pantofles is 'to affect an air of superiority; to behave pompously or conceitedly' (*OED*).

[262] turn the cat in the pan] 'to reverse the order of things so dexterously as to make them appear the very opposite of what they really are; to turn a thing right about [. . .] To change one's position, change sides, from motives of interest, etc.' (*OED*). Mabbe's 'And above all [. . .] and turn the cat in the pan' (not in the original) substitutes Celestina's explicit acknowledgment of her intense past

of whom they were entreated; they endure torment for him, whom before they had tormented; they are servants to those whose mistresses they were; they break through stone walls, they open windows, feign sickness; if the hinges of their doors chance to creak, they anoint and supple them with oil, that they may perform their office without any noise. I am not able to express unto thee the great impression of that sweetness, which the primary and first kisses of him they love, leaveth imprinted in their hearts. They are enemies of the mean, and whole set upon extremes.

Sempronio. Mother, I understand not these terms.

Celestina. Marry, I say, that a woman either loveth, or hateth him much, of whom she is beloved, so that if she entertain not his love, she cannot dissemble her hate; there are no reins strong enough to bridle their dislike. And because I know this to be true, it makes me go more merrily and cheerfully to Melibea's house, than if I had her fast in my fist already. For I know, that though at the first I must be forced to woo her, yet in the end, she will be glad to sue to me. And though at present perhaps she threaten me, and flatly fall out with me; yet at last will she be well pleased, and fall as much a flattering, as she did a reviling me. Here in this pocket of mine, I carry a little parcel of yarn, and other such like trinkets, which I always bear about me; that I may have some pretence at first to make my easier entrance and free access, where I am not throughly known: as gorgets, coifs, fringes, rolls,° fillets, hair-laces, nippers, antimony,[263] ceruse,° and sublimated mercury,[264] needles and pins; they shall not ask that thing, which I shall not have for them. To the end, that look whatsoever they shall call for, I may be ready provided for them. And this bait upon the first sight thereof shall work my acceptance, and hold fast the fish which I mind to take.

---

sexual activity, and of her still lingering desire: 'Camino es, hijo, que nunca me harté de andar; nunca me vi cansada, y aún así vieja como soy, sabe Dios mi buen deseo; cuánto más éstas que hierven sin fuego' (Lobera *et al.*, eds, 2000, p. 103).

[263] antimony] used for cosmetic purposes, *antimony* here translates *alcohol*, which probably refers to the '*al-koḥ'l*' of the Arabs, used to stain the eyelids' (*OED*).

[264] sublimated mercury] Spanish 'solimán', a mercury-based cosmetic.

Sempronio. Mother, look well about you. Take heed what you do. For a bad beginning can never make a good ending. Think on her father, who is noble and of great power and courage; her mother jealous and furious, and thou, suspicion itself. No sooner seen, but mistrusted. Melibea is the only child to them both, and she miscarrying, miscarrieth with her all their happiness; the very thought whereof makes me quake and tremble. Go not to fetch wool, and come home shorn yourself; seek not to pluck her wings, and [come back] yourself without your plumes.

Celestina. Without my plumes, my son?

Sempronio. Or rather emplumed, mother, which is worse.

Celestina. Now by my fay,° in an ill hour had I need of thee to be my companion. As though thou couldst instruct Celestina in her own trade? As if I knew not better what to do, than thou canst teach me? Before ever thou wast borne, I did eat bread with crust. Oh, you are a proper man to make a commander, and to marshal other men's affairs, when thyself art so dejected with sinister divinations, and fear of ensuing harms.

Sempronio. Marvel not, mother, at my fear, since it is the common condition of all men; that what they most desire, they think shall never come to pass. And the rather, for that in this case now in hand, I dread both thine, and my punishment; I desire profit; I would that this business might have a good end; not because my master thereby might be rid of his pain, but I of my penury. And therefore I cast more inconveniences with my small experience, than you with all your aged art and cunning.

Elicia. I will bless myself, Sempronio, come. I will make a streak in the water,[265] I will score it up. This is news indeed: I had thought to have strewed green rushes against your coming.[266] What? Come hither twice? Twice in one day?

---

[265] a streak in the water] 'una raya en el agua', denoting something impossible, or highly unusual.

[266] green rushes] 'fresh rushes spread on the floor of a house in honour of an esteemed guest who is a stranger; hence formerly as an exclamation of surprise or welcome on seeing a person who has been absent a long while' (*OED*).

Celestina. Peace, you fool. Let him alone. We have other thoughts (iwis°) to trouble our heads withal, matters of more importance, than to listen to your trumperies. Tell me, is the house clear? Is the young wench gone, that expected the young novice?

Elicia. Gone? Yes; and another come, since she went, and gone too.

Celestina. Say'st thou me so, girl? I hope then it was not in vain.

Elicia. How in vain? No by my fay° it was not; it was not in vain; for though he came late, yet better late than never. And little need he to rise early, whom his stars have a purpose to help.[267]

Celestina. Go, hie you up quickly to the top of all the house, as high as you can go, and bring me down hither the bottle of that oil of serpents, which you shall find fastened to that piece of rope, which I brought out of the fields with me that other night, when it rained so fast, and was so dark;[268] then open my chest where the paintings be, and on your right hand you shall find a paper written with the blood of a bat, or flitter-mouse; bring it down also with you, together with that wing of the dragon, whereof yesterday we did cut off the claws. And take heed, you do not shed the May-dew,[269] which was brought me for to make my confection.

Elicia. It is not here, mother; you never remember where you lay your things.

Celestina. Do not reprove me, I pray thee, in mine old age; misuse me not, Elicia. Do not you feign untruths, though Sempronio be here, be not you proud of it. For he had rather have me for his counsellor, than you for his play-fellow, for all you love him so well. Enter into the chamber where my ointments be, and there in the skin of a black cat, where I willed you to put the eyes of the she-wolf, you shall not fail to find it; and bring

---

[267] A translation of the Spanish proverb (truncated in the original) 'Más vale a quien Dios ayuda, etc. [que a quien mucho madruga]'. Mabbe completes the full sense of the proverb, but eliminates the reference to God, and uses 'stars' instead.

[268] Oil of serpent was a concoction made of snakes, used for medicinal purposes, but also with obvious satanic connotations; 'that piece of rope', i.e. a hangman's rope.

[269] May-dew] dew formed or gathered on May Day or in the month of May, popularly supposed to have medicinal and cosmetic properties.

down the blood of the he-goat, and that little piece of his beard which you yourself did cut off.

Elicia. Take it to you, mother. Lo, here it is; while you stay here, I will go up, and take my Sempronio with me.

Celestina. I conjure thee (thou sad god Pluto) Lord of the infernal deep, emperor of the damned court, captain general and proud commander of the wicked spirits, grand signor of those sulphurous fires, which the flaming hills of Aetna flash forth in most fearful and most hideous manner; governor and supervisor both of the torments, and tormenters of those sinful souls that lie howling in Phlegeton;[270] prince and chief ruler of those three hellish furies, Tisiphone, Megaera and Allecto;[271] administrator of all the black things belonging to the kindgoms of Styx and Dis,[272] with all their pitchy lakes, infernal shades, and litigious Chaos; maintainer of the flying Harpies, with all the whole rabblement of frighful Hydras;[273] I Celestina, thy best known, and most noted client, conjure thee by the virtue and force of these red letters, by the blood of this bird of the night, wherewith they are charactered, by the power and weight of the names and signs which are contained in this paper, by the fell and bitter poison of those vipers, whence this oil was extracted, wherewith I anoint this clew[274] of yarn, thou come presently without delay to obey my will, to envelop, and wrap thyself therein, and there to abide, and never depart thence, no, not the least moment of time, until that Melibea, with that prepared opportunity, which shall be offered unto her, shall buy it of me, and with it, in such sort be entangled and taken, that the more she shall behold it, the more may her heart be mollified, and the sooner wrought to yield to my request: That thou wilt open her heart to my desire, and wound her very soul with the love of Calisto; and in that extreme and violent

---

[270] Phlegeton] one of the rivers in Hades; not in the Spanish original.
[271] Tesiphone, Meghera and Alecto] the three Furies, the Eumenides.
[272] Styx and Dis] translation of the Spanish 'Dite', according to Lobera *et al.* (2000, p. 109, n. 134) the name of a Roman god identified with Pluto.
[273] Hydras] mythological creatures; the hydra was a many-headed snake whose heads grew back as fast as they were cut off.
[274] clew] ball.

manner, that despising all honesty, and casting off all shame, she may discover herself unto me, and reward both my message, and my pains; do this and I am at thy command, to do what thou wilt have me: but if thou do not do it, thou shalt forthwith have me by thy capital foe, and professed enemy. I shall strike with light thy sad and darksome dungeons; I shall cruelly accuse thy continual lyings, and daily falsehoods. And lastly, with my charming words and enchanting terms, I will chain and constringe° thy most horrible name. Wherefore, again and again; once, twice, and thrice, I conjure thee to fulfil my command. And so presuming on my great power, I depart hence, that I may go to her with my clew of yarn; wherein I verily believe, I carry thyself enwrapped.

Actus IV
The Argument

Celestina, going on her way, talks to herself, till she comes to Pleberio's gate, where she meets with Lucrecia, one of Pleberio's maid-servants; she boards[275] her, and enters into discourse with her, who being over-heard by Alisa, Melibea's mother, and understanding it was Celestina, causes her to come near the house. A messenger comes to call away Alisa, she goes her ways; Celestina in the mean while being left alone with Melibea, discovers unto her the cause of her coming.

INTERLOCUTORS
Celestina, Lucrecia, Alisa, Melibea

Celestina. Now that I am all alone, I will, as I walk by myself, weigh and consider that which Sempronio feared, concerning my travel° in this business. For, those things which are not well weighed, and considered, though sometimes they take good effect, yet commonly fall out ill. So that much speculation brings forth much good fruit; for although I dissembled with him, and did set a good face on the matter, it may be, that if my drift and intent should chance to be found out by Melibea's father, it would cost me little less than my life: or at least, if they should not kill me, I should rest much impaired in my credit, either by their tossing me in a blanket, or by causing me to be cruelly whipped; so that my sweetmeats shall have sour sauce: and my hundred crowns in gold be purchased at too dear a rate. Ay wretched me! Into what a labyrinth have I put myself? What a trap am I like to fall into, through my own folly? For that I might show myself solicitous and resolute, I have put myself upon the hazard of the dice. Woe is me, what shall I do? To go back, is not for my profit; and to go on, stands not with my safety. Shall I persist? Or shall I desist? In what a strait am I? In what a doubtful and strange perplexity? I know not which I were best to choose. On my daringness dependeth manifest danger; on my cowardice shameful damage. Which

---

[275] boards] approaches.

way shall the ox go, but he must needs plough?²⁷⁶ Every way, go which way I will, discovers to my eyes deep and dangerous furrows; desperate downfalls; if I be taken in the manner; if the theft be found about me, I shall be either killed, or carted, with a paper-crown set upon my head, having my fault written in great text-letters. But in case I should not go, what will Sempronio then say? Is this all thou canst do? Thy power, thy wisdom, thy stoutness, thy courage, thy large promises, thy fair offers, thy tricks, thy subtleties, and the great care (forsooth) thou wouldst take, what? are they all come to this? And his master Calisto, what will he say? What will he do? Or what will he think? Save only this; that there is much deceit in my steps; and that I have discovered this blot to Pleberio, like a prevaricating sophistress,²⁷⁷ or cunning ambidexter°, playing the traitor on both sides, that I might gain by both? And if he do not entertain so hateful a thought, he will rail upon me like a madman; he will upbraid me to my face, with most reproachful terms; he will propose a thousand inconveniences, which my hasty deliberation was the cause of, saying, 'out you old whore; why didst thou increase my passions with thy promises? False bawd as thou art; for all the world besides, thy feet can walk, for me only thy tongue; others can have works; I only words. Others can have remedy at thy hands, I only the man that must endure torment. To all others, thy force can extend itself; and to me is it only wanting. To all others thou art light; to me darkness. Out thou old treacherous, disloyal wretch;²⁷⁸ why didst thou offer thyself and service unto me? For it was thy offer that did put me in hope: and that hope did delay my death, prolonged my life, and did put upon me the title of a glad man. Now, for that thy promises have not proved effectual, neither shalt thou want punishment, nor I woeful despair.

---

[276] '¿Adónde irá el buey que no are?' Proverbial expression which asks 'Whither shall the ox that cannot plough go?', the implicit answer being: 'to the slaughter-house' (see Lobera *et al.*, eds, 2000, p. 112, n. 11). Mabbe continues with the *ox and plough* metaphor a few words later by translating 'barrancos' (i.e., gully, ravine) as 'furrows', which in turn (and following a frequent technique of his), he reduplicates with 'desperate downfalls'.

[277] sophistress] the *OED* only lists three quotations, the earliest of which is its use here.

[278] 'Wertike' in the 1631 text, which Fitzmaurice-Kelly (whom I follow here) corrects to 'wretch' in his edition.

So that, look I on which side I will (miserable man that I am) it is ill here, and it is ill there: pain and grief on either hand'. But when extremes shall want their mean, and no means to avoid either the one or the other, of two evils, it is the wiser course to incline to the lesser. And therefore I had rather offend Pleberio, than displease Calisto. Well then, I will go. For greater will my shame be, to be condemned for a coward, than my punishment, in daring to accomplish what I promised. Besides, fortune still friendeth those that are bold and valiant. Lo, yonder's the gate; I have seen myself in greater danger than this in my days. *Coraggio, coraggio*,[279] Celestina; be of good cheer, be not dismayed, for there are never suitors wanting for the mitigating and allaying of punishment. All divinations are in my favour, and show themselves propitious in my proceedings; or else I am nobody in this my art, a mere bungler, an idiot, an ass. Of four men that I meet by the way, three of them were Johns; whereof two were cuckolds. The first word that I heard, passing along the street, was a love complaint. I have not stumbled since I came forth, as at other times I used to do. Methinks the very stones of the street did sunder themselves one from another, to give me way as I passed. Nor did the skirts of my clothes crumple up in troublesome folds, to hinder my feet. Nor do I feel any faintness, or weariness in my legs. Every one saluteth me. Not a dog that hath once barked at me;[280] I have neither seen any bird of a black feather, neither thrush, nor crow; nor any other of the like unlucky nature; and which is a better sign of good luck than all this, yonder do I see Lucrecia, standing at Melibea's gate, which is kinswoman to Elicia: it cannot but go well with us; it is impossible we should miss our purpose. All is cock-sure.

---

[279] *Coraggio, coraggio*] *sic* in Italian, 'Courage, courage'; it translates a similar expression, 'esfuerza, esfuerza' in the Spanish original.
[280] These omens of good luck contrast with Parmeno's former description of Celestina as she walked about town (see 1.612–43 above). Later, on her way back from Melibea's house, Celestina fails to identify the crumpling of her petticoats around her legs as a bad omen (see 5.21–24; also 11.24–28).

Lucrecia. What old witch is this, that comes thus trailing her trail on the ground? Look how she sweeps the streets with her gown! Fie, what a dust she makes!
Celestina. By your leave, sweet beauty.
Lucrecia. Mother Celestina, you be welcome. What wind, I trow, drives you this way? I do not remember that I have seen you in these parts this many a day. What accident hath brought you hither?
Celestina. My love, daughter, my love, and the desire I have to see all my good friends; and to bring you commendations from your cousin Elicia, as also to see my old and young mistress, whom I have not seen since I went from this end of the town.
Lucrecia. Is this your only errand from home? Is it possible, you should come so far for this? I promise you, you make me much to marvel; for I am sure you were not wont to stir your stumps, but you knew wherefore; nor to go afoot forth out of doors unless it were for your profit.
Celestina. What greater profit, you fool, would you have, than a man to comply with his desires? Besides, such old women as we never want business: especially myself, who having the breeding of so many men's daughters as I have,[281] I go to see if I can sell a little yarn.
Lucrecia. Did I not tell you so before? I wote well what I said; you never put in a penny, but you take out a pound: be your pains never so little, you will be sure you will be well paid for it. But to let that pass, my old mistress hath begun a web; she hath need to buy it, and thou hast need to sell it. Come in, and stay here awhile, you and I will not fall out.[282]
Alisa. Lucrecia, who is that you talk withal?
Lucrecia. With that old woman forsooth, with the scotch on her nose, who sometimes dwelt hard by here in Tanners Row, close upon the riverside.
Alisa. Now I am further to seek than I was before. If thou wilt give me to understand an unknown thing, by a thing that is less known, is to take up water in a sieve.

---

[281] Celestina is referring to her wenches (who address her as mother): ironically, Celestina portrays herself here as a responsible step-mother.
[282] Mabbe here mistranslates the original, which reads 'no os desavenirés', i.e. 'I am sure you and my lady will not fail to reach an agreement [on the purchase of the yarn]'.

Lucrecia. Madame![283] Why, this old woman is better known than the herb rue. Do not you remember her that stood on the pillory for a witch? That sold young wenches by the great and by the wholesale? And that hath marred many thousands of marriages, by sundering man and wife, and setting them at odds?

Alisa. What trade is she of? What is her profession? It may be, by that I shall know her better.

Lucrecia. Forsooth, she perfumes coifs,[284] veils, and the like; she makes your sublimate mercury, and hath some thirty several trades besides; she is very skilful in herbs; she can cure little children; and some call her, the old woman, the lapidary, for her great dealing in stones.

Alisa. All this makes me never a whit the wiser. Tell me her name, if thou knowst it.

Lucrecia. If I knew it? Why, there is neither young nor old in all this city, but knows it. And should not I then know it?

Alisa. If you know it so well, why then do not you tell it me?

Lucrecia. I am ashamed, forsooth.

Alisa. Go to, you fool; tell me her name; do not anger me by this your delay.

Lucrecia. Her name, saving your reverence, is Celestina.

Alisa. He, he, he! Now beshrew your fingers; Oh my heart! Oh my sides! I am not able to stand for laughing, to see that the loathing which you have of this poor old woman should make thee ashamed to name her unto me. Now I call her to mind; go to, you are a wag;° no more of this. She, poor soul, is come to beg somewhat of me. Bid her come up.

Lucrecia. Aunt, it is my mistress's pleasure, you come up.

Lucrecia. My good lady, all blessings abide with you, and your noble daughter. My many griefs and infirmities have hindered my visiting of this your house, as in duty I was bound to do; but heaven knows how fair are the entrails of my inward affection, how free from any spot of foulness. It knows the sincerity of my heart, and trueness of my love. For, distance of place

---

[283] 'Jesu!' in the original.
[284] The 1631 text reads 'calls'; in part following the Alnwick Manuscript (Martínez Lacalle, ed. p. 168), I have changed it to 'coifs'; the original reads 'tocas', i.e. 'wimple' or a similar type of female head-dress. As is his wont, Mabbe here reduplicates in his translation by adding 'veils'.

displaceth not that love which is lodged in the heart. So that what heretofore in myself I did much desire, now my necessity hath made me to perform. And amongst other my many crosses and miseries in this life, my crosses in my purse grow daily less and less;[285] so that I have no better remedy to help myself withal, and to relieve this my poor estate, than to sell this little parcel of yarn of mine own spinning to make coifs and kerchiefs; and understanding by your maid, that you had need thereof (howbeit I am poor in everything, I praise my fate, save the richness of this grace) it is wholly at your command, if either it or I may do you any service.

Alisa. Honest neighbour, thy discourse and kind offer move me to compassion, and so move me, that I had rather light upon some fit occasion whereby I might supply thy wants, than diminish thy web,[286] still thanking thee for thy kind offer; and if it be such as will serve my turn, I shall pay you well for it.

Celestina. Madame, by my life, as I am true old woman, or by any other oath you shall put me to, it is such as all the whole town is not able to match it. Look well upon it: it is as fine as the hair of your head, even and equal, as nothing more strong as the strings of a viol; white as a flake of snow, spun all with mine own fingers; reeled and wound up with mine own hands. Look you, Lady, on some of the same in skeins: did you ever see better? Three royals, as I am true woman, I received no longer ago than yesterday for an ounce.

Alisa. Daughter Melibea, I will leave this honest woman with you; for methinks it is now high time, if I have not stayed too long, to go visit my sister, wife unto Chremes, for I have not seen her since yesterday; and besides, her page is now come to call me, and tells me that her old fit hath already been on her this pretty while.

---

[285] Mabbe creates a pun in English on the double meaning of 'cross': a metonymy for *coin* (*OED* III.20) and also in its figurative meaning as *misfortune* (*OED* I.10:b).

[286] some fit occasion whereby I might supply thy wants, than diminish thy web] Mabbe's translation of 'en tiempo de poder complir tu falta, que menguar tu tela', i.e. I'd prefer to provide what you lack without having to reduce your goods (in this case, to help her in exchange for the yarn that Celestina is offering). See Lobera *et al.*, eds (2000), p. 117, n. 55.

Celestina. (Now does the devil go preparing opportunity for my stratagem, by reinforcing this sickness upon the other. Go on, my good friend, stand stiffly to your tackling; be strong and shrink not. For now is the time or never; see you leave her not and remove away this woman from me. But soft: I fear she hears me.)

Alisa. Say, friend, what is that thou sayst?

Celestina. I say, madam, cursed be the devil and my evil fortune, that your sister's sickness is grown now upon her in such an unlucky hour, that we shall have no fit time to dispatch our business: but I pray, what is her sickness?

Alisa. A pain in her side, which takes her in such grievous manner, that if it be true which her page tells me, I fear me it will cost her her life. Good neighbour, let me entreat you for my sake to recommend her recovery unto your best devotions and prayers.

Celestina. Here, lady, I give you my faithful promise, that as soon as I go hence, I will hie me to my vestals, where I have many devout virgins, my friends, upon whom I will lay the same charge as you have laid upon me.[287]

Alisa. Do you hear, Melibea? Content our neighbour, and give her that which is reason for her yarn. And you mother, I pray hold me excused, for I doubt not, but you and I shall have another day, when we shall have more leisure to enjoy one another.

Celestina. Madame, there is no need of pardon, where there is no fault committed. Jove pardon you, and I do. For I thank you, you have left me here with very good company. Jove grant she may long enjoy her noble youth, and this her flourishing prime; a time wherein more pleasures and delights are found, than in this old decayed carcass of mine, which is nothing else but a very spittlehouse[288] of diseases, an inn full of infirmities, a storehouse, or magazine of sad and melancholy thoughts, a friend to brangling° and brawling, a continual grief and incurable plague, pitying that which is past, punished in that which is present, and full of wretched care in that which is to come;

---

[287] In the original Celestina promises to visit several monasteries and friars of her acquaintance, whom she will engage in prayers for the health of Alisas's sister. Celestina vows to pray four rosaries herself too.

[288] spittlehouse] a hospital for the indigent and the sick.

a near neighbour unto death, a poor cabin without one bough of shelter, whereinto it rains on all sides; a stick of willow, a staff of weak osiers, which is doubled with any the least stress you put it to.

Melibea. Tell me, mother, why do you speak so ill of that, which the whole world so earnestly desireth to enjoy and see?

Celestina. They desire so much their more hurt, they desire so much their more grief, they desire to live to be old because by living to be old, they live. And life (you know) is sweet; and living they come to be old. Hence it is, that your children desire to be men; and your men to be old men; and your old men, to be more and more old; and though they live in never so much pain, yet do they still desire to live. For (as it is in the proverb) fain would the hen live, for all her pip:[289] she would not be put out of her life, to be put out of her pain. But who is he, lady, that can recount unto you the inconveniences of old age? The discommodities it brings with it? Its torments, its cares, its troubles, its infirmities, its colds, its heats, its discontentments, its brawls, its janglings, its griefs, which like so many weights lie heavy up on it? Those deep furrows and deep wrinkles in the face? That change and alteration in the hair? That fading of fresh and lively colour? That want of hearing? That weakness of sight? That hollowness in the eyes? Seeing, as if they were shut up in a shade? That sinking and falling of the jaws? That toothlessness of the gums? That failingness of force and of strength? That feebleness of legs? That slowness in feeding? Besides, madam, which makes me sigh to think upon it, when all these miseries I have told you of come accompanied with poverty, all sorrows to this must stoop and strike sail, when the appetite shall be great and the provision small, the stomach good and the diet naught; for I never knew any worse habit, than that of hunger.

---

[289] fain would the hen live, for all her pip] translates '[. . .] viva la gallina con su pepita': the 'pepita' (i.e. 'pip') is a tumor which grows in old hens' tongues; this proverbial expression refers to the fact that people prefer old age (with its inherent decrepitude and infirmities) to death (Lobera *et al.*, eds, 2000, p. 119, n. 73). As he does in other cases, Mabbe first informs his readers that this is a proverb, and then proceeds to rephrase its meaning.

Melibea. I perceive, so goes the market, as it goes with you. And as you find your penniworths, so you speak of the fair.[290] And though you perhaps complain, the rich will sing another song.
Celestina. Daughter, and mistress, there is no way so fair, but hath some foul; if you have one mile of good, you have three of bad. At the foot of every hill, you have three leagues of ill follows.[291] And of a thousand that live contentedly, you have ten thousand do the contrary. True contentedness, rest, renown, glory, and quietness, run from the rich by other by-conduits,[292] and gutters of subtlety and deceit; which pipes, whereby they are conveyed, are never perceived, because they are paved and bricked over with smooth and well wrought flatteries. He is rich that hath God's blessing. Ay marry! that is wealth indeed. And shall I tell you, lady? Safer it is with him that is despised, than with him that is feared. And a far better sleep doth the poor man take than he who is bound to keep that with care which he hath gotten with labour, and must leave with sorrow. My friend will not dissemble with me, but the rich man's will with him; I am loved for mine own sake; the rich man for his wealth's sake. A rich man shall never hear the truth; every one will flatter him, and seek to please his humour in whatsoever he shall say. Besides, he lies open to every man's envy; and you shall scarce find one rich man amongst a thousand, but will ingeniously confess, that it had been better for him to have been in a middling estate, or in good honest poverty. For riches make not a man rich but busied; not a master, but a steward. More are they that are possessed by their riches, than they that possess their riches. To many they have been a means of their death; and most men they have robbed of their pleasure, and their good and commendable qualities; and to say the truth, they are enemies to all goodness. Have you not heard say, men have lain down and dreamed of

---

[290] as you find your penniworths, so you speak of the fair] translates '[. . .] hablas de la feria según te va en ella', a saying still in common use. Mabbe again reduplicates the phrase to clarify its original sense.

[291] The sense appears to be reasonably clear: Mabbe expands the original 'a cada cabo hay tres leguas de mal quebranto' into three different rephrasings of the same idea, the last of which is somewhat confusing as a result of the ill-fitting 'followes', which I have regularized as 'follows' (the Alnwick manuscript reads 'fallows', which does not make much sense either).

[292] by-conduits] Mabbe's use of this word is the only example in the *OED*.

their riches, and behold, they have waked, and found nothing in their hands? Every rich man hath a dozen of sons, or nephews, which repeat no other prayer, nor tender any other orison to God, but that he would be pleased to take him out of this world; and desire nothing more, than to see the hour that they may come to enjoy his estate; to see him under ground, and what was his, in their hands; and with a small charge, to lay him up in his last and everlasting mansion here on earth.

Melibea. Methinks, mother, it should be a great grief unto you, to think upon those good days of yours, which are past and gone. Would you not be willing to run them over again?

Celestina. That traveller, lady, were a fool, who having tired out himself with a hard day's travel, would, to begin his journey again, desire to return to the same place from whence he came. For all those things whose possession is no whit pleasing, it is better to enjoy them as they are than to desire their longer stay. For then they are so much the nearer to their end, by how much the farther they are from their beginning. Nor is there anything in the world more sweet, or more pleasing to him that is truly weary, than his inn, wherein he may rest himself. So that though youth be a thing very jocund,[293] yet he that is truly old, doth not desire it. But he indeed that wants reason and true understanding, that man in a manner loves nothing else but the days that are past and gone.[294]

Melibea. Were it but only to live, it is good to desire that which I say.

Celestina. As soon, lady, dies the young lamb as the old sheep; they go both to the shambles together;[295] there is no man so old, but he may live one year more; nor no man so young, but he may die today: so that in this you have little, or no advantage of us.

---

[293] jocund] cheerful, merry.

[294] This and the previous paragraphs contain numerous echoes from Petrarch's *De remediis* and *Familiares*, as well as Aristotle, in combination with some popular *sayings* — all of which Celestina puts to good use in her attempt to persuade Melibea (for further details, see Lobera *et al.*, eds, 2000, pp. 119–121, and their footnotes).

[295] Another reduplication of the original proverb, 'Tan presto, señora, se va el cordero como el carnero'.

Melibea. Thou hast scared me with thy words; thy reasons put me in remembrance that I have seen thee heretofore. Tell me, mother, art not thou Celestina, that dwelt in Tanners Row, near the river?

Celestina. Even the very same.

Melibea. By my fay, you are an old woman. Well, I see it is a true saying, that days go not away in vain. Now, never trust me, I did not know you; neither should I, had it not been for that slash over your face; then were you fair, now wonderfully altered.

Lucrecia. (She changed? He, he, he! The devil she is: she was fair when she met with him (saving your reverence)[296] that scotched her over the nose.)

Melibea. What sayst thou fool? Speak, what is it thou sayst? What laughest thou at?

Lucrecia. As though I did not know mother Celestina.

Celestina. Madam, take you hold on time, that it slip not from you. As for my complexion, that will never change: have you not read what they say? The day will come when thou shalt not know thyself in a glass? Though I am now grown grey before my time, and seem double the years I am of,[297] of four daughters which my mother had, myself was the youngest. And therefore, I am sure, I am not so old as you take me to be.

Melibea. Friend Celestina, I am very glad both to see and know thee; and I have taken great pleasure in thy discourse. Here, take your money and farewell, for thou lookest, poor soul, as if you hadn't eaten nothing all this day.

Celestina. Oh more than mortal image! Oh precious pearl! How truly have you guessed! Oh with what a grace do thy words come from thee! I am ravished hearing thee speak. But yet it is not only eating that maintains a man or woman; especially me, who use to be fasting a whole day, nay, two days together, in

---

[296] Saving your reverence] Mabbe's somewhat confusing translation of 'Dios os salve', a common slang expression used to name a scar, and which the servant ironically uses to refer to Celestina's 'scotch' in 'hermosa era, con aquel su "Dios os salve" que traviesa la media cara' (Lobera *et al.*, eds, 2000, p. 121, n. 94), i.e. 'she was beautiful indeed, with that scotch of hers across half of her face'.

[297] Both the 1631 text and the *Alnwick* manuscript omit a reference to the enjoyment of the pleasures of youth: 'que ansí gocé desta alma pecadora y tú dese cuerpo gracioso'.

soliciting other folks' businesses. For I intend no other thing, my whole life is nothing else, but to do good offices for the good, and (if occasion serve) to die for them. And it was evermore my fashion, rather to seek trouble to myself by serving of others, than to please and content myself. Wherefore, if you will give me leave, I will tell you the necessitated cause of my coming, which is another manner of matter than any you have yet heard; and such as we were all undone, if I should return in vain, and you not know it.

Melibea. Acquaint me, mother, with all your necessities and wants, and if I can help you in them, or do you any good, I shall willingly do it, as well out of our old acquaintance, as out of neighbourhood, which in good and honest minds, is a sufficient bond to tie them thereunto.

Celestina. My wants, madame? My necessities do you mean? Nay, others', as I told you, not mine. For mine own, I pass at home with myself in mine own house, without letting the whole country to know them, eating when I may, and drinking when I can get it. For, for all my poverty, I never wanted a penny to buy me bread, nor a quart, that is, the eighth part of sixpence, to send for wine, no, not all this time of my widowhood. For before, I never took thought for any, but had always a good vessel still in my house. And when one was empty, another was full. I never went to bed, but I did first eat a toast well steeped in wine, and two dozen of draughts, sipping still the wine after every sop, for fear of the mother,[298] wherewith I was then wont to be troubled. But now, that I husband all things myself, and am at mine own finding, I am fain to fetch my wine in a little poor jar, which will scarce hold a pottle.[299] And sometimes in punishment of my sins (which cross I am willing to bear) I am forced to go six times a day with these my silver hairs about my shoulders, to fill and fetch my wine myself at the tavern. Nor would I by my good will die, till I see myself have a good roundlet or terse[300] of mine own within mine own doors. For,

---

[298] mother] *Hysterica passio*, often referred to as 'the mother', was a complaint thought to rise up from the uterus, leading to shortness of breath or a feeling of suffocation.

[299] pottle] unit of capacity, equivalent to half a gallon.

[300] a good roundlet or terse] this is Mabbe's translation of 'un cuero o tinajica', which denote two different types of containers for wine ('cuero' made of animal

on my life, there is no provision in the world like unto it. For as the saying is, it is bread and wine, not the young man that is spruce and fine,[301] that makes us ride the way, and travel with mettle; yet let me tell you, that where the good man is missing, all other good is wanting. For ill does the spindle move when the beard does not wag above. And this I thought good to tell you by the way, upon those speeches which I used concerning others' and not mine own necessities.

Melibea. Ask what thou wilt, be it either for thyself, or anybody else, whom it pleaseth thee.

Celestina. My most gracious and courteous lady, descended of high and noble parentage, your sweet words, and cheerful gesture, accompanied with that kind and free proffer, which you are pleased to make to this poor old woman, gives boldness to my tongue, to speak what my heart even longeth to utter. I come lately from one, whom I left sick to the death, who only with one word, which should come from your noble mouth, and entrusted in this my bosom to carry it hence with me, I verily assure myself, it will save his life, so great is the devotion which he bears to your gentle disposition, and the comfort he would receive by this so great a kindness.

Melibea. Good woman, I understand thee not, unless thou deliver thy mind unto me in plain terms. On the one side thou dost anger me, and provoke me to displeasure; on the other thou doest move and stir me to compassion. Neither know I how to return thee a convenient answer, because I have not fully comprehended thy meaning. I should think myself happy if my words might carry that force as to save the life of any man, though never so mean. For to do good is to be like unto the Deity.[302] Besides, he that doth a benefit, receives it when it is done to a person that desires it. And he that can cure one

---

skin, 'tinajica' being a small earthen jar); the *OED* defines 'rundlet' as a cask or vessel of varying capacity, or the quantity of liquid contained in this, often used as a measure for wine or spirits; 'terse' is probably used here to denote 'claret' (see *OED*, terse †4. Applied to claret; also *absol.* as n. *Obs.*).

[301] it is bread and wine, not the young man that is spruce and fine] Mabbe's remarkable translation of the Spanish proverb, 'Pan y vino anda camino, que no mozo garrido' (Lobera *et al.*, eds, 2000, p. 123).

[302] Mabbe translates the original 'para salud de algún cristiano' as the more neutral 'to save the life of any man', and 'Dios' as the more abstract 'Deity' (Lobera *et al.*, eds, 2000, p. 124).

that is sick, not doing it, is guilty of his death. And therefore give not over thy petition, but proceed and fear nothing.

Celestina. All fear fled (fair lady) in beholding your beauty. For I cannot be persuaded that nature[303] did paint in vain one face fairer than another, more enriched with grace and favour, more fashionable and more beautiful than another, were it not to make them magazines[304] of virtue, mansions of mercy, houses of compassion and pity, ministers of her blessings, and dispensers of those good gifts and graces, which in her bounty she hath bestowed upon them, and upon yourself in a more plentiful manner. Besides, sithence we are all mortal, and borne to die; as also, that it is most certain, that he cannot be said truly to be born who is only born for himself. For then should men be like unto brute beasts, if not worse, amongst which there are some that are very pitiful, as your unicorn, of whom it is reported that he will humble and postrate himself at the feet of a virgin. And your dog, for all his fierceness, and cruelness of nature, when he comes to bite another, if he throw himself down at his feet, he will let him alone and do him no harm, and this is all out of pity. Again, to come to your birds and fowls of the air, your cock eateth not anything but he first calleth his hens about him, and gives them part of his feeding. The pelican, with her beak breaketh up her own brest, that she may give her very bowels and entrails to her young ones to eat. The storks maintain their aged parents as long in the nest as they did give them food, when they were young and unable to help themselves.[305] Now, if God and Nature gave such knowledge unto beasts and birds, why should we that are men, be more cruel one to another? Why give we not part of our graces, and of our persons, to our neighbours? Especially when they are involved and afflicted with secret infirmities, and those such, that where the medicine is, thence was the cause of the malady?

Melibea. For God's love, without any more dilating, tell me who is this sick man, who feeling such great perplexity hath both

---

[303] Mabbe translates 'Dios' as 'nature' here.
[304] magazine] storehouse or repository.
[305] Storks had been used as examples of filial piety since Aristotle and Pliny the Elder (*Natural History*, 10.63). For more details, see Lobera *et al.*, eds (2000), p. 126, n.126, and their long note, pp. 620–21.

his sickness and his cure flowing from one and the self-same fountain?

Celestina. You cannot choose, lady, but know a young Gentleman in this city, nobly descended, whose name is *Calisto*.

Melibea. Enough, enough; no more, good old woman. Not a word, not a word more, I would advise you. Is this the sick patient for whom thou hast made so many prefaces to come to thy purpose? For what, or whom cam'st thou hither? Cam'st thou to seek thy death? Know'st thou for whom, thou bearded impudent, thou hast trodden these dangerous steps? What ails this wicked one, that thou pleadest for him with such passion? He is fool-sick, is he not? Is he in his wits, I trow? What would'st thou have thought, if thou should'st have found me without some suspicion and jealousy of this fool? What a windlass° hast thou fetched, with what words hast thou come upon me? I see it is not said in vain, that the most hurtful member in a man or woman is the tongue. I will have thee burned, thou false witch, thou enemy to honesty, thou causeress of secret errors. Fie upon thee filth. Lucretia! Out of my sight with her! Send her packing! Away with her, I pray! She makes me ready to swound°... ay me, I faint, I die. She has not left me one drop of blood in my body. But I well deserve this, and more, for giving ear to such a paltry housewife as she is. Believe me, were it not that I regarded mine honour, and that I am unwilling to publish to the world his presumptuous audaciousness and boldness, I would so handle thee, thou accursed hag, that thy discourse and thy life, should have ended both together.

Celestina. (In an ill hour came I hither. If my spells and conjuration fail me.) Go to, go to. I wot well enough to whom I speak. This poor gentleman, this your brother, is at the point of death, and ready to die.

Melibea. Darest thou yet speak before me? And mutter words between thy teeth, for to augment my anger, and double thy punishment? Wouldst thou have me soil mine honour, for to give life to a fool, to a madman? Shall I make myself sad, to make him merry? Wouldst thou thrive by my loss? And reap profit by my perdition? And receive remuneration by my error? Wouldst thou have me overthrow and ruin my father's house and honour for to raise that of such an old rotten bawd as thou

490 art? Dost thou think I do not perceive thy drift? That I do not track thee step by step? Or that I understand not thy damnable errand? But I assure thee, the reward that thou shalt get thereby shall be no other save that I may take from thee all occasion of farther offending heaven, to give an end to thy evil days. Tell me, traitor as thou art, how didst thou dare to proceed so far with me?

Celestina. My fear of you, madam, doth interrupt my excuse; but my innocency puts new courage into me: your pretense again disheartens me, in seeing you so angry. But that which grieves 500 and troubles me most is that I receive displeasure without any reason, and am hardly thought on without a cause. Give me leave, good lady, to make an end of my speech, and then will you neither blame it, nor condemn me; then will you see, that I rather seek to do good service than endeavour any dishonest course; and that I do it more to add health to the patient, than to detract anything from the fame and worth of the physician. And had I thought that your ladyship would do easily have made this bad construction out of your late noxious suspicion, your licence should not have been sufficient warrant to have 510 emboldened me to speak anything, that might concern Calisto, or any other man living.

Melibea. Let me hear no more of this madman, name not this fool unto me, this leaper over walls, this hobgoblin, this night-walker, this phantastical spirit, long-shanked like a stork; in shape and proportion like a picture in arras that is ill-wrought or an ill-favoured fellow in an old suit of hangings. Say no more of him, unless you would have me to fall down dead where I stand. This is he who saw me the other day, and began to court me with I know not what extravagant phrases, as if he 520 had not been well in his wits, professing himself to be a great gallant. Tell him, good old woman, if he think that I was wholly his, and that he had won the field, because it pleased me rather to consent to his folly than correct his fault and yield to his errand, than chastise his error; that I was willing rather to let him go like a fool as he came, than to publish this his presumptuous enterprise. Moreover, advise him, that the next way to have his sickness leave him, is to leave off his loving and wholly to relinquish his purpose, if he purpose to impart health to himself; which if he refuse to do, tell him from me, that he 530 never bought words all the days of his life at a dearer rate.

Besides, I would have him know that no man is overcome, but he that thinks himself so to be. So shall I live secure, and he contented. But it is evermore the nature of fools to think others like themselves. Return thou with this very answer unto him, for other answer of me shall he none, nor never hope for any; for it is but in vain to entreat mercy of him, of whom thou canst not have mercy. And for thine own part, thou mayst thank God, that thou scapest hence scot-free; I have heard enough of you heretofore, and of all your good qualities, though it was not my hap to know you.

Celestina. (Troy stood out more stoutly, and held out longer. And many fiercer dames have I tamed in my days. Tush, no storm lasteth long.)

Melibea. You mine enemy, what say you? Speak out, I pray, that I may hear you. Hast thou anything to say in thy excuse, whereby thou mayst satisfy my anger, and clear thyself of this thy error and bold attempt?

Celestina. Whilst your choler lives, my cause must needs die. And the longer your anger lasteth, the less shall my excuse be heard. But wonder not that you should be thus rigorous with me: for a little heat will serve to set young blood a-boiling.

Melibea. Little heat, say you? Indeed thou mayst well say little, because thyself yet lives, whilst I with grief endure thy great presumption. What words canst thou demand of me for such a one as he is, that may stand with my good? Answer to my demand, because thou sayst thou hast not yet concluded. And perhaps thou mayst pacify me for that which is past.

Celestina. Marry, a certain charm, madame, which (as he is informed by many of his good friends) your ladyship hath, which cureth the toothache, as also that same admirable girdle of yours, which is reported to have been found and brought from Cumae the cave there, and was worn, 'tis thought, by the Sibyl, or prophetess of that place; which girdle they say, hath such a singular and peculiar property and power, with the very touch to abate and ease any ache or anguish whatsoever.[306] Now this gentleman I told you of, is exceedingly pained with

---

[306] The Sibyl of Cumae was a prophetess from Greek and Roman mythology. A new instance of Mabbe's paganization of the text: in the original, Celestina requests a special prayer to Saint Polonia, and a girdle that had touched all the reliques in Rome and Jerusalem (see Lobera *et al.*, eds, 2000, p. 129).

the toothache, and even at death's door with it. And this was the true cause of my coming: but since it was my ill hap to receive so harsh and unpleasing an answer, let him still for me continue in his pain, as a punishment due unto him, for sending so unfortunate a messenger. For since in that muchness of your virtue I have found much of your pity wanting; I fear me, he would also want water, should he send me to the sea to fetch it. And you know, sweet lady, that the delight of vengeance and pleasure of revenge endureth but a moment, but that of pity and compassion continueth for ever and ever.

Melibea. If this be that thou would'st have, why did'st thou not tell me of it sooner? Why went'st thou about the bush with me? What needed all those circumstances? Or why did'st thou not deliver it in other words?

Celestina. Because my plain and simple meaning made me believe that though I should have proposed it in any other words whatsoever, had they been worse than they were, yet would you not have suspected any evil in them. For, if I were failing in the fitness of my preface, and did not use so due and convenient a preamble as I should have done, it was, because truth needeth no colours. The very compassion that I had of his pain and the confidence of your magnificence did choke in my mouth, when I first began to speak the expression of the cause. And for that you know, lady, that sorrow works turbation, and turbation doth disorder and alter the tongue, which ought always to be tied to the brain. For heaven's love, lay not the fault on me; and if he hath committed an error, let not that redound to my hurt; for I am no farther blameable of any fault, than as I am the messenger of the faulty. Break not the rope where it is weakest. Be not like the cobweb, which never shows its force but on poor little flies. No humane law condemns the father for the son's offence, nor the son for the father's. Nor indeed, lady, is it any reason that this presumption should occasion my perdition; though considering his desert, I should not greatly care, that he should be the delinquent, and myself be condemned, since that I have no other trade to live by, save to serve such as he is. This is my occupation, this I make my happiness. Yet withal, madame, I would have you to conceive that it was never in my desire to hurt one, to help another, though behind my back your ladyship hath perhaps been otherwise informed of me. But the best is, it is not the vain breath of the vulgar, that can blast the truth; assuredly I mean nothing in this, but only plain and honest dealing. I do little harm to any, I have as few enemies in this city as a woman can have. I keep my word with all men; and what I undertake, I perform as faithfully as if I had twenty feet, and so many hands.

Melibea. I now wonder not, that your ancients were wont to say; that one only teacher of vice was sufficient to mar a great city.[307] For I have heard such and so many tales of thy false and cunning tricks, that I know not whether I may believe thy errand was for this charm.

Celestina. Never let me pray: or if I pray, let me never be heard, if you can draw any other thing from me, though I were to be put to a thousand torments.

Melibea. My former late anger will not give me leave to laugh at thy excuse. For I wot very well, that neither oath nor torment shall make thee so speak the truth. For it is not in thy power to do it.

Celestina. You are my good lady and mistress, you may say what you list, and it is my duty to hold my peace; you must command, and I must obey, but your rough language (I hope) will cost your ladyship an old petticoat.

Melibea. And well hast thou deserved it.

Celestina. If I have not gained it with my tongue, I hope I have not lost it with my intention.

Melibea. Thou dost so confidently plead thy ignorance, that thou makest me almost ready to believe thee; yet will I in this thy so doubtful an excuse, hold my sentence in suspense, and will not dispose of thy demand upon the relish of so light an interpretation. Neither for all this would I have thee to think much of it, nor make it any such wonder, that I was so exceedingly moved; for two things did concur in thy discourse, the least of which was sufficient to make me run out of my wits. First, in naming this gentleman unto me, who thus presumed to talk with me: then, that thou should'st entreat me for him, without any further cause given; which could not but engender a strong suspicion of intention of hurt to my honour. But since all is well meant, and no harm intended, I pardon all that is past; for

---

[307] 'Voluptatis magister unus in magno populo satis est', Petrarch, *Index* to his *Opera latina* (Lobera *et al.*, eds, 2000, p. 131, n. 181).

my heart is now somewhat lightened, sithence it is a pious, and a holy work, to cure the sick, and help the distressed.

Celestina. Ay, and so sick, madam, and so distressed, that did you know it as well as I, you would not judge him by the man which in your anger you have censured him to be. By my fay, the poor gentleman hath no gall at all, no ill meaning in his heart. He is endowed with thousands of graces; for bounty, he is an Alexander, for strength, a Hector; he has the presence of a prince; he is fair in his carriage, sweet in his behaviour, and pleasant in his conversation; there is no melancholy, or other bad humour, that reigns in him; nobly descended, as yourself well know, a great tilter; and to see him in his armour, it becomes him so well, that you would take him to be another Saint George. Hercules had not that force and courage as he hath; his disportment, his person, his feature, his disposition, his agility, and activeness of body, had need of another manner of tongue to express it, than mine. Take him altogether, and for all in all, you shall not find such another; and for admired form, a miracle: and I am verily persuaded, that that fair and gentle Narcissus, who was enamoured of his own proper beauty, when as in a glass he viewed himself, in the water was nothing so fair as he, whom now one poor tooth, with the extremity of its pain, doth so torment, that he doth nothing but complain.

Melibea. The ague, I pray, how long hath he had it?

Celestina. His age, madam? Marry, I think he is about some three and twenty. For here stands she who saw him born and took him up from his mother's feet.

Melibea. This is not that which I ask thee, nor do I care to know his age. I ask thee how long he hath been troubled with his toothache?

Celestina. Some eight days, madam, but you would think he had had it a year, he is grown so weak with it, and the greatest ease, and best remedy he hath is to take his viol, whereto he sings so many songs and in such doleful notes, that I verily believe, they did far exceed those, which that great emperor and musician Hadrian composed concerning the soul's departure from the body; the better to endure without dismay, his approaching death.[308] For though I have but little skill in music, methinks

---

[308] Rojas also took this reference to the Roman emperor Hadrian from Petrarch's *Index* (Lobera *et al.*, eds, 2000, p. 133, n. 203).

he makes the viol, when he plays thereon, to speak; and when he sings thereunto, the birds with a better will listen unto him than to that musician of old, which made the trees and stones to move. Had he been borne then, Orpheus had lost his prey. Weigh then with yourself, sweet lady, if such a poor old woman as I am, have not cause to count myself happy, if I may give life unto him, to whom the heavens have given so many graces? Not a woman that sees him, but praiseth Nature's[309] workmanship, whose hand did draw so perfect a piece; and if it be their hap to talk with him, they are no more mistresses of themselves, but are wholly at his disposing; and of commanders, desire to be commanded by him. Wherefore, seeing I have so great reason to do for him, conceive, good lady, my purpose to be fair and honest, my courses commendable, and free from suspicion and jealousy.

Melibea. Oh how I am fallen out with mine own impatience! How angry with myself, that he being ignorant and thou innocent of any intended ill, thou hast endured the distemperature of my enraged tongue! But the great reason I had for it frees me from any fault of offence, urged thereunto by thy suspicious speeches: but in requital of thy sufferance, I will forthwith fulfil thy request, and likewise give thee my girdle. And because I have not leisure to write the charm, till my mother comes home, if this will not serve the turn, come secretly for it tomorrow morning.

Lucrecia. (Now, now is my mistress quite undone. All the world cannot save her. She will have Celestina come secretly tomorrow. I smell a rat, there is a pad in the straw... I like not this come secretly tomorrow... I fear me, she will part with something more than words.)

Melibea. What sayst thou, Lucrecia?

Lucrecia. Marry, I say, madam, you have worded well. For it is now somethat late.

Melibea. I pray, mother, say nothing to this gentleman of what hath passed between you and me, lest he should hold me either cruel, sudden or dishonest.

Lucrecia. (I did not lie even now; I see well enough how ill the world goes.)

---

[309] 'Dios' in the original.

Celestina. Madam, I much marvel you should entertain any the least doubt of my service. Fear you not: for I can suffer, and cover anything; and well I perceive, that your great jealousy and suspicion of me made you, as commonly it doth, to interpret my speeches to the worst sense. Well, I will take my leave, and go hence with this girdle so merrily, as if I did presently see his heart leaping for joy, that you have graced him with so great a kindness; and I doubt not, but I shall find him much eased of his pain.

Melibea. I will do more for your sick patient than this, if need require, in requital of your great patience.

Celestina. (We shall need more, and you must do more than this, though perhaps you will not so well like of it, and scarce thank us for it.)

Melibea. Mother, what's that thou talkest of thanks?

Celestina. Marry, I say, madam, that we both give you thanks that we are both at your service; and rest both deeply indebted to your ladyship, and that the payment is there most certain, where the party is most bound to satisfy.

Lucrecia. (Here's cat in the pan.[310] What chop-logic have we here?)

Celestina. (Daughter Lucrecia, hold thy peace; come hither to me. If tomorrow I may see thee at my house, I will give thee such a lye[311] as shall make thy hair as yellow as gold, but tell not your mistress of it. Thou shalt also have a powder of me to sweeten thy breath, which is a little of the strongest. There is not any in this kingdom, that can make it but myself. And there is not anything in a woman that can be worse than a stinking breath.

Lucrecia. A blessing on your aged heart; for I have more need of this, than of my meat.

Celestina. And yet, you fool, you will be talking and prating against me. Hold thy peace, for thou knowst not what need thou mayst have of me. Do not exasperate your mistress, and make her more angry now than she was before. But let me go hence in peace.)

Melibea. What sayst thou to her, mother?

Celestina. Nothing, madame, we have done already.

---

[310] cat in the pan] see note to 3.206 above.
[311] lye] a hair dye.

760 *Melibea*. Nay, you must tell me what you said to her; for I cannot abide that anybody should speak anything in my presence, and I not have a part therein. And therefore, without any more ado, let me know it.

Celestina. I entreated her to put your ladyship in mind of the charm, that it might be writ out ready for me, and that she should learn of me to temper herself in the time of your anger, putting her in mind of that ancient adage: from an angry man, get thee gone, but for a while, but from an enemy forever. But you, madam, had only a quarrel to those words of mine which 770 you suspected, and not any enmity to my person. And say, they had been such as you conceited them, yet were they not so bad, as you would have made them to be. For it is every day's experience, to see man pained and tormented for women; and woman as much for men. And this, Nature worketh, and Nature, you know, is craft's master, and works nothing that is ill.[312] So that my demand, you see, was (as my desire was it should be) in itself commendable, as having its growth from so good a root. Many the like reasons could I render you, were not prolixity tedious to the hearer, and hurtful to the speaker.

780 *Melibea*: Thou hast thrown a great deal of temper, as well in saying little, when thou saws't me angry, as also in thy great and singular sufferance.

Celestina. Madam, I endured your chiding with fear, because I knew you were angry with reason. Besides, a fit of anger is but like a flash of lightning; which made me the more willing to give way, till your heat were overpast.

Melibea. This gentleman is beholding unto you, whom I recommend to your care.

Celestina. Not so madam. His deserts challenge more at my 790 hands. And if by my entreaties, I have done him any good, I fear me, by my over-long stay, I have done him as much harm. And therefore, if your ladyship will license me, I will haste to see how he does.

---

[312] Mabbe omits once again Rojas's reference to God as Nature's inherently benevolent master in this passage: 'esto obra la natura, y la natura ordénola Dios, y Dios no hizo cosa mala' (Lobera *et al.*, eds, 2000, p. 136). Note the implicit contrast between this statement about God and Nature, and the inherent chaos and strife described in the introduction.

Melibea. Hadst thou spoke for it sooner, sooner hadst thou been sped. Go thy ways, and a good luck with thee: for neither thy coming hither hath done me any good, nor thy going hence can do me any harm; thy message being as bootless[313] as thy departure shall be harmless.

---

[313] bootless] unavailing, useless.

Actus V
The Argument

Celestina having taken her leave of Melibea, trudges along the street mumbling and muttering to herself. Being come home, there she found Sempronio, who stayed expecting her return. They go both talking together, till they come to Calisto's house. And being spied by Parmeno, he tells it [to] his master, who wills him to open the door.

INTERLOCUTORS
Celestina, Sempronio, Parmeno, Calisto

Celestina. Oh cruel encounter! Oh daring and discreet attempt! Oh great and singular sufferance! Oh how near had I been to my death, if my much subtlety and cunning craft had not shifted in time the sails of my suit! Oh braving menaces of a gallant lady! Oh angry and enraged damsel! Oh thou devil whom I conjured! Oh how well hast thou kept thy word with me in all that I desired! I am much bound unto thee; so handsomely hast thou appeased this cruel dame by thy mighty power, and afforded me so fit a place and opportunity, by reason of her mother's absence, to utter my mind unto her. Oh thou old Celestina; cheer up thy heart, and think with thyself; that things are half ended, when they are well begun! Oh thou oil of serpents! Oh thou delicate white thread, how have you bestirred yourselves in my business, whose favourable furtherance if I had not found, I would utterly have broken and destroyed all the enchantments which either I have already, or hereafter are to be made; nor would I ever any more have had any belief in herbs, stones, or words. Be merry then, old stinkard, frolic with thyself, old wench, for thou shall get more by this one suit, than by soldering of fifteen cracked maidenheads. A pox upon these long and large playthings in my petticoats; fie how they rumple and fold themselves about my legs, hindering my feet from hasting thither whither I desire my good news should come.[314] Oh good fortune, what a friend art

---
[314] Celestina fails to interpret this rumpling of her petticoats around her legs as a bad omen (see above 4.74–76).

thou to the valiant! What a foe to those that are fearful! Nor by flying doth the coward fly death. Oh how many failed of that which I have effected! How many have struck at, but missed, that nail which myself only have hit on the head! What in so strong and dangerous a strait as this would these young graduates in my art have done? Perhaps [they would] have bolted out some foolish word or other to Melibea, whereby they would have lost as much by their prattling, as I have gained by my silence. And therefore it is an old saying: let him play that hath skill, and that the better physician is he that hath experience, than he that hath learning; for experience and frequent warnings make men artists in their professions; and it must be such an old woman as I am, who at every little channel holds up her coats, and treads the streets with leisurely steps, that shall prove a proficient in her trade. Oh girdle, my pretty girdle, let me hug thee a little! Oh how my heart leaps in looking upon thee! If I live, I will make thee bring her to me by force, who is so unwilling to come to me of her own accord, that I had much ado to get a good word from her.

Sempronio. Either mine eyes are not matches, or that is Celestina. Now the devil go with her; how her gown comes dragging on the ground! How the skirts of her coat trouble her![315] How her mouth goes! Sure, she is muttering something to herself.

Celestina. Why dost thou keep such a crossing of thyself? I believe thou blessest thyself to see me.

Sempronio. I will tell thee: why? Rarity, you know, is the mother of admiration; and admiration being conceived in the eyes, entreth straight into the mind: and the mind is informed again by the eyes, to discover itself by these outward signes.[316] Who did ever see thee walk the streets before with thy head hanging in thy bosom; with thy eyes cast down to the ground? Who did ever see thee go thus mumbling of thy words to thyself? And to come in such post-haste,[317] as if thou wert going to get a benefice? So that the rarity and strangeness thereof makes

---

[315] Further proof of the ominous crumpling of Celestina's skirts around her legs.

[316] 'Admiratio in animum descendit per oculos. Admirationis mater est raritas' (Petrarch, *Index*, see Lobera et al., eds, 2000, p. 138, n. 19, and their long note, p. 630).

[317] post-haste] speed, hurry.

those who know thee, to wonder what it should mean? But to let this pass, tell me of all loves, what good news thou bringst. Say: is it a son, or a daughter? That is, whether we have sped well or ill? For ever since one of the clock I have waited here for you; all which while, I have had no greater or better token of comfort, than that of your long staying.

Celestina. This foolish rule, my son, is not always true; for had I stayed but one hour longer, I might perhaps have left my nose behind me, and two other noses, had I had them, and my tongue to boot: so that the longer I had stayed, the dearer it would have cost me.

Sempronio. Good mother, as you love me, go not hence, till you have told me all.

Celestina. Sempronio, my friend, neither have I time to stay here, nor is this a fit place to tell it thee. Come, go along with me to Calisto, and thou shalt hear wonders, my bully.[318] For by communicating myself to many, I should as it were deflower my embassage, whose maidenhead I mean to bestow on your master; for I will that from mine own mouth, he hear what I have done; for though thou shalt have parcel of the profit, I mind to have all the thanks for my labour.

Sempronio. What? Are you at your parcels now? Do you think, Celestina, to put me to my parcels? 'Though you shall have your parcel'; marry, come up: I tell you plainly, I do not like this word, that I do not. And therefore parcel me no more of your parcels.

Celestina. Go to, you fool. Hold your peace, be it part or parcel, man, thou shalt have what thou wilt thyself. Do but ask, and have; what is mine, is thine: let us laugh and be merry, and benefit ourselves the best that we can. Hang all this trash, this putrified dirt, rather than thou and I should fall out about dividing the spoil; yet must I tell you, which is no more than yourself know, that old folks have more need than the young; especially you, who live at full table, upon free cost.

Sempronio. There goes more, iwis,[319] to a man's life than eating and drinking.

Celestina. What, son? A dozen of points, a hat, or a stone-bow,[320] to go from house to house shooting at birds, aiming at other

---

[318] bully] a term of endearment, i.e. my good friend, my fine fellow.
[319] iwis] certainly, indeed.

birds with your eye, that take their standing in windows. I mean pretty wenches, you fool, such birds, you mad-cap, as have no wings to fly from you: you know my meaning, sir. For there is no better bawd, for them, than a bow: under colour whereof thou mayst enter any house whatsoever, making it thy excuse to seek after some bird thou shootest at, etc. It is your only delicate trick you can use. But woe, Sempronio, unto her, who is to uphold and maintain her credit, and begins to grow old, as I now do.

Sempronio. (Oh cogging° old hag! Oh old bawd, full filled with mischief! Oh covetous and greedy cormorant!³²¹ Oh ravenous glutton! I perceive she would as willingly cozen me, as I would my master, and all to enrich herself. But seeing she is so wickedly minded, and cares not who perish, so as she may thrive, I will mar her market, I will look to her water hereafter; I will keep her from fingering any more crowns, nor will I any longer rent out the gains to her, which I make of my master, but reserve the profits for myself: or rather (which is the surer and more honest course) seek to save his purse, and play the good husband for him. For he that riseth by lewd and unlawful means, comes tumbling down faster than he clambered up. Oh how hard a thing it is to know man! True is that vulgar saying, no manner of merchandise, or beast, is half so hard to be known. Cursed old witch, she is as false as truth is truth; I think the devil brought me acquainted with her: it had been better for me to have fled from this venomous viper, than to put her, as I have done, in my bosom; but it was mine own fault, I can blame nobody but myself: and therefore let her gain what she can gain, be it by right or wrong, I will keep my word with her.)³²²

---

³²⁰ stone-bow] a kind of cross-bow or catapult used for shooting stones.
³²¹ cormorant] a greedy and rapacious person (by analogy with the cormorant, a large and voracious sea-bird), *OED*.
³²² This paragraph features two consecutive *adagia* freely translated by Rojas from the alphabetical *Index* to Petrarch's *Opera latina* of 1496: 'Animal nullum, nulla merx difficilior cognitu quam homo' (i.e. '¡Oh qué mala cosa es de conocer el hombre! ¡Bien dicen que ninguna mercaduría ni animal es difícil', rendered by Mabbe as 'Oh how hard a thing it is to know man! True is that vulgar saying, no manner of merchandise, or beast, is half so hard to be known')

Celestina. What sayst thou, Sempronio? Whom doth thou talk to? Goest thou gnawing of my skirts? What is that thou grumblest at? Why comest thou not forward?

Sempronio. That which I say, mother Celestina, is this: that I do not marvel that you are mutable, for therein you do but as others have done before you, following that common track that many more have trod in. You told me you would defer this business, leading my master along in a fool's paradise; and now thou runn'st head-long without either sense or wit, to tell Calisto of all that hath passed. Knowest thou not, that men esteem those things most, which are most difficult to be achieved? And prize them the more, the more hardly they come by them? Besides, is not every day of his pain, unto us a double gain?

Celestina. A wise man alters his purpose, but a fool persevereth in his folly:[323] a new business requires new counsel, and various accidents, various advice. Nor did I think, son Sempronio, that fortune would have befriended me so soon. Besides, it is the part of a discreet messenger, to do that which the time requires; especially when as the quality of the business cannot conceal or admit of dissembled time. And moreover, I know that thy master, as I have heard, is liberal and somewhat of a womanish longing; and therefore will give more for one day of good news, than for a hundred, wherein he is pained. And with his pain, mine will be increased: his in loving, and mine in trudging to and fro. For your quick and speedy pleasures beget alteration; and great alteration doth hinder deliberation. Again, where will you find goodness, but in that which is good? and nobleness of blood, but in large and long continued rewards? Peace, you fool, let me alone with him, and you shall see how your old woman will handle him.

---

and 'Animalia venenosa tutius est vitare quam capere' ('Más seguro me fuera huir de esta venenosa víbora que tomalla', which Mabbe translates as 'it had been better for me to have fled from this venomous viper, than to put her, as I have done, in my bosom'). See Lobera *et al.*, eds (2000), p. 140. For a similar case see the note to 1.423 above.

[323] 'El propósito muda el sabio; el necio persevera': another literal translation from Petrarch, this time from *Bucolicum carmen* VIII.12 (see Lobera *et al.*, eds, 2000, p. 141, n. 41, and their long note, pp. 631–32).

Sempronio. Then tell me what passed concerning that noble lady. Acquaint me but with one word of her mouth, for trust me, I long as much to know her answer, as my master doth.

Celestina. Peace, you fool. What? Does your complexion change? Does your colour alter? I know by your nose, what porridge you love.[324] You had rather have the taste than scent of this business. Come I prithee, let us hie us, for thy master will be ready to run mad if we stay overlong.

Sempronio. And I am little better, because you will not stay and tell me.

Parmeno. Master, master!

Calisto. What's the matter, you fool?

Parmeno. I see Sempronio and Celestina coming towards the house. And at every step they make a stop; and look where they stand still, there Sempronio, with the point of his sword, makes streaks and lines in the ground. It is some earnest matter sure that they are debating, but what it should be, I cannot devise.

Calisto. Oh thou careless absurd ass! Canst thou descry land, and not make to the shore? See them coming, and not hie thee to open the door? Oh thou supreme deity:[325] with what come they? What news do they bring, whose stay hath been so long, that I have longed more for their coming, than the end of my remedy? Oh my sad ears, prepare yourselves for that which you are now to hear: for in Celestina's mouth rests either my present case, or eternal heart-grief. Oh that I could fall into a slumber, and pass away this short, this little, little space of time in a dream wherein I might see the beginning and ending of her speech. Now I verily believe that more painful to a felon is the expecting of that his cruel and capital sentence than the act itself of his certain and foreknown death. Oh leaden-heeled Parmeno, slower than the snail, dead-handed as thou art,

---

[324] Mabbe's translation of 'Yo lo veo en ti que querrías más estar al sabor que al olor deste negocio', i.e. I can see that you would prefer to participate directly in this affair, rather than remain a mere spectator. (Parmeno appears to share his master's interest for Melibea.)

[325] 'Oh alto Dios, oh soberana deidad' in the original (Lobera *et al.*, eds, 2000, p. 142).

190   dispatch, I say, and unbolt this troublesome door, that this honourable woman may enter in, in whose tongue lies my life.

Celestina. (Dost thou hear him, Sempronio? Your master is now of another temper; these words are of another tune, than those we lately heard both of Parmeno, and him, at our first coming hither. The matter I see is well amended; there is never a word I shall tell him, but shall be better to old Celestina, than a new petticoat.

Sempronio. Make at your coming in as though you did not see Calisto, using some good words as you go.

200   *Celestina.* Peace, Sempronio. Though I have hazarded my life for him, yet Calisto's own worth, and his, and your joint entreaties, merit much more than this. And I hope, he will well reward me for my pains, being so frank and noble a gentleman as he is.)

Actus VI
The Argument

Celestina being entered in Calisto's house, Calisto with great affection and eartnessness demandeth of her what had happened betwixt her and Melibea. While they continue talking together Parmeno hearing Celestina speak wholly for herself, and her own private profit, turning himself toward Sempronio, at every word he gives her a nip, for the which he is reprehended by Sempronio. In the end, old Celestina discovers to Calisto all the whole business, and shows him the girdle she brought from Melibea. And so taking her leave of Calisto, she gets her home to her own house, taking Parmeno along with her.

INTERLOCUTORS
Calisto, Celestina, Parmeno, Sempronio

Calisto. What good news, mother? Speak, dear mother.

Celestina. Oh my good lord and master Calisto, how is it? How is it with you? Oh my new lover, and not without just cause, of fairest Melibea! How canst thou make this old woman amends, who hath hazarded her life in thy service? What woman was ever driven to such narrow shifts? The very thought whereof makes my heart to faint, emptying my vital veins of all their blood. I would have given my life for less than the price of this old trotted[326] mantle, which you see here on my back.

Parmeno. (Thou art all, I see, for thyself. That is it thou shoot'st at. Thou art like a lettuce, that grows betwixt two coleworts.[327] If thou be let alone, thou will over-top them. The next word I look for is that she beg a kirtle for her mantle: thou art all, I perceive, for thyself, and wilt not ask anything whereof others may have part. The old woman will unplume him, not leaving him so much as one feather; how cunningly does she work him! How craftily pitch her nets to catch me and my master, seeking

---

[326] trotted] Mabbe's translation of '*raído*', i.e. ragged from overuse.

[327] Thou art like a lettuce, that grows betwixt two coleworts] Mabbe's somewhat too literal translation of the Spanish proverb 'Entre col y col una lechuga', which in this context refers to the fact that mixed with the information she provides about Melibea, Celestina indirectly requests her own rewards.

to make me faithless, and him foolish! Do but mark her, Sempronio, be still, and give her but the hearing, and you shall see, she will not demand any money of my master, because it is divisible.)

Sempronio. (Peace, thou despairful fellow, lest Calisto kill thee, if he chance to hear thee.)

Calisto. Good mother, either cut off thy discourse, or take thou this sword and kill me.

Parmeno. (Now, what a devil ails he? He shakes and quivers like a fellow that hath had his senses over-touched with quicksilver. Look, he cannot stand on his legs, would I could help him to his tongue, that I might hear him speak again: sure, he cannot live long, if this fit continue. We shall get well by this his love, shall we not? Every man his mourning weed, and there's an end.)

Celestina. Your sword, sir. Now I hope not. What? Take your sword and kill you? There's a word indeed to kill my heart. No, let your sword serve to kill your enemies, and such as wish you harm. As for me, I will give thee life, man, by that good hope, which I have in her, whom thou lovest best.

Calisto. Good hope, mother?

Celestina. Ay, good hope; and well it may be called so, since that the gates are set open for my second return. And shall I tell you? She will sooner receive me in this poor trotted gown and kirtle, than others in their silks and cloth of gold.

Parmeno (Sempronio, sow me up this mouth, for I can no longer hold. A pox on her, she hath hedged in the kirtle to her gown. Could not one alone have contented her?)

Sempronio. (You will hold your peace, will you not? By Jove you were best be quiet, or I shall set you hence in a devil's name. What? Is there no ho with you?[328] Say she beg her apparel of him, what's that to thee? She does well in it, and I commend her for it, having such need thereof as she has. And thou know'st, where the flamen sings, there hath he his offerings; he must have food and raiment.)[329]

Parmeno. (True, he hath so; but as his service is, so is his allowance. He sings all the year long for it: and this old jade would in one day, for treading some three steps, cast off all her

---

[328] Is there no ho with you?] i.e. 'Won't you stop? Is there no end with you?'

[329] Mabbe translates Rojas's 'abad' (i.e. abbot) as 'flamen' (i.e. a pagan priest).

rugged hairs, and get her a new coat, which is more than she could well do these fifty years.)

Sempronio. (Is this all the good she taught thee? Is all your old acquaintance come to this? Is this all the obligation you owe her for her pains in breeding you up? Sure, she has brought her hogs to a good market, in bestowing so great kindness on so very a pig.)

Parmeno. (I could be well content, that she should pill and poll,[330] ask and have, shave and cut, but not cut out all the cloth for her own coat.)

Sempronio. (It is her fault, I must confess, but other vice hath she none, save only that she is a little too covetous. But let her alone, and give her leave to provide straw, first, for to thatch her own walls, and to lay the joists first of her own house, then afterwards shall she board ours; else had it been better for her she had never known us.)

Calisto. Mother, as you love goodness, if you be a good woman, tell me what was she doing? How got you into the house? How was she apparelled? On which side of the house did you find her? What countenance did she show thee at thy first entrance? How did she look on thee?

Celestina. With such a look and countenance as your brave fierce bulls vie towards those that cast sharp darts against them, when they come for to be baited. Or like your wild boars when they make towards those mastiffs which set upon them.

Calisto. Be these thy good hopes? These signs of health? What then are those that are mortal? Why, death itself could not be half so deadly. For that would ease and rid me of this my torment, than which none is greater, none more grievous.

Sempronio. (These are my master's former fires; he renews afresh his wonted flames. What a strange kind of man is he! He hath not the patience to stay to hear that which so earnestly he had desired.)

Parmeno. (Now, sir, who talks now? I must not speak a word, but did my master hear you, he would cudgel your coat, as well as mine.)

---

[330] pill and poll] Mabbe's phonetically accurate translation of the alliterating 'pida y pele' (Lobera *et al.*, eds, 2000, p. 145): here he triplicates the original Spanish expression.

Sempronio. (Some evil fire consume thee: for thou speakest prejudicially of all; but I offend no man. Let some intolerable mortal disease, or some pestilent plague seize upon thee, and consume thee. Thou quarrelsome, contentious, envious, and accursed caitiff. Is this thy friendship, this the amity thou hast contracted with Celestina and me? Go with the devil's name, if this be thy love.)

Calisto. If thou wilt not, thou that art sole queen and sovereign of my life, that I die desperate, and that my soul go condemned from hence to perpetual pain, so impatient am I of hearing these things, delay me no longer, but certify me briefly, whether thy glorious demand had a happy end, or not? As also whether that cruel and stern look of that impious face, whose frowns murder as many as they are bent against, sorted to a gentle entertaining of thy suit? For all that I have heard hitherto, are rather tokens of hate, than of love.

Celestina. The greatest glory which is given to that secret office of the bee — which little creature of nature the more discreet sort ought to imitate — is that whatsoever he toucheth he converteth it into a better substance. With those coy and squeamish speeches of Melibea, and all other her scornful and disdainful behaviours, all her sour looks and words I turned into honey; her anger into mildness, her fury into gentleness, and her running from me into running to me. Tell me, man, what didst thou think Celestina went thither for? What would she make there, whom you have already rewarded beyond her desert, unless it were to pacify her fury, to oppose myself to all accidents, to be your shield and buckler in your absence, to receive upon my mantle all the blows that were struck at you, to endure those revilings, bitter tauntings, and those disdainful terms which, such as she is, usually make show of, when they are first sued unto for their love? Only to the end that what they give may the better be esteemed and therefore they still speak worst of him, whom they love best; and make a show of most dislike, where they like most. Which if it should not be so, there would be no difference between the love of a common whore and an honest damsel that stands upon her honour, if everyone should say 'yea' as soon as she is asked. And therefore, when they see a man loves them (though themselves burn and fry in the liveliest flames of love) yet for modesty's sake, they will outwardly show a coldness of affection, a sober countenance, a pleasing kind of strangeness, a constant mind, a chaste intent, and pour forth words as sharp as vinegar, that their own tongues wonder at this their great sufferance, making them forcibly to confess that with their mouths, whose contrary is contained in their hearts. But because I would have thee have some ease of thy sorrows, and take some repose, whilst I relate at large unto thee all the words that passed between her and me, and by what means, I made my first entrance into Melibea's house, know for thy comfort that the end of her discourse was very good.

Calisto. Now, dear mother, that you have given me assurance, that I may boldly with comfort expect the extremest vigour of her answer, say what thou wilt, and I shall be attentive thereunto. Now my heart is at rest; now my thoughts are quiet, now my veins receive and recover their lost blood, now have I lost my fear, now do I find some joy, now am I cheerful. Let us, if it please you, go up, where in my chamber you shall report that at full, which I have heard in brief.

Celestina. With all my heart, sir, come, let us go.

Parmeno. (Oh[331] what starting holes does this fool seek for to fly from us, that he may at his pleasure weep for joy with Celestina and discover unto her a thousand secrets of his light and doting appetite! First, to ask her I know not how oft of every particular, and then have her answer him to the same, six several times one after another, and never to make an end, by over, and over, and over with it again, having nobody by to tell him how tedious he is. Fie upon him, I am sick to think upon it. Go your ways, you fool, get you up with a murrain,[332] but we will not stay long after you.)

Calisto. Mark, mother, how Parmeno goes mumbling to himself, see how the slave crosses himself, to hear what thou hast brought to pass by thy great diligence! Observe in what a maze he stands! Look, look, Celestina: dost thou see what he is doing? See, and the villain does not cross himself again? Come up, up, up, and sit you down (I pray) whilst I on my knees give ear to thy sweet answer. Say on, and tell me quickly by what means thou gotst into the house?

---

[331] Mabbe omits here the exclamation '¡Oh santa María!' in the original.
[332] Get you up with a murrain] a plague upon you.

170 *Celestina.* By selling a parcel of thread which I had, by which trick I have taken in my days more than thirty of as good worth and quality as herself — so it pleased fortune to favour me in this world — and some better women, iwis, and of greater rank, were she more honourable than she is.

Calisto. Greater, mother, perhaps in body, but not in nobleness of birth, not in estate, not in beauty, not in discretion, not in estateliness, linked with gracefulness and merit, not in virtue, nor in speech.

Parmeno. (Now the fool's steel begins to strike fire, now his bells
180 begin to jangle, mark how his clock goes, it never strikes under twelve, the finger of his dial point is still upon high noon, and upon the most. Sempronio, tell the clock, keep true reckoning, how standst thou gazing like a wide-mouthed drivelling fool, hearing his fooleries and her lies?)[333]

Sempronio. (Oh thou venomous-tongued villain; thou railing rascal; why shouldst thou alone stop thy ears at that to which all the world besides is willing to harken?[334] And say they are but tales and fables which she tells him? Yet were it only but for this, that their discourses are of love, though oughtst to
190 lend them a willing attention.)

Celestina. Noble Calisto, let thy ears be open to that which I shall tell thee, and thou shalt see what thy good fortune and my great care have effected for thee. For when I was about to pitch a price of my thread, and to sell it, Melibea's mother was called away to go visit a sister of hers, that lay exceeding sick: and because she could not stay with me herself (so necessary was her absence) she left Melibea to conclude the bargain, and to drive such a price with me, as she should think fit.

Calisto. Oh joy beyond compare! Oh singular opportunity! Oh
200 seasonable time! Oh that I had lain hid underneath thy mantle,

---

[333] Rojas uses the metaphor of a dysfunctional clock to describe Calisto's madness (see Lobera *et al.*, eds, 2000, p. 148, n. 51, ff.)

[334] Mabbe here slightly alters the wording in the original, which runs '¿por qué cierras las orejas a lo que todos los del mundo las aguzan, hecho serpiente que huye la voz del encantador?' (Lobera *et al.*, eds, 2000, p. 148, see also n. 55 and their long note, p. 634). Rojas's source here is *Psalms* LVIII.4–5 ('Their poison is like the poyson of a serpent; they are like the deafe adder that stoppeth her eare: Which will not hearken to the voyce of charmers, charming neuer so wisely', KJB).

that I might have heard her but speak, on whom heaven hath
so plentifully poured forth the fullness of his graces!

Celestina. Under my mantle, noble sir? Alack, poor soul as I am,
what would you have done there? Why, she must needs have
seen you at least through thirty holes, should not fortune give
me a better.

Parmeno. (Well, I will get me gone. I say nothing, Sempronio.
Hear you all for me: I will be hanged if the fool my master do
not measure with his thoughts how many steps there be
between this and Melibea's house, and if he not contemplate
every kind of action and gesture she might use, as how she
looked, how she stood, when she was bargaining for the
thread. All his senses, all the powers and faculties of his soul
are wholly taken up and possessed with her. But he will find in
the end that my counsel would have done him more good than
all the cunning tricks and cozenages of Celestina.)

Calisto. What's the matter with you there? I am hearing of a
cause that concerns no less than my life, and you keep a-
tattling and a-prattling there — as you still use to do — to
trouble and molest me in my business, and provoke me to
anger. As you love me, hold your tongues, and you will die
with delight: such pleasure will you take in the repetition of her
singular diligence. Go on, dear mother, what didst thou do,
when thou saw'st thou wast left all alone?

Celestina. Oh sir, I was so overjoyed that whosoever had seen me,
might have read in my face the merriment of my heart.

Calisto. It is so now with me. But how much more had a man
beforehand conceived some such image in his mind? But tell
me, wast thou not strucken dumb with this so sudden and
unexpected an accident?

Celestina. No. But rather grew thereby the bolder to utter my
mind unto her; it was the thing that I desired; it was even as I
would have wished it. There was nothing could have fell out so
pat for me, as to see myself all alone with her. Then began I to
open the very bowels and entrails of my heart. Then did I
deliver my embassage, and told her in what extreme pain you
lived, and how that one word of her mouth, proceeding
favourably from her, would ease you of your mighty torment.
And as one standing in suspense, looking wisely and steadily
upon me, somewhat amazed at the strangeness of my message,
hearkening very attentively, till she might come to know who

this should be, that for want of a word of her mouth, lived in such great pain, and what manner of man he might be, whom her tongue was able to cure? In naming you unto her, she did cut off my words, and with her hand stroke herself a blow on the breast, as one that had heard some strange and fearful news; charging me to cease my prattle, and to get me out of her sight, unless I would her servants should become my executioners, and make short work with me in these my old and latter days; aggravating my audacious boldness, calling me witch, sorceress, bawd, old whore, false baggage°, bearded miscreant, the mother of mischief, and many other more ignominious names, wherewithal they fear[335] children. And when she had ended with her bug-bears, she began to fall into often swoonings and trances, making many strange gestures, full of fear and amazement, all her senses being troubled, her blood boiling within her, throwing herself this way and that way, bearing in a strange kind of manner the members of her body one against another; and then in a strong and violent fashion, being wounded with that golden shaft, which at the very voicing of your name, had struck her to the heart, writhing and winding her body, her hands and fingers being clinched one within another, like one struggling and striving for life, that you would have thought she would have rent them asunder, hurling and rolling her eyes on every side, striking the hard ground with her tender feet. Now, I all this while stood me still in a corner, like a cloth that is shrunk in the wetting, as close as I could for my life, not saying so much as any one word unto her, yet glad with all my heart to see her in this cruel and pitiful taking. And the more her throes and pangs were, the more did I laugh in my sleeve at it, because I thereby knew her yielding would be the sooner and her fall the nearer: yet must I tell you, that whilst her anger did foam out its froth, I did not suffer my thoughts to be idle, nor give them leave to run a wool-gathering, but recollecting myself, and calling my wits about me, I took hold on times fore-top and found a salve to heal that hurt, which myself had made.

Calisto. Dear mother, thou hast told me that, which whilst I was hearing thee, I had forecasted in mine own judgement, I did

---

[335] fear] To inspire with fear; to frighten. *Obs.* exc. *arch.* or *vulgar* (*OED*).

still dream it would come to this; but I do not feel how thou couldst light upon a fit excuse, that might serve the turn, and prove good enough to cover and colour the suspicion of thy demand; though I know, that thou art exceeding wise, and in all that thou dost (to my seeming) more than a woman. Sithence, that as thou didst prognosticate her answer, so didst thou in time provide thee of thy reply. What could that Tuscane champion (so much famoused throughout all Italy) have done more, whose renown (hadst thou then been living) had been quite lost; who three days before she died, divined of the death of her old husband, and her two sons?[336] Now do I believe that, which is so commonly spoken; that a woman is never to seek for an answer; and though it be the weaker sex, yet is their wit more quick and nimble than that of men.

Celestina. Say you me so, sir? Well, let it be so then. I told her, your torment was the toothache, and that the word which I craved of her was a kind of prayer, or charm, which she knew to be very good, and of great power against that pain.

Calisto. Oh admirable craft! Oh rare woman in thy art! Oh cunning creature! Oh speedy remedy! Oh discreet deliverer of a message! What humane understanding is able to reach unto so high a means of help? And I verily persuade myself, that if our age might purchase those years past, wherein Aeneas and Dido lived, Venus would not have taken so much pains, for to attract the love of Elisa to his son, causing Cupid to assume the form of Ascanius, the better to deceive her, but would (to make short work of the business) have made choice of thee to mediate the matter.[337] And therefore do I hold my death happily employed, since that I have put it into such hands, and I shall evermore be of this mind, that if my desire obtain not its wished effect, yet know I not what could be done more, according to nature, for my good and welfare. What think you now, my masters? What can ye imagine more? Was there ever the like woman born in this world? Had she ever her fellow?

---

[336] The 'Tuscane champion' whose name Mabbe omits here is Adelecta, a famous Italian witch, whose story Petrarch recounts in his *Rerum memorandum libri* IV.39 (Lobera *et al.*, eds, 2000, p. 151, note 82, and their long note, p. 635).
[337] Calisto is comparing Celestina with Venus: in Virgil's *Aeneid* (I.657–756), Dido, Queen of Carthage (also known as Elisa), fell in love with the hero Aeneas, through the intervention of Venus and her son Cupid — who took the form of Ascanius, Aeneas's son to perform this ploy.

Celestina. Sir, do not stop me in the course of my speech. Give me leave to go on, for night draws on. And you know, he that does ill hateth the light.

Calisto. How? What's that? No, by no means. For heaven's sake, do not offer it, you shall have torches, you shall have pages, any of my servants, make choice of whom you will to accompany you home.

Parmeno. (Oh yes, in any case! I pray take care of her, because she is young and handsome, and may chance to be ravished by the way. Sempronio, thou shalt go with her, because she is afraid of the crickets, which chirp in the dark, as she goes home to her house.)

Calisto. Son Parmeno, what's that thou said'st?

Parmeno. I said, sir, it were meet, that I and Sempronio should accompany her home. For it is very dark.

Calisto. It is well said, Parmeno. You shall by and by. Proceed, I pray, in your discourse; and tell me what farther passed between you. What answer made she for the charm?

Celestina. Marry, that with all her heart I should have it.

Calisto. With all her heart? Oh Jove! How gracious and how great a gift!

Celestina. Nay, this is not all; I craved more than this.

Calisto. What, my honest old woman?

Celestina. Her girdle, which continually she wore about her, affirming that it was very good for the allaying of your pain; because of some supereminent influence from the *Sibylla Cumanae*.[338]

Calisto. But what said she?

Celestina. Give me *albricias*:[339] reward me for my good news, and I will tell you all.

---

[338] *Sic*, in Latin, i.e. the well-known prophetess of Greek and Roman mythology (see note to 4.565 above). In the original, the girdle has miraculous powers because it had been in touch with numerous reliques ('porque había tocado muchas reliquias', Lobera *et al.*, eds, 2000, p. 153). On the reasons why Mabbe may have wished to avoid this irreverent use of an object endowed with the miraculous power of Catholic reliques see Pérez Fernández's 'Translation, Diplomacy and Espionage: New Insights into James Mabbe's Career' (forthcoming in *Translation and Literature*).

[339] *albricias*] *sic*, as in the original Spanish. As Mabbe himself explains, 'albricias' denotes a present or reward for someone who bears good news.

Calisto. Take my whole house, and all that is in it, on condition you tell me, or else besides what thou wilt.
Celestina. Give but this poor old woman a mantle, and I will give that into thy hand, which she wears about her.
Calisto. What dost thou talk of a mantle? Tut, a kirtle, a petticoat, anything, all that I have.
Celestina. It is a mantle that I need; that alone shall content me. Enlarge not therefore your liberality. Let not any suspectful doubt interpose itself in my demand. My request is reasonable, and you know, it is a common saying, to offer much to him that asketh but a little is a kind of denial.
Calisto. Run, Parmeno, call hither my tailor and let him presently cut her out a mantle and a kirtle of that fine pure cloth, which he took to cottoning.[340]
Parmeno. (So, so . . . all for the old woman, because like the bee, she comes home laden with lies, as he does with honey.[341] As for me, I may go work out my heart, and go hang myself when I have done, whilst she with a pox must have every day change of raiment.)
Calisto. Now the devil go with him, with what an ill will does he go? I think there is not any man living so ill served as I am; maintaining men that devise nothing but mischief, murmurers, grudgers of my good, repiners of my prosperity, and enemies to my happiness. Thou villain, what does thou mumbling to thyself? Thou envious wretch, what is that thou sayst? For I understand thee not. Do as I command you, you were best, and that quickly too. Get you gone with a murrain, and vex me no more, for I have grief enough already to bring me to my grave. There will as much of the piece be left (which remnant you may take for yourself) as will serve to make you a jerkin.
Parmeno. I say nothing, sir, but that it is too late to have the tailor for to come tonight.
Calisto. And have not I told you, that I would have you not divine of things aforehand, but to do as I bid you? Let it alone

---

[340] cottoning] to cotton, *v.* 'To form a down or nap on; to furnish with a nap, to frieze. *Obs.*' (*OED*). The *OED* quotes a near-contemporary definition in Florio's *Worlde of Wordes*, as originating in the Italian '*Cotonare*, to cotton, to bumbace, to thrum, or set a nap vpon'.

[341] The bee was used as an emblem of deceitful flattery, since the honey in her mouth could actually conceal her venomous sting.

then till tomorrow; and for you, mother, let me entreat you out of your love to me, to have patience until then; for that is not auferred[342] which is but deferred. Now I pray let me see that glorious girdle, which was held so worthy to engird so goodly a body, that these my eyes, together with the rest of my senses, may enjoy so great a happiness, since that together they have all of them been a little affected with passion. My afflicted heart shall also rejoice therein, which hath not had one minute of delight, since it first knew that lady. All my senses have been wounded by her, all of them have brought whole basketfulls of trouble to my heart. Every one of them hath vexed and tormented it all they could; the eyes, in seeing her; the ears in hearing her; and the hands in touching her.

Celestina. Ha! What's that? Have you touched her with your hands? You make me startle.

Calisto. Dreaming of her, I say in my sleep.

Celestina. Oh, in your dreams, that's another matter.

Calisto. In my dreams have I seen her oft, night by night, that I fear me, that will happen unto me, which befell Alcibiades who dreamed that he was himself enwrapped in his mistress' mantle, and was the next day murdered, and found none to remove him from forth the common street, no, nor any to cover him, save only she who did spread her mantle over him.[343] Though I, for my part, be it alive or dead, would any way be glad to see myself clothed with anything that is hers.

Celestina. You have punishment, sir, enough already, for when others take their rest in their beds, thou preparest thyself to suffer thy next day's torment. Be of good courage, sir. Pluck up your heart. After a tempest, follows a calm; afford thy desire some time; take unto thee this girdle: for if death prevent me not, I will deliver the owner thereof into thy hands.

Calisto. Oh new guest! Oh happy girdle! Which hast had such power and worth in thee, as to hedge in that body, and be its

---

[342] auferred] Aufer, v. 'To take away, withdraw, remove.' The *OED* illustrates its use with only two examples, one of which is this quotation from *The Spanish Bawd*.

[343] Calisto's ominous dream, skilfully rendered by Mabbe in a series of balanced, and subtly modulated periods. Rojas took the story, once more, from Petrarch's *Index* ('Alcibiades occisus, nullo miserante insepultus iacens, amicae obvolutus est amiculo ut prius somniaverat', Lobera *et al.*, eds, 2000, p. 155, n. 109).

enclosure, which myself am not worthy to serve. Oh ye knots of my passion, it is you that have entangled my desires. Tell me, if you were present at that uncomfortable answer of fairest she, whom thou servest, and I adore. And yet the more I torment myself for her sake, mourning and lamenting night and day, the less it avails me, and the less it profits me.

Celestina. It is an old proverb: he that labours least, oftentimes gets most. But I will make thee by thy labouring to obtain that which by being negligent, thou shouldst never achieve. For Zamora was not wonne in an hour;[344] yet did not her besiegers for all this despair. No more was Rome built in one day; nor Troy ruined in a year.

Calisto. Oh unfortunate that I am! For cities are encircled, and walled in with stones, and stones by stones are easily overthrown. But this my dear lady hath her heart environed with steel, there is no mettle that can prevail against her; no shot of that force, as to make a breach. And should ladders be reared to scale the walls, she hath eyes which let fly darts of repulsion, and a tongue which dischargeth whole volleys of reproaches, if you once approach, forcing you to stand farther off, and so inaccessible is her castle, that you cannot come near it by half a league.

Celestina. No more, good sir, no more; bridle your passion, for the stout courage, and hardy boldness of one man, did get Troy. Doubt not then, but one woman may work upon another, and at last win her unto thee; thou hast little frequented my house, thou art ignorant of my courses, thou knows't not what I can do.

Calisto. Say, mother, what thou wilt, and I will believe thee, since thou hast brought me so great a jewel, as is this. Oh thou glory of my soul, and encircler of so incomparable a creature; I behold thee, and yet believe it not. Oh girdle, girdle, thou lovely lace! Wast thou mine enemy too? Tell me the truth, if thou wert, I forgive thee: for it is proper unto good men, to forgive; but I do not believe it. For hadst thou likewise been my foe, thou wouldst not have come so soon to my hands,

---

[344] 'Zamora [also spelled Çamora in early modern usage] no se conquistó en una hora': a traditional Spanish refrain, still in common use, signifying that important and difficult endeavours take time to accomplish. I have corrected the misspelling 'Camora' to Zamora.

unless thou hadst come to disblame and excuse thy doings. I conjure thee, that thou answer me truly, by the virtue of that great power, which thy lady hath over me.

450 *Celestina.* Cease, good sir, this vain and idle humour; for my ears are tired with attention, and the girdle almost worn out with your often handling.

Calisto. Oh wretch that I am! Far better had it been for me had the heavens made me so happy that thou hadst been made and woven of these mine own arms, and not of silk as now thou art, that they might have daily rejoiced in clasping and enclosing with due reverence those members which thou without sense or feeling, not knowing what it is to enjoy so great a glory, holdest still in strict embracements. Oh what secrets

460 shouldst thou then have seen of that so excellent an image?

Celestina. Thou shalt see more, and enjoy more, in a more ample and better manner, if thou lose it not by talking as thou dost.

Calisto. Peace, good mother, give me leave a little; for this and I well understand one another. Oh my eyes, call to your remembrance how that ye were the cause of my ill and the very door through which my heart was wounded; and that he is seen to do the hurt, who doth give the cause of the harm. Call to your remembrance, I say, that ye are debtors to my welfare. Look here upon your medicine, which is come home to your own

470 house to cure you.

Sempronio. Sir, it is not your rejoicing in this girdle that can make you to enjoy Melibea.

Calisto. How like a fool thou pratest, without either wit or reason! Thou disturber of my delight, what meanest thou by this?

Sempronio. Marry, that by talking and blabbing so much as you do, you kill both yourself, and those which hear you. And so by consequence, overthrow both thy life and understanding; either of which to want is sufficient to leave you darkling, and

480 say good night to the world. Cut off your discourse therefore, and listen unto Celestina, and hear what she will say unto thee.

Calisto. Mother, are my words troublesome unto you? Or is this fellow drunk?

Celestina. Howbeit they be not, yet should you not talk thus as you do, but rather give an end to these your long complaints. Use a girdle like a girdle, that you may know to make a difference of your words, when you come to Melibea's presence; let not your tongue equal the apparel with the person, making no distinction betwixt her, and her garments.

Calisto. Oh my much honoured matron, my mother, my comfortress! Let me glad myself a little with this messenger of my glory. Oh my tongue! Why doest thou hinder thyself in entertaining any other discourse? Leaving off to adore that present excellency, which, peradventure,[345] thou shalt never see in thy power? Oh ye my hands! With what presumption, with what slender reverence do you touch that treacle,[346] which must cure my wound? Now that poison cannot hurt me, wherewith that cruel shot of Cupid hath its sharp point deeply indipped. For now I am safe, since that she who gave me my wound gives me also my medicine. Oh dear Celestina! Thou that art the delight of all old dames, the joy of young wenches, the ease of the afflicted, and comfort of such comfortless wretches as myself, do not punish me more with fear of thee than I am already punished with shame of myself; suffer me to let loose the reins of my contemplation; give me leave to go forth into the streets with this jewel, that they who see me, may know that there is not any man more happy than myself.

Sempronio. Do not infistulate[347] your wound, by clapping on it still more and more desire. Sir, it is not this string nor this girdle alone, wherein your remedy must depend.

Calisto. I know it well, yet have I not the power to abstain from adoring so great a relic? So rich a gift?

Celestina. That's a gift which is given *gratis*; but you know that she did this for to ease your toothache,[348] and to close up your wounds, and not for any respect or love, which she bears to you. But if I live, she shall turn the leaf, ere I leave her.

Calisto. But the charm you talked of?

Celestina. She hath not given it me yet.

Calisto. And what was the cause why she did not?

---

[345] peradventure] perhaps, possibly.
[346] treacle] medicine.
[347] infistulate] to convert into a fistula; the *OED* only gives two examples of this verb, one from Florio's 1611 *Queen Anna's New World of Words* ('*Infistolare*, to infistulate, to fester.') and this one in Mabbe's text.
[348] Mabbe omits here the original 'lo hizo por amor de Dios' (Lobera *et al.*, eds, 2000, 158), i.e. she did it for the love of God.

520 *Celestina.* The shortness of time, and therefore will'd me that if your pain did not decrease, I should return to her again tomorrow.
Calisto. Decrease? Then shall my pain decrease, when I see a decrease of her cruelty.
Celestina. Sir, content yourself with that, which hath hitherto been said and done; she is already bound, I have showed you, how (as far-forth as she is able) she will be ready to yield you any help for this infirmity of yours, which I shall crave at her hands. And tell me, I pray, if this be not well for the first bout.
530 Well, I will now get me home. And in any case, have a care, that if you chance tomorrow to walk abroad, that you go muzzled about the cheeks with a cloth, that she seeing you so bound about the chaps,° may not accuse me of petitioning a falsehood.
Calisto. Nay, to do you service, I will not stick to clap on four double clothes. But of all loves tell me, passed there anything more between you? For I die out of longing for to hear the words which flow from so sweet a mouth. How dids't thou dare, not knowing her, be so bold, to show thyself so familiar,
540 both in thy entrance, and thy demand?
Celestina. Not knowing her? They were my neighbours for four years together; I dealt with them; I conversed with them; I talked with them; and laughed together with them day and night. Oh, how merry we have been! Her mother, why she knows me better than her own hands, and Melibea too, though now she be grown so tall, so great, so courteous, and discreet a Lady.
Parmeno. (Sempronio, a word with you in your ear.
Sempronio. Say on: what's the matter?
550 *Parmeno.* Marry, this: Celestina's attention gives matter to our master to enlarge his discourse; give her a touch on the toe, or make some sign to her that she may be gone, and not wait thus, as she doth upon his answers. For, there is no man, be he never so much a fool, that speaks much when he is all alone.)
Calisto. Didst thou say Melibea was courteous? I think it was but in a mock. Was the like ever borne into the world? Did God ever create a better, or more perfect body? Can the like proportion be painted by any pencil? Is she not that paragon of beauty, from whence all eyes may copy forth a true pattern of
560 inimitable excellence? If Helen were now alive, for whom so

great a slaughter was made of Greeks and Troyans, or fair Polixena,[349] both of them would have done their reverence to this lady for whom I languish. If she had been present in that contention for the apple with the three goddesses, the name of contention had never been questioned.[350] For without any contradiction they would all of them have yielded, and jointly have given their consent that Melibea should have born it from them, so that it should rather have been called the apple of concord than of discord. Besides, as many women as are now born and do know her, curse themselves and their fortune, complaining of heaven because it did not remember them, when it made her, consuming as well their bodies as their lives with envy, being ready to eat their own flesh for very anger, still augmenting martyrdoms to themselves, thinking to equal that perfection by art which Nature had bestowed upon her without any labour. They pill°, and dishair[351] their eyebrows with nippers, with plasters of pitch or barm and other the like instruments. They seek after wallwort and the like herbs, roots, sprigs and flowers to make lyes, wherewithal to bring their hair to the colour of hers, spoiling and martyring their faces, clothing them with divers colourings, glistenings, paintings, unctions, ointments, strong waters, white and red pargetings, which, to avoid prolixity, I repeat not. Now judge then, whether she whom Nature hath so richly beautified, be worthy the love and service of so mean a man as myself?

Celestina. (Sempronio, I understand your meaning, but give him leave to run on, for he will fall anon from his ass, and then his journey will be at an end. You shall see, he will come by and by to a full point, and so conclude.)

---

[349] Polixena] the beautiful daughter of Priam, king of Troy.

[350] Calisto refers here to the episode that led to the Trojan war, in which Paris (son of King Priam) was appointed to decide which of three goddesses (Hera, Athene, and Aphrodite) was to receive a golden apple as the trophy for being the most beautiful of the three. Aphrodite promised Paris the most beautiful woman in the world if he chose her. He did, and won Helen of Troy as his reward. Since Helen was married to the Spartan King Menelaus, this brought about enmity between Greeks and Trojans, and also between the three goddesses (who also took sides in the war). Hence the reference to Paris's trophy as the apple of discord.

[351] dishair] to deprive of hair, remove the hair from; the *OED* only lists this example.

Calisto. In her, Nature, as in a glass did wholly behold herself; that she might make her most absolutely perfect; for those graces, which she has diffused unto divers, she had jointly united them in her, and overviewed this her work with so curious an eye, that nothing might be added to make it fairer. To the end that they might know, who had the happiness to see her, the worthiness and excellency of her painter. Only a little fair fountain-water with a comb of ivory is sufficient (without any other slibber-slabbers) to make her surpass all other of her sex in beauty and courtesy. These are her weapons, with these she kills and overcomes, and with these hath she bound me in so hard and strong a chain that I must for ever remain her prisoner.

Celestina. Sir, put a period to your words, trouble yourself no more; for this chain which shackles thee, is not so strong, but my file is as sharp to cut it in sunder, which I will do for thee, that thou mayst be at liberty. And therefore give me now licence to take my leave of you, for it grows very late, and let me have the girdle along with me. For you know, I must needs use it.

Calisto. Oh disconsolate that I am! My misfortunes still pursue me, for with thee, or with this girdle, or with both, I would willingly have been accompanied all this dark and tedious night. But because there is no perfect happiness in this our painful and unhappy life, let solitariness wholly possess my soul, and cares be my continual companions. What ho? Where be these men? Why, Parmeno, I say!

Parmeno. Here, sir.

Calisto. Accompany this matron home to her house, and as much pleasure and joy go with her, as sorrow and woe doth stay with me.

Celestina. Sir, fare you well. Tomorrow I shall make my return, and visit you again, not doubting but my gown and her answer shall meet here together; for now time doth not serve. And in the interim, let me entreat you to be patient. Settle your thoughts upon some other thing, and do not so much as once think upon her.

Calisto. Not think upon her? It is impossible. Nay, it were profane to forget her, for whom my life only pleaseth me.

JOSÉ MARÍA PÉREZ FERNÁNDEZ

Actus VII
The Argument

Celestina talks with Parmeno, inducing him to concord, and amity with Sempronio. Parmeno puts her in mind of the promise she made him, for the having of Areusa, whom he exceedingly loved. They to go Areusa's house, where that night Parmeno remained. Celestina hies her home, to her own house, and knocking at the door, Elicia opens it unto her, blaming her for her tarrying so long.

INTERLOCUTORS
Celestina, Parmeno, Areusa, Elicia

Celestina. Parmeno, my son, since we last talked together, I have not had any opportunity to express unto thee the infiniteness of that love which I bear unto thee, and as all the world can well witness for me, how well I have spoken of thee in thy absence. Every man's ear hath been filled with the good reports I have made of thee. The reason thereof I need not to repeat, for I ever held thee to be my son, at least by adoption, and therefore thought thou wouldst have showed thyself more natural and loving towards me. But instead thereof, thou gav'st me bad payment, even to my face: crossing whatsoever I said, thinking ill of all that I spoke, whispering and murmuring against me in the presence of Calisto. I was well persuaded that after thou hadst once yielded to my good counsel, that you would not have turned your heel and kicked against me as you did, nor have fallen off from your promise. But notwithstanding all this, I perceive some old relic yet still remaining of thy former folly. And so speaking rather to satisfy thine own humour than that thou canst render any reason for it, thou dost hinder thyself of profit to give thy tongue contentment. Hear me, my son, if thou hast not heard me already. Look, I say, and consider with thyself, that I am old, and well struck in years, and good counsel only lodgeth with the elder sort, it being proper to youth to follow pleasure and delight. But my hope is, that of this thy error, thy youth only is in fault: and I trust that you will bear yourself better towards me hereafter and that you will alter your ill purpose together with your tender years. For as it is in the proverb, our customs suffer change, together with our hairs, and we vary our disposition as we vary our years. I speak this, my son, because as we grow in age, so grow we in experience, new things offering themselves to our view: for youth looks no farther than to things present, occupying his eye only in that he sees set before him, but riper years omit neither things present, things past, nor things to come.[352] And son Parmeno, if you would but bethink yourself of the love I have heretofore born you, I know it cannot escape your knowledge, that the first night's lodging that you took when you were a stranger, and came newly to this city, was in my house. But you young men care not for us that are old, but govern yourselves according to the savour and relish of your own palates; you never think that you have or shall have need of us; you never think upon sickness; you never think that this flower of your youth shall fade. But do you hear me, my friend, and mark what I say unto you, that in such cases of necessity, as these, an old woman, (be she well experienced) is a good help, a comforter, a friend, a mother; nay, more than a mother: a good inn, to give ease and rest to a sound man, and a good hospital for to cure a sick man, a good purse in time of need, a good chest to keep money in prosperity, a good fire in winter, environed with spits of good roastmeat, a good shade in summer and a good tavern to eat and drink in. Now my pretty little fool, what sayst thou to all this? What dost thou think of it? I know, thou art by this time ashamed of that which thou hast spoken today; thou can'st not say B to a battledoor,[353] thou art struck so dumb, and so dead. And therefore I will press thee no further, nor crave any more at thy hands,[354] than that which friendship craves of thee,

---

[352] Celestina again employs her remarkable oratorical skills to dispel Pármeno's reticence, and win him to her cause. As is his wont, Rojas has resorted again here to Petrarch's *adagia* on the wisdom of old age (*Bucolicum carmen* VIII.9, 12, 75–77, and *De remediis* II.43; see Lobera *et al.*, eds, 2000, p. 164, notes 7 and 9, and their long notes, p. 641). Once again, Rojas concentrates in the same passage consecutive adagia taken from a single page in Petrarch's *Index* — in this case, from its first page (see also notes to Prologue 17, 5.126, 8.117).

[353] A proverbial expression, 'to open one's mouth in speech' (*OED*).

[354] Mabbe omits here the original 'Pues no quiero más de ti, que Dios no pide más del pecador de arrepentirse y emendarse' (Lobera *et al.*, eds, 2000, p. 164), i.e. 'I will not demand anything else from you, since God only expects

which is look upon Sempronio. Next under heaven myself have made him a man. I could wish you would live and love together as brothers and friends: for being in league with him, thou shalt live in the favour and love of thy master, and in good repute with all the world. For Sempronio, I tell thee, is well beloved, he is diligent, a good courtier, a proper servant, a fellow of a good fashion, and one that is willing to embrace thy friendship, which will turn to both your profits, if you will but hand-fast your affections to each other. Besides, you know, that you must love, if you will be beloved. Trouts cannot be taken with dry breeches. And if the cat will have fish, she must wet her foot. Nor does Sempronio owe this of right unto thee, nor is he bound to love thee, unless thou exchange love for love: it is mere simplicity, not to be willing to love, and yet look to be beloved of others.[355] And as great folly, to repay friendship with hatred.

Parmeno. Mother, I confess my second fault, and craving pardon for what is passed, I offer myself to be ordered by you in all my future proceedings. But yet methinks it is impossible that I should hold friendship with Sempronio: he is frappish,[356] and I cannot bear [that]; he is choleric, and I can carry no coals.[357] How then is it possible to make a true contract betwixt two such contrary natures?

Celestina. But you were not wont to be thus forward.

Parmeno. In good fay, mother, you say true. But the more I grow in years, the less I grow in patience. Tush, I have forgotten that lesson, as if I had never known what it meant. I am (I confess)

---

repentance and amends from sinners.' He does translate, however, Parmeno's confession in his response, whose wording in the original echoes formulaic expressions used in confession: 'Madre, mi segundo yerro te confieso, y con perdón de lo pasado quiero que ordenes lo por venir' (Lobera *et al.*, eds, 2000, p. 165).

[355] An excellent example of Rojas's interweaving of popular refrains ('Trouts cannot be taken with dry breeches [...] if the cat will have fish, she must wet her foot') with authoritative adagia ('it is mere simplicity, not to be willing to love, and yet look to be beloved of others '), this time from Petrarch's *De remediis* I.50. A few lines later ('A sure friend is known in a doubtful matter', etc.), Celestina invokes Senecan adagia on the value of friendship, also transmited through Petrarch's *Index*.

[356] frappish] fretful, peevish; this is the only sample listed in the *OED*.

[357] I can carry no coals] To do dirty or degrading work, submit to humiliation or insult.

not the man I was, nor is Sempronio himself; neither can he, nor will he stead[358] me in anything. I never yet tasted any the least kindness from him.

Celestina. A sure friend is known in a doubtful matter, and in adversity is his faith proved. Then comes he nearest unto him, when he is farthest from comfort; and with greater desire doth he then visit his house, when as prosperous fortune hath forsaken it. What shall I say unto thee, son, of the virtues of a good and fast friend? There is nothing more to be beloved, nothing more rare, he refuseth no burden. You two are equals, and parity of persons, similitude of manners, and sympathy of hearts are the main props that uphold friendship.[359] Take heed, my son, for if thou hast anything, it is safely kept for thee. Be thou wise to gain more, for this is gained already to your hands. Your father, oh what pains took he for it! But I may not put it into your hands, till you lead a more reposed life, and come to a more complete and full age.

Parmeno. Mother, what do you call a reposed life?

Celestina. Marry, son, to live of yourself. Not to go through other men's houses, nor to set thy foot under another man's table: which thou shalt still be enforced to do unless thou learn to make profit of thy service, for out of very pity to see thee go thus trotted and torn, not having a rag almost to hang on thy breech, did I get that mantle which thou saw'st, of Calisto, not so much for the mantle's sake, as for that there being a tailor belonging to the house, and thou before being without a jerkin, he might bestow it upon thee. So that I speak not for mine own profit (as I heard you say) but for thy good. For, if you rely only upon the ordinary wages of these gallants, it is such that what you get by it after ten years' service, you may put it in your eye and never see the worse. Enjoy thy youth, good days, good nights, good meat and good drink; when thou may'st have these things, lose them not; let that be lost that will be lost. Do not thou mourn for the wealth which was left thy

---

[358] stead] be of use, or advantageous to.

[359] Celestina again deftly manipulates the rhetoric of mutual benefit, the communication of interests and goods, as the best means to achieve personal autonomy and a life of ease. Parmeno's subsequent question ('Mother, what do you call a reposed life?') gives this exchange the tone of a Socratic dialogue, with the old bawd posing as a philosopher imparting wisdom to the young servant.

master (for that will but shorten thy days) sithence we can enjoy it no longer than we live. Oh, son Parmeno (and well can I call thee son, since I had the breeding of thee so long a time), follow my counsel, seeing it proceeds out of pure love, and an earnest desire to see thee grow up in honour. Oh, how happy should I be, might I but see thee and Sempronio agree; see you two friends, and sworn brothers in everything, that yee may come to my poor house to be merry, and to see me now and then, and to take your pleasure each of you with his wench!

Parmeno. His wench, mother?

Celestina. Ay, his wench, and a young one too. As for old flesh, myself am old enough, and such a wench as Sempronio would be glad of with all his heart, with the one half of that regard and affection which I show to thee. What I speak comes from my entrails, and the very bowels of me.

Parmeno. Mother, you shall not be deceived in me.

Celestina. And if I should, the matter is not great, for what I do, I do for charity,[360] and for that I see thee here alone in a strange land, and for the respect which I bear unto those bones of her, who recommended thee unto me. When you are more man, you will think of all this and come to a truer knowledge of things and then thou wilt say, that old Celestina gave me good counsel.

Parmeno. I know that as well now, though I am but young, as if I were elder; and howbeit I spoke against you today, it was not because I thought that to be ill spoken which you said, but because I saw, when I told my master the truth, and advised him for the best, he ill-treated me, and therefore henceforth let us shake hands, and use him accordingly. Do what thou wilt unto him, I will hold my peace, for I have already too much offended, in not crediting thee in this business concerning him.

Celestina. In this and all other, thou shalt not only trip, but fall, as long as thou shalt not take my counsel with thee, which comes from thy true and faithful friend.

Parmeno. Now, I bless the time wherein I served thee: counting those days happy under which thou bredst me up of a child, since old age brings with it such store of fruit.[361]

---

[360] 'Por amor de Dios' in the original (Lobera *et al.*, eds, 2000, p. 167).
[361] Although Mabbe emphasizes the fact that Celestina has apparently obtained

Celestina. Son, no more. For mine eyes already run over, and my tears begin to break over those banks, which should bound them in. Oh had I in all this world, but such another friend? Such another companion? Such a comfortress in my troubles? Such an easer, and lightener of my heart's heaviness? Who did supply my wants? Who knew my secrets? To whom did I discover my heart? Who was all my happiness, and quietness, but thy mother? She was nearer and dearer unto me, than my gossip, or mine own sister. Oh, how well favoured was she, and cheerful of countenance? How lusty? How quick? How neat? How portly and majestical in her gate? How stout and manly? Why, she would go at midnight without or pain, or fear, from churchyard to churchyard, seeking for implements appertaining to our trade, as if it had been day. Nor did she omit either Christians, Moors or Jews, whose graves and sepulchres she did not visit. By day she would watch them, and by night she would dig them out, taking such things as should serve her turn. So that she took as great pleasure in darkness of the night as thou dost comfort in the brightness of the day. She would usually say that the night was the sinful man's cloak, that did hide and cover all his rogueries that they might not be seen, though perhaps she had not the like dexterity and skill in all the rest of those tricks that appertained to her trade. Yet one thing shall I tell thee, because thou shall see what a mother thou hast lost, though I was about to keep it in. But it makes no matter, it shall out to thee. She did pull out seven teeth out of a fellow's head that was hanged with a pair of pincers, such as you pull out stubbed hairs withal, whilst I did pull off his shoes. She was excellent at a circle, and would enter it far better than myself, and with great boldness, though I also was very famous for it in those days, more iwis than I am now, who have

---

Parmeno's credit ('I have already too much offended, in not crediting thee in this business'), he omits here Parmeno's pious reference to his father and mother. This prompts Celestina's tears, and the tenor of her reponse: 'Yo rogaré a Dios por el alma de mi padre, que tal tutriz me dejó, y de mi madre, que a tal mujer me encomendó' (Lobera *et al.*, eds, 2000, p. 168), i.e. 'I shall pray to God for the soul of my father, who left me in the hands of such tutor, and of my mother, who entrusted me to the care of such a woman'. As a result of this omission, the reader misses the sarcasm implicit in praying for the soul of a witch, and in the fact that his parents have left Parmeno under Celestina's guardianship.

together with her lost almost my cunning. What shall I say more unto thee, but that the very devils themselves did live in fear of her? She did hold them in horror, and dread, making them to tremble and quake when she began to exercise her exorcisms, her spells, her incantations, her charms, her conjurations, and other words of most horrisonous roaring, and most hideous noise. She was as well known to them all, as the beggar knows his dish, or as thyself in thine own house. One devil coming tumbling in upon the neck of another, as fast as it pleased her to call them up, and not one of them durst tell her a lie, such power had she to bind them. So that ever since she died I could never attain to the truth of anything.

Parmeno. (May this woman no better thrive, than she pleased me with those her wordy praises.)[362]

Celestina. What sayst thou, my honest Parmeno? My son, nay, more than my son.

Parmeno. I say, how should it come to pass, that my mother should have this advantage of you, being the words which she and you spoke were both one?

Celestina. How? Make you this so great a wonder? Know you not, the proverb tells us that there is a great deal of difference betwixt Peter and Peter?[363] Trust me truly, we cannot all be alike in all. We cannot all of us attain to those good gifts and graces of my deceased gossip. And have not you yourself seen amongst your artisans some good, and some others better than they? So likewise was it betwixt me and your mother. She was the only woman in our art, she had not her fellow. And for such a one was she of all the world both known and sought after, as well of *cavalleroes*,[364] as married men, old men, young men, and children besides, maids and damsels, who did as earnestly pray for her life, as for that of their own fathers and mothers. She had to do with all manner of persons, she talked with all sorts of people. If we walked the streets, as many as we met they were all of them her godsons. For her chiefest

---

[362] Although he has outwardly accepted Celestina's wisdom, in this aside Parmeno expresses his disgust at the old bawd's description of his mother as an accomplished witch.

[363] there is a great deal of difference betwixt Peter and Peter] A literal translation of 'Mucho va de Pedro a Pedro' (Lobera *et al.*, eds, 2000, p. 169).

[364] *cavalleroes*] i.e. gentlemen, *sic*, in Spanish.

220   profession for some sixteen years together was to play the midwife. So that albeit thou knew'st not these secrets, because thou wast then but young, now it is fit that thou should'st know them, sithence that she is dead, and thou grown up to be a man.

Parmeno. Tell me, mother: when the justice sent officers to apprehend you, at which time I was then in your house, was there any great acquaintance between you?

Celestina. Any great acquaintance? You are disposed to jest. Our cases were both alike, they took us both alike, they accused us both alike, and they did punish us both alike, which — if I be not deceived — was the first punishment that ever we had. But thou wast a little one then. I wonder how thou shouldst remember it, for, it is a thing of all other the most forgotten that hath happened in this city; so many, and so daily in this world are those new occurrents,° which obliterate the old. If you go but out into the marketplace, you shall every day see *peque y pague*, the peccant and his punishment.[365]

Parmeno. It is true, but the worser part of wickedness is the perseverance therein.

Celestina. (How deadly the fool bites! He hath hit me home, and pricked me to the quick. I will therefore be now Tom tell-truth, and assure thyself, sithence thou hast galled me, I will wring thee till I make thee winch and fling. I will tickle thee on the right vein.)

Parmeno. What say you, mother?

Celestina. Marry I say, son, that besides this, your mother was taken four several times, she herself alone. And once she was accused for a witch; for she was found one night by the watch with certain little candles in her hand, gathering I know not what earth in a cross-way, for which she stood half a day in the open marketplace upon a scaffold with a high paper hat, like the coffin° of a sugar-loaf painted full of devils, whereon her fault was written, being brought thither riding through the streets upon an ass, as the fashion is in the punishment of

---

[365] *peque y pague*] *sic*, in Spanish, which Mabbe immediately translates: the idea is that events like this — the public punishment of witches, prostitutes, and other heretics — are so common that they are soon forgotten. A few lines later, Celestina describes the details of one such public punishment which Parmeno's mother underwent.

bawds and witches. Yet all this was nothing, for men must suffer something in this wicked world for to uphold their lives and their honours. And mark, I pray, what small reckoning they made of it, because of her great wisdom and discretion. For she would not for all this give over her old occupation, and from that day forward followed it the more earnestly than she did before and with happier proof. This I thought good to tell you to cross that opinion of yours touching perseverance in that wherein we have once already erred: for all that she did, did so well become her, and such a grace had she with her, that upon my conscience, howbeit she stood thus disgracefully upon the scaffold, every one might perceive that she cared not a button for those that stood beneath staring and gazing upon her; such was her behaviour and carriage at that instant: look they might their fill, but I warrant you, she was not a farthing in debt, no not to the proudest of them all, wherein I thought fit to instance, to show thereby unto you that they who have anything in them as she had and are wise and of worth, fall far more easily and sooner into error than any other. Do but weigh and consider with yourself, what a manner of man Virgil was: how wise in all kind of knowledge. And yet I am sure you have heard how in a wicker basket he was hung out from a tower, all Rome looking upon him. Yet for all this was he neither the less honoured, neither lost he the name of Virgil.[366]

Parmeno. That is true which you say, but it was not enjoined by the justice.

Celestina. Peace, you fool. Thou art ignorant what a sinister and coarse kind of justice was used and rigorously executed upon thy mother to the most extremity which, as all men confess, is a mere injury. And the rather, because it was commonly spoken of all men, that wrongfully and against all right and reason, by suborning of false witnesses and cruel torments, they enforced her to confess that which in reality of truth was not.[367] But because she was a woman of great spirit, and good

---

[366] This was a famous and apocryphal medieval legend about Virgil, which can also be found in Piccolomini's *Historia de duobus amantibus* (see Ravasini, ed. 2003, p. 316, ll. 356–59).

[367] Here Mabbe omits another irreverent passage, in which Celestina recounts how Parmeno's mother was consoled by the priest while she was being punished. This said priest invoked the Sermon of the Mount, which turned the

courage, and her heart had been accustomed to endure, she made matters lighter than they were. And of all this, she reckoned not a pin: for a thousand times have I heard her say: 'if I broke my leg, it was all for my good; for this made me better known than I was before'. And certainly so she was, and the more noted and respected, nay, and thrived the better by it, both she and I, and the more plentiful our harvest and incomes of customers of the best, and we loved and lived merrily together to her last. And be but thou unto me, as she was; that is to say, a true and faithful friend, and withal, endeavour thyself to be good, since thou hast so good a pattern to follow. And for that which thy father left thee, thou hast it safely kept for thee.

Parmeno. Let us now leave talking of the dead, and of patrimonies, and let us parley of our present businesses, which concerns us more than to draw things past unto our remembrance. If you be well remembered, it is not long since that you promised me I should have Areusa, when as I told you at my master's house, that I was ready to die for love, so fervent is my affection towards her.

Celestina. If I did promise thee, I have not forgot it; nor would I you should think that I have lost my memory with my years. For I have thrice already, and better, given her the check concerning this business in thy absence. But now I think the matter is grown to some ripeness. Let us walk towards her house, for now, do what she can, she shall not avoid the mate.[368] For this is the least thing of a thousand that I will undertake to do for thee.

Parmeno. I was quite out of hope ever to have her; for I could never come to any conclusion with her, no, not to find so much favour, as but to speak with her, or to have but a word with her. And as it is in the proverb: in love it is an ill sign to see his mistress fly, and turn the face. And this did much dishearten me in my suit.

Celestina. I marvel not much at thy discouragement, considering I was then a stranger unto thee; at least, not so well acquainted

---

witch into a victim of persecution for righteousness' sake. Celestina thus sets forth Claudina as an example of the sort of penance required to achieve salvation.

[368] Like *check*, before, *mate* here — as in chess.

with thee as now I am; and that thyself did not then know, (as now thou dost) that thou may'st command her who is the doctress of this art. But now you shalt see, what favour thou shalt find for my sake, what power I have over these wenches, how much I can prevail with them, and what wonders I can work in matters of love. But hush, tread softly. Lo, here's the door, let us enter in with still and quiet steps, that the neighbours may not hear us. Stay, and attend me here at the stairs' foot, whilst I go up and see what I shall be able to do with her, concerning the business we talked of. And it may be we shall work more with her, than either thou or I did ever dream of.

Areusa. Who's there? Who is that, that at this time of night comes up into my chamber?
Celestina. One, I assure you, that means you no ill; one that never treads step but she thinks on thy profit; one that is more mindful of thee than of herself; one that loves thee as her life, though I am now grown old.
Areusa. (Now the devil take this old trot!) What news with you, that you come thus stealing like a ghost, and at so late an hour? How think you, gentlewoman, is this a fair hour to come to one's chamber? I was even putting off my clothes to go to bed.
Celestina. What? To bed with the hen, daughter? So soon to roost? Fie for shame, is this the way to thrive? Think you ever to be rich, if you go to bed so timely? Come, walk a turn or two, and talk with me a little. Let others bewail their wants, not thou. Herbs seed them that gather them. Who but would, if he could, lead such a life?
Areusa. How cold it is! I will go put on my clothes again. Beshrew me if I am not cold at my very heart.
Celestina. Nay, by my fay shall you not; but if you will go into your bed, do; and so shall we talk more conveniently together.
Areusa. Yes indeed, I have need so to do; for I have felt myself very ill all this day; so that necessity, rather than laziness, hath made me thus early to take my sheets, instead of my petticoat, to wrap about me.
Celestina. Sit not up, I pray, any longer, but get you to bed, and cover yourself with clothes, and sink lower in, so shall you be the sooner warm. Oh how like a siren doest thou look! How fair, how beautiful! Oh how sweetly everything smells about

thee, when thou heavest and turnest thyself in thy bed! I assure you, everything is in very good order. How well I have always been pleased with all thy things, and thy doings? You will not think, how this neatness, this handsomeness of yours in your lodging doth delight me; to see everything so trim and tricksy about you. I promise you, I am even proud of it. Oh how fresh dost thou look! What sheets! What quilts be here! What pillows! Oh how white they be! Let me not live, if everything here doeth not like me wonderful well: my pearl, my jewel of gold, see whether I love you or no, that I come to visit you at this time of night! Let my eye take its fill in beholding of thee, it does me much good to touch thee, and to look upon thee.

Areusa. Nay, good mother, leave, do not touch me, pray you do not, it doth but increase my pain.

Celestina. What pain, sweet heart, tell me, pretty duck. Come, come, you do but jest, I am sure.

Areusa. Jest? Let me never taste of joy, if I jest with you. It is scarce four hours since, that every minute I was ready to die with pain of the mother,° which rising in my breast, swelled up to my throat, and was ready to stifle me; that I still looked when I should leave the world, and therefore am not so gamesome and wanton as you think I am: now have I little mind of that.

Celestina. Go to, give me leave a little to touch you; and I will try what I can do. For I know something of this evil, which everyone calls the mother, and the passion thereunto belonging.

Areusa. Lay your hand higher up towards my stomach.

Celestina. Alack, poor heart, how I pity thee. That one so plump, so fair, so clear, so fresh, so fragrant, so delicate, so dainty a creature, that art indeed the very abstract of beauty, the most admired model for complexion, feature, comeliness, and rarest composure; every limb, every lineament carrying such extraordinary lustre and ornament by reflection from thee.[369] I say, how do I pity thee, that any ache, sickness, or infirmity should dare to seize, or presume to usurp over such a peerless potent,

---

[369] Mabbe tones down Celestina's voluptuous description of Areusa's body, which concludes with old bawd's expression of regret that she is not a man, and consequently unable to enjoy Areusa ('¡Oh quien fuera hombre y tanta parte alcanzara de ti para gozar tal vista!', Lobera *et al.*, eds, 2000, p. 175).

400   a commanding power, as thy imperious unparalleled beauty! But I dare say, it is not so, not so; no, no, your disease is self-conceited, and the pride of your good parts, this puffs you and makes you flight and contemn all. Go to, go to, daughter, you are to blame if it be so, and I tell you, it is a shame for you, that it is, not to impart these good graces and blessings, which heaven hath bestowed upon you, to as many as wish you well; for they were not given you in vain, that you should let them wither, and lose the flower of your youth under six linings of woollen and linen; have a care, that you be not covetous of
410   that, which cost you but little; do not, like a miser, hoard up your beauty; make not a hidden treasure of it, sithence in its own nature it is as communicable, and as commonly current as money from man to man.[370] Be not the mastiff in the garden, nor the dog in the manger, and since thou canst not take any pleasure in thyself, let others take their pleasure, and do not think thou was born for nothing: for when thou wast born, man was born, and when man was born, woman was born; nothing in all this wide world was created superfluous, nor which nature did not provide for with very good consonancy
420   and well suiting with reason. But think on the contrary, that it is a fault to vex and torment men, when it is in thy power to give them remedy.

Areusa. Tush, mother, these are but words, and profit me nothing; give me something for my evil, and leave your jesting.

Celestina. In this so common a grief, all of us (the more misfortune ours) are in a manner physicians to ourselves; that which I have seen practised on others, and that which I found good in myself, I shall plainly deliver unto you. But as the states of our bodies are diverse, and the qualities differing, so are the
430   medicines also diverse, and the operations different. Every strong scent is good: as pennyroyal,[371] rue, wormwood, smoke

---

[370] Mabbe's expanded but nevertheless accurate translation of the original 'Cata que no seas avarienta de lo que poco te costó; no atesores tu gentileza, pues es de su natura tan comunicable como el dinero' (Lobera *et al.*, eds, 2000, p. 175), i.e. 'Be not greedy of what cost you so little; do not hoard up your gentleness, since by nature it is as communicable as money'. For Celestina, desire and money should both be common currency (see also my notes to 8.196 and 8.325 below).

[371] pennyroyal] a type of mint (*Mentha pulegium*).

of partridge feathers, of rosemary, and of the soles of old shoes, and of muskroses, of incense, of strong perfumes, received kindly, fully, and greedily, doth work much good, much slacketh and easeth the pain, and by little and little returns the mother to its proper place. But there is another thing that passeth these, and that I ever found to be better than anyone, or all of them put together; but what it is, I will not tell you, because you make yourself such a piece of niceness.

Areusa. As you love me, good mother, tell me: see'st thou me thus pained, and concealest thou thyself?

Celestina. Go to, go to, you understand me well enough; do not make yourself more fool than you are.

Areusa. Well, well, well; now trust me no more, if I understood thee. But what is it thou wouldst have me to do? You know that my friend went yesterday with his captain to the wars; would you have me to wrong him?

Celestina. Oh, take heed! Great wrong, I promise you!

Areusa. Yes indeed, for he supplies all my wants; he will see I shall lack nothing; he holds me honest; he does love me, and uses me with that respect, as if I were his lady and mistress.

Celestina. Suppose all this to be true, be it in the best sort it may be, yet what all of this? This retiredness is no cure for your disease; you must be free and communicable[372], for I must tell you, there are griefs and pangs cannot easily be posted off and dispossessed, and some not to be removed but by being a mother, (you know my meaning), and such is your disease, and you can never recover it, but by living sole and simple (as you now do) without company.

Areusa. It is but my ill hap, and a curse laid upon me by my parents, else had I not been put to prove all this misery and pain which I now feel. But to let this pass, because it is late, tell me I pray, what wind drove you hither?

Celestina. You know already what I have said unto you concerning Parmeno, who complains himself unto me, that you refuse to see him; that you will not vouchsafe him so much as a look: what should be the reason, I know not, unless because you know that I wish him well, and make account of him, as of my

---

[372] free and communicable] Mabbe insists on the idea of communicability, absent from the Spanish original — which he has expanded in his English rendering.

son. I have a better care of your matters, and regard your friends in a kinder fashion. Not a neighbour that dwells near you, but she is welcome unto me, and my heart rejoiceth as often as I see them, and all because they converse with thee, and keep thee company.

Areusa. It is true, aunt, that you say, and I acknowledge my beholdingness.

Celestina. I know not whether you do or no, dost thou hear me, girl? I must believe works, for words are wind, and are sold everywhere for nothing, but love is never paid but with pure love, and works with works. Thou know'st the alliance between thee and Elicia, whom Sempronio keeps in my house. Parmeno and he are fellows and companions, they both serve the gentleman you wot of, and by whom you may gain great good and grace unto yourself. Do not therefore deny him that, the granting whereof will cost thee so little; you are kinswomen, and they companions: see, how pat all things fall! Far better than we ourselves could have wished; and to tell you truly, I have brought him along with me: how say you? Shall I call him up?

Areusa. Now, heavens forbid. Fie! What did you mean? Ay me, I fear me he hath heard every word.

Celestina. No, for he stays beneath. I will call to him to come up, for my sake show him good countenance; take notice of him; speak kindly unto him; entertain him friendly; and if you think fit, let him enjoy you, and you him, and both one another, for though he gain much, I am sure, you shall lose nothing by the bargain.

Areusa. Mother, I am not ignorant, that as well these, as all other your former speeches unto me, have ever been directed to my good and benefit; but how is it possible, that I should do this, that you would now have me? For you know to whom I am bound to give an account, as already you have heard; and if he know I play false, he will kill me. My neighbours, they are envious and malicious, and they will straightaway acquaint him therewith. And say, that no great ill should befall me, save only the losing of his love; it will be more than I shall gain by giving contentment to him, for whom you entreat, or rather command me.

Celestina. For this fear of yours, myself have already provided for we entered in very softly.

510 *Areusa.* Nay, I do not speak for this night, but for many other that are to come. Tush, were it but for one night, I would not care.

Celestina. What? Is this your fashion? Is this the manner of your carriage? And you use these niceties you shall never have a house with a double room, but live like a beggar all the days of your life. What? Are you afraid of our sweetheart now he is absent? What would you then do, were he now in town? It hath ever been my ill fortune to give counsel unto fools, such as cannot see their own good; say what I will, they will err, still 520 stand in their own light. But I do not much wonder at it; for though the world be wide, yet there are but few wise in it. Great is the largeness of the earth, but small the number of those that have experience. Ha, daughter! Did you but see your cousin's wisdom, or but know what benefit my breeding and counsel hath brought her, how cunning, how witty, and what a mistress in her art, you would be of another mind; say what I will unto her, she patiently endured my reprehensions, she hearkens to my advice, and does all that I will have her do; she will sometimes boast that she hath at one time had one in bed with her, 530 another waiting at the door, and a third sighing for her within the house; and yet hath given good satisfaction to them all. And art thou afraid, who hast but two to deal withal? Can one cock° fill all thy cisterns? One conduit-pipe water all thy court? If this be your diet, you may chance to rise a-hungered, you shall have no meat left against another time, I will not rent your fragments; I cannot live upon scraps. One could never please me, I could never place all my affection upon one, two can do more than one: they give more, and they have more to give. It goes hard, daughter, with that mouse that hath but one 540 hole to trust to, for if that be stopt, she hath no means to hide herself from the cat. He that hath but one eye, you see in what danger he goes? One sole act maketh not a habit. It is a rare, and strange thing to see a partridge fly single. To feed always upon one dish, brings a loathing to the stomach; one swallow makes not a summer; one witness alone is of no validity in law. He that hath but one suit of clothes, and she that hath but one gown to her back, quickly wears them out. What would you do, daughter, with this number of one? Many more inconveniences can I tell thee of this single sole number (if one may be 550 a number). If you be wise, be never without two, for it is a laudable and commendable company, as you may see it in yourself, who hath two ears, two feet, and two hands, two sheets upon one bed, and two smocks wherewith to shift you. And the more you have, the better it is for you, for still (as it is in the proverb) the more moors, the better market.[373] And honour without profit, is no other but as a ring upon the finger. And because one sack cannot hold them both apply yourself to your profit. Son, Parmeno, come up.

Areusa. Oh let him not come up if you love me: the pox be my death, if I am not ready to swoon, to think on it. I know not what to do for very shame. Nay, fie, mother, what mean you to call him up? You know that I have no acquaintance with him, I never exchanged a word with him, in all my life. Fie, how I am ashamed!

Celestina. I am here with thee, wench, I who will stand betwixt him and thee, I will quit thee of this shame, and will cover thee close, and speak for you both. For he is as bashful as you, for your life.

Parmeno. Gentlewoman, heavens preserve this gracious presence of yours.[374]

Areusa. You are welcome, gentle sir.

Celestina. Come hither, you ass, whither go you now, to sit moping down in a corner? Come, come, be not so ashamed, for it was the bashful man whom the devil brought to court: for he was sure, he should get nothing there. Hearken both of you, what I shall now say unto you: you, my friend Parmeno, know already what I promised you, and you, daughter, what I entreated at your hands. Laying aside therefore the difficulty in drawing thee to grant that which I defined, few words I conceive to be best, because the time will not permit me to be long. He for his part hath hitherto lived in great pain and grief for your sake; and therefore you seeing his torment, I know you will not kill him; and I likewise know, that yourself liketh

---

[373] 'Mientras más moros, más ganancia' (Lobera *et al.*, eds, 2000, p. 180): during the frontier wars, Moors captured as prisoners were sold as slaves by the Christians, hence the proverb.

[374] 'Señora, Dios salve tu graciosa presencia', in the original (Lobera *et al.*, eds, 2000, p. 180).

so well of him that it shall not be amiss that he stay with you here this night in the house.

Areusa. For my maidenhead's sake, mother, let it not be so, pray do not command it me.

Parmeno. (Mother, as you love my life, as you love goodness, let me not go hence until we be well agreed: for she hath wounded me with her eyes to death, and I must die through love, unless you help me. Offer her all that which my father left with you for me; tell her I will give her all that I have besides, do you hear? Tell her, that methinks she will not vouchsafe to look upon me.)

Areusa. What doth this gentleman whisper in your ear? Thinks he that I will not perform ought of your request?

Celestina. No, daughter, no such matter; he says that he is very glad of your good love and friendship, because you are so honest, and so worthy, and that any benefit shall light well that shall fall upon you. Come hither, modesty, come hither you bashful fool.[375]

Areusa. He will not be so uncivil as to enter into another body's ground without leave, especially when it lies in several.[376]

Celestina. So uncivil? Do you stand upon leave? Would you have him stand with cap in hand, and say, 'I pray shall I, will you give me leave, forsooth', and I know not what fiddle-come-faddles?[377] Well, I will stay no longer with you: and I will pass my word, that you shall rise tomorrow painless.[378]

---

[375] Mabbe here omits the old bawd's explicit remarks encouraging Parmeno to have intercourse with Areusa, since Celestina herself wants to witness his skills: 'que quiero ver para cuánto eres antes de que me vaya. Retózala en esta cama' (Lobera *et al.*, eds, 2000, p. 181). The Alnwick manuscript does translate this as 'for I will see before I goe what metall you be made of. Come playe the wag a little with her, and tickle her as she lyes in her bed' (Martínez Lacalle, ed., p. 198).

[376] especially when it lies in several] these concluding words — the actual meaning of which is rather obscure — do not feature in the Spanish original.

[377] fiddle-come-faddles] trivial matters.

[378] Some more saucy remarks are omitted here: 'Mas como es un putillo, gallillo, barbiponiente, entiendo que en tres noches no se le demude la cresta; destos me mandaban a mí comer en mi tiempo los médicos de mi tierra cuando tenía mejores dientes' (Lobera *et al.*, eds, 2000, p. 181). The Alnwick manuscript translates it as: 'And because he is but a younge wanton wagg, a *Ganimede*, a little Cockerell, a dawe of the first downe but now beginninge to put out his bearde, I make no question but in 3 nightes, his Combe will be cutt.

Areusa. Nay, fie, good sir, for modesty's sake, I beseech you let me alone: content yourself, I pray, I pray let be. If not for my sake, yet look back upon those grey hairs of that reverend old dame, which stands by you, and forbear for her sake. Get you gone, I say, for I am none of those you take me to be. I am none of your common hackneys that hire out their bodies for money. Would I might never stir, if I do not get me out of the house, if you do but touch so much as a cloth about me.

Celestina. Why, how now Areusa? What's the matter with you? Whence comes this strangeness? Whence this coyness of yours? This niceness? Why, daughter, do you think that I know not what this means? Did I never see a man and woman together before? And that I know not all their tricks and devices? What they say, and what they do? I am sorry to hear that I do. Besides, I must tell you, I was once as wanton as you are now, and thought my penny as good silver as yours; and many a friend I had that came unto me, yet did I never in all my life exclude either old man, or old woman out of my company, or that ever I refused their counsel, were it public or private. By my little honesty, I had rather thou hadst given me a box on the ear, than to hear what I hear. You make of me, as if I had been born but yesterday. Oh how cunning forsooth! How close you be! For to make yourself seem honest, you would make me a fool. I must be a kind of *ignoramus*, without shame, secrecy and experience. Ye would discredit me in my trade, for to win yourself credit in your own. But the best is, betwixt pirate and pirate, there is nothing to be got but blows and empty barrels. And well I wot, that I speak far better of thee, behind my back, than thou canst think of thyself before me.

Areusa. Mother, if I have offended, pardon me, for I had rather give contentment to you, than to myself. I would not anger you for a world.

Celestina. No, I am not angry, I do but tell you this against another time, that you may beware you do so no more. And so good night, for I will be gone, I will get me away alone by myself.[379]

Marke yf he be not crestfallen ere 3 nightes come to an ende' (Martínez Lacalle, ed., p. 198).

[379] As usual, the Alnwick manuscript is more explicit here, by reproducing the original more faithfully — and in this case, it even amplifies it with the final

Areusa. Good night, aunt.

Parmeno Mother, will you that I wait upon you? Shall I accompany you home?

Celestina. No, marry, shall you not; that were but to strip one, and cloath another;[380] or again, it needs not, for I am old and therefore not to be forced in the streets. I am past all danger of ravishing.[381]

Elicia. The dog barks. The old witch comes hobbling home.

Celestina. Tha, tha, tha.

Elicia. Who is there? Who knocks at the door?

Celestina. Daughter, come down, and open the door.

Elicia. Is this a time to come in? You are disposed still to be out thus a-nights. To what end, I trow,[382] walk you thus late? What a long time, mother, have you been away? What do you mean by it? You can never find the way home when you are once abroad. But it is your old wont, you cannot leave it, and so as you may pleasure one, you care not, and you leave a hundred discontented. You have been sought after today, by the father of her that was betrothed, which you brought from the prebendary upon Easter day, whom he is purposed to marry within these three days, and you must needs help her, according as you promised, that her husband may not find her virginity cracked.

Celestina. Daugher, I remember no such matter. For whom is it that you speak?

Elicia. Remember no such matter? Sure, you have forgot yourself. Oh what a weak memory have you! Why, yourself

---

Trojan metaphor: 'Well, I will begon, and so god be with you. You doe but sett my teeth an edge with your kissinge, your smackinge, your ticklinge, for I haue some inward fellinge in my gummes: the tast stickes in my mouth still, as old as I am; I haue not lost that touche togeather with my teeth. There be some reliques of old *Troye* still remaininge, though I am not nowe so trewe a *Troian* as I haue bene' (Martínez Lacalle, ed. pp. 198–99).

[380] to strip one [saint], and cloath another] Mabbe's translation of the Spanish proverbial expression 'quitar un santo por poner en otro', i.e. by accompanying Celestina, Areusa would be leaving Parmeno alone, and the old bawd's recent endeavours would have been in vain. Note that Mabbe omits the reference to the saint.

[381] ravishing] used here as a noun, i.e. rape, violation.

[382] trow] according to the *OED*, this expression appears parenthetically, in questions, with a meaning equivalent to 'I suppose' or 'I believe'; here it seems to have the force of 'I wonder'.

told me of it when you took her hence, and that you had renewed her maidenhead seven times at the least.

Celestina. Daughter, make it not so strange, that I should forget. For he that scattereth his memory into many parts can keep it steadfast in no part. But tell me, will he not return again?

Elicia. See whether he will return or no? He hath given you a bracelet of gold, as a pledge for your pains: and will he not then return again?

Celestina. Oh wast he that brought the bracelet? Now I know whom you mean. Why did you not prepare things in a readiness, and began to do something against I came home? For in such things you should practise yourself when I am absent, and try whether you can do that by yourself, which you so often have seen me do; otherwise, you are like to live all your lifetime like a beast, without either art, or income. And then when you grow to my years you will too late lament your present laziness; for an idle and lazy youth brings with it a repentful and a painful old age. I took a better course iwis, when your grandmother showed me her cunning: for, in the compass of one year, I grew more skilful than herself.

Elicia. No marvel, for many times, (as it is in the proverb) a good scholar goes beyond his master; and it is all in the will and desire of him that is to learn; for no science can be well employed on him who hath not a good mind and affection thereunto. But I had as lief die as go about it. I am sick, methinks, when I set myself to it, and you are never well, but when you are at it.

Celestina. You may say what you like. But believe me, you will die a beggar for this. What? Do you think to live always under my wing? Think you never to go from my elbow?

Elicia. Pray let us leave off this melancholy talk; now is now, and then is then. When time serves, we will follow your counsel, but now let us take our pleasure, while we may. As long as we have meat for today, let us not think on tomorrow. Let tomorrow care for itself: as well dies he that gathers much, as he that lives but poorly, the master, as the servant, he that is of a noble lineage, as he that is of a meaner stock, and thou with thy art, as well as I without it. We are not to live forever, and therefore let us laugh and be merry for few are they that come to see old age; and they who do see it, seldom die of hunger. I desire nothing in this world, but meat, drink and clothing, and a part in pleasure. And though rich men have better means to attain to this glory than he that hath but little, yet there is not one of them that is contented, not one that says to himself: 'I have enough'. There is not one of them with whom I would exchange my pleasures for their riches. But let us leave other men's thoughts and cares to themselves; and let us go sleep, for it is time. And a good sound sleep without fear will fat me more, and do me more good, than all the treasure and wealth of Venice.

JOSÉ MARÍA PÉREZ FERNÁNDEZ

Actus VIII
The Argument

The day appears. Parmeno departs, and takes his leave of Areusa, and goes to his master Calisto. He finds Sempronio at the door. They enter into amity, go jointly to Calisto's chamber; they find him talking with himself; being risen, he goes to church.

INTERLOCUTORS
Parmeno, Areusa, Calisto, Sempronio

Parmeno. It is day. Oh what a sight is this? Whence is it, that it is so light in the chamber?
Areusa. What do you talk of day? Sleep, sir, and take your rest; for it is even now since we lay down. I have scarce shut mine eyes yet, and would you have it to be day? I pray you open the window by you, the window there by your bed's head, and you shall then see whether it be so or no.
Parmeno. Gentlewoman, I am in the right. It is day. I see it is day, I am not deceived. No, no. I knew it was broad day, when I saw the light come through the chinks of the door. Oh what a villain am I! Into how great a fault am I fallen with my master! I am worthy of much punishment. Oh how far days is it![383]
Areusa. Far days?
Parmeno. Ay, far days; very far days.
Areusa. Never trust me. Alas, I am not eased of my mother yet. It pains me still. I know not what should be the reason of it.
Parmeno. Dear love, what would's thou have me to do?
Areusa. That we talk a little on the matter concerning my indisposition.
Parmeno. What should we talk, love, any more? If that which hath been said already be not sufficient, excuse that in me, which is more necessary; for it is now almost high noon: and if I stay any longer, I shall not be welcome to my master. Tomorrow is a new day, and then I will come to see you again, and as often afterwards as you please: and therefore was one day made after another, because that which could not be

---

[383] how far days is it!] how far into the day it is, i.e. it's late.

performed in one day, might be done in another: as also, because we should see one another the oftener. In the meanwhile, let me entreat you to do me the favour, that you will come and dine with us today at Celestina's house.

Areusa. With all my heart, and I thank you too. Farewell, good luck be with you. I pray pull the door after you.

Parmeno. And fare you well too. Oh singular pleasure! Oh singular joy! What man lives there this day that can say he is more fortunate than I am? Can any man be more happy? Any more successful than myself, that I should enjoy so excellent a gift? So curious a creature, and no sooner ask than have? Believe me, if my heart could brook[384] this old woman's treasons, I could creep upon my knees to do her a kindness. How shall I be able to requite her? Oh heavens![385] To whom shall I impart this my joy? To whom shall I discover so great a secret? To whom shall I discover some part of my glory? It is true that the old woman told me: that of no prosperity the possession can be good without company, and that pleasure not communicated is no pleasure. Oh, who can have so true a feeling of this my happiness, as myself?[386] But lo, yonder is Sempronio, standing at our door; he hath been stirring betimes; I shall have a piteous life with my master, if he be gone abroad; but I hope he is not; if he be, he hath left his old wont. But being he is not now himself, no marvel if he break custom.

Sempronio. Brother Parmeno, if I knew that country where a man might get wages by sleeping, it should go hard, but I would make a shift to get thither. For, I would not then come short of any man; I would scorn to be put down, but would gain as much as another man, be he who he will be that bears a head. But what is the matter that thou, like a careless and reckless fellow, loitering I know not where, hast been so negligent, and slow in thy return? I cannot devise what should be the cause of this thy so long stay, unless it were to give old Celestina a

---

[384] brook] profit by (but also put up with, tolerate).
[385] '¡Oh alto Dios!' in the original (Lobera *et al.*, eds, 2000, p. 188).
[386] There are echoes of Terence's *Eunuchus* here (ll. 549–556, 1031–1033; for further details see Lobera *et al.*, eds, 2000, p. 188, note 10, and their long note, p. 655).

warming tonight; or to rub her feet, as you were wont to do, when you were a little one.

Parmeno. Oh Sempronio, my good friend, I pray thee do not interrupt, or rather, corrupt my pleasure. Do not intermix thy anger with my patience. Do not involve thy discontentment with my quiet. Do not soil with such troubled water the clear liquor of those gladsome thoughts which I harbour in my heart. Do not sour with thy malicious taunts and hateful reprehensions the sweetness of my delight. Receive me cheerful, embrace me with joy, and I shall tell thee wonders of my late happy proceedings.

Sempronio. Come, out with it. Is it anything touching Melibea? Say, lad, hast thou seen her?

Parmeno. What talk'st thou to me of Melibea? It is touching another, that I wish better unto than Melibea. And such a one (if I be not deceived) as may compare with her both in handsomeness and beauty. Melibea? Why, she is not worthy to carry her shoes after her: as though forsooth the world and all that therein is, be it beauty or otherwise, were only enclosed in Melibea?

Sempronio. What means this fellow? Is he mad? I would fain laugh, but I cannot. Now I see, we are all in love: the world is at an end. Calisto loves Melibea; I, Elicia; and thou out of mere envy hast found out someone with whom thou might'st lose that little wit thou hast.

Parmeno. Is it folly, say you, to love? Then am I a fool. But if foolishness were a pain, some in every house would complain.

Sempronio. I appeal to thyself; by thine own judgment thou art no better: for myself have heard thee give vain and foolish counsel to Calisto, and to cross Celestina in every word she spoke, to the hindrance of both our profits. Oh sir, you were glad of this; it was meat alone to you. Who, you? No, not for a world, would you bear a part with us. But since I have caught you in my clutches, I will hamper you i'faith. Now, that thou are in those hands, that may hurt thee, they shall do it; assure thyself they shall.

Parmeno. It is not, Sempronio, true courage, nor manly valour, to hurt or hinder any man, but to do good, to heal, and help him: and far greater is it to be willing so to do. I have evermore made reckoning of thee, as of mine own brother. Let not that be verified of thee, which is commonly spoken amongst us: that a slight cause should part true friends. I tell you, you do not use me well. Nay, you deal very ill with me. I know not whence this rancor should arise. Do not vex me, Sempronio, torment me not with these thy wounding words. And shall I tell you? It is a very strange and strong kind of patience, which sharp taunts and scoffs, which like so many needles and bodkins set to the heart, cannot pierce and prick through.

110 *Sempronio*. I say nothing, but that now you have your wench, you will allow one pilchard more to the poor boy in the stable.[387]

Parmeno. You cannot hold, your heart would burst, if you should not vent your choler. Well, I will give way, and should you use me worse, I will pocket up all your wrongs: and the rather, because it is an old saying, no humane passion is perpetual.[388]

Sempronio. But you can use Calisto worse, advising him to that which thou thyself seek'st to shun, never letting him alone but
120 still urging him to leave loving of Melibea, wherein thou art just like unto a sign in an inn, which gives shelter to others, and none to itself. Oh Parmeno, now may'st thou see how easy a thing it is to find fault with another man's life, and how hard to amend his own. I say no more, yourself shall be your own judge, and from this day forward we shall see how you behave yourself, sithence you have now your porringer,[389] as well as other folks. If thou hadst been my friend (as thou professest) when I stood in need of thee, thou should'st then have favoured me, and made show of thy love, and assisted
130 Celestina in all that had been for my profit, and not to drive in at every word a nail of malice. Know moreover that as wine in

---

[387] A translation of an idiomatic expression, 'echa otra sardina, que otro ruin viene' (used when some unexpected guest requires a share in the meal). Rojas paraphrases it as 'que se eche otra sardina para el mozo de caballos', i.e. now that everyone is in love, and has a share in the action, even the stable boy will want to have his own paramour too.

[388] 'No humane passion is perpetual' is another adage from the *Index* of Petrarch's *Opera latina* (see Lobera *et al.*, eds, 2000, p. 190, n. 26, also their long note, p. 656). A few lines before, with 'It is a very strange and strong kind of patience...' we find another adage taken from the same *Index*, where both refrains appear consecutively. See notes to Prologue 17, 5.126.

[389] porringer] small bowl or basin, or the contents thereof (usually food), here used metaphorically.

the lees, when it is drawn to the very dregs, driveth drunkards from the tavern, the like effect hath necessity or adversity with a feigned friend; and false mettle, that is gilded but slightly over, quickly discovers itself to be but counterfeit.

Parmeno. I have often-times heard it spoken and now by experience I see it is true that in this wretched life of ours there is no pleasure without sorrow, no contentment without some cross, or counterbuff of fortune. We see our fairest days, our clearest sunshines are overcast with clouds, darkness and rain; our solaces and delights are swallowed up by dolours and by death; laughter, mirth and merriment are waited on by tears, lamentations, and other the like mortal passions. In a word, sweet meat will have sour sauce, and much ease and much quietness much pain and much heaviness.[390] Who could come more friendly or more merrily to a man than I did now to thee? And who could receive a more unkind welcome, or unfriendly salutation? Who lives there that sees himself, as I have seen myself, raised with such glory to the height of my dear Areusa's love? And who that sees himself more likely to fall from thence, than I, being so ill-treated as I am of thee? Nay, thou wilt not give me leave to tell thee, how much I am thine, how much I will further thee in all I am able, how much I repent me of that which is past, and what good counsel and reprehensions I have received of Celestina, and all in favour of thee, and thy good, and the good of us all. And now that we have our master's and Melibea's game in our own hands, now is the time that we must thrive or never.

Sempronio. I like your words well, but should like them better were your works like unto them, which as I see the performance, so shall I give them credence; but tell me, I pray thee, what's that me thought, I heard you talk even now of Areusa? Do you know Areusa, that is cousin to Elicia?

Parmeno. Why, what were all the joy I now enjoy, did I not enjoy her?

Sempronio. (What does the fool mean? He cannot speak for laughing.)[391] What doest thou call this thy enjoying of her? Did

---

[390] Rojas closely adapts here from Petrarch's *Bucolicum carmen* VIII.96–99 (Lobera *et al.*, eds, 2000, p. 191, n. 35).

[391] In the original it is Sempronio who cannot speak because of laughter (see Lobera *et al.*, eds, 2000, p 192).

she show herself unto thee out at a window? Or what is the matter?

170 *Parmeno.* No great matter. Only I have left her in doubt whether she be with child or no.

Sempronio. Thou hast struck me into a maze. Continual travail may do much: often dropping makes stones hollow.

Parmeno. How? Continual travail? Why, I never thought of having her till yesterday; then did I work her; and now she is mine own.

Sempronio. The old woman had a finger in this business, had she not?

Parmeno. Why should you think so?

180 *Sempronio.* Because she told me how much she loved you, how well she wished you, and that she would work her for you. You were a happy man, sir: you had no more to do but to come and take up. And therefore they say, it is better with him whom fortune helpeth, than with him that riseth early. But was she the godfather to this business?

Parmeno. No, but she was the godmother, which is the truer of the two. And you know, when a man comes once to a good tree he will stay a while by it and take the benefit of the shade.[392] I was long a coming, but when I came, I went quickly

190 to work: I dispatched it in an instant. Oh brother, what shall I say unto thee of the graces that are dwelling in that wench, of her language, and beauty of body? But I will defer the repetition thereof to a fitter opportunity.

Sempronio. She can be no other but cousin to Elicia: thou canst not say so much of her, but that this other hath as much, and somewhat more. But what did she cost thee?[393] Hast thou given her anything?

Parmeno. No, not anything. But whatsoever I had given her, it had been well bestowed, for she is capable of every good thing.

200 And such as she are by so much the better esteemed by how much the dearer they are bought, and like jewels are the higher

---

[392] Mabbe's explicit, and expanded, translation of the Spanish proverb (which appears truncated in the original) 'quien a buen árbol se arrima… [buena sombra le cobija]' (Lobera *et al.*, eds, 2000, p. 193, n. 45).

[393] Mabbe emphasises the mercantile implication in Sempronio's question, whereas Rojas's original was more neutral: '¿Hasle dado algo?' (Lobera *et al.*, eds, 2000, p. 193), i.e. 'Did you give her anything?'

prized the more they cost us. But, save in this my mistress, so rich a thing was never purchased at so low a rate. I have invited her today to dinner to Celestina's house, and if you like of it, let us all meet there.

Sempronio. Who, brother?

Parmeno. Thou and she, and the old woman and Elicia; and there we will laugh and be merry.

Sempronio. Oh good heavens, how glad a man hast thou made me! Thou art frank, and of a free and liberal disposition, I will never fail thee. Now I hold thee to be a man; now my mind gives me that fate hath some good in store for thee; all the hatred and malice which I bore thee for thy former speeches is now turned into love; I now doubt not but that the league which thou hast made with us shall be such as it ought to be. Now I long to embrace thee. Come, let us now live like brothers, and let the devil go hang himself. All those contentitous words notwithstanding, whatsoever have passed between us, let there be now no falling out, and so have peace all the year long, for, the falling out of friends is everymore the renewing of love. Let us feast and be merry, for our master will fast for us all.

Parmeno. What does the man in desperation do?

Sempronio. He lies where you left him last night, stretching himself all along upon his pallet by his bedside. But the devil a wink that he sleeps, and the devil a whit that he wakes, but lies like a man in a trance between them both, resting, and yet taking no rest. If I go in unto him, he falls a-routing[394] and a-snorting; if I go from him, he either sings or raves; nor can I for my life comprehend (so strange is his carriage therein) whether the man be in pain or ease; whether he take grief or pleasure in it.

Parmeno. What a strange humour is this? But tell me, Sempronio, did he never call for me? Did he not remember me when I was gone?

Sempronio. He remembered not himself, why should he then remember you?

Parmeno. Even in this also fortune hath been favourable unto

---

[394] a-routing] the *OED* documents this expression only twice: in Chaucer (*c.* 1390), and then again in 1399. Its meaning is uncertain, although in this case something can be gleaned from the context.

me. And since all things go so well, whilst I think on it, I will send thither our meat, that they may the sooner make ready our dinner.

Sempronio. What hast thou thought upon to send thither, that those pretty fools may hold thee a complete courtier, well bred and bountiful?

Parmeno. In a plentiful house a supper is soon provided: that, which I have here at home in the larder is sufficient to save our credit. We have good white bread, wine of Monviedro,³⁹⁵ and good gammon of bacon, and some half dozen couple of dainty chicken, which my master's tenants brought him the other day when they came to pay their rent; which if he chance to ask for, I will make him believe that he hath eaten them himself; and those turtledoves which he willed me to keep against today I will tell him that they were a little to blame, and none of the sweetest, and that they did so stink that I was fain to throw them away; and you shall justify it, and bear me witness. We will take order, that all that he shall eat thereof, shall do him no harm; and that our own table (as good reason it is it should) be well furnished; and therewith the old woman, as oft as we meet, we will talk more largely concerning this his love, to his loss, and our profit.

Sempronio. Callst thou it love? Thou may'st call it sorrow with a vengeance. And by my fay, I swear unto thee that I verily think that he will hardly now escape either death or madness. But since it is, as it is, dispatch your business, that we may go up, and see what he does.

Calisto.   In peril great I live,
            And strait of force must die:
            Since what desire doth give,
            That, hope doth me deny.

Parmeno. Hark, hark, Sempronio! Our master is a-rhyming: he is turned poet, I perceive.

Sempronio. Oh whoreson sot!° What poet, I pray? The great Antipater Sidonius,³⁹⁶ or the great poet Ovid,³⁹⁷ who never

---

³⁹⁵ wine of Monviedro] i.e. wine from Sagunto, in the region of Valencia.
³⁹⁶ Antipater of Sidon was a Greek poet from the second-century BC. Towards the end of his life he moved to Rome, where he gained a reputation as a skilful improviser. He is mentioned by Cicero in his *De oratore*, and also by Petrarch in his *Index*.
³⁹⁷ The *Index* does not say anything about Ovid — the famous Roman poet,

spoke but in verse? Ay, it is he, the very same: we shall have the devil turn poet too shortly, he does but talk idly in his sleep; and thou think'st the poor man is turned poet.
Calisto. This pain, this martyrdom.
Oh heart, well dost thou prove,
Since thou so soon wast won
To Melibea's love.
Parmeno. (Lo, did I not tell thee he was turned true rhymer?)
Calisto. Who is that, that talks in the hall? Why, ho?
Parmeno. Anon, sir.
Calisto. How far night is it? Is it time to go to bed?
Parmeno. It is rather, sir, too late to rise.
Calisto. What sayst thou fool? Is the night passed and gone then?
Parmeno. Ay, sir, and a good part of the day too.
Calisto. Tell me, Sempronio, does not this idle-headed knave lie in making me believe it is day?
Sempronio. Put Melibea, sir, a little out of your mind, and you will then see that it is broad day; for through that great brightness and splendour which you contemplate in her clear shining eyes, like a partridge dazzled with a buffet, you cannot see, being blinded with so sudden a flash.[398]
Calisto. Now I believe it, and 'tis far day too. Give me my clothes; I must go to my wonted retirement to the myrtle-grove, and there beg of Cupid,[399] that he will direct Celestina and put my remedy into Melibea's heart, or else that he will shorten my sorrowful days.
Sempronio. Sir, do not vex yourself so much. You cannot do all that you would in an hour, nor is it discretion for a man to desire that earnestly that may unfortunately fall upon him. If you will have that concluded in a day which is well if it be effected in a year, your life cannot be long.

---

and author *inter alia* of the *Metamorphoses* — as an improviser of poetry. However, Ovid himself recalled his natural facility with verse, 'et quod temptabam scribere versus erat' ('whatever I tried to write was verse') in *Tristia* IV.10.26.

[398] buffet] translates 'calderuela', i.e. a lamp used as a flash to blind and hunt for partridges and other fowl at night (Lobera *et al.*, eds, 2000, p. 196, n. 74).

[399] 'Iré a la Madalena, rogaré a Dios...' (Lobera *et al.*, eds, 2000, p. 196). Mabbe translates the church of Mary Magdalen into a myrtle-grove and God into Cupid; see also 11.3, 11.15, 12.300–01.

Calisto. I conceive your meaning; you would infer that I am like squire *Gallego*'s boy,[400] who went a year without breeches, and when his master commanded a pair to be cut out for him, he would have them made in a quarter of an hour.

Sempronio. Heaven forbid, sir, I should say so. For you are my master, and I know besides that as you will recompense me for my good counsel, so you will punish me if I speak amiss; though it be a common saying, that the commendation of a man's good service, or good speech, is not equal to the reprehension and punishment of that which is either ill done or spoken.

Calisto. I wonder, Sempronio, where thou got so much philosophy?

Sempronio. Sir, all that is not white which differs from black, nor is all that gold which glisters. Your accelerated, and hasty desires, not being measured by reason, make my counsels to seem better than they be. Would you that they should yesterday, at the first word, have brought Melibea manacled and tied to her girdle, as you would have sent into the market for any other merchandize? Wherein there is no more to do, than to go into the market, and take the pains to buy it.[401] Sir, be of good cheer, give some ease and rest to your heart; for no great happiness can happen in an instant. It is not one stroke that can fell an oak; prepare yourself for sufferance, for wisdom is a laudable blessing, and he that is prepared may withstand a strong encounter.

Calisto. Thou hast spoken well, if the quality of my evil would consent to take it so.

Sempronio. To what end serves understanding, if the will shall rob reason of her right?

Calisto. Oh thou fool, thou fool! The sound man says to the sick: 'heaven send thee thy health'. I will no more counsel, no more hearken to thy reasons: for, they do but revive and kindle those

---

[400] squire *Gallego*'s boy] 'El mozo del escudero gallego', i.e. 'The Galician squire's boy'. Mabbe expands the original, and clarifies the significance of the Spanish saying.

[401] A significant trope that construes Melibea as one of those communicable goods that are mentioned elsewhere in the text (see the note to 2.16 above). Tropes related to trade, merchandise, as well as communication and its cognates abound in the original. Frequently Mabbe amplifies or emphasizes them (see, for instance, my notes to 7.413 and 8.189).

flames afresh, which burn and consume me. I will go and invocate Cupid;[402] and will not come home till you call me and crave a reward of me for the good news you shall bring me, upon the happy coming of Celestina; nor will I eat anything, till Phoebus his horses shall feed and graze their fill in those green meadows where they use to bait,° when they come to their journey's end.

Sempronio. Good sir, leave off these circumlocutions; leave off these poetical fictions: for that speech is not comely which is not common unto all, which all men partake not of as well as yourself, of which few do but understand. Say: 'till the sun set', and everyone will know what you mean. Come, eat in the meanwhile some conserves or the like confection that you may keep some life in you till I return.

Calisto. Sempronio, my faithful servant, my good counsellor, my loyal follower: be it as thou wilt have it, for I assure myself (out of the unspottedness of thy pure service) that my life is as dear unto thee as thine own.

Sempronio. (Dost thou believe it, Parmeno? I wot well that thou wilt not swear it. Remember, if you go for the conserves, that you nim° a barrel for those you wot of; you know who I mean. And to a good understanding everything will light in his lap: or — as the phrase is — fall into his codpiece.)[403]

Calisto. What say'st thou, Sempronio?

Sempronio. I speak, sir, to Parmeno, that he should run quickly and fetch you a slice of conserves, of citron, or of lemon.

Parmeno. Lo, sir, here it is.

Calisto. Give it me hither.

Sempronio. (See, how fast it goes down! I think the devil makes him make such quick work. Look, if he does not swallow it whole, that he may the sooner have done.)

Calisto. My spirits are returned unto me again; I promise you it hath done me much good. My sons both, farewell. Go look after the old woman and wait for good news that I may reward you for your labour.

---

[402] In the original Calisto declares his intention to go mass ('Yo me voy solo a misa', Lobera *et al.*, eds, 2000, p. 198), which Mabbe translates as an invocation to the God of Love. The Alnwick manuscript was, as usual, closer to the original: 'I will goe alone by my selfe to *Masse*' (Martínez Lacalle, ed., p. 204).
[403] I.e. Sempronio advises Parmeno to hide the filched food inside his breeches.

Parmeno. So, now he is gone.[404] The devil and ill fortune follow thee, for in the very same hour hast thou eaten this citron, as Apuleius did that poison which turned him into an ass.[405]

---

[404] This *de facto* stage direction is Mabbe's.
[405] A reference to Apuleius's novel *Asinus Aureus* (*The Golden Ass*) whose protagonist is transformed into an ass after rubbing his body with a magic ointment. Parmeno mistakes the author of the novel, Apuleius (born *c*. AD 125), for the protagonist and first-person narrator, Lucius.

JOSÉ MARÍA PÉREZ FERNÁNDEZ

Actus IX
The Argument

Sempronio and Parmeno go talking each with other to Celestina's house; being come thither, they find there Elicia and Areusa. They sit down to dinner; being at dinner, Elicia and Sempronio fall out; being risen from table, they grow friends again. In the meanwhile comes Lucrecia, servant to Melibea, to call Celestina to come and speak with Melibea.

INTERLOCUTORS
Sempronio, Parmeno, Celestina, Elicia, Areusa, Lucrecia

Sempronio. Parmeno, I pray thee bring down our cloaks, and our rapiers, for I think it be time for us to go to dinner.

Parmeno. Come, let us go presently, for I think they will find fault with us for staying so long. Let us not go through this but that other street, that we may go in by the Vestals, so shall we see whether Celestina have ended her devotions, and take her along with us.[406]

Sempronio. What? Do you think to find her at her theme now? Is this a fit hour? This a time for her to be at her orisons?[407]

10 *Parmeno.* That can never be said out of time, which ought to be done at all times.[408]

Sempronio. It is true, but I see you know not Celestina. When she has anything to do she never thinks upon heaven, the devil a whit that she cares then for devotion. When she hath anything in the house to gnaw upon, farewell all holiness, farewell all prayers; and indeed, her going to any of these ceremonies is but to spy and pry only upon advantages for such persons as she may prevaricate and make for her profit. And though she bred thee up, I am better acquainted with her qualities than you are.

---

[406] In the original, Parmeno and Sempronio search for Celestina in church, not 'by the Vestals': 'por que nos entremos por la iglesia, y veremos si hobiere acabado Celestina sus devociones' (Lobera *et al.*, eds, 2000, p. 201).
[407] orisons] prayers.
[408] Another adage from Petrarch's *Index* (which also features in his *De remediis* II.48; see Lobera *et al.*, eds, 2000, p. 201, n. 5), used here with obvious sarcastic overtones.

That which she doth ruminate: how many cracked maidenheads she hath then in cure, how many lovers in this city, how many young wenches are recommended unto her, what stewards afford her provision, which is the more bountiful, and how she may call every man by his name that when she chanceth to meet them she may not salute them as strangers. When you see her lips go, then is the inventing of lies, and devising of sleights and tricks for to get money. Then doth she thus dispute with herself: 'in this manner will I make my speech', 'in this fashion will I cloze° with him', 'thus then will he answer me', 'and to this I must thus reply'. Thus lives this creature, whom we so highly honour.

Parmeno. Tush, this is nothing; I know more than this. But because you were angry the other day, when I told Calisto so much, I will forbear to speak of it.

Sempronio. Though we may know so much for our own good, yet let us not publish it to our own hurt; for to have our master to know it were but to make him discard her for such a one as she is, and not to care for her; and so leaving her, he must needs have another of whose pains we shall reap no profit, as we shall be sure to do by her, who by fair means or by foul shall give us part of her gains.

Parmeno. Well, and wisely hast thou spoken; but hush, the door is open, and she in the house. Call before you go in; peradventure they are not yet fully ready; or things are not in that order as they would have it, and then will they be loth to be seen.

Sempronio. Go in, man, never stand upon those niceties, for we are all of a house. Now, just now, they are covering the table.

Celestina. Oh my young amorous youths, my pearls of gold! Let the year go about as well with me as you are both welcome unto me.

Parmeno. (What compliments has the old bawd! Brother, I make no question, but you well enough perceive her foistings°, and her flatteries.

Sempronio. Oh, you must give her leave, it is her living. But I wonder what devil taught her all her knacks and her knaveries.

Parmeno. What? Marry, I will tell you: necessity, poverty, and hunger, than which there are no better tutors in the world, no better quickeners, and revivers of the wit. Who taught your pies° and your parrots to imitate our proper language, and tone, with their slit tongues, save only necessity?)

Celestina. Hola! Wenches! Girls! Where be you, fools? Come down! Come hither quickly, I say! For there are a couple of young gallants that would ravish me!

Elicia. Would they would never have come hither for me! Oh, it is a fine time of day! Is this a fit hour, when you have invited your friends, to a feast? You have made my cousin to wait here these three long hours: but this same lazy-gut Sempronio was the cause, I warrant you, of all this stay, for he has no eyes to look upon me.

Sempronio. Sweetheart, I pray thee be quiet. My life, my love! You know full well that he that serves another is not his own man. He that is bound must obey. So that my subjection frees me from blame. I pray thee be not angry. Come, let us sit down, and fall to our meat.

Elicia. Ay, it is well, you are ready at all times to sit down and eat, as soon as the cloth is laid, with a clean pair of hands but a shameless face.

Sempronio. Come, we will chide and brawl after dinner: now let us fall to our victuals. Mother Celestina, will it please you to sit down first?

Celestina. No, first sit you down (my son) for here is room enough for us all. Let every one take their place as they like and sit next whom he loves best. As for me, who am a sole woman, I will sit me down here by this jar of wine, and this good goblet. For I can live no longer than while I talk with one of these two. Ever since that I was grown in years I know no better office at board than to fall a-skinking,[409] and to furnish the table with pots and flagons. For he that handles honey, shall feel it still clinging to his fingers. Besides, in a cold winter's night you cannot have a better warming-pan. For, when I toss off two of these little pots, when I am even ready to go into my bed, why, I feel not a jot of cold all the night long. With this, I fur all my clothes at Christmas. This warms my blood, this keeps me still in one estate, this makes me merry wherever I go, this makes me look fresh and ruddy as a rose. Let me still have store of this in my house and a fig for a dear year.[410] It

---

[409] to fall a-skinking] to pour or serve drinks.
[410] a dear year] a year of dearth.

shall never hurt me, for one crust of mouse-eaten bread will serve me three whole days. This drives away all care and sorrow from the heart better than either gold or coral. This gives force to a young man and vigour to an old woman. It adds colour to the discoloured, courage to the coward, diligence to the slothful. It comforteth the brain, it expels cold from the stomach, it takes away the stinking of the breath, it makes cold constitutions to be potent and active, it makes husbandmen endure the toil of tillage, it makes your painful and weary mowers to sweat out all their watrish ill humours, it remedies rheums and cures the toothache. This may you keep long at sea without stinking, so can you not water. I could tell you more properties of this wholesome liquor than all of you have hairs on your head. So that I know not the man whom it doth not delight to hear it but mentioned, the very name of it is so pleasing. Only it has but this one fault: that that which is good costs us dear, and that which is bad does us hurt. So that what maketh the liver sound, the same maketh the purse light. But for all this I will be sure to seek after the best, for that little which I drink, which is only some dozen times a meal. Which number I never pass, unless now when I am feasted, or so.

Parmeno. It is the common opinion of all: that thrice in a dinner is good, honest, competent, and sufficient for any man. And all that do write thereof do allow you no more.

Celestina. Son, the phrase is corrupted: they have put three times, instead of thirteen.[411]

Sempronio. Aunt, we all like well of your gloss. Let us eat, and talk, and talk and eat. For else we shall not afterwards have time to discourse of the love of our lost master, and of that fair, handsome, and courteous Melibea, lovely gentle Melibea.

Elicia. Get thee out of my sight, thou distasteful companion, thou disturber of my mirth; the devil choke thee with that thou hast eaten. Thou hast given me my dinner for today. Now as I live I am ready to rid my stomach and to cast up all that I have in my body, to hear that thou shouldst call her fair and courteous, lovely, and gentle. I pray thee how fair, how lovely, how courteous, how gentle is she? It angers me to the heart-blood to see

---

[411] Celestina turns to philological analysis to justify her heavy drinking. Mabbe expands the metaphor into Sempronio's retort, in which he approves of Celestina's gloss.

you have so little shame with you. How gentle, how fair is she, more than other women? Believe me, if she be as thou reportest her, nay, if she have any jot in her of beauty, or any the least gracefulness. But I see there are some eyes that make no difference betwixt Ione[412] and my lady, and that it is with every one as he likes, as the good man said, when he kissed his cow. Draff[413] I perceive is good enough for swine. I will cross myself in pity of thy great ignorance, and want of judgement. Who I pray, had any mind to dispute with you, touching her beauty, and her gentleness? Gentle Melibea? Fair Melibea? And is Melibea so gentle, is she so fair as you make her to be? Then it must be so; and then shall both these hit right in her, when two Sundays come together . . .[414] All the beauty she hath may be bought at every peddler's or painter's shop for a pennymatter, or the like trifle. And believe me, I myself, upon mine own knowledge, know that in that very street where she dwells there are four maidens at the least, if not more, to whom Nature hath imparted a greater part of beauty and other good graces in greater abundance than she hath on Melibea; and if she have any jot of handsomeness in her, she may thank her good clothes, her neat dressings, and costly jewels, which if they were hung upon a post, thou wouldst as well say by that too, that it were fair and gentle. And by my fay (be it spoken without ostentation) I think my penny to be as good silver as hers, and that I am every way as fair as your Melibea.

Areusa. Oh sister! Hadst thou seen her as I have seen her (I tell thee no lie) if thou shouldst have met her fasting, thy stomach would have taken such a loathing, that all that day thou wouldst not have been able to have eaten any meat. All the year long, she is mewed up at home, where she is daubed over

---

[412] Ione] the *OED* defines Ione as 'a generic name for a female rustic'; Mabbe's use of it here (with no equivalent in the original) is somewhat obscure; perhaps Elicia complains that Sempronio is so blind that he cannot distinguish between Melibea and a female rustic — and will fall for both, as some kiss their cows, and as swine enjoy draff. There is also possibly an allusion to Io who was turned into a heifer by Jupiter to divert the wrath of his jealous wife, Juno.

[413] draff] wash or swill given to swine.

[414] when two Sundays come together] Mabbe's translation of the proverbial 'cuando andan a pares los diez mandamientos', an obscure expression on whose meaning there is some controversy (see Lobera *et al.*, eds, 2000, p. 206, n. 57, and their long note, p. 668).

with a thousand sluttish slibber-slabbers; all which, forsooth, she must endure, for once perhaps going abroad in a twelvemonth to be seen: she anoints her face with gall and honey, with parched grapes and figs crushed and pressed together, with many other things, which for manners sake, and reverence of the table, I omit to mention. It is their riches that make such creatures as she to be accounted fair; it is their wealth that causeth them to be thus commended, and not the graces and goodly features of their bodies. For she has such breasts, being a maid, as if she had been the mother of three children, and are for all the world like nothing more than two great pompions°, or big bottled-gourds.[415] Her belly I have not seen, but judging by the rest I verily believe it to be as slack and as flaggy[416] as a woman of fifty years old. I know not what Calisto should see in her, that for her sake he should forsake the love of others whom he may with great ease obtain and far more pleasure enjoy, unless it be, that like the palate that is distasted, he thinketh sour things the sweetest.

Sempronio. Sister, it seemeth here unto me, that every peddler praises his own needles; but I assure you, the quite contrary is spoken of her throughout the whole city.

Areusa. There is nothing farther from the truth than the opinion of the vulgar, and nothing more false than the reports of the multitude, nor shall thou ever live a merry life, if thou govern thyself by the will of the common people. And these conclusions are uncontrollable, and infallibly true: that whatsoever thing the vulgar thinks is vanity, whatsoever they speak is falsehood, what they reprove, that is good, what they approve, that is bad. And since this is a true rule and common custom amongst them, do not judge Melibea's either goodness or beauty by that which they affirm.

Sempronio. Gentlewomen, let me answer you in a word. Your ill-tongued multitude, and prattling vulgar, never pardon the faults of great persons, no, not of their sovereign himself, which makes me to think that if Melibea had so many defects as you tax her withal, they would e're this have been discovered by those who know her better than we do. And howbeit I

---

[415] The *OED* only documents this compound (under the entry for *bottle* n.) in 1861, with the form *bottle-gourd*.
[416] flaggy] soft and flabby.

should admit all you have spoken to be true, yet pardon me if
I press you with this particular. Calisto is a noble gentleman,
Melibea the daughter of honourable parents,⁴¹⁷ so that it is
usual with those that are descended of such a high lineage to
seek and enquire each after other; and therefore it is no marvel
if he rather love her than another.

Areusa. Let him be base that holds himself base; they are the
noble actions of men that make men noble. For in conclusion,
we are all of one making: flesh and blood all. Let every man
strive to be good of himself, and not go searching for his virtue
in the nobleness of his ancestors.

Celestina. My good children, as you love me, cease this contentitous kind of talk. And you Elicia, I pray you come to the table
again, sit you down, I say, and do not vex and grieve yourself
as you do.

Elicia. With this condition, that my meat may be my poison and
that my belly may burst with that I eat. Shall I sit down and
eat with this wicked villain, that hath stoutly maintained it to
my face, and nobody must say him nay, that Melibea, that
dish-clout° of his, is fairer than I?

Sempronio. I prithee, sweet-heart, be quiet, it was you that made
the comparison; and comparisons, you know, are odious: and
therefore it is you that are in the fault, and not I.

Areusa. Come, sister, come, and sit with us. I pray, come eat with
us. Have you no more wit, than to be angry with such a cross
fool as he? I would not do him so much pleasure, as to forbear
my meat for him; let him go hang, if he be peevish, will you be
peevish too? I pray you sit down, unless you will have me
likewise to rise from the table.⁴¹⁸

Elicia. The necessity which I have imposed upon myself, to please
thee in all things, and in all thy request, makes me against my
will, to give contentment to this enemy of mine; and to carry
myself out of my respect to this good company more fairly
towards him, than otherwise I would.

Sempronio. Ha, ha, he.

---

⁴¹⁷ 'Calisto es caballero, Melibea hijadalgo'; see Lobera *et al.*, eds, 2000, p. 208, n. 71. See also the note to Argument 4 above.

⁴¹⁸ Mabbe's very expanded translation of the much shorter original, which reads: 'Ven, hermana, a comer; no hagas agora ese placer a estos locos porfiados. Si no, levantarme he yo de la mesa' (Lobera *et al.*, eds, 2000, p. 209).

Elicia. What dost thou laugh at? Now the evil canker eat and consume that unpleasing and offensive mouth of thine.

Celestina. Son, I pray thee no more. Do not answer her, for then we shall never make an end. This is nothing to the present purpose. Let us follow our business, and attend that which may tend to our good. Tell me, how does Calisto? How happed it you left him thus all alone? How fell it out, that both of you could slip away from him?

Parmeno. He flung from us with a vengeance, fretting and fuming like a madman, his eyes sparkling forth fire, his mouth venting forth curses, despairful, discontented in mind, and like one that is half besides himself, and is now gone to Saint Mary Magdalens, to desire of God that thou mayst well and truely gnaw the bones of these chicken, vowing never to come home till he hears that thou art come with Melibea in thy lap.[419] Thy gown and kirtle, and my cassock are cocksure. For the rest let the world slide. But when we shall have it, that I know not, all the craft is in the catching.

Celestina. Let it come when it will come, it shall be welcome, whenever it comes. A cassock is good wear after winter. And sleeves are good after Easter. Everything makes the heart merry that is gotten with ease and without any labour, especially coming from thence, where it leaves so small a gap, and from a man of that wealth and substance, who with the very bran and scraps of his house would make me of a beggar to become rich. Such is the surplus and store of his goods. And such as he, it never grieves them what they spend, considering the cause wherefore they give, for they feel it not. When they are in the heat and passion of their love, it pains them not: they neither see nor hear; which I judge to be true by others that I have known to be less passionate and less scorched in the fiery flames of love than Calisto is. In so much, that I have seen them neither eat nor drink, neither laugh nor weep, neither sleep nor wake, neither speak nor hold their peace, neither live in pain, nor yet find ease, neither be contented, nor yet complain of discontentment, answerable to the perplexity of that sweet and cruel wound of their hearts. And if natural necessity forceth them to any one of these, they are so wholly forgetful of

---

[419] This literal translation, with the explicit reference to the church of St Mary Magdalen, proves Mabbe's inconsistent paganization of the original text.

themselves, and struck into such sudden senselessness of their present being and condition, that eating, their hands forget to carry their meat to their mouths. Besides, if you talk with them, they never answer you directly. Their bodies are there with you, but where they love there are their hearts and their senses. Great is the force of love. His power doth not only reach over the earth, but passeth also over the seas. He holds an equal command over all mankind. He breaks through all kind of difficulties and dangers whatsoever. It is a tormentful thing, full of fear, and of care. His eye rolls every way, nothing can escape him.[420] And if any of you that be here were ever true lovers and did love faithfully indeed, he will say I speak the truth.

Sempronio. Mother, you and I are both of a mind. For here is she present who caused me once to become another Calisto, desperate and senseless in my doings, weary in my body, idle in my brain, sleeping ill adays, and watching too well a nights, up by break of day, playing the fool with thousands of gesticulations, and odd antic tricks, leaping over walls, putting my life every day in haphazard and manifold dangers, standing in harm's way before bulls, running-horses, throwing the bar, tossing the pike, tiring out my friends, cracking of blades, making ladders of ropes, putting on armour, and a thousand other idle acts of a lover, making ballads, penning of sonnets, painting mottoes, making purposes and other the like devices. All which I hold well spent and think myself happy in them, sithence they gained me so great and fair a jewel.

Elicia. You do well to persuade yourself so. But howsoever you conceit you have gained me, I assure thee, thy back is no sooner turned but another is presently with me, whom I love better than thee and is a properer man than thou art, and one that will not go vexing and angering me as thou dost. It is a year ere your worship, forsooth, can find in your heart to come and see me, and then as good have your room, as your company, unless it were better.

Celestina. Son, give her leave to ease her stomach, let her speak her mind, for the wench, (I think) is mad. And the more she

---

[420] 'Great is the force of love [. . .] nothing can escape him': this tirade of proverbs on love have been documented in Petrarch's *Index* (Lobera *et al.*, eds, 2000, p. 210, n. 94).

talks thus lavishly and wildly, assure thyself, she is the more confirmed in thy love. All this stir is because you commended Melibea so highly, and she, poor soul, knows not how to be even with you but to pay you home in this coarse kind of coin, and hard language. And I believe, I shall not see her eat yet a while, for a thing that I know. And this other her cousin here, I know her meaning well enough. Go to, my masters, take the benefit of your youth, enjoy the flower of this your fresh and lively age. For he that will not when he may, when he would he shall have nay. And repentance shall be the recompense of his tarriance, who hath time and will not take it, as I myself do not repent me of those hours which I sometimes lost when I was young, when men did esteem of me, and when they loved me. For now, the worse luck mine, I am a decayed creature, I wax old, withered, and full of wrinkles. Nobody will now look after me, yet my mind is still the same and want rather ability than desire. Fall to your flap,° my masters, kiss and clip.[421] As for me, I have nothing else to do but to look on and please mine eye. It is some comfort to me yet to be a spectator of your sports. Never stand upon nice terms, for whil'st you sit at board, it is lawful to do anything from the girdle upwards. All play above board is fair and pardonable; when you are alone by yourselves, close together at it in a corner, I will not clap a fine on your heads, because the king doth not impose any such taxation. And as for these young wenches, I know, they will never accuse you of ravishment. And as for old Celestina, because her teeth will be on edge, she will mumble with her dull and empty gums the crumbs off the napkins.

Elicia. Mother, somebody knocks at the door.

Celestina. Daughter, look who it is.

Elicia. Either the voice deceives me, or else it is my cousin Lucrecia.

Celestina. Open the door and let her come in, for she also understands somewhat touching that point whereof we discoursed last; though being shut up so close at home, as she is, she is mightily hindered in the fruition of her friculation,[422] and cannot enjoy her youth with the like liberty as others do.

---

[421] clip] embrace.
[422] friculation] copulation, or intercourse. Not in the *OED*. Probably related to *fricatrice* ('a lewd woman', *OED*) and *frication* ('The action of rubbing the

350 *Areusa.* Now I see it is most true that these same chamber-maids, these forsooth that wait upon ladies, enjoy not a jot of delight nor are acquainted with the sweet rewards of love. They never converse with their kindred, nor with their equals, with whom they may say 'thou for thou'; or 'so hail fellow, well met', as to ask in familiar language 'wench, what hast thou to supper?' 'Art thou with child yet?' 'How many hens dost thou keep at home?' 'Shall we go make our bever[423] at thy house? Come, let us go laugh and be merry there'. 'Sirrah, show me thy sweetheart, which is he?' 'Oh wonderful!' 'How long is it since I saw
360 thee last?' 'How is it with thee, wench? How hast thou done this great while?' 'Tell me, I pray thee, who are thy neighbours now?' And a thousand other the like unto these. Oh aunt! How hard a name it is, how troublesome, and how proud a thing to carry the name of a lady up and down continually in one's mouth![424] And this makes me to live of myself ever since I came to years of understanding and discretion. For I could never endure to be called by any other name, than mine own; especially by these ladies we have nowadays. A wench may wait upon them, and spend in their service the better part of their
370 time, and with an old cast-gown, which hath scarce e're a whole piece in it, they make payment of ten years' service. They will revile their maids and call them all to naught. They will use them extreme hardly and keep them in such awe and continual slavery that they dare as well be hanged as to speak but one word before them. And when they see the time draw on that they be ready and ripe for marriage and that they should both in reason and conscience do them some good that ways, they take occasion to wrangle and fall out with them, and falsely to object unto them, that they have trod their shoe awry,[425] either
380 with some one of her ladyship's servants, or with her son, or

---

surface of one body against that of another', *OED*). See 'Fricatrice' in William Gordon, *A Dictionary of Sexual Language and Imagery in Shakespearean and Stuart Literature*, 3 vols (London: The Athlone Press, 1994).

[423] bever] Mabbe's translation of *merienda*, i.e. a small snack between meals.
[424] Note that one of the consequences, and an index, of submission to a lady is the exclusion from conversational exchanges with one's peers, like those described here by Areusa. Note the similarity between this description, and Celestina's similar arguments when she is persuading Parmeno to establish a community of interests with Sempronio towards the end of act I.
[425] trod their shoe awry] fallen from virtue, broken the law of chastity.

put jealousies betwixt her and her husband, or that they bring men privily into her house, or that they have stolen such a goblet, or lost such a ring. For which they will not stick to strip them, and lamme[426] them soundly, bestowing perhaps 100 stripes upon them, and afterwards thrust them out of doors with their hair about their ears, and their fardles at their backs, rating them in most vile manner, crying: 'Out of my doors, you thief, you whore, you strumpet, this is no place for such paltry baggages. Thou shalt not spoil my house, I will not be thus dishonoured by thee'. So that instead of expected recompense, they receive nothing but bitter revilements. Where they expect to go preferred out of the house, they go prejudiced out of the house. And where they expect to be well married, they are quite marred in their reputation. And where they expect jewels and wedding apparel, there are they sent out naked and disgraced. These are their rewards, these their benefits, and these the payments they receive for their service. They are bound to give them husbands, and in lieu thereof, they strip them of their clothes. The greatest grace and honour which they have in their ladies' house is to be employed in walking the streets from one lady to another, and to deliver their ladies' message, as: 'My lady hath sent to know how you do?' How you did rest tonight?' 'How your physic wrought with you, and how many occasions it gave your ladyship?', &c. They never hear their own name out of their ladies' mouth, but the best they can call them by is 'Come hither, you whore', 'Get you gone, you drab, or I'll set you going', 'Whither gad you now, you mangy harlotry, you pocky slut', 'What have you done today, you loitering quean?' 'Why did you eat this, you ravening thing, you gorbelly,° you greedy cormorant?'[427] 'Ah you, filthy sow, how clean this frying pan is kept? This pisspot, minion, it is well scoured, is it not?' 'Why, you lazy bones, did you not brush my clothes, when I left them off, and make clean my mantle?', 'Why said you thus and thus, you sot, you foolish ass?' 'Who lost the piece of plate, you scattergood, you draggle-tail?'[428] 'What's

---

[426] lamme] beat soundly, trash.
[427] cormorant] a sea-bird thought of as large and voracious; see note to 5.103 above.
[428] draggle-tail] 'A draggle-tailed person; a woman whose skirts are wet and draggled, or whose dress hangs about her untidily and dirty; a slut' (*OED*).

become of my handkerchief, you purloining thief? You have given it to one of your copemates,[429] some sweet-heart of yours, that must help to make you a whore', 'Come hither, you foul flaps,[430] say, where is my hen, my crammed hen, that I cannot find her? You were best look her me out, and that quickly too, unless you mean I shall make you pay for her, when I come to pay you your wages'. And besides all this, her pantofles shall walk about her ears a thousand times a day; pinchings, cudgelings, and scourgings shall be as common to her as her meat and drink. There is not any that knows how to please and content them; not any that can endure their tartness and cursedness. Their delight is to speak loud, their glory to chide and to brawl, and the better one does, and the more one seeks to please them, the less are they contented. And this, mother, is the reason why I have rather desired to live free from controlment,° and to be mistress in a poor little house of mine own, than to live a slave, and at command in the richest palace of the proudest lady of them all.

Celestina. Thou art in the right, my girl. I will take no care for you, you will shift for yourself. I perceive you know what you do, you need not to be told on which side your bread is buttered, you are no baby, I see. And wise men tell us, that better is a crust of bread and a cup of cold water with peace and quietness, than a houseful of dainties, with brabbling[431] and wrangling. But now let us leave this argument, for here comes Lucrecia.

Lucrecia. Much good to you, good aunt, and to all this fair company and great meeting.

Celestina. So great, daughter? Hold you this so great a meeting? It appears that you have not known me in my prosperity, which is now some twenty years since. There be those that have seen me in better case than I am now. And he that now sees

---

[429] copemates] 'A partner or colleague in power, office, etc.; an associate, companion, comrade' (*OED*).

[430] flaps] *OED* defines a 'flap' as 'A woman or girl of light or loose character'; three examples are quoted, two of which come from *The Spanish Bawd*, whereas the third one dates from 1892.

[431] brabbling] quarrelling.

me, I wonder his heart doth not burst with sorrow. I tell thee, wench, I have seen at this table, where your kinswomen now sit, nine gallant young wenches, much about your age, for the eldest was not above eighteen, and not one of them under fourteen. But such is this world, it comes and goes upon wheels. We are like pots in a water-wheel, or like buckets in a well: one up, and another down, one full, and another empty. It is fortune's law that nothing can continue any long time in one and the selfsame state of being. Her order is alteration, her custom, change. I cannot without tears deliver unto you the great honour I then lived in; though now, such is my ill fortune, by little and little it hath gone decaying. And as my days declined, so diminished and decreased my profit. It is an old saying, that whatsoever is in this world, it doth either increase or decrease. Everything hath its limits; everything its degrees of more or less: my honour did mount to that height as was fitting for a woman of my quality to rise unto, and now of force it must descend and fall as much. By this I know, that I am near to my end, and that the lease of my life is now expiring, and all my years are almost spent and gone. And I also well know, that I did ascend that I might descend, that I flourished for to wither; that I had joy that I might have sorrow, that I was born to live, lived to grow, grew to grow old, and grow old to die. And though it did always appear unto me that I ought in this respect to suffer my misery the more patiently, yet as I am formed of flesh and blood, and bear this heavy mass of sin about me, I cannot but think on it now and then with grief, nor can I wholly as I would blot every thought thereof out of the woeful roll of my wretched remembrance.

Lucrecia. Methinks, mother, it could not choose but be wondrous troublesome unto you to have the charge of so many young wenches. For they are very dangerous cattle to keep, and will ask a great deal of pains.

Celestina. Pains, sweet-heart? Nay, they were an ease, and pleasure unto me. They did all of them obey me, they did all of them honour me, they did all of them reverence me, not one of them that would swerve from my will. What I said stood for a law, it was good and current amongst them. Not any one of them to whom I gave entertainment ever made their own choice any further than it stood with my liking, were he lame, crooked, squint-eyed, or crippled, all was one, he was the welcomest and the soundest that brought me the soundest gains: mine was the profit, and their the pains. Besides, I needed no servants, for in keeping them, I had servants enough. Why, your noblemen, your knights, your old men, your young men, your learned men, men of all sorts and dignities, from the highest to the lowest, why, they were all at my service. And when I came to a feast, my foot was no sooner in, but I had presently as many bonnets vailed unto me, as if I had been a duchess. He that had least acquaintance, least business with me, was held the most vile and basest fellow. They spying me almost a league off, they would forsake their most earnest occasions, one by one, two by two, and come to me to see if I would command them any service, and withal, ask me severally, how his love, how his mistress did? When they saw me once pass by, you should have such a shuffling and scraping of feet, and all in such a general gaze,[432] and so out of order, that they did neither doe nor say anything aright. One would call me mistress, another aunt, others their love, others honest old woman. There they would consent when they should come to my house. There they would agree when I should go unto theirs. There they would offer me money. There they would make me large promises, there likewise present me with gifts, some kissing the lappet of my coat, and some other my cheek, that by these kindnesses they might give me contentment and work me to their will. But now fortune hath brought me to so low a place in her wheel, that you may say unto me, 'mich you good dich you with your old ware, your hinges are now grown rusty for want of oiling'.[433]

Sempronio. Mother, you make my hair stand on end, to hear these strange things, which you recount unto us; would your nobles, your knights, and learned men fall so low? I am sure, they are not all of them so bad as you make them to be.

Celestina. No, my son, Jove forbid that I should raise any such report, or lay a general scandal upon any of their rank. For, there were many old good men amongst them, with whom I

---

[432] In such a general gaze] i.e. in wonder, expectancy, or bewilderment.

[433] mich you good dich you] the *OED* documents a very similar expression, dating from 1630, under *dich* (which it defines as: 'A corrupt or erroneous word, having apparently the sense *do it*'): 'So mich God dich you with your sustenancelesse sauce' (tr. G. Botero, *Relations Famous Kingdomes World*, 87).

had but small dealings, and could scarce endure to see me. But amongst the greatest, as they grew great in number, so had I a great number of them: some of one sort, and some of another, some I found very chaste, and some that took the charge upon them to maintain such traders as myself. And I am still of this belief, that of these there is no lack. And these, forsooth, would send their squires and young men to wait upon me, withersoever I went. And I should scarce have set my foot within mine own doors, but straight at the heels of me, you should have one come in with chicken, another with hens, a third with geese, a fourth with ducks. This man sends me in partridges, that man turtledoves, he a gammon of bacon, such a one a tart, or a custard, and some good fellow or other a good suckling pig or two. For everyone, as soon as he had a convenient present, so they came presently to register them in my house that I and those their pretty souls might merrily eat them together. And as for wine, we wanted none. The best that a man could lay his lips to in the whole city was sent unto me from divers parts and corners of the town: as that of Monviedro, of Luque, of Toro, or Madrigal, or San Martin, and many other towns and villages.[434] And indeed so many that albeit I still keep the differences of their taste and relish in my mouth, yet do I not retain the diversity of their soils in my remembrance. For it is enough for such an old woman as I, that when a good cup of wine comes near my nose, I can be able to say, this is such a wine, or it comes from such a place, or person. Why, your presents from all parts, from all sorts came upon me as thick as hops, as flies to a pot of honey, or as stones that are thrown upon a stage. Boys came tumbling in at my door, with as much provision as they could carry on their backs.[435] But now those good days are past, I have eaten all my white bread in my youth, and know not how in the world to live, being fallen from so happy an estate.

Areusa. Since we are come hither to be merry, good mother, do not weep, I pray, do not vex yourself. Be of good cheer, pluck

---

[434] All these are famous wine-producing regions, some of which (like Toro) still produce excellent wines.

[435] Mabbe expands the original text to clarify the meaning. The original reads: 'Espesos como piedras a tablado entraban mochachos cargados de provisiones por mi puerta' (Lobera *et al.*, eds, 2000, p. 217).

up your heart like a woman. The world while we are in it, is bound to keep us all, and no doubt but you shall have enough.

Celestina. Oh daughter! I have cause enough, I think, to weep, when I call to mind those pleasant days that are past and gone, that merry life which then I led, and how I had the world at will, being served, honoured, and sought to of all. Why, then there was not any new fruit, or any the like dainty, which I had not in my hands before others knew they were scarce blossomed. In those days, they were sure to be found in my house, if any one with child should long for such a toy.

Sempronio. Mother, the remembrance of the good time we have had doth profit us nothing when it cannot be recovered again, but rather brings grief and sorrow to ourselves, as this interrupting discourse hath done. But mother, we will go off and solace ourselves, whilst you stay here: and give this maid her answer.

Celestina. Daughter Lucrecia, passing over our former discourse, I pray you tell me what is the cause of your happy coming hither?

Lucrecia. Believe me, I had almost forgot my chief errand unto you, with thinking on that merry time which you talked of. Methinks I could continue fasting almost a whole year in harkening unto thee, and thinking on that pleasant life, which those young wenches led. Methinks that with the very talking thereof I have a conceit with myself, that at this present, I feel myself in the same happiness with them. I shall now, mistress, give you to understand the cause of my coming: I am sent unto you for my lady's girdle, and moreover, my lady entreats you, that you would come and visit her, and that out of hand, for she feels herself very ill, and much pained and troubled with griefs and pangs about the heart. I assure you, she is very heart-sick.

Celestina. Oh these petty griefs, the report is more than the pain. It's about the heart, say you? I marvel (I promise you) that so young a gentlewoman as she is should be pained at the heart.

Lucrecia. (Would thou were as well dragged along the streets, thou old traitorous hag, as thou know'st well enough what she ails. The subtil old bawd comes, and does her witcheries, and her tricks, and then goes her ways, and afterwards when one comes unto her for help, she makes forsooth as if she knew no such matter, it is news forsooth to her.)

Celestina. What sayst thou, daughter?
Lucrecia. Marry, I say, mother, would we were gone [at] once, and that you would give me the girdle.
Celestina. Come, let us go. I will carry it along with me.

Actus X
The Argument

Whilst Celestina and Lucrecia go onward on their way, Melibea talks and discourses with herself. Being come to the door, first enters Lucrecia, anon after, [she] causes Celestina to come in. Melibea, after some exchange of words, opens her mind to Celestina, telling her how fervently she has fallen in love with Calisto. They spy Alisa, Melibea's mother coming. They take their leave each of other. Alisa asks her daughter Melibea what business she had with Celestina and what she made there, dissuading her from conversing with her and forbidding her her company.

INTERLOCUTORS
Melibea, Celestina, Alisa, Lucrecia

Melibea. Oh wretch that I am! Oh unfortunate damsel! Had I not been better yesterday to have yielded to Celestina's petition and request when in the behalf of that gentleman, whose sight hath made me his prisoner, I was so earnestly sued unto, and to have contented him and cured myself, than to be thus forcibly driven to discover my heart, when haply he will not accept of it? When as already disaffianced[436] in his hope, for want of a good and fair answer, he hath set both his eyes and his heart upon the love and person of another? How much more advantageous unto me would an entreated promise have been than a forced offerture?° To grant being requested, than to yield being constrained? Oh my faithful servant, Lucrecia, what wilt thou say of me, what wilt thou think of my judgment and understanding, when thou shalt see me to publish that, which I would never discover unto thee? How wilt thou stand astonished of my honesty and modesty, which (like a recluse, shut up from all company) I have ever hitherto kept inviolable? I know not whether thou hast suspected or no, whence this my sorrow proceedeth, or whether thou art now coming with that

---

[436] dissafianced] i.e. to put out of affiance, trust, or confidence; the *OED* lists only this example in *The Spanish Bawd* to illustrate the meaning of this verb; also used as a noun in 2.198 above.

20   solicitress of my safety? Oh thou high and supreme power![437] Thou unto whom all that are in misery and affliction call and cry for help, the appassionated beg remedy, the wounded crave healing; thou, whom the heavens, seas, earth, and the centre of hell itself doth obey; thou who submittedst all things unto men ... I humbly beseech thee, that thou wilt give sufferance and patience to my wounded heart whereby I may be able to dissemble my terrible passion. Let not this leaf of my chastity lose its gilding, which I have laid upon this amorous desire, publishing my pain to be otherwise than that, which indeed
30   tormenteth me. But how shall I be able to do it, that poisoned morsel so cruelly tormenting me which the sight of that gentleman's presence gave me? Oh sex of womankind, feeble and frail in thy being! Why was it not granted as well unto women to discover their tormentful and fervent flames, as unto men? For then neither should Calisto have cause to complain, nor I to live in pain.

Lucrecia. Aunt, stay here awhile behind this door, whilst I go in,
40   and see with whom my mistress is talking. Come in, she is talking alone to herself.
Melibea. Lucrecia, make fast the door there and pull down the hanging over it. Oh wise and honest old dame! You are exceeding welcome. What think you, that chance should so dispose of things and fortune so bring about her wheel, that I should stand in need of this wisdom, and crave so suddenly of you that you would pay me in the self-same coin the courtesy which was by you demanded of me for that gentleman whom you were to cure by the virtue of my girdle?
50 *Celestina*. Say, lady, what is your disease, that you so lively express the tokens of your torment in those your maiden blushes?
Melibea. Truly, mother, I think there be some serpents within my body, that are gnawing upon my heart.[438]

---

[437] '¡Oh soberano Dios!' in the original (Lobera *et al.*, eds, 2000, p. 219).
[438] Fiammetta's passion was also kindled by the sting of a serpent; see Boccaccio, *Amorous Fiammetta*, [trans. by Bartholomew Yong] (London: John Charlewood for Thomas Gubbin and Thomas Newman), 1587, 2_r–2_v: 'like as that little hydden Viper did pricke Euridices tender foote, eyen so a lurking and

Celestina. (It is well, even as I would have it. I will be even with you, you fool, for your yesterday's anger, I will make you pay for it with a witness.)

Melibea. What's that you say? Have you perceived by my looks any cause from whence my malady proceedeth?

Celestina. You have not, madam, told me the quality of your disease, and would you have me divine of the cause? That which I say is this, that I am heartily sorry to see your ladyship so sad and so ill.

Melibea. Good old woman, do thou make me merry then. For I have heard much of thy wisdom.

Celestina. Madam, as far as human knowledge can discern of inward grief, I dare presume. And for as much as for the health and remedy of infirmities and diseases, these graces were imparted unto men, for the finding out of fit and convenient medicines, whereof some were attained to by experience, some by art, and some by a natural instinct; some small portion of these good gifts, this poor old creature myself have gotten, who is here present to do you the best service she can.

Melibea. Oh, how acceptable and pleasing are thy words to mine ears! It is a comfortable thing to the sick patient to see his physician to look cheerfully upon him. Methinks I see my heart broken between thy hands in pieces, which with a little labour, and by power and virtue of thy tongue, thou art able (if thou wilt) to joine together and make it whole again, even as easily as Alexander that great king of Macedon dream't of that wholesome root in the mouth of a dragon, wherewith he healed his servant Ptolemy, who had been bitten by a viper.[439] And therefore, for the love of Jove, disrobe yourself that you may more easily and more diligently look into the nature of my disease, and afford me some remedy for it.

---

creeping Serpent did likewyse appeare to my sight, as I lay upon the soft and thicke grasse, the which (me thought) with her cruell tongue sting me vnder the left pappe [. . .] hauing after a good while sucked a great quantitie of my vitall blood, me thought, that [. . .] she went also away wyth my fainting soule'. A few lines later, Melibea describes the symptoms of her disease thus: 'My pain is about my heart, its residence near unto my left pap, but disperseth itself over every part of my body' (10.111–13).

[439] Rojas found the episode of Alexander's dream in Petrarch's *Index* (Lobera *et al.*, eds, 2000, p. 221, n. 21).

Celestina. A great part of health is the desiring of health. And a good sign of mending to be willing to mend. For which reason I reckon your grief is less, and hold it the less dangerous. But that I may minister a wholesome medicine unto you, and such as one as may be agreeable to your disease it is requisite that you first satisfy me in these three particulars. The first is on which side of you body your pain doth lie most? The second, how long you have had this pain, whether it hath taken you but of late, or no? For your newly growing infirmities are sooner cured in the tenderness of their growth, than when they have taken deep rooting by over-long persevering in their office; so beasts are sooner tamed when they are young and more easily brought to the yoke than when their hide is thoroughly hardened; so far better do those plants grow up and prosper which are removed when they are young and tender, than those that are transplanted, having long borne fruit. The third is, whether this your evil hath proceeded of any cruel thought which hath taken hold on you. This being made known, you shall see me set myself roundly to work about your cure; for it is very fit and convenient, that you should open the whole truth, as well to your physician, as your confessor.

Melibea. Friend Celestina, thou wise matron, and great mistress in thy art, thou hast well opened unto me the way by which I may manifest my malady unto thee. Believe me, you have questioned me like a wise woman, and like one that is well experienced in these kind of sicknesses. My pain is about my heart, its residence near unto my left pap, but disperseth itself over every part of my body.[440] Secondly, it hath been so but of late, nor did I ever think that any pain whatsoever could have so deprived me of my understanding as this doth: it troubles my sight, changes my countenance, takes away my stomach, I cannot sleep for it, nor will it suffer me to enjoy any kind of pleasure. Touching the thought, which was the last thing you demanded concerning my disease, I am not able to deliver it unto you, and as little the cause thereof; for neither death of kinsfolk, nor loss of temporal goods, nor any sudden passion upon any vision, nor any doting dream, nor any other thing can I conjecture to be the cause of it, save only a kind of alteration, caused by yourself upon your request, which I suspected

---

[440] See note to 10.54 above.

in the behalf of that gentleman Calisto, when you entreated me for my charm.

Celestina. What, madam? Is Calisto so bad a man? Is his name so bad, that only but to name him should, upon the very sound thereof, send forth such poison? Deceive not yourself. Do not believe that this is the cause of your grief. I have another thing in the wind, there is more in it than so. But since you make it so dainty, if your ladyship will give me leave, I will tell you the cause of it.

Melibea. Why, how now, Celestina, what a strange request is this that thou mak'st unto me? Needest thou to crave leave of me, who am to receive help from thee? What physician did ever demand such security, for to cure his patient? Speak, speak what you please, for you shall always have leave of me to say what you will; always excepted that you wrong not my honour with your words.

Celestina. I see, lady, that on the one side you complain of your grief, and on the other side, I perceive that you fear your remedy, your fear strikes fear into me, which fear causeth silence, and silence truce betwixt your malady and my medicine. So that yourself will be the cause that your pain shall not cease, nor my cunning cure you.

Melibea. By how much the longer you defer my cure, by so much more do you increase my pain and augment my passion. Either thy medicines are of the powder of infamy, and of the juice of corruption, confectionated with some other more cruel pain than that which thy patient already feels, or else thy skill is nothing worth. For if either the one or the other did not hinder thee, thou woulds't tell me of some other remedy boldly and without fear, sithence I entreat thee to acquaint me therewith, my honour full preserved.

Celestina. Madam, think it not strange, that it is harder for him that is wounded to endure the torment of hot-scalding turpentine, and the sharp incisions which gall the heart and double the pain, than the wound that is newly inflicted on him that is whole. And therefore, if you be willing to be cured, and that I should discover unto you the sharp point of my needle, without any fear at all, frame for your hands and feet a bond of patience and of quietness; for your eyes, a veil of pity and compassion; for your tongue a bridle of silence; for your ears, the bombast or stuffing of sufferance and bearing. And then shall you see what effects this old mistress in her art will work upon your wounds.

Melibea. Oh how thou killest me with delays! For God's love, speak what thou wilt, do what thou wilt, exercise thy skill, put thy experience in practice. For there is not any remedy so sharp, as can equal the bitterness of my pain and torment. No, though it touch upon mine honour, tough it wrong my reputation, though it afflict my body, though it rip and break up my flesh for to pull out my grieved heart. I give thee my faith to do what thou wilt securely; and if I may find ease of my pain, I shall liberally reward thee.

Lucrecia. (My mistress hath lost her wits: she is exceeding ill: this same sorceresss hath captivated her will.)

Celestina. (One devil or other is still haunting me. One while here, another while there. I have escaped Parmeno, and have fallen upon Lucrecia.)

Melibea. Mother, what is it you say, what said the wench unto you?

Celestina. I cannot tell, lady, I did not well hear her. But let her say what she will, yet let me tell you that there is not anything more contrary in great cures, before strong and stout-hearted surgeons, than weak and fainting hearts who with their great lamentations, their pitiful words, and their sorrowful gestures strike a fear into the patient, make him despair of his recovery, and anger and trouble the surgeon, which trouble makes him to alter his hand, and direct his needle without any order. By which you may clearly know, that it is very necessary for your safety, that there be nobody about you; no, not so much as Lucrecia. And therefore, it is very meet that you command her absence: daughter Lucrecia, you must pardon me.

Melibea. Get you out quickly, be gone.

Lucrecia. (Well, well, we are all undone.) I go, madam.

Celestina. Your great pain and torment doth likewise put boldness into me, as also that I perceive by your suspicion, you have already swallowed some part of my cure. But notwithstanding, it is needful that we bring a more manifest remedy, and more wholesome mitigation of your pain from the house of that worthy one Calisto.

Melibea. Mother, I pray you, good now hold your peace; fetch not anything from his house that may work my good. If you love me, do not so much as once name him unto me.

Celestina. Madam, I pray be patient. That which is the chief and principal pillar must not be broken. For then all our labour is lost. Your wound is great and hath need of a sharp cure. And hard with hard, doth smooth and mollify more effectually and more delicately. And wise men say that the cure of a lancing surgeon leave behind it the greater scar. And that without danger, no danger is overcome. Have patience then with yourself. For seldom is that cured without pain which in itself is painful. One nail drives out another. And one sorrow expels another. Do not conceive hatred nor disaffection, nor give your tongue leave to speak ill of so virtuous a person, as Calisto, whom, if you did but know him . . .

Melibea. Oh you kill me! No more of him, for God's sake no more. Did not I tell you, that you should not commend him unto me? And that you should not speak a word of him neither good nor bad?

Celestina. Madam, this is that other and main point in my cure which, if you by your impatience will not consent unto, my coming can little profit you. But if you will, as you promised, be patient, you shall remain sound and out of doubt, and Calisto be well apaid, and have no cause to complain. I did before acquaint you with my cures, and with this invisible needle, which before it come at you to stitch up your wound, you feel it, only but having it in my mouth and naming it unto you.

Melibea. So often wilt thou name this gentleman unto me, that neither my promise nor the faith I plighted thee will suffice to make me any longer to endure your words. Wherein should he be well apaid? What do I owe unto him? Wherein am I bound unto him? What charge have I put him to? What hath he ever done for me? What necessity is there, that we must be driven to use him as the instrument of my recovery? More pleasing would it be unto me that you would tear my flesh and sinews asunder, and tear out my heart, than to utter such words as these.

Celestina. Without any rupture, or renting of your garments, love did lance your breast; and therefore [I][441] will not sunder your flesh to cure your sore.

---

[441] Not in the 1631 text. The whole paragraph translates a Spanish proverb that

Melibea. How call you this grief, that hath seized on the better part of my body?
Celestina. Sweet love.
Melibea. Tell me, then, what thing this sweet love may be? For only in the very hearing of it named, my heart leaps for joy.
Celestina. It is a concealed fire, a pleasing wound, a savoury poison, a sweet bitterness, a delightful grief, a cheerful torment, a sweet, yet cruel hurt, and a gentle death.
Melibea. Oh wretched that I am! For if thy relation be true, I rest doubtful of my recovery. For according to the contrariety which these names do carry, that which shall be profitable for one, shall to another bring more passion.
Celestina. Let not your noble youth be diffident of recovery; be of good cheer. Take a good heart to you and doubt not of your welfare, for where heaven gives a wound, there it gives a remedy; and as it hurts, so it heals; and so much the sooner, because I know where the flower grows, that will free you from all this torment.
Melibea. How is it called?
Celestina. I dare not tell you.
Melibea. Speak, and spare not.
Celestina. Calisto. Oh Madam Melibea! Ah woe is me, why woman, what mean you? What a cowardly heart have you? What a fainting is here? Oh miserable that I am, hold up your head, I pray lift it up! Oh accursed old woman! Must my steps end [in][442] this? If she go thus away in a swound,° they will kill me; if she revive, she will be much pained, for she will never endure to publish her pain, nor give me leave to exercise my cure. Why, Melibea, my sweet lady, my fair angel, what's the matter, sweet-heart? Where is your grief? Why speak you not unto me? What is become of your gracious and pleasing speech? Where is that cheerful colour that was wont to beautify your cheeks? Open those brightest lamps that ever nature tinded,° open your eyes, I say, those clear suns that are able to

---

describes the emotional turmoil inflicted without accompanying physical violence: 'Sin te romper las vistiduras se lanzó en tu pecho el amor; no rasgaré yo tus carnes para le curar' (Lobera *et al.*, eds, 2000, p. 226, n. 57, and their long note, p. 681, document it in several sources).

[442] Not in the 1631 text: added by Fitzmaurice-Kelly (p. 181, whom I follow here). Another alternative reading could be 'must my steps end thus?'

280   give light to darkness. Lucrecia, Lucrecia, come hither quickly, come quickly, I say, you shall see your lady lie here in a swound° in my arms; run down quickly for a jar of water.

Melibea. Softly, speak softly I pray; I'll see if I can rise. In no case do not trouble the house.

Celestina. Ay me! Sweet lady, doe not sink any more: speak, speak unto me as you were wont.

Melibea. I will, and much more than I was wont. But peace, I pray, awhile, and do not trouble me.

Celestina. What will you have me to do, my precious pearl? Whence arose this sudden qualm? I believe, my points are broken.[443]

Melibea. No, it is my honesty that is broken, it is my modesty that is broken, my too much bashfulness and shamefastness occasioned my swooning, which being my natural and familiar friends and companions could not sleightly absent themselves from my face, but they would also carry away my colour with them for a while, my strength, my speech, and a great part of my understanding. But now, my good mistress, my faithful secretary, since that which thou so open knowst, it is in vain for me to seek to smother it. Many, yea, many days are now overpassed since that noble gentleman motioned his love unto me, whose speech and name was then as hateful as now the reviving thereof is pleasing unto me. With thy needles thou hast stitched up my wound; I am come to thy bent; it is in thy power to do with me what thou wilt. In my girdle, thou carriedst away with thee the possession of my liberty. His anguish was my greater torment, his pain my greater punishment. I highly praise and comment your singular sufferance, your discreet boldness, your liberal pains, your solicitous and faithful steps, your pleasing speech, your good wisdom, your excessive solicitude, and your profitable importunity. The gentleman is much bound unto you, and myself more; for my reproaches and revilings could never make thee to slack thy courage, thy strong continuance and forcible perseverance in thy suit, relying still on thy great subtlety and strength of wit, or rather bearing thyself like a most faithful and trusty servant, being then most diligent, when thou wast most reviled; the

---

[443] point] translates the Spanish 'puntos', i.e. the metaphorical suture stitches that Celestina has used to heal Melibea's wound.

more I did disgrace thee, the more wast thou importunate; the harsher answer I gave thee, the better didst thou seem to take it: when I was most angry, then wast thou most mild and humble: and now, by laying aside all fear, thou hast gotten that out of my bosom, which I never thought to have discovered unto thee, or to any other whosoever.

Celestina. My most dear both lady and friend, wonder not so much at this, for those ends, that have their effect, give me daringness to endure those craggy and dangerous byways, by which I come to such recluses as yourself. True it is, that until I had resolved with myself, as well on my way hitherwards, as also here in your house, I stood in great doubt whether were I best discover my petition unto you or no. When I did think on the great power of your father, then did I fear; but then withal I weighed the nobleness of Calisto, then I grew bold again; when I observed your discretion, I waxed timorous; but when I considered your virtue, and your courtesy, I recovered new courage: in the one, I found fear, in the other, safety. And since, madam, you have been willing to grace me with the discovery of so great a favour, as now you have made known unto me, declare your will unto me, lay your secrets in my lap, put into my hands the managing of this matter, and I will give it such a form, as both you and Calisto shall very shortly accomplish your desires.

Melibea. Oh my Calisto! My dear lord, my sweet and pleasing joy, if thy heart feel the like torment as mine, I wonder how thy absence gives thee leave to live. Oh thou, both my mother, and mistress, so handle the business that I may presently see him, if you desire I should live.

Celestina. See him? You shall both see him and speak with him.

Melibea. Speak with him? It is impossible.

Celestina. Nothing is impossible to a willing mind.

Melibea. Tell me how.

Celestina. I have it in my head: marry, thus, within the doors of this house.

Melibea. When?

Celestina. This night.

Melibea. Thou shalt be glorious in mine eyes, if thou compass this. But soft, at what hour?

Celestina. Just when the clock strikes twelve.

Melibea. Go, be gone, hie you, good mistress, my faithful friend,

and talk with that gentleman and will him that he come very
softy at this appointed hour, and then we will conclude of
things as himself shall think fit to order them.

Celestina. Farewell. Lo, yonder is your mother making hitherward.
Melibea. My friend Lucrecia, my loyal servant, and faithful
secretary, you have here seen that I have no power over myself,
and what I have done, lies not in my hands to help it. Love
hath made me prisoner to that gentleman. I entreat thee, for
pity's sake, that you will sign what you have seen with the seal
of secrecy, whereby I may come to the enjoying of so sweet a
love. In requital whereof, thou shalt be held by me in that high
regard as thy faithful service deserves.
Lucrecia. Madam, long afore this I perceived your wound, and
sounded your desire. I did much pity your torment; for, the
more you sought to hide from me the fire which did burn you,
the more did those flames manifest themselves in the colour of
your face, in the little quietness of your heart, in the restlessness
of your members, in your tossing to and fro, in eating
without appetite, and in your unableness to sleep. So that I did
continually see from time to time, as plainly as if I had been
with you, most manifest and apparent signs of your wretched
estate. But because in that instant when, as will reigneth in
those whom we serve, or a disordinate appetite, it is fitting for
us that are servants to obey them with bodily diligence and not
to check and control them with the artificial counsels of the
tongue, and therefore did I suffer with pain, held my peace
with fear, concealed with fidelity — though I always held it
better to use sharp counsel than smooth flattery. But since that
your ladyship hath no other remedy for your recovery, but
either to die or to live, it is very meet, that you should make
choice of that for the best, which in itself is best.

Alisa. How now neighbour? What's the matter with you, that you
are here thus day by day?
Celestina. I wanted yesterday a little of my weight in the thread
I sold, and now I am come, according to my promise, for to
make it up. And now that I have delivered it, I am going away.
Jove have you in his good keeping.

Alisa. And you too. Daughter Melibea, what would this old woman have?

400 *Melibea.* She would have sold me a little sublimated mercury.

Alisa. Marry, I rather believe this than that which the old lewd hag told me. She was afraid I would have been angry with her, and so she popped me in the mouth with a lie. Daughter, take heed of her. For she is an old crafty fox, and as false and the devil. A whole country cannot afford you such another treacherous housewife. Take you heed therefore, I say, of her. For your cunning and crafty thieves go always prowling about your richest houses. She knows by her treasons and false merchandise how to change chaste purposes. She causeth an ill
410 report, bringeth a bad name and fame upon those that have anything to do with her. If she be but seen to have entered one house thrice, it is enough to engender suspicion.

Lucrecia. (My old lady's counsel comes too late.)

Alisa. I charge you, daughter, upon my blessing, and by that love which I bear unto you, that if she come hither any more, when I am out of the way, that you do not give her any entertainment, no manner of welcome, no, not so much as to show her the least countenance of liking, lest it should encourage her to come again. Let her find that you stand upon your honesty and
420 reputation. And be you round and short with her in your answers, and she will never come at you again. For true virtue is more feared than a sword.

Melibea. Is she a blade of that making?[444] Is she such a whipster?[445] Is she one of those, you know what? She shall never come at me more. And believe me, madam, I much joy in your good advice, and that you have so well instructed me, of whom I ought to beware.[446]

---

[444] Is she a blade of that making?] Is she made of that sort of mettle?

[445] whipster] wanton and lascivious person.

[446] Mabbe slightly expands the paragraphs that contain Alisa's warning, to emphasize the dramatic effect between the scene just witnessed, in which Melibea finally agrees to meet Calisto, and the stern advice provided by her mother.

Actus XI
The Argument

Celestina having taken her leave of Melibea, goes mumbling and talking along the streets to herself. She spies Sempronio and Parmeno, who are going to Saint Mary Magdalens to look out [for] their master. Sempronio talks with Calisto.[447] In the meanwhile comes in Celestina. They go all to Calisto's house. Celestina delivereth her message, and the means for their meeting appointed by Melibea. In the interim that Celestina and Calisto are discoursing together, Sempronio and Parmeno fall a-talking between themselves. Celestina takes her leave of Calisto, and gets her home to her own house. She knocks at the door. Elicia opens it unto her. They sup, and then go to take their rest.

INTERLOCUTORS
Celestina, Sempronio, Calisto, Parmeno, Elicia

Celestina. Oh thrice happy day! Would I were at home with all my joy, wherewith I go laden. But I see Parmeno and Sempronio going to the myrtle-grove:[448] I will after them. And if I meet with Calisto there, we will all along together to his house, to demand a reward for the great good news that I bring him.

Sempronio. Take heed, sir, lest by your long stay you give occasion of talk to the world. For your honesty have a care, that you make not yourself become a by-word to the people. For nowadays, it is commonly spoken amongst them, he is an hypocrite that is too devout. For, what will they say of you, if

---

[447] There is an inconsistency here: in 8.296–97, Calisto has declared that he was going to pray in a myrtle-grove: the argument here is more faithful to the original (11.3 and 11.12–15 below also mention the myrtle-grove, instead of the church of St. Mary Magdalen, see also 8.296–97, 12.298–301).

[448] The St Mary Magdalen of the argument becomes again the myrtle-grove of Act VIII (see also 8.296–97, 11.13, 12.298–301). The original here reads: 'A Párterno y Sempronio veo ir a la Madalena' (Lobera *et al.*, eds, 2000, p. 231), which the Alnwick manuscript translates literally as 'I see Parmeno and Sempronio goinge to Saint Marie Magdalen' (Martínez Lacalle, ed., p. 219).

they see you thus, but scoff in derision at you, and say, 'he is gone to the myrtle-grove to sacrifice some half-score hecatombs of sighs and ay-me's to Venus's son, to prosper and prefer him to the favour and fruition of some mistress?'[449] If you are oppressed with passion, endure it at home in your own house, that the world may not perceive it. Discover not your grief unto strangers, since the drum is in their hands who know best how to beat it, and your business in her hands who knows best how to manage it.

Calisto. In whose hands?

Sempronio. In Celestina's.

Celestina. Who is that names Celestina? What sayst thou of this slave of Calisto's? I have come trudging all along the Augur's street,[450] to see if I could overtake you, I did put my best leg foremost, but all would not do: the skirts of my petticoat were so long, and did so often interfold themselves between my feet.[451]

Calisto. Oh thou joy of the world! Thou ease of my passions, thou relieveress of my pain, my eyes' looking-glass, my heart doth even exult for joy in beholding so honoured a presence, an age so ennobled with years. Tell me, what is it thou com'st with, what good news dost thou bring? For I see thou lookst cheerfully, and yet I know not of what terms my life doth stand, in what it consisteth.

Celestina. In my tongue.[452]

Calisto. What sayst thou then? Speak, thou that art my glory and comfort. Deliver it more at large unto me.

---

[449] In a much expanded paragraph, Mabbe paganizes the original idiomatic expression 'royendo los santos' (Lobera *et al.*, p. 231), literally 'gnawing upon saints' (which denotes a disproportionate and frequent display of public devotion) into equally exaggerated sacrifices offered to Cupid, Venus's son. In ancient Greece and Rome, a hecatomb was a great public sacrifice. Strictly speaking it involved a hundred oxen — note the etymology < Greek ἑκατόμβη, properly, 'an offering of a hundred oxen' (< ἑκατόν hundred + βοῦς ox) (*OED*).

[450] 'Calle del Arcediano' (Archdeacon's Street) in the original (Lobera *et al.*, eds, 2000, p. 232).

[451] Celestina fails once more to interpret the ill-omen that these folding skirts portend (see 4.74–76 and 5.21–24 above).

[452] Celestina is here as blunt as she is honest.

Celestina. Sir, let us first go more privately, and as we go home to your house, I will tell you that which shall make you glad indeed.⁴⁵³

Parmeno. (Brother, the old woman looks merrily. Sure, she hath sped well today.)
Sempronio. (Soft, listen what she says.)
Celestina. All this day, sir, have I been labouring in your business, and have neglected other weighty and serious affairs which did much concern me. Many do I suffer to live in pain only that I may yield you comfort. Besides, I have lost more by it than you are aware of, but farewel it. All is well lost, sithence I have brought my business to so good an end. And hear you me, for I will tell it you in few words, for I love to be short: Melibea is wholly at your service.
Calisto. Oh, what do I hear?
Celestina. Nay, she is more yours than her own: more at your service and command than of her father Pleberio.
Calisto. Speak softly, good mother, take heed what you say; let not my men hear you, lest they should call thee fool. Melibea is my mistress, Melibea is my desire, Melibea is my life, I am her servant, I am her slave.
Sempronio. Sir, with this distrustfulness of yours, with this undervaluing of yourself, you intersert° such doubts as cut off Celestina in the midst of her discourse; you would tire out a whole world with your disordered and confused interruptions. Why do you cross and bless yourself? Why do you keep such a wondering? It were better you would give her something for her pains. For these words are worthy better payment, and expect no less at your hands.
Calisto. Well hast thou spoken, dear mother. I wot full well that my small reward can no ways reward your pains, but instead of a gown and a kirtle (because tradesmen shall not share with

---

⁴⁵³ Mabbe again omits an important piece of information about the location of this dialogue. The original reads: 'Salgamos, señor, de la iglesia, y de aquí a la casa te contaré algo con lo que te alegres de verdad' (Lobera *et al.*, eds, 2000, p. 323). This conversation has been taking place inside the church of St. Mary Magdalen.

you)[454] take this little chain, put it about your neck, and go on with your discourse and my joy.

Parmeno. (Call you that a little chain? Heard you him, Sempronio? This spendthrift makes no reckoning of it; but I assure you, I will not give my part thereof for half a mark of gold, let her share it never so ill.

Sempronio. Peace, I say, for should my master have overheard you, you should have had work enough to pacify him, and to cure yourself; so offended is he already with your continual murmuring. As you love me, brother, hear, and hold your peace, for to this end thou hast two ears, and but one tongue.

Parmeno. He hath hanged himself so fast to that old woman's mouth that he is both deaf, dumb and blind, like a body without a soul or a bell without a clapper; insomuch that if we should point at him scornfully with our fingers, he would say we lifted up our hands to heaven, imploring his happy success in his love.

Sempronio. Peace, hearken, listen well unto Celestina. On my soul, she deserves it all, and more too, had he given it her. She speaks wonders.)

Celestina. Noble Calisto, to such a poor weak old woman as myself you have showed yourself exceeding frank and liberal. But as every gift is esteemed great, or little in regard of him that gives it, I will not therefore compare therewith my small desert, which it surpasseth both in quality and quantity, but rather measure it with your magnificence, before which it is nothing. In requital whereof I restore unto thee thy health, which was upon losing, thy heart, which was upon fainting, and thy wits, which were upon turning. Melibea is pained more for you than you for her. Melibea loves you, and desires you. Melibea spends more hours in thinking upon you, than on herself. Melibea calls herself thine, and this she holds as a title of liberty, and with this, she allays that fire which burns more in her than thyself.

Calisto. You my servants, am I here? Hear I this? Look whether I am awake or not. Is it day, or is it night? Oh thou great God of heaven, I beseech thee this may not prove a dream. Sure, I

---

[454] 'por que no se dé parte a oficiales' (Lobera *et al.*, eds, 2000, p. 233), i.e. Calisto does not give Celestina cloth as a reward so she does not have to share part of it with the tailors who will turn it into garments.

do not sleep; methinks I am fully awake. Tell me, mother, dost thou make sport with me, in paying me with words? Fear nothing, but tell me the truth, for thy going to and fro deserveth a great deal more than this.

Celestina. The heart that is wounded with desire never entertaineth good news for certain; nor bad for doubtful. But whether I jest or no yourself shall see, by going this night to her house, herself having agreed with me about the time, appointing you to be just there as the clock strikes twelve that you may talk together through the chinks of the door; from whose own mouth, you shall fully know my solicitude, and her desire, and the love which she bears unto you, and who hath caused it.

Calisto. It is enough. Is it possible I should hope for so great a happiness? Can so great a blessing light upon Calisto? I die till that hour come. I am not capable of so great a glory. I do not deserve so great a favour nor am I worthy to speak with so fair a lady, who of her own freewill should afford me so great a grace.

Celestina. I have often heard that it is harder to suffer prosperous than adverse fortune, because the one hath never any quietude, and the other still taketh comfort. It is strange, sir, that you will not consider who you are, nor the time that you have spent in her service, nor the person whom you have made to be your means; and likewise, that hitherto thou hast ever been in doubt of having her, and yet didst still endure all with patience, and now, that I do certify unto thee the end of thy torment, wilt thou put an end to thy life? Consider, consider, I pray, with thyself, that Celestina is on thy side, and that although all should be wanting unto thee which in a lover were to be required, I would sell thee for the most complete gallant of the world; for I would make for thee mountains of most craggy rocks to grow plain and smooth. Nay, more, I would make thee go through the deepest channel, or the highest swelling sea, without wetting of thy foot. You know not on whom you have bestowed your largesse.

Calisto. Remember yourself, mother, did you not tell me that she would come to me of her own accord?

Celestina. Yes, and that upon her very knees.

Sempronio. Pray heaven it be not a false alarm, one thing rumoured, another purposed. It may be a false firework to blow us all up. I fear me, it is a false train,° a made match, and a trap purposely set to catch us all. Bethink yourself, mother, that so men use to give crooked pins wrapped up in bread; poisonsome pills rolled up in sugar, that they may not be seen and perceived.

Parmeno. I never heard thee speak better in my life. The sudden yielding of this lady, and her so speedy consenting to all that Celestina would have her, engenders a strong suspicion within me and makes me fear that deceiving our will with her sweet and ready words, she will rob us on the wrong side, as your gypsies use to do when they look in our hands to tell us our fortunes. Besides, mother, it is an old saying: that with fair words, many wrongs are revenged, and the counterfeit stalking horse, which is made but of canvas with his dissembled gate, and the alluring sound of the tinkling of a bell, drives the partridges into the net. The song of the sirens deceive the simple mariner with the sweetness of their voices. Even so, she with her exceeding kindness and sudden concession of her love, will seize handsmooth° on a whole drove of us at once, and purge her innocency with Calisto's honour and our deaths. Being like herein to the teatling[455] lamb, which sucks both her dam's teat and that of another ewe, she by securing us will be revenged both of Calisto and all of us. So that with the great number of people which they have in the house, they may catch both the old ones and the young one together in the nest, whilst she shrugging and rubbing herself by the fireside may safely say: 'he is out of gun-shot, that rings the bell to the battle'.

Calisto. Peace, you knaves, you villains, you suspicious rascals. Will you make me believe that angels can do ought that is ill? I tell you, Melibea is but a dissembled angel, that lives here amongst us.

Sempronio. (What? Will you still play the heretic?[456] Hearken to him, Parmeno. But take thou no care at all, let it not trouble thee. For, if there be any double dealing, or that the play prove foul, he shall pay for all, for our feet be good, and we will betake us to our heels.)

---

[455] teatling] suckling; this is the only sample in the *OED*.
[456] Sempronio seems to have detected the Scriptural echoes (John I.14) in the original, and also in the translation. 'Melibea ángel disimulado es que vive entre nosotros' (Lobera *et al.*, eds, 2000, p. 236, n. 56).

Celestina. Sir, you are in the right, and these in the wrong; overloading their thoughts with vain suspicions and jealousies. I have done all that I was enjoined, and so I leave you to your joys. Good angels defend you and direct you. As for myself, I am very well satisfied. And if you shall have further occasion to use me, either in this particular, or anything else, you shall find me ever ready to do you the best service I can.
Parmeno. (Ha, ha, he.
Sempronio. I pray thee, why dost thou laugh?
Parmeno. To see what haste the old trot makes to be gone: she thinks every hour a year, till she be gone clear away with the chain. She cannot persuade herself that it is as yet sure enough in her hands, for she knows that she is as little worthy of that chain as Calisto is of his Melibea.
Sempronio. What would you have such an old whorish bawd as she to do? Who knows and understands that which we silence and keep secret, and useth to patch up seven virginities at a clap for two pieces of silver? And now, that she sees herself to be laden with gold, what, I say, would you have her to do, but to make it safe and sure, by taking possession thereof, for fear lest he should take it from her again, after that he hath had his desire? But let us beware of the devil, and take heed that we go not together by the ears, when we come to divide the spoil.)[457]
Calisto. Mother, fare you well. I will lay me down to sleep and rest myself awhile, that I may redeem the nights past and satisfy the better for that which is to come.

Celestina. Tha, ta, ta.
Elicia. Who knocks?
Celestina. Daugher Elicia, open the door.
Elicia. How chance you come so late? It is not well done of you, being an old woman as you are, for you may hap to stumble where you may so fall, that it may be your death.
Celestina. I fear not that, wench, for I consult with myself in the day which way I shall go in the night. For I never go near any

---

[457] The original threat sounds more aggressive and — in the light of the subsequent events — ominous: 'Pues guárdese del diablo que sobre el partir [i.e. repartir] no le saquemos el alma' (Lobera *et al.*, eds, 2000, p. 237), i.e. 'Let her beware of the devil, lest we rip off her soul over our share'.

bridge, bench, pit or causey.° For, as it is in the proverb, he goes not safe, nor never shall, who goes too close unto the wall.[458] And he goes still most safe and sound, whose steps are placed on plainest ground. And I had rather foul my shoes with dirt, than bebloody my handkerchief at every wall's corner. But does it not grieve thee to be here?

Elicia. Why should it grieve me?

Celestina. Because the company I left here with you is gone, and you are all alone.

Elicia. It is some four hours ago since they went hence, and would you have me to think on that now?

Celestina. Indeed, the sooner they left you, the more reason you had to think thereon. But let us leave to talk of their speedy going, and of my long staying, and let us first provide for our supper, and then for our sleep.

---

[458] A somewhat inaccurate translation of the popular refrain, 'No da paso seguro quien corre por el muro', which refers to those who walk upon the wall, not close to it.

Actus XII
The Argument

Midnight being come, Calisto, Sempronio, and Parmeno, being well armed, go towards the house of Melibea. Lucrecia and Melibea stand at the door, watching for Calisto. Calisto comes. Lucrecia first speaks unto him. She calls Melibea, Lucrecia goes aside; Melibea and Calisto talk together, the door being betwixt them; Parmeno and Sempronio withdraw themselves a little ways off. They hear some people coming along the street; they prepare themselves for flight. Calisto takes his leave of Melibea, leaving order for his return the next night following; Pleberio awakened with the noise which he heard in the street, calls to his wife Alisa; they ask of Melibea who that was, that walked up and down in her chamber? Melibea answers her father, by feigning she was athirst. Calisto with his servants go talking home to his house. Being come home, he lays him down to sleep; Parmeno and Sempronio go to Celestina's house, they demand their share of her pains; Celestina dissembles the matter, they fall a wrangling; they lay hands on Celestina, they murder her. Elicia cries out; the justice comes, and apprehends them both.

INTERLOCUTORS
Calisto, Lucrecia, Melibea, Parmeno, Sempronio,
Pleberio, Alisa, Celestina, Elicia

Calisto. Sirs, what's a clock?
Sempronio. It struck now ten.
Calisto. Oh how it discontents me, to see servants so reckless! Oh my much mindfulness for this night's meeting and your much unmindfulness, and extreme carelessness! There might have been had some indifferent both remembrance and care. How inconsiderately (knowing how much it importeth me to be either ten or eleven) dost thou answer me at haphazard, with that which comes first to mouth. Oh unhappy I, if by chance I had overslept myself, and my demand had depended on the answer of Sempronio, to make of eleven ten, and of twelve but eleven! Melibea might have come forth, I had not gone out, and she returned back: so that neither my misery should have had an end, nor my desire have taken effect. And therefore it

is not said in vain, that another man's harm hangs out by one hair, no man caring whether he sink or swim.

Sempronio. Methinks it is as great an error in a man to ask what he knows as to answer to what he knows not. It were better, sir, that we should spend this hour that remaineth in preparing weapons than in propounding questions.

Calisto. The fool says well, I would not at such a time receive a displeasure. I will not think on that which may be, but on that which hath been; not on the harm which may arise by his negligence, but on the good which may come by my carefulness. I will give leisure to my anger, and will either quite dismiss it, or force it to be more remiss. Parmeno, take down my corslets, and arm yourselves, so shall we go the safer: for it is in the proverb, half the battle is then waged, when a man is well prepared.

Parmeno. Lo, sir, here they be.

Calisto. Come help me here to put them on. Do you look on, Sempronio, and see if anybody be stirring in the street.

Sempronio. Sir, I see not any, and though there were, yet the darkness of the night is such, and so great, that it is impossible for any that shall meet us, either to see or know us.

Calisto. Let us along then. Here, my masters, this way; for though it be somewhat about, yet it is the more private way, and the lesser frequented. Now it strikes twelve, a good hour.

Parmeno. We are near unto the place.

Calisto. We are come in very good time. Go thou, Parmeno, and peep in at the door, to see if that lady be come or no.

Parmeno. Who, I, sir? God forbid, that I should mar that which I never made. Much better were it, sir, that your presence should be her first encounter, lest in seeing me she should be moved to anger, in seeing so many acquainted with that which she so secretly desires to be done, and undergoes with so great fear; as also, because she may haply imagine that you mock her.

Calisto. Oh how well hast thou spoken! Thou hast given me my life, by giving me this sound advice. For there needeth nothing more to bear me home dead to my house, than that she through my improvidence should have gone her ways back. I will go thither myself, and do you stay here.

Parmeno. What dost thou think, Sempronio, of the fool our master, who thought to have made me to be his target for to receive the encounter of this first danger? What do I know who stands between or behind the doors? What know I if there be any treason intended, or no? What can I tell, whether Melibea have plotted this to cry quittance with our master for this his great presumption? Besides, we are not sure whether the old trot told him truth or no. Thou knowst not, Parmeno, how to speak. Thy life shall be taken from thee, and thou ne'r the wiser for it: thy soul shall be let forth, and thou not know who was he that did it. Do not thou turn flatterer nor soothe up thy master in everything, that he would have thee, and then thou shalt never have cause to weep for other men's woes, or to mourn for other's miseries. Do thou not follow Celestina's counsel in that which is fit and convenient for thee, and you wert as good go break thy neck blindfold. Go on with thy good persuasions, and faithful admonitions, and thou shalt be well cudgelled for thy labour. Turn the leaf now no more, lest thou be forced to bid the world good night before thou be willing to leave it. I will solemnize this as my birthday, since I have escaped so great a danger.

Sempronio. Hush, I say, softly, Parmeno, softly. Do not you keep such a leaping and skipping, nor for joy make such a noise, lest you may hap to be heard.

Parmeno. Content yourself, brother, hold your peace, I pray, for I cannot contain myself for very joy to think that I should make him believe that it was most fit for him to go to the door, when as indeed, I did only put him on because I held it fittest for mine own safety. Who could ever have brought a business more handsomely about for his own good than I myself have done? Thou shalt see me do many such things, if thou shalt hereafter but observe me, which every man shall not know of, as well towards Calisto himself, as all those who shall any way intermeddle or interpose themselves in this business. For, I am assured that this damsel is but the bait to this hook, whereat he must hang himself, or that flesh which is thrown out to vultures, whereof he that eateth is sure to pay soundly for it.

Sempronio. Let this pass, ne'r trouble thy head with these jealousies, and suspicions of thine; no, though they should happen to be true. But prepare thyself, and like a tall soldier, be in readiness upon the first alarm or word given to betake thee to thy heels. Do like the men of *Villa-Diego*, who being besieged, ran away by night with their breeches in their hands.[459]

Parmeno. We have read both in one book, and are both of the same mind. I have not only their breeches, but their light easy buskins, that I may run away the nimbler and outstrip my fellows. And I am glad, good brother, that thou hast advised me to that which otherwise, even for very shame and fear of thee, I should never have done. As for our master, if he chance to be heard, or otherwise discovered, he will never escape, I fear me, the hands of Pleberio's people; whereby he may hereafter demand of us, how we behaved ourselves in his defence, or that he shall ever be able to accuse us, that we cowardly forsook him.

Sempronio. Oh my friend, Parmeno, how good and joyful a thing it is for fellows and companions to live together in love and unity! And though Celestina should prove good to us in no other thing, save only this, yet in this alone hath she done us service enough, and deserved very well at our hands.[460]

Parmeno. No man can deny that which in itself is manifest. It is apparent that we for modesty's sake, and because we would not be branded with the hateful name of cowardice, we stayed here expecting together with our master no less than death, though we did not so much deserve it as he did.

Sempronio. Melibea should be come. Hark, methinks I hear them whispering each to other.

Parmeno. I fear rather that it is not she, but some one that counterfeits her voice.

Sempronio. Heavens defend us from the hands of traitors; I pray God, they have not betaken themselves to that street through which we were resolved to fly. For I fear nothing else but that.

---

[459] Mabbe's free version of a Spanish saying ('tomar las de Villadiego'), signifying 'to run away in haste'. This expression, still in common current use, is documented for the first time in *La Celestina*.

[460] The opening paragraphs in this act are full of ironic and ominous passages. This is one of the most remarkable among them: Sempronio here celebrates the mutual friendship that Celestina has created between the two servants, unaware that this community is about to destroy all three of them.

Calisto. (This stirring and murmur which I fear is not of one single person alone. Yet will I speak, come what will come, or be who as will be there). Madam, mistress, be you there?

Lucrecia. (If I be not deceived, this is Calisto's voice. But for the more surety, I will go a little nearer.) Who is that that speaks? Who is there without?

Calisto. He that is come addressed to your command.

Lucrecia. (Madam, why come you not? Come hither, I say, be not afraid, for here is the gentleman you wot of.

Melibea. Speak softly, you fool, mark him well, that you may be sure it is he.

Lucrecia. Come hither, I tell you, it is he. I know him by his voice.)

Calisto. (I fear me I am deluded, it was not Melibea that spoke unto me. I hear some whispering: I am undone. But live or die, I have not the power to be gone.)

Melibea. (Lucrecia, go a little aside, and give me leave to call unto him.) Sir, what is your name? Who willed you to come hither?

Calisto. She that is worthy to command all the world, she whom I may not merit to serve. Let not your ladyship fear to discover herself to this captive of your gentle disposition, for the sweet sound of those your words, which shall never fall from my ears, gives me assurance that you are that lady Melibea, whom my heart adoreth; I am your servant Calisto.

Melibea. The strange and excessive boldness of thy messages hath enforced me, Calisto, to speak with thee, who having already received my answer to your reasons, I know not what you may imagine to get more out of my love than what I then made known unto you. Banish therefore from thee those vain and foolish thoughts, that both my honour and my person may be secured from any hurt they may receive by an ill suspicion. For which purpose I am come hither to take order for your dispatch, and my quietness. Do not, I beseech you, put my good name and reputation upon the balance of back-biting and detracting tongues.

Calisto. To hearts prepared with a strong and dauntless resolution against all adversities whatsoever nothing can happen unto them that shall easily be able to shake the strength of their wall. But what unhappy man who, weaponless and disarmed, not thinking upon any deceit or ambuscade,° puts himself within the door of your safe-conduct and protection.

Whatsoever in such a case falls out contrary to my expectation, it cannot in all reason but torment me, and pierce through the very soul of me, breaking all those magazines and storehouses wherein this sweet news was laid up. Oh miserable and unfortunate Calisto! Oh how hast thou been mocked and deluded by thy servants! Oh thou cozening and deceitful Celestina, thou mightst at least have let me alone, and given me leave to die, and not gone about to revive my hope, to add thereto more fuel to the fire which already doth sufficiently waste and consume me. Why didst thou falsify this my lady's message? Why hast thou thus with thy tongue given cause to my despair and utter undoing? Why didst thou command me to come hither? Was it that I might receive disgrace, interdiction, diffidence, and hatred, from no other mouth but that which keeps the keys of my perdition or happiness? Oh thou enemy to my good! Didst not thou tell me that this my lady would be favourable, and gracious unto me? Didst not thou tell me that of her own accord she had commanded this her captive to come to this very place where now I am? Not to banish me afresh from her presence, but to repeal that banishment whereunto she had sentenced me by her former command? Miserable that I am, whom shall I trust, or in whom may I hope to find any faith? Where is truth to be had? Who is void of deceit? Where doth not falsehood dwell? Who is he that shows himself an open enemy? Or who is he that shows himself a faithful friend? Where is that place wherein treason is not wrought? Who, I say, durst[461] trespass so much upon my patience, as to give me such cruel hope of destruction?

Melibea. Cease, good sir, your true and just complaints. For neither my heart is able to endure it, nor mine eyes any longer to dissemble it. Thou weepest out of grief, judging me cruel, and I weep out of joy, seeing thee so faithful. Oh my dearest lord, and my life's whole happiness, how much more pleasing would it be unto me to see thy face than to hear thy voice. But sithence that at this present we cannot enjoy each other as we would, take thou the assignment and seal of those words which I sent unto thee, written, and engrossed in the tongue of that thy diligent and careful messenger. All that which I then said,

---

[461] durst] archaic past tense of *dare*.

I do thee anew confirm. I acknowledge it as my deed, and hold the assurance I have made thee to be good and perfect. Good sir, do not you weep, dry up your tears, and dispose of me as you please.

Calisto. Oh my dear lady! Hope of my glory, easeress of my pain, and my heart's joy. What tongue can be sufficient to give thee thanks, that may equal this so extraordinary and incomparable a kindness, which in this instant of so great and extreme a sorrow thou hast been willing to confer upon me? In being willing, I say, that one so mean, and unworthy as myself, should be by thee enabled to the enjoying of thy sweetest love, whereof, although I was evermore most desirous, yet did I always deem myself unworthy thereof, weighing thy greatness, considering thy estate, beholding thy perfection, contemplating thy beauty, and looking into my small merit, and thy great worth, besides other thy singular graces, thy commendable, and well-known virtues? Again, oh thou great God, how can I be ungrateful unto thee, who so miraculously hast wrought for me so great and strange wonders? Oh how long ago did I entertain this thought in my heart, and as a thing impossible, repelled it from my memory, until now, that the bright beams of thy most clear shining countenance gave light unto my eyes, inflamed my heart, awakened my tongue, enlarged my desert, abridged my cowardice, unwreathed my shrunk-up spirits, reinforced my strength, put life and metal into my hands and feet, and, in a word, infused such a spirit of boldness into me that they have born me up by their power unto this high estate wherein, with happiness, I now behold myself, in hearing this thy sweet-pleasing voice, which if I had not heretofore known, and scented out the sweet and wholesome favour of thy words, I should hardly have believed they would have been without deceit. But now, that I am well assured of thy pure and noble both blood and actions I stand amazed at the gaze of my good, and with a stricter eye begin to view and look upon myself, to see whether I am that same Calisto whom so great a blessing hath befallen?

Melibea. Calisto, thy great worth, thy singular graces, and thy nobleness of birth, have ever since I had true notice of thee wrought so effectually with me, that my heart hath not so much as one moment been absent from thee. And although now these many days I have striven and striven again to dissemble it, yet could I not so smother my thoughts, but that as soon as that woman returned thy sweet name unto my remembrance I discovered my desire and appointed our meeting at this very place and time, where I beseech thee to take order for the disposing of my person according to thine own good will and pleasure. These doors debar us of our joy, whose strong locks and bars I curse, as also mine own weak strength. For were I stronger, and they weaker, neither shouldst thou be displeased, nor I discontented.

Calisto. What, madam, is it your pleasure that I should suffer a paltry piece of wood to hinder our joy? Never did I conceive that anything, save thine own will, could possibly hinder us. Oh troublesome and sport-hindering doors, I earnestly desire that you may be burned with as great a fire as the torment is great, which you give me, for then the third part thereof would be sufficient to consume you to ashes in a moment. Give me leave, sweet lady, that I may call my servants, and command them to break them open.

Parmeno. (Hark, hark, Sempronio. Hearest thou not what he says? He is coming to seek after us, we shall make a bad year of it, we shall run into a peck[462] of troubles. I tell you surely, I like not of his coming. This love of theirs, I verily persuade myself, was begun in an unlucky hour. If you will go, go, for I'll stay here no longer.

Sempronio. Peace, hark; she will not consent we come.)

Melibea. What means my love? Will you undo me? Will you wound my reputation? Give not your will the reins. Your hope is certain, and the time short, even as soon as yourself shall appoint it. Besides, your pain is single, mine double; your for yourself, mine for both. You only feel your own grief, I both your own and mine. Content yourself therefore, and come you tomorrow at this very hour, and let your way be by the wall of my garden. For if you should now break down these cruel doors, though haply we should not be presently heard, yet tomorrow morning there would arise in my father's house a terrible suspicion of my error. And you know besides, that by so much the greater is the error, by how much the greater is the party that erreth, and in the turning of a hand, will be noised through the whole city.

---

[462] peck] a great deal.

Sempronio. (In an unfortunate hour came we hither this night; we shall stay here, till the day hath overtaken us, if our master go on thus leisurely, and make no more haste. And albeit fortune hath hitherto well befriended us in this business, yet I fear me, if we stay overlong we shall be overheard, either by some of Pleberio's household, or of his neighbours.

Parmeno. I would have had thee been gone two hours ago; for he will never give over, but still find some occasion to continue his discourse.)

Calisto. My dear lady, my joy and happiness, why dost thou style this an error, which was granted unto me by the destinies, and seconded by Cupid himself, to my petitions in the myrtle-grove?[463]

Parmeno. Calisto talks idly, surely, he is not well in his wits. I am of the belief, brother, that he is not so devout. That which that old traitorous trot, with her pestiferous sorceries hath compassed and brought about, he sticks not to say that the destinies have granted, and wrought for him. And with this confidence he would adventure to break ope these doors; who shall no sooner have given the first stroke, but that presently he will be heard, and taken by her father's servants, who lodge hard by.

Sempronio. Fear nothing, Parmeno, for we are far enough off. And upon the very first noise that we hear, we will betake us straight to our heels and make our flight our best defence. Let him alone, let him take his course, for if he do ill, he shall pay for it.

Parmeno. Well hast thou spoken; thou knowst my mind, as well as if thou hadst been within me. Be it as thou hast said; let us shun death, for we are both young, and not to desire to die nor to kill is not cowardice, but a natural goodness. Pleberio's

---

[463] '¿Por qué llamas yerro a aquello que por los santos de Dios me fue concedido? Rezando hoy ante el altar de la Madalena me vino con tu mensaje alegre aquella solícita mujer' (Lobera *et al.*, eds, 2000, p. 247), i.e. 'Why do you call this an error, which God's saints have bestowed upon me? For I was praying today before the altar of St. Mary Magdalen when that obsequious woman came to me with your gladsome message'. See also 11.3, 11.15, and line 3 in the argument of act 11.

320   followers, they are but fools and mad-men, they have not that mind to their meat and their sleep as they have to be brabbling[464] and quarrelling. What fools then should we be to fall together by the ears with such enemies, who do not so much affect victory and conquest as continual war and endless contention? Oh, if thou didst but see, brother, in what posture I stand, thou wouldst be ready to burst with laughing. I stand sideling, my legs abroad, my left foot foremost ready to take the start, the skirts of my cassock tucked under my girdle, my buckler clapped close to my arm, that it may not hinder me;
330   and I verily believe, that I should outrun the swiftest buck, so monstrously am I afraid of staying here.

Sempronio. I stand better, for I have bound my sword and buckler both together, that they may not fall from me when I run; and have clapped my casque in the cape of my cloak.

Parmeno. But the stones you had in it, what hast thou done with them?

Sempronio. I have turned them all out, that I might go the lighter, for I have enough to do to carry this corselet, which your importunity made me put on; for I could have been very well
340   content to have left it off, because I thought it would be too heavy for me, when I should run away. Hark, hark, hearest thou Parmeno? The business goes ill with us, we are but dead men. Put on! Away! Be gone! Make towards Celestina's house, that we may not be cut off, by betaking us to our own house.

Parmeno. Fly! Fly! You run too slowly! Passion of me! If they should chance to overtake us, throw away thy blucker and all.

Sempronio. Have they killed our master? Can you tell?

Parmeno. I know not. Say nothing to me, I pray. Run, and hold your peace; as for him, he is the least of my care.
350   *Sempronio.* Zit, zit,[465] Parmeno, not a word; turn, and be still, for it is nothing but the *alguazil*'s[466] men, who make a noise as they pass through this other street.

Parmeno. Take your eyes in your hand, and see you be sure. Trust not, I say, too much to those eyes of yours: they may mistake, taking one thing for another. They have not left me one drop

---

[464] brabbling] dispute, quarrel.
[465] zit, zit] hush, hush.
[466] *alguazil*] thus, in Spanish. An 'alguazil' is the officer in charge of executing the orders of the local judiciary.

of blood in my body. Death had e'n almost swallowed me up; for methought still as I ran, they were cutting and carbonading° my shoulders. I never in my life remember that I was in the like fear, or ever saw myself in the like danger of an affront,° though I have gone many a time through other men's houses, and through places of much peril, and hard to pass. Nine years I was servant to Guadalupe,[467] and a thousand times myself and others were at buffets, cutting one another for life, yet was I never in that fear of death, as now.

Sempronio. And did not [I], I pray, serve at Saint Michael's?[468] And mine host in the marketplace? And Molleias the gardener. I also (I trow) was at fisty cuffs with those which threw stones at the sparrows, and other the like birds, which sat upon a green poplar that we had, because with their stones, they did spoil the herbs in the garden. But God keep thee, and every good man from the sight of such weapons as these: these are shrewd tools, this is true fear indeed. And therefore it is not said in vain; laden with iron, laden with fear. Turn, turn back; for it is the *alguazil*, that's certain.

Melibea. What noise is that, Calisto, which I hear in the street? It seems to be the noise of some that fly and are pursued. For your own sake and mine, have a care of yourself. I fear me, you stand in danger.

Calisto. I warrant you, madam, fear you nothing; for I stand on a safeguard. They should be my men, who are madcaps, and disarm as many as pass by them; and belike, someone hath escaped them, after whom they hasten.

Melibea. Are they many, that you brought?

Calisto. No, madam, no more but two. But should half a dozen set upon them, they would not be long in disarming them, and make them fly: they are such a couple of tall lusty fellows. They are men of true and well approved mettle, choice lads for the nonce. For I come not hither with a fire of straw, which is no

---

[467] 'Nueve años serví a los frailes de Guadalupe' (Lobera *et al.*, eds, 2000, p. 249), i.e. 'For nine years I served the friars of Guadalupe'. Mabbe omits the reference to the friars.

[468] '¿no serví al cura de San Miguel?' (Lobera *et al.*, eds, 2000, p. 250). Mabbe omits the reference to the priest.

sooner in, but out. And were it not in regard of your honour, they should have broken these doors in pieces. And in case we had been heard, they should have freed both yourself and me from all your father's servants.

Melibea. Oh, of all loves! Let not any such thing be attempted. Yet it glads me much that you are so faithfully attended. That bread is well bestowed which such valiant servants eat. For that love, sir, which you bear unto me, since Nature hath enriched them with so good a gift, I pray make much of them, and reward them well, to the end that in all things they may be trusty and secret, that concern thy service. And when for their boldness and presumption thou shalt either check or correct them, intermix some favours with thy punishments, that their valour and courage may not be daunted and abated,[469] but be stirred and provoked to outdare dangers, when thou shalt have occasion to use them.

Parmeno. Sist, sist![470] Hear you sir? Make haste and begone, for here is a great company coming along with torches. And unless you make haste, you will be seen and known, for here is not any place where you may hide yourself from their view.

Calisto. Oh unfortunate that I am! How am I enforced, lads, against my will to take my leave! Believe me, the fear of death would not work so much upon me, as the scare of your honour doth. But since it is so, that we must part, angels be the guardians of thy fair person. My coming, as you have ordered it, shall be by the garden.

Melibea. Be it so, and all happiness be with you.
Pleberio. Wife, are you asleep?
Alisa. No, sir.
Pleberio. Do not you hear some noise, or stirring in your daughter's withdrawing chamber?
Alisa. Yes, marry do I. Melibea, Melibea?
Pleberio. She does not hear you. I will call a little louder. Daughter Melibea?
Melibea. Sir.

---

[469] abated] defeated, discouraged (see note to 1.40 above).
[470] Sist, sist] Hush, hush (see the similar 'zit, zit' above).

Pleberio. Who is that, that tramples up and down there, and makes that stirring to and fro in your chamber?

Melibea. It is Lucrecia, sir, who went forth to fetch some water for me to drink, for I was very thirsty.

Pleberio. Sleep again, daughter, I thought it had been something else.

Lucrecia. (A little noise, I perceive, can wake them; methought they spoke somewhat fearfully, as if all had not been well.

Melibea. There is not any so gentle a creature, who with the love or fear of its young, is not somewhat moved. What would they have done, had they had certain and assured knowledge of my going down?)

Calisto. My son, shut the door. And you, Parmeno, bring up a light.

Parmeno. You were better, sir, to take your rest, and that little that it is till day, to take it out in sleep.

Calisto. I will follow thy counsel, for it is no more than needeth. I want sleep exceedingly. But tell me, Parmeno, what dost thou think of that old woman, whom thou didst dispraise so much unto me? What a piece of work hath she brought to pass? What could we have done without her?

Parmeno. Neither had I any feeling of your great pain, nor knew I the gentleness and well-deservingness of Melibea, and therefore am not to be blamed. But well did I know both Celestina, and all her cunning tricks and devices; and did thereupon advise you, as became a servant to advise his master, and as I thought, for the best. But now I see, she is become another woman, she is quite changed from what she was, when I first knew her.

Calisto. How? Changed? How dost thou mean?

Parmeno. So much that had I not seen it, I should never have believed it. But now, heaven grant you may live as happy, as this is true.

Calisto. But tell me: didst thou hear what passed between me and my mistress? What did you do all that while? Were you not afraid?

Sempronio. Afraid, sir? Of what? All the world could not make us afraid. Did you ever find us to be fearful? Did you ever see any such thing in us? We stood waiting for you well provided, and with our weapons in our hands.

Calisto. Slept you not a whit? Took you not a little nap?

Sempronio. Sleep, sir? It is for boys and children to sleep. I did not so much as once sit down, nor put one leg over another, watching still as diligently as a cat for a mouse; that if I had heard but the least noise in the world, I might presently have leapt forth, and have done as much as my strength should have been able to perform. And Parmeno, though till now he did not seem to serve you in this business with any great willingness, he was as glad when he spied the torches coming as the wolf when he spies the dust of a drove of cattle, or flock of sheep, hoping still that he might make his prey, till he saw how many they were.

Calisto. This is no such wonder, Sempronio, never marvel at it; for it is natural in him to be valiant. And though he would not have bestirred himself for my sake, yet would he have laid about him because such as he cannot go against that which they be used unto. For though the fox change his hair, yet he never changeth his nature; he will keep himself to his custom, though he cannot keep himself to his colour. I told my mistress Melibea, what was in you, and how safe I held myself, having you at my back for my guard. My sons, I am much bound unto you both, pray to heaven for our welfare and good success. And doubt not, but I will more fully guerdon[471] your good service. Good night, and heaven send you good rest.

Parmeno. Whither shall we go, Sempronio. To our chamber and go [to] sleep, or to the kitchen and break our fast?

Sempronio. Go thou whither thou wilt, as for me, ere it be day, I will get me to Celestina's house, and see if I can recover my part in the chain. She is a crafty hilding[472] and I will not give her time to invent some one villainous trick or other whereby to shift us off, and cozen us of our shares.

Parmeno. It is well remembered, I had quite forgot it. Let us go both together, and if she stand upon points[473] with us, let us

---

[471] guerdon] reward.
[472] hilding] a jade, a baggage. It translates Rojas's more explicit 'puta vieja' (Lobera *et al.*, eds, 2000, p. 253).
[473] stand upon points] to act scrupulously or punctiliously.

put her into such a fear, that she may be ready to bewray herself. For money goes beyond all friendship.

Sempronio. (Cist, cist,[474] not a word, for her bed is hard by this little window here. Let me knock her up.) Tha, tha, tha, mistress Celestina, open the door.

Celestina. Who calls?

Sempronio. Open [the] door, your sons be here.

Celestina. I have no sons that be abroad at this time of night.

Sempronio. It is Parmeno and Sempronio. Open the door, we are come hither to break our fast with you.

Celestina. Oh ye mad lads, you wanton wags. Enter, enter, how chance you come so early? It is but now break of day. What have you done? What hath past? Tell me, how goes the world? Calisto's hopes, are they alive or dead? Has he her, or has he her not? How stands it with him?

Sempronio. How, mother? Had it not been for us, his soul ere this had gone seeking her eternal rest. And if it were possible to prize the debt wherein he stands bound unto us, all the wealth he hath were not sufficient to make us satisfaction. So true is that trivial saying that the life of man is of more worth than all the gold in the world.[475]

Celestina. Have you been in such danger since I saw you? Tell me, how was it? How was it I pray?

Sempronio. Marry in such danger that as I am an honest man, my blood still boils in my body, to think upon it.

Celestina. Sit down, I beseech you, and tell me how it was.

Parmeno. It will require a long discourse. Besides, we have fretted out our hearts, and are quite tired with the trouble and toil we have had. You may do better to provide something for his and my breakfast. It may be, when we have eaten, our choler will be somewhat allayed. For I swear unto thee, I desire not now to meet that man that desires peace. I should now glory to light upon someone on whom I might revenge my wrath, and stanch my anger, for I could not do it on those that caused it, so fast did they fly from my fury.

---

[474] cist, cist] hush, hush (see 'sist, sist' and 'zit, zit' above).

[475] The reference to gold (which introduces a vague threat, by indirectly referring to the golden chain they purport to share) does not appear in the original, which reads 'la vida y persona es más digna y de más valor que otra cosa ninguna' (Lobera *et al.*, eds, 2000, p. 254).

Celestina. The pox canker out my carcass to death, if thou makest me not afraid to look on thee, thou lookest so fierce and so ghastly. But for all this, I do believe you do but jest. Tell me, I pray thee Sempronio, as thou lov'st me what hath befallen you?

Sempronio. By heavens, I am not myself, I come hither I know not how, without wit or reason. But as for you, fellow Parmeno, I cannot but find fault with you, for not tempering of your choler, and using more moderation in your angry mood. I would have thee look otherwise now, and not carry that sour countenance here, as thou didst there, when we encountered so many. For mine own part, before those that I knew could do but little I never made show that I could do much. Mother, I have brought hither my arms all broken and battered in pieces, my buckler without its ring of iron, the plates being cut asunder, my sword like a saw, also behacked and hewed, my casque strangely bruised, beaten as flat as a cake, and dented in with the blows that came hammering on my head, so that I have not anything in the world to go further with my master, when he shall have occasion to use me. For it is agreed on, that my master shall this night have access unto his mistress by the way of her garden. Now for to furnish myself anew, if my life lay on it, I know not where to have one penny or farthing.

Celestina. Since it is spoiled and broken in your master's service, go to your master for more, let him, a God's name, pay for it. Besides, you know how it is with him, but ask and have; he will presently furnish you, I warrant you. For he is none of those who say to their servants: live with me, and look out some other to maintain thee. He is so frank and of so liberal a disposition, that he will not give thee money for this only, but much more, if need be.

Sempronio. Tush, what's this to the purpose? Parmeno's be also spoiled and marred. After this reckoning, we may spend our master all that he hath in arms. How can you in conscience think, or with what face imagine, that I should be so importunate as to demand more of him than what he hath already done of his own accord? He for his part hath done enough, I would not it should be said of me that he hath given me an inch, and that I should take an ell.[476] There is a reason in all things. He

---

[476] ell] a measure of length, equivalent to 45 inches.

hath given us a hundred crowns in gold; he hath given us, besides, a chain; three such picks more, will pick out all the wax in his ear;[477] he hath, and will have a hard market of it. Let us content ourselves with that which is reason; let us not lose all, by seeking to gain more than is meet; for he that embraced much, holdeth little.[478]

Celestina. (How wittily this ass thinks he hath spoken!) I swear to thee, by the reverence of this my old age, had these words been spoken after dinner, I should have said that we had all of us taken a cup too much, that we had been all drunk. Art thou well in thy wits, Sempronio? What has thy remuneration to do with my reward? Thy payment with my merit? Am I bound to buy you weapons? Must I repair your losses, and supply your wants? Now I think upon it, let me be hanged, or die any other death, if thou hast not taken hold of a little word, that carelessly slipped out of my mouth the other day, as we came along the street. For, as I remember, I then told you that what I had was yours, and that I would never be wanting unto you in anything, to the utmost of my poor ability; and that if fortune did prosper my business with your master, that you should lose nothing by it. But you know, Sempronio, that words of compliment and kindness are not obligatory, nor bind me to do, as you would have me. All is not gold that glitters, for then it would be a great deal cheaper than it is. Tell me, Sempronio, if I have not hit the right nail on the head? Thou mayst see by this, that though I am old, that I can divine as much as thou canst imagine. In good faith, son, I am as full of grief, as ever my heart can hold, I am even ready to burst with sorrow and anguish. As soon as ever I came from your house, and was come home, I gave the chain I brought hither with me to this fool Elicia, that she might look upon it and cheer herself with the sight thereof. And she, for her life, cannot as yet call to mind what she hath done with it. And all this live-long night, neither she nor I have slept one wink, for very thought and grief thereof. Not so much for the value of the chain —for it

---

[477] three such picks more, will pick out all the wax in his ear] Mabbe's literal translation of the Spanish saying 'A tres tales aguijones, no terná cera en el oído' (Lobera *et al.*, eds, 2000, p. 255), i.e. if he continues at this rate, he will be left without any further rewards to bestow upon us.

[478] Mabbe somewhat expands the original here.

was not much worth — but to see that she should be so careless in the laying of it up, and to see the ill luck of it. At the very same time that we missed it, came in some friends of mine that had been of my old and familiar acquaintance, and I am sorely afraid lest they have lighted upon it, and taken it away with them, meaning to make use of that vulgar saying, *si spie it, tum sporte fac; si non spie it, packe and away Jack*.[479] But now, my sons, that I may come a little nearer unto you both, and speak home to the point: if your master gave me anything, what he gave me, that, you must think, is mine. As for your cloth of gold doublet, I never asked you any share out of it, nor ever will. We all of us serve him, that he may give unto us all, as he sees we shall deserve. And as for that which he hath given me, I have twice endangered my life for it. More blades have I blunted in his service than you both. More material and substantial stuff have I wasted, and have worn out more hose and shoes. And you must not think, my sons, but all this costs me good money. Besides, my skill, which I got not playing or sitting still, or warming my tail over the fire, as most of your idle housewives do, but with hard labour and painstaking, as Parmeno's mother could well witness for me, if she were living. This I have gained by mine own industry and labour; as for you, what have you done? If you have done anything for Calisto, Calisto is to requite you. I get my living by my trade and my travail; you, yours, with recreation and delight; and therefore, you are not to expect equal recompence, enjoying your service with pleasure, as I, who go performing it with pains. But whatsoever I have hitherto said unto you, because you shall see, I will deal kindly with you: if my chain be found again, I will give each of you a pair of scarlet breeches, which is the comeliest habit that young men can wear. But if it be not found, you must accept of my good will, and myself be content to sit down with my loss. And all this I do out of pure love, because you were willing that I should have the benefit of

---

[479] Mabbe here translates, half into colloquial English, half into mock-Latin, the sense of the original proverb used by Celestina (which in the original appears truncated, leaving the reader with the understanding of the rest): 'Si te vi, burleme [si no me viste, calleme]' (Lobera *et al.*, eds, 2000, p. 257). It could be rephrased as 'if you catch me red-handed [*si spie it*], then I shall pretend I was only joking [*tum sporte fac*], if you do not, then I'll get away with it'.

managing this business before another. And if this will not content you, I cannot do withal. To your own harm be it.

Sempronio. This is not the first time that I have heard it spoken how much in old folks the sin of avarice reigns. As also that other: 'when I was poor, then I was liberal, when I was rich, then I was covetous'. So that covetousness increaseth with getting and poverty with coveting: and nothing makes the covetous man poor but his riches.[480] Oh heavens! How doth penury increase with abundance and plenty! How often did this old woman say that I should have all the profit that should grow from this business? Thinking then perhaps that it would be but little: but now she sees how great it grows, she will not part with anything, no, not so much as the parings of her nails, that she may comply with that common saying of your little children: of a little, a little, of much, nothing.

Parmeno. Let her give thee that which she promised, let her make that good, or let us take it all from her. I told you before, would you have believed me, what an old cozening companion you should find her.

Celestina. If you are angry either with yourselves, your master, or your arms, wreck not your wrath upon me. For I wot well enough whence all this grows, I wind[481] you where you are. I now perceive on which foot you halt, not out of want of that which you demand, nor out of any covetousness that is in you, but because you think I will tie you to rack and manger, and make you captives all your lifetime to Elicia, and Areusa, and provide you with no other fresh ware, you make all this ado, quarrel thus with me for money, and seek by fearing me, to force me to a parting and sharing of stakes. But be still, my boys, and content yourselves: for she who could help you with these will not stick to furnish you with half a score of handsome wenches apiece, fairer than these by far, now that I see that you are grown to greater knowledge and more reason, and a better deservingness in yourselves. And whether or no,

---

[480] Characteristically, Rojas uses both popular sayings ('cuando pobre, franca, cuando rica, avarienta') and *adagia* from more authoritative sources, such as Petrarch's *Index* ('cómo crece la necesidad con la abundancia'). Lobera *et al.* (2000, p. 257, n. 167 and 168) document them in Correas, as well as in Petrarch's *De remediis* I.36, (and in the *Index* too).

[481] wind] get wind of, perceive.

in such a case as this, I am able to be as good as my word, let Parmeno speak for me. Speak, speak, Parmeno, be not ashamed, man to tell what did betide us, with that wench you wot of, that was sick of the mother.

Sempronio. I go not for what which you think. You talk of chalk, and we of cheese. Do not think to put us off with a jest; our demands desire a more serious answer. And assure yourself, if I can help it, you shall take no more hares with this greyhound. And therefore lay aside these tricks, and do not stand arguing any longer on the matter. I know your fetches too well: to an old dog, a man need not cry, now, now. Come off therefore quickly and give us two parts of that which you have received of Calisto. Dispatch, I say, and do not drive us to discover what you are. Come, come, exercise your wits upon some other. Flap those in the mouth, you old filth with your coggings and foistings,[482] that know you not, for we know you too well.

Celestina. Why, what am I, Sempronio? What do you know me to be? Did you take me out of the *puteria*?[483] Broughtst thou me, as a whore, out of the stews?[484] Bridle your tongue for shame, and do not dishonour my hoary hairs. I am an old woman of God's making, no worse than all other women are. I live by my occupation as other women do, very well, and handsomely. I seek not after those who seek not after me; they that will have me, come home to my house to fetch me. They come home, I say, and entreat me to do this or that for them. And for the life that I lead, whether it be good or bad, heaven knows my heart. And do not think out of your choler to misuse me, for there is law and justice for all, and equal to all; and my tale, I doubt not, shall be as soon heard, though I am an old woman, as yours, for all you be so smoothly kembed.[485] Let me alone, I pray, in mine own house, and with mine own fortune. And you, Parmeno, doe not you think that I am thy

---

[482] coggings and foistings] frauds and rogueries.
[483] out of the stews] 'Puteria', in Spanish, whoredom. The original reads: '¿Quitásteme de la putería?' (Lobera *et al.*, eds, 2000, p. 259), as usual, Mabbe expands and paraphrases the original sense to clarify the meaning, hence: 'Boughtst thou me, as a whore, out of the stews?'
[484] stews] brothels.
[485] kembed] well-kempt, well groomed.

slave, because thou knowst my secrets, and my life past, and all those matters that happened betwixt me and that unfortunate mother of thine. For she was also wont to use me on this fashion, when she was disposed to play her pranks with me.

Parmeno. Do not hit me in the teeth with these thy idle memorials of my mother, unless thou meanst I should send thee with these thy tidings unto her, where thou mayst better make thy complaint.

Celestina. Elicia, Elicia, arise and come down quickly, and bring me my mantle; for by heaven I will hie me to the justice, and there cry out and rail at you, like a mad woman. What is it you would have? What do you mean, to menace me thus in mine own house? Shall your valour and your bravings be exercised on a poor silly innocent sheep? On a hen, that is tied by the leg, and cannot fly from you? On an old woman of sixty years of age? Get you, get you, for shame, amongst men, such as yourselves; go and wreak your anger upon such as are girt with the sword, and not against me and my poor weak distaff.[486] It is an infallible note of great cowardice to assail the weak and such as have but small or very little power to resist. Your filthy flies bite none but lean and feeble oxen, and your barking curs fly with greater eagerness and more open mouth upon your poorest passengers. If she that lies above there in the bed, would have hearkened unto me, this house should not have been, as not it is, without a man in the night; nor we have slept, as we do, by the naked shadow of a candle. But to pleasure you, and to be faithful unto you, we suffer this solitude; and because you see we are women, and have nobody here to oppose you, you prate,[487] and talk, and ask I know not what without any reason in the world, which you would as soon have been hanged as once dared to have proffered it, if you had heard but a man stirring in the house. For, as it is in the proverb, a hard adversary appeaseth anger.

Sempronio. Oh thou old covetous crib,[488] that art ready to die

---

[486] distaff] staff or 'rock' of a hand spinning-wheel, upon which the flax to be spun is placed (*OED*), used here as a metonymy for the female condition.

[487] prate] chatter, speak boastfully or foolishly.

[488] crib] a close-fisted person (the *OED* documents this particular meaning with an expression from Mabbe's *The Rogue*, his translation of Alemán's *Guzmán de Alfarache*).

with the thirst of gold! Cannot a third part of the gain content thee?

Celestina. What third part? A pox on you both. Out of my house in the devil's name! You and your companion with you! Do not you make such a stir here as you do. Cause not our neighbours to come about us, and make them think we be mad. Put me not out of my wits, make me not mad: you would not, I trow,[489] would you, that Calisto's matters and yours should be proclaimed openly at the cross? Here's a stir indeed.

Sempronio. Cry, bawl, and make a noise; all's one, we care not: either look to perform your promise, or to end your days. Die you must, or else do as we will have you.

Elicia. Ah, woe is me! Put up your sword! Hold him, hold him, Parmeno, for fear lest the fool should kill her in his madness!

Celestina. Justice, justice! Help, neighbours! Justice, justice! For here be ruffians that will murder me in my house. Murder, murder, murder!

Sempronio. Ruffians, you whore? Ruffians, you old bawd? Have you no better terms? Thou old sorceress! Thou witch, thou! Look for no other favour at my hands, but that I send thee post unto hell! You shall have letters thither! You shall! You old enchantress! And that speedily too! You shall have a quick dispatch!

Celestina. Ay me! I am slain! Ay, ay, confession, confession!

Parmeno. So, so: kill her! Kill her! Make an end of her! Since thou hast begun, be brief, be brief with her; lest the neighbours may chance to hear us. Let her die! let her die! LET us draw as few enemies upon us as we can.

Celestina. Oh, oh, oh!

Elicia. Oh cruel-hearted as you are! Enemies in the highest nature! Shame and confusion light upon you! The extremity of justice fall upon you, with its greatest vigours, and all those that have had a hand in it! My mother is dead, and with her, all my happiness!

Sempronio. Fly, fly, Parmeno! The people begin to flock hitherward. See, see, yonder comes the *alguazil*!

---

[489] I trow] I believe, I trust.

Parmeno. Ay, wretch that I am! There is no means of escape for us in the world, for they have made good the door, and are entering the house.

Sempronio. Let us leap out at these windows, and let us die rather so, than fall into the hands of justice!

Parmeno. Leap then, and I will follow thee.

Actus XIII
The Argument

Calisto awakened from sleep, talks a while with himself; anon after he calls unto Tristan, and some other of his servants. By and by Calisto falls asleep again. Tristan goes down, and stands at the door. Sosia comes weeping unto him. Tristan, demanding the cause, Sosia delivers unto him the death of Sempronio and Parmeno. They go and acquaint Calisto with it, who knowing the truth thereof, maketh great lamentation.

INTERLOCUTORS
Calisto, Tristan, Sosia

Calisto. Oh how daintily have I slept! Ever since that sweet short space of time, since that harmonious discourse I enjoyed, I have had exceeding ease, taken very good rest. This contentment and quietude hath proceeded from my joy. Either the travail of my body caused so sound a sleep; or else the glory and pleasure of my mind. Nor do I much wonder, that both the one and the other should link hands, and join together to close the lids of mine eyes, since I travailed the last night with my body and person, and took pleasure with my spirit and senses. True it is that sorrow causeth much thought, and overmuch thought much hindreth sleep, as it was mine own case within these few days, when I was much discomfited and quite out of heart, of ever hoping to enjoy that surpassing happiness, which I now possess. Oh my sweet lady, and dearest love, Melibea, what dost thou think on now? Art thou asleep or awake? Thinkst thou on me, or somebody else? Art thou up and ready, or art thou not yet stirring? Oh most happy, and most fortunate Calisto, if it be true, and that it be no dream, which hath already passed! Dreamt I, or dreamt I not? Was it a mere phantasy, or was it a real truth? But now I remember myself, I was not alone, my servants waited on me, there were two of them with me; if they shall affirm it to be no dream, but that all that was past was true, I am bound to believe it. I will command them to be called, for the further confirmation of my joy. Tristanico! Why ho! Where are my men? Tristanico! Hie you and come up! Arise, I say! Get you up quickly and come hither!

Tristan. Sir, I am up and here already.
Calisto. Go, run, and call me hither Sempronio and Parmeno.
Tristan. I shall, sir
30 *Calisto.*   Now sleep, and take thy rest,
                        Once griev'd, and pained wight;
                        Since she now loves thee best,
                        Who is thy heart's delight.
                        Let joy be thy soul's guest;
                        And care be banish't quite;
                        Since shee hath thee expressed
                        To be her favourite.
Tristan. There is not so much as a boy in the house.
Calisto. Open the windows, and see whether it be day or no.
40 *Tristan.* Sir, it is broad day.
Calisto. Go again, and see if you can find them; and see you wake me not, till it be almost dinner-time.

Tristan. I will go down and stand at the door, that my master may take out his full sleep; and to so many as shall ask for him, I shall answer that he is not within. Oh what an outcry do I hear in the marketplace! What's the matter a God's name? There is some execution of justice to be done, or else they are up so early to see some bull-baiting. I do not know what to make of this noise, it is some great matter, the noise is so great; but lo,
50 yonder comes Sosia, my master's foot-boy;[490] he will tell me what the business is. Look how the rogue comes pulling and tearing of his hair. He hath tumbled into one tavern or other, where he hath been scuffling. But if my master chance to scent him, he will cause his coat to be well cudgelled; for though he be somewhat foolish, punishment will make him wise. But methinks he comes weeping. What's the matter, Sosia? Why dost thou weep? Whence com'st thou now? Why speak'st thou not?
Sosia. Oh miserable that I am! What misfortune could be more?
60 Oh what a great dishonour to my master's house! Oh what an unfortunate morning is this! Oh unhappy young men!
Tristan. What's the matter, man? Why dost thou keep such ado? Why griev'st thou thus? What mischief hath befallen us?

---

[490] foot-boy] page-boy.

Sosia. Sempronio, and Parmeno!

Tristan. What of Sempronio and Parmeno? What means this fool? Speak a little plainer, thou torment'st me with delays.

Sosia. Our old companions, our fellows, our brethren.

Tristan. Thou art either drunk or mad, or thou bringest some ill news along with thee. Why dost thou not tell me what thou hast to say, concerning these young men?

Sosia. That they lie slain in the street.

Tristan. Oh unfortunate mischance! Is it true? Didst thou see them? Did they speak unto thee?

Sosia. No. They were e'en past all sense. But one of them with much ado, when he saw I beheld him with tears, began to look a little towards me, fixing his eyes upon me, and lifting up his hands to heaven, as one that is making his prayers unto God, and looking on me, as if he had asked me if I were not sorry for his death. And straight after, as one that perceived whither he was presently to go, he let fall his head with tears in his eyes, giving thereby to understand that he should never see me again till we did meet at that day of the great judgement.

Tristan. You did not observe in him, that he would have asked you whether Calisto were there or no? But since thou hast such manifest proofs of this cruel sorrow, let us haste with these doleful tidings to our master.

Sosia. Master, master, do you hear, sir?

Calisto. What, are you mad? Did not I will you I should not be wakened?

Sosia. Rouse up yourself, and rise, for if you do not stick unto us we are all undone. Sempronio and Parmeno lie beheaded in the marketplace as public malefactors, and their fault proclaimed by the common crier.

Calisto. Now heaven help me! What is it thou tell'st me? I know not whether I may believe thee, in this thy so sudden and sorrowful news. Didst thou see them?

Sosia. I saw them, sir.

Calisto. Take heed what thou sayst, for this night they were with me.

Sosia. But rose too early to their deaths.

Calisto. Oh my loyal servants! Oh my chiefest followers! Oh my faithful secretaries and counsellors in all my affairs. Can it be, that this should be true? Oh unfortunate Calisto! Thou art dishonoured as long as thou hast a day to live. What shall become of thee, having lost such a pair of trusty servants? Tell me, for pity's sake, Sosia, what was the cause of their deaths? What spoke the proclamation? Where were they slain? By what justice were they beheaded?

Sosia. The cause, Sir, of their deaths, was published by the cruel executioner, or common hangman, who delivered with a loud voice: 'justice hath commanded that these violent murderers be put to death'.

Calisto. Who was it they so suddenly slew? Who might it be? It is not four hours ago since they left me. How call you the party whom they murdered? What was he for a man?

Sosia. It was a woman, sir, one whom they call Celestina.

Calisto. What's that thou sayest?

Sosia. That which you heard me tell you, sir.

Calisto. If this be true, kill thou me too, and I will forgive thee. For sure, there is more ill behind, more than was either seen or thought upon, if that Celestina be slain that hath the slash over her face.

Sosia. It is the very same, sir, for I saw her stretched out in her own house, and her maid weeping by her, having received in her body above thirty several wounds.

Calisto. Oh unfortunate young men! How went they? Did they see thee? Spake they unto thee?

Sosia. Oh sir, had you seen them, your heart would have burst with grief. One of them had all his brains beaten out in most pitiful manner, and lay without any sense or motion in the world. The other had both his arms broken, and his face so sorely bruised, that it was all black and blue, and all of a gore-blood. For, that they might not fall into the *alguazil's* hands, they leapt down out of a high window; and so, being in a manner quite dead, they chopped off their heads, when, I think, they scarce felt what harm was done them.

Calisto. Now I begin to have a taste of shame and to feel how much I am touched in mine honour. Would I had excused them and had lost my life, so I had not lost my honour, and my hope of achieving my commenced purpose, which is the greatest grief and distaste that in this case I feel. Oh my name and reputation, how unfortunately dost thou go from table to table, from mouth to mouth! Oh ye my secret, my secret actions, how openly will you now walk through every public street, and open marketplace? What shall become of me? Whither shall I go? If I go forth to the dead, I am unable to recover them, and if I stay here it will be deemed cowardice. What counsel shall I take? Tell me, Sosia, what was the cause they killed her?

Sosia. That maid, Sir, of her, which sat weeping and crying over her made known the cause of her death to as many as would hear it, saying that they slew her because she would not let them share with her in that chain of gold which you had lately given her.

Calisto. Oh wretched and unfortunate day! Oh sorrow, able to break even a heart of adamant! How go my goods from hand to hand, and my name from tongue to tongue? All will be published and come to light, whatsoever I have spoken, either to her or them, whatsoever they knew of my doings, and whatsoever was done in this business. I dare not go forth of doors. I am ashamed to look any man in the face. Oh miserable young men! That ye should suffer death by so sudden a disaster. Oh my joys, how do you go declining, and waning from me! But it is an ancient proverb, that the higher a man climbs, the greater is his fall. Last night I gained much, today I have lost much. Your sea-calms are rare and seldom. I might have been listed in the roll of the happy, if my fortune would but have allayed these tempestuous winds of my perdition. Oh Fortune! How much, and through how many parts hast thou beaten me! But howsoever thou dost shake my house, and how opposite soever thou art unto my person, yet are adversities to be endured with an equal courage. And by them the heart is proved whether it be of oak or elder, strong or weak. There is no better say or touchstone in the world to know what fineness, or what carats of virtue or of fortitude remain in man. And therefore come what will come, fall back, fall edge, I will not desist to accomplish her desire, for whose sake all this hath happened. For it is better for me to pursue the benefit of that glory which I expect than the loss of those that are dead. They were proud, and stout, and would have been slain at some other time, if not now. The old woman was wicked and false, as it seems, in her dealing, not complying with that contract which she had made with them: so that they fell out about the true man's cloak, taking it from the true owner to share it amongst themselves. But this was a just judgment of God upon

190　　her, that she should receive this payment for the many adulteries which by her intercession and means have been committed. Sosia and Tristianico shall provide themselves, they shall accompany me, in this my desired walk. They shall carry the scaling-ladders, for the walls are very high. Tomorrow I will abroad, and see if I can revenge their deaths; if not, I will purge my innocency with a feigned absence, or else feign myself mad, that I may the better enjoy this so tasteful a delight of my sweet love, as did that great captain Ulysses, to shun the Trojan war, that he might lie dulcing[491] at home with his wife Penelope.

---

[491] dulcing] from dulce, *v.* sweeten, (Latin *dulcis*, sweet), i.e. resting pleasantly and enjoying the company of his wife. When the Trojan war broke out, Ulysses feigned madness to avoid being dragged into the conflict.

ACTUS XIV
THE ARGUMENT

Melibea is much afflicted. She talks with Lucrecia concerning Calisto's slackness in coming, who had vowed that night to come and visit her, the which he performed. And with him came Sosia and Tristan, and after that he had accomplished his desire, they all of them betook them to their rest. Calisto gets him home to his palace, and there begins to complain and lament that he had stayed so little awhile with Melibea; and begs of Phoebus that he would shut his beams, that he might the sooner go to renew his desire.

INTERLOCUTORS
Melibea, Lucrecia, Sosia, Tristan, Calisto

Melibea. Methinks the gentleman whom we look for, stays very long. Tell me, Lucrecia, what think'st thou? Will he come or no?

Lucrecia. I conceive, madam, he hath some just cause of stay, and it is not in his power to come so soon as you expect.

Melibea. Good spirits be his guard and preserve his person from peril. For his long stay doth not so much grieve me, but I am afraid lest some misfortune or other may befall him as he is on his way unto us. For who knows, whether he coming so willingly to the place appointed, and in that kind of fashion as such gentleman as he on the like occasion and the like hour use to go, whether or no, I say, he may chance to light upon the night-watch or be met by the *alguazils*, and they not knowing him have set upon him and he to defend himself hath either hurt them or they him? Or whether some roguish cur or other with his cruel teeth — for such dogs as they make no difference of persons — have perhaps unfortunately bit him? Or whether, he hath fallen upon the causey,° or into some dangerous pit, whereby he may receive some harm? But, ay me, these are but inconveniences which my conceived love brings forth and my troubled thoughts present unto me. Goodness forbid that any of these misfortunes should befall him! Rather let him stay as long as it shall please himself from coming to visit me. But hark, hark, what steps are those that I hear in the street? And to my thinking likewise I hear somebody talking on this side of the garden.

Sosia. Tristan, set the ladder here, for though it be the higher yet I take it to be the better place.
Tristan. Go up, sir. And I will along with you. For, we know not who is there within, they are talking (I am sure) whoever they be.
Calisto. Stay here, you fool, I will in alone, for I hear my lady and mistress.

Melibea. Your servant, your slave, Calisto, who prices more yours than her own life. Oh my dear lord! Take heed how you leap, leap not down so high; you kill me, come down gently, I pray. Take more leisure in coming down the ladder; as you love me, come not so fast.
Calisto. Oh divine image! Oh precious pearl, before whom the whole world appeareth foul! Oh my lady and my glory! I embrace and hug thee in mine arms, and yet I not believe it: such a turbation[492] of pleasure seizes on my person, that it makes me not feel the fulness of that joy I possess.
Melibea. My lord, sithence I have instructed myself in your hands, since I have been willing to comply with your will, let me not be worse thought of for being pitiful, than if I had been coy and merciless. Nor do not work my undoing, for a delight so momentary and performed in so short a space. For, actions that are ill, after they are committed, may easier be reprehended than amended. Rejoice thou in that, wherein I rejoice, which is to see and draw near unto thy person, to view and touch thee. But do not offer either to ask or take that which being taken away is not in thy power to restore. Take heed, sir, that you go not about to overthrow that which with all the wealth in the world you are not able to repair.
Calisto. Dear lady, since for to obtain this favour I have spent my whole life, what folly were it in me to refuse that which you have so kindly conferred upon me? Nor, madam, do I hope

---

[492] turbation] confusion, agitation.

that you will lay so hard a command upon me, or if you should, yet have I not power to contain myself within the limits of your command. Do not impose such a point of cowardice upon me. For I tell you, it is not in any man that is a man to forbear in such a case and to condition so hard with himself, much less in me, loving as I do, and having swum, as I have done all my life long, through this sea of thy desire and mine own love. Will you then after my so many travels, deny me entrance into that sweet haven, where I may find some ease of all my former sorrows?

Melibea. As you love me, Calisto, though thy tongue take liberty to talk what it will, yet, I prithee, let not thy hands do all what they can. Be quiet, good sir, since I am yours, suffice it you content yourself in the enjoying of this outwardness, which is the proper fruit of lovers, and not to rob me of the greatest jewel which nature hath enriched me with. Consider, besides, that it is the property of a good shepherd to fleece, but not to slay his sheep; to shear them, but not to uncase them.

Calisto. Madam, what mean you by this? That my passions should not be at peace? That I shall run over my torments anew? That I shall return to my old yoke again? Pardon, sweet lady, these my impudent hands, if too presumptuously they press upon you, which once did never think — so all together were they unworthy — not to touch, no not so much as any part of thy garments, that they now have leave to lay themselves with a gentle palm on this dainty body of thine, this most white, soft, and delicate flesh.

Melibea. Lucrecia, go aside a little.

Calisto. And why, madam? I should be proud to have such witness as she of my glory.

Melibea. So would not I, when I do amiss. And had I but thought that you would have used me thus, or been but half so violent, as I now see you are, I would not have trusted my person with such a rough and cruel conversation.

Sosia. Tristan, thou hear what hath past, and how the gear goes.

Tristan. I hear so much that I hold my master the happiest man that lives. And I assure thee (though I am but a boy to speak of) methinks I could give as good account of such a business as my master.

Sosia. To such a jewel as this who would not reach out his hand? But allow him this flesh to his bread, and much good may it do him, for he hath paid well for it: for a couple of his servants served to make sauce for this his love.

Tristan. I had quite forgot that. But let them die, as instruments of their own destruction, and let others as many as will play the fools upon affiance° to be defended. But for mine own part, I well remember when I served the count, that my father gave me this counsel: that I should take heed how I killed a man, of all other things, that I should beware of that. For (quoth he) you shall see the master merry and kindly embraced, when his man (poor soul) shall be hanged an disgraced.

Melibea. Oh my life and my dear lord, how could you find in your heart that I should lose the name and crown of a virgin, for so momentary and so short a pleasure? Oh my poor mother, if thou didst but know what we have done, with what willingness wouldst thou take thine own death? And with what violence and enforcement give me mine? How cruel a butcher wouldst thou become of thine own blood? And how doleful an end should I bee of thy days? Oh my most honourable father, how have I wronged thy reputation? And given both opportunity and place to the utter overthrowing and undoing of thy house? Oh traitor that I am! Why did I not first look into that great error, which would ensue by thy entrance, as also that great danger, which I could not but expect?

Sosia. You should have sung this song before. Now, it comes too late. You know, it is an old saying: when a thing is done, it cannot be undone. There is no fence for it, but what, if the fool Calisto should hap to hear me?

Calisto. Is it possible? Look and it be not day already. Methinks we have not been here above an hour, and the clock now strikes three.

Melibea. My lord, for Jove's sake, now that all that I have is yours; now that I am your mistress; now that you cannot deny my love; deny me not your sight. And on such nights as

you shall resolve to come, let your coming be by this secret place, and at the self-same hour: for then shall I still look for you prepared with the same joy, wherewith I now comfort myself in the hopeful expectation of those sweet nights that are to come. And so for this present, I will take my leave. Farewell, my lord, my hope is that you will not be discovered, for it is very dark, nor I heard in the house, for it is not yet day.
Calisto. Do you hear there? Bring hither the ladder.
Sosia. Sir, it is here ready for you to come down.
Melibea. Lucrecia, come hither, I am now all alone. My love is gone, who hath left his heart with me, and hath taken mine with him. Didst thou not hear us, Lucrecia?
Lucrecia. No madam, I was fast asleep.

Sosia. Tristan, we must go very softly, and not speak a word. For just about this time, rise your rich men, your covetous money-mongers, your penny-fathers, your venereans and love-sick souls, such as our master; your day-labourers, your plough-men and your shepherds, who about this time unpen their sheep and bring them to their sheepcots to be milked. And it may be, they may hear some word escape us, which may wrong either Calisto's or Melibea's honour.
Tristan. Now you silly ass, you whoreson horse-currier,[493] you would have us make no noise, not a word, but mum, and yet thyself dost name her. Thou art an excellent fellow, to make a guide or leader to conduct an army in the moor's country: for that prohibiting, thou permittest; covering, thou discoverest; defending, offendest; bidding others hold their peace, you thyself speak'st aloud, nay, proclaims it; and proclaiming, makes answer thereunto. But though you are so subtle-witted and of so discreet a temper, you shall not tell me in what month our lady day in harvest falls. For we know that we have more straw in the house this year, than you art able to eat.[494]

---

[493] horse-currier] i.e. one who curries (combs or rubs down) horses, a stable boy.
[494] we have more straw in the house this year, than you art able to eat] Tristan is calling Sosia an ass.

Calisto. My masters, what a noise make you there? My cares and yours are not alike. Enter softly, I pray, and leave your prattling, that they in the house may not hear us. Shut this door, and let us go take our rest. For I will up alone to my chamber, and there disarm me. Go get you to bed.

Calisto. Oh wretch that I am, how suitable and natural unto me is solitariness, silence, and darkness! I know not whether the cause of it be that there cometh now to mind the treason that I have committed in taking my leave of that lady whom I so dearly love before it was further day, or whether it be the grief which I conceive of my dishonour by the death of my servants ... Ay, ay, this is it that grieves me, this is that wound whereof I bleed. Now, that I am grown a little cooler, now that blood waxeth cold, which yesterday did boil in me, now that I see the decaying of my house, my want of service, the wasting of my patrimony, and the infamy which lights upon me by the death of my servants. What have I done? How can I possibly contain myself? How can I forbear any longer, but that I should presently express myself as a man much wronged, and show myself a proud and speedy revenger of that open injury which hath been offered me? Oh the miserable sweetness of this most short and transitory life! Who is he so covetous of thy countenance who will not rather choose to die presently, than to enjoy a whole year of a shameful life, and to prorogue it with dishonour, losing the good report and honourable memory of his noble ancestors? Especially, sithence that in this world, we have not any certain or limited time: no, not so much as a moment or a minute. We are debtors without time: we stand continually bound to present payment. Why have I not gone abroad, and made all the inquiry I can, after the secret cause of my open perdition? Oh thou short delight of the world, how little do thy pleasures last and how much do they cost! Repentance should not be bought so dear. Oh miserable that I am! When shall I recover so great a loss? What shall I do? What counsel shall I take? To whom shall I discover my disgrace? Why do I conceal it from the rest of my servants and kinsfolk? They clip[495] and note my good name in their council-

---

[495] clip] shear, cut off hair; it translates the original 'trasquilar' (shear): i.e. Calisto's name is being subject to the same infamy that some individuals underwent by having their hair clipped, as a form of punishment. The expression

house and public assembly, and make me infamous throughout the whole kingdom: and they of mine own house and kindred must not know of it. I will out amongst them. But if I go out and tell them that I was present, it is too late, if absent, it is too soon. And to provide me of friends, ancient servants, and near allies, it will ask some time, as likewise that we be furnished with arms, and other preparations of vengeance. Oh thou cruel judge, what ill payment hast thou made me of that my father's bread, which so often thou hast eaten? I thought, that by thy favour I might have killed a thousand men without controlment.° Oh thou falsifier of faith, thou persecutor of the truth, thou man moulded of the baser sort of earth! Truly is the proverb verified in thee, that for want of good men thou wast made a judge. Thou shouldst have considered that thyself and those thou didst put to death were servants to my ancestors and me, and thy fellows and companions. But when the base to riches doth ascend, he regardeth neither kindred nor friend. Who would have thought, that thou wouldst have wrought my undoing? But there is nothing more hurtful than an unexpected enemy. Why wouldst thou that it should be verified of thee, that that which came out of Aetna, should consume Aetna, and that I hatched the crow which picked out mine eyes? Thou thyself art a public delinquent, and yet punishest those that were private offenders. But I would have thee to know, that a private fault is less than a public, and less the inconvenience and danger, at least according to the laws of Athens, which were not written in blood, but do show that it is a lesse[r] error not to condemn a delinquent than to punish the innocent.[496] Oh how hard a matter it is, to follow a just cause before an unjust judge! How much more this excess of my servants, which was not free from offence! But consider with all spite of all stoical paradox, their guilt was not equal, though their sufferings alike. What deserved the one, for that which the other did? That only because he was his companion, thou shouldst doom them both to death? But why do I talk

---

'trasquilar en concejo', i.e. to shear one's name or reputation in public councils had a certain tradition in Castilian proverbs (see Lobera *et al.*, eds, 2000, p. 278, n. 70).
[496] This legal principle appears in Petrarch's *Familiares* V.iii.17 (Lobera *et al.*, eds, 2000, p. 280, n. 83).

thus? With whom do I discourse? Am I in my right wits? What's the matter with thee, Calisto? Dream'st thou, sleep'st thou, or wak'st thou? Stand'st thou on thy feet? Or liest thou all along? Consider with thyself that thou art in thy chamber. Doest thou not see that the offender is not present? With whom doest thou contend? Come again to thyself, weigh with thyself that the absent were never found just. But if thou wilt be upright in thy judgement, thou must keep an ear for either party. Doest thou not see, that the law is supposed to be equal unto all? Remember that Romulus, the first founder of Rome, killed his own brother, because he transgressed the law. Consider that Torquatus the Roman slew his own son because he exceeded his commission.[497] And many other like unto these did this man do. Think likewise with thyself, that if the judge were here present, he would make thee this answer: that the principal and the accessary, the actor and consenter, do merit equal punishment. Howbeit, they were both notwithstanding executed, for that which was committed but by one. And if that other had not his pardon, but received a speedy judgment, it was because the fault was notorious, and needed no further proofs, as also that they were taken in the very act of murder, and that one of them was found dead of his fall from the window. And it is likewise to be imagined, that that weeping wench which Celestina kept in her house made them to hasten the more by her woeful and lamentable noise, and that the judge, that he might not make a hurly burly of it, that he might not defame me, and that he might not stay till the people should press together, and hear the proclaiming of that great infamy which could not choose but follow me, he did sentence them so early as he did; and the common hangman, which was the crier, could do no other wise, that he might comply with their execution and his own discharge. All which, if it were

---

[497] The exemplary story of Romulus, who executed his own brother for trespassing over the imaginary line that established the boundary of the future Rome, was common stock in law books, both ancient and medieval. According to Livy (*Ab Urbe Condita*, 1.7), Remus jumped over the newly constructed walls. Titus Manlius Imperiosus Torquatus was a Roman consul (fourth century BC), whose severity led him to execute his own son for fighting a duel against orders. This story was well known in antiquity, and was first documented in the historian Ennius. Through Cicero it passed on to Petrarch and also Juan de Mena's *Laberinto de Fortuna*.

done as I conceive it to be, I ought rather to rest his debtor, and think myself bound unto him the longest day of my life, not as to my father's sometimes servant, but as to my true and natural brother. But put case it were not so, or suppose I should not construe it in the better sense, yet call, Calisto, to mind the great joy and solace thou hast had, bethink thyself of thy sweet lady and mistress, and thy whole and sole happiness; and since for her sake thou esteemest thy life as nothing for to do her service, thou art not to make any reckoning of the death of others, and the rather, because no sorrow can equal thy received pleasure. Oh my lady and my life, that I should ever think to offend thee in thy absence! And yet in doing as I do, methinks it argues against me, that I hold in small esteem that great and singular favour which I have received at thy hands. I will now no longer think on grief. I will no longer entertain friendship with sorrow. Oh incomparable good! Oh insatiable contentment! And what could I have asked more of heaven, in requital of all my merits in this life (if they be any) than that which I have already received? Why should I not content myself with so great a blessing? Which being so, it stands not with reason that I should be ungrateful unto him who hath conferred upon me so great a good. I will therefore acknowledge it, I will not with care craze my understanding, lest that being lost, I should fall from so high and so glorious a possession. I desire no other honour, no other glory, no other riches, no other father nor mother, no other friends nor kinsfolks. In the day I will abide in my chamber. In the night, in that sweet paradise, in that pleasant grove, that green plot of ground amidst those sweet trees and fresh and delightsome walks. Oh night of sweet rest and quiet! Oh that thou hadst made thy return! Oh bright shining Phoebus, drive on thy chariot apace, make haste to thy journey's end. Oh comfortable and delightful stars, break your wont, and appear before your time, and out of your wonted and continued course! Oh dull and slow clock, I wish to see thee burned in the quickest and loveliest fire that love can make. For didst thou but expect that which I do, when thou strikest twelve, thou wouldst never endure to be tied to the will of the master that made thee! Oh ye hiematical[498]

---

[498] hiematical] hiemal, i.e. belonging to winter; the *OED* uses this example from Mabbe to illustrate the definition of this adjective.

and winterly months, which now hide your heads, and live in darkness and obscurity! Why haste ye not to cut off these tedious days with your longer nights? Methinks it is almost a year since I saw that sweet comfort and most delightful refreshing of my travails. But what do I ask? Why like a fool do I, out of impatience, desire that which never either was or shall be? For your natural courses did never learn to wheel away. For to all of them there is an equal course, to all of them one and the self-same space and time. Not so much as to life and death, but there is a settled and limited end. The secret motions of the high firmament of heaven, of the planets and the North-star, and of the increase and wane of the moon, all of these are ruled with an equal rein, all of these are moved with an equal spur. Heaven, earth, sea, fire, wind, heat and cold. What will it benefit me, that this clock of iron should strike twelve, if that of heaven do not hammer with it? And therefore though I rise never so soon, it will never the sooner be day. But thou my sweet imagination, thou, who canst only help me in this case, bring thou unto my fantasy the unparalleled presence of that glorious image. Cause thou to come unto my ears that sweek music of her words, those her unwilling handings off without profit, that her pretty 'I prithee leave off', 'forbear, good sir, if you love me, touch me not', 'do not deal so discourteously with me', out of whose ruddy lips, methinks, I hear these words still sound, 'do not seek my undoing', which she would evermore be out withal. Besides, those her amorous embracements betwixt every word; that her losing of herself from me, and clipping me again; that her flying from me and her coming to me; those her sweet sugared kisses; and that her last salutation wherewith she took her leave of me. Oh with what pain did it issue from her mouth! With what resuscitation of her spirits! With how many tears, which did seem to be so many round pearls, which did fall without any noise from her clear and resplendent eyes!

Sosia. What thinkst thou of Calisto? How hath he slept? It is now upon four of the clock in the afternoon, and he hath neither as yet called us, nor eaten anything.

Tristan. Hold your peace, for sleep requires no haste. Besides, on the one side, he is oppressed with sadness and melancholy for his servants, and on the other side transported with that gladsome delight and singular great pleasure, which he hath enjoyed with his Melibea. And thou knowst, that where two such strong and contrary passions meet, in whomsoever they shall house themselves, with what forcible violence they will work upon a weak and feeble subject.

Sosia. Dost thou think that he takes any great grief and care for those that are dead? If he did not grieve more, whom I see here out of the window go along the street, she would not wear a veil of that colour as she does.

Tristan. Who is that, brother?

Sosia. Come hither and see her, before she be past. Seest thou that mournful maid, which wipes the tears from her eyes? That is Elicia, Celestina's servant, and Sempronio's friend. She is a good, pretty, handsome, well-favoured wench, though now, poor soul, she be left to the wide world, and forsaken of all. For she accounted Celestina her mother, and Sempronio her chiefest and best friends. And in that house, where you see her now enter, there dwells a very fair woman, she is exceeding well-favoured, very fresh and lovely, she is half courtezan; yet happy is he, and counts himself to be, that can purchase her favour at an easy rate, and win her to be his friend. Her name is Areusa, for whose sake, I know, that unfortunate and poor Parmeno endured many a miserable night. And I know that she, poor soul, is nothing pleased with his death.

JOSÉ MARÍA PÉREZ FERNÁNDEZ

Actus XV
The Argument

Areusa utters injurious speeches to a ruffian, called Centurio, who takes his leave of her, occasioned by the coming in of Elicia, which Elicia recounts unto Areusa the deaths, which had ensued upon the love of Calisto and Melibea. And Areusa and Elicia agree, and conclude together, that Centurio should revenge the death of all those three upon the two young lovers. This done, Elicia takes her leave of Areusa, and would not be entreated to stay because she would not lose her market at home in her accustomed lodging.

INTERLOCUTORS
Elicia, Centurio, Areusa

Elicia. What ails my cousin, that she cries and takes on as she does? It may be she hath already heard of that ill news which I came to bring her. If she have, I shall have no reward of her for my heavy tidings. So, weep, weep on, weep thy belly-full; let thine eyes break their banks and overflow thy bosom with an eternal deluge, for two such men were not everywhere to be had. It is some ease yet unto me, that she so resents the matter, and hath so true a feeling of their deaths. Do, tear, and rend thy hair, as (I poor soul) have done before thee, and think, and
10   consider with thyself, that to fall from a happy life is more miserable than death itself. Oh how I hug her in my heart! How much more, than ever heretofore, do I now love her; that she can express her passion in such lively colours, and paint forth sorrow to its perfect and true life!

Aerusa. Get thee out of my house, thou ruffianly rascal! Thou lying companion! Thou cheating scoundrel! Thou hast deluded me, thou villain! Thou hast played bob-fool[499] with me by thy vain and idle offers, and with thy fair words and flattering speeches — a pox on that smooth tongue of thine! — thou hast

---

[499] played bob-fool] made a fool of, befooled.

robbed me of all that I have. I gave thee, you rogue, a jerkin and a cloak, a sword and a buckler, and a couple of shirts wrought with a thousand devices, all of needle-work. I furnished thee with arms and a horse, and placed thee with such a master as thou wast not worthy to wipe his shoes. And now that I entreat thee to do a business for me, thou makest a thousand frivolous excuses.

Centurio. Command me to kill ten men, to do you service, rather than to put me to walk a league on foot for you.

Areusa. Why then did you play away your horse? You must be a dicer with a murrain;[500] had it not been for me, thou hadst been hanged long since. Thrice I have freed thee from the gallows; four times have I disimpawned[501] thee, first from this, and then from that ordinary, when as thou might'st have rotted in prision had not I redeem'd thee and paid thy debts. Oh that I should have anything to do with such a villain! That I should be such a fool! That I should have any affiance° in such a false-hearted, white-livered slave! That I should believe him and his lies! That I should once suffer him to come within my doors! What a devil is there good in him? His hair is curled, and shagged like a water spaniel; his face scotcht, and notcht; he hath been twice whipped up and down the town; he is lame on his sword-arm, and hath some thirty whores in the common stews. Get thee out of my house, and that presently too. Look me no more in the face; speak not to me; no not a word. Neither say thou that thou did'st ever know me, lest, by the bones of my father, who begot me, and of my mother, who brought me forth, I cause 2000 bastinadoes to be laid upon that miller's back of thine. For, I would thou shouldst know, I have a friend in a corner that will not stick to do a greater matter than that for me, and come off handsomely with it, when he has done.

Centurio. The fool is mad, I think. But do you hear, dame? If I be nettled, I shall sting somebody; if my choler be moved, I shall draw tears from some; I shall make somebody put finger in the eye, I shall, i'faith. But for once, I will go my way and

---

[500] a dicer with a murrain] i.e. a gambler with a pestilence, a lousy, incompetent gambler.
[501] disimpawned] redeemed, taken out of pawn; this is the only example listed in the *OED*.

say nothing. I will suffer all this at your hands, lest somebody may come in, or the neighbours chance to hear us.

Elicia. I will in, for that is no true sound of sorrow, which sends forth threatenings and revilings.

Areusa. Oh wretch that I am! Is it you, my Elicia? I can hardly believe it. But what means this? Who hath clothed thee thus in sorrow? What mourning weed is this? Believe me, cousin, you much affright me. Tell me quickly, what's the matter? For I long to know it. Oh what a qualm comes over my stomach! Thou hast not left me one drop of blood in my body.

Elicia. Great sorrow, great loss. That which I show is but little to that which I feel and conceal. My heart is blacker than my mantle, my bowels than my veil. Ah, cousin, cousin . . . I am not able to speak through hoarseness; I cannot for sobbing send my words from out my breast.

Areusa. Ay miserable me; why dost thou hold me in suspense? Tell me, tell me, I say, do not you tear your hair, do not you scratch and martyr your face. Deal not so ill with yourself. Is this evil common to us both? Appertains it also unto me?

Elicia. Ay, my cousin, my dear love! Sempronio and Parmeno, are now no more. They live not. They are no longer of this world: dead, alas, they are dead.

Areusa. What dost thou tell me? No more I entreat thee, for pity hold thy peace, lest I fall down dead at thy feet.

Elicia. There is yet more ill news to come unto thine ears. Listen well to this woeful wight and she shall tell thee a longer tale of woe. Thy sorrows have not yet their end. Celestina, she whom thou knewst well; she whom I esteemed my mother; she who did cocker° me as her child, she who did cover all my infirmities; she who made me to be honoured amongst my equals; she by whose means I was known through all the city and suburbs of the same, stands now rendering up an account of all her works. I saw her with these eyes stabbed in a thousand places. They slew her in my lap, I folding her in mine arms.

Areusa. Oh strong tribulation! Oh heavy news worthy our bewailing! Oh swift-footed misfortunes! Oh incurable destruction! Oh irreparable loss! Oh how quickly hath Fortune turned about her wheel! Who slew them? How did they die? Thou hast made me almost besides myself with this thy news, and to stand amazed as one, who hears a thing that seems to be impossible. It is not eight days ago since I saw them all alive. Tell me, good friend, how did this cruel and unlucky chance happen?

Elicia. You shall know. I am sure, cousin, you have already heard tell of the love betwixt Calisto and that fool Melibea. And you likewise saw how Celestina, at the intercession of Sempronio, so as she might be paid for her pains, undertook the charge of that business and to be the means to effect it for him; wherein she used such diligence, and was so careful in the following of it, that she drew water at the second spitting.[502] Now when Calisto saw so good and so quick a dispatch, which he never hoped to have effected, amongst divers other things, he gave this my unfortunate aunt a chain of gold. And as it is the nature of that metal that the more we drink thereof the more we thirst, she, when she saw herself so rich, appropriated the whole gain to herself and would not let Sempronio and Parmeno have their parts, it being before agreed upon between them that whatsoever Calisto gave her they should share it alike. Now, they being come home weary one morning from accompanying their master, with whom they had been abroad all night, being in great choler and heat, upon I know not what quarrels and brawls, as they themselves said, that had betided them, they demanded part of the chain of Celestina, for to relieve themselves therewith. She stood upon denial of any such covenant or promise made between them, affirming the whole gain to be due to her; and discovering withal other petty matters of some secrecy, for — as it is the proverb — when gossips brawl, then out goes all. So that they being mightily enraged, on the one side necessity did urge them, which rends and breaks all the love in the world; on the other side, the great anger and weariness they brought thither with them, which many times works an alteration in us. And besides, they saw that they were forsaken in their fairest hopes, she breaking her faith and promise with them. So that they knew not in the world what to do, and so continued a great while upon terms with her, some hard words passing to and fro between them. But in the end perceiving her covetous disposition, and finding that she still

---

[502] She drew water after just two attempts with the spade ('a la segunda azadonada sacó agua', Lobera *et al.*, eds, 2000, p. 288).

persevered in her denial, they laid hands upon their swords, and hacked and hewed her in a thousand pieces.

Areusa. Oh unfortunate woman! Wast thou ordained to end thy days in so miserable a manner as this? But for them, I pray what became of them? How came they to their end?

Elicia. They, as soon as ever they had committed this foul murder, that they might avoid the justice, the *alcalde*[503] passing by by chance at that very instance, made me no more ado, but leapt presently out of the windows; and being in a manner dead with the fall, they presently apprehended them, and without any further delay, chopped off their heads.

Areusa. Oh my Parmeno, my love, what sorrow do I feel for thy sake? How much doth thy death torment me? It grieves me, for that my great love, which in so short a space I had settled upon him, sithence it was not my fortune to enjoy him longer. But being that this ill success hath ensued, being that this mischance hath happened, and being that their lives now lost cannot be bought or restored by tears, do not thou vex thyself so much in grieving and weeping out thine eyes. I grieve as much and believe thou hast but little advantage of me in thy sorrowing, and yet thou seest with what patience I bear it and pass it over.

Elicia. Oh, I grow mad! Oh wretch that I am, I am ready to run out of my wits! Ay me, there is not anybody's grief that is like to mine, there is not anybody that hath lost that which I have lost! Oh how much better, and more honest, had my tears been in another person's passion, than mine own! Whither shall I go? For I have lost both money, meat, drink, and clothes. I have lost my friend, and such a one, that had he been my husband, he could not have been more kind unto me. Oh thou wise Celestina, thou much honoured matron, and of great authority! How often did'st thou cover my faults by thy singular wisdom! Thou took'st pains, whil'st I took pleasure; thou went'st abroad, whil'st I stayed at home; thou went'st in tatters and rags, whil'st I did ruffle in silks and satins; thou still camest home like a bee, continually laden, whil'st I did nothing but spend and play the unthrift, for I knew not else what to do. Oh thou worldly happiness and joy, which whilst thou art

---

[503] *alcalde*] the local justice.

possessed, are the less esteemed! Nor dost thou ever let us know what thou art till we know that thou art not, finding our loss greater by wanting than in enjoining thee, never knowing what we have till we have thee not. Oh Calisto and Melibea, occasioners of so many deaths! Let some ill attend upon your love, let your sweet meat have some sour sauce, your pleasure pain, let your joy be turned into mourning, the pleasant flowers whereon you took your stolen solace let them be turned into serpents and snakes, your songs let them be turned into howlings, the shady trees of the garden let them be blasted and withered with your looking on them, your sweet scenting blossoms and buds let them be black and dismal to behold.

Areusa. Good cousin, content yourself, I pray, be quiet; enjoin silence to your complaints; stop the conduit-pipes to your tears; wipe your eyes; take heart again unto you. For when fortune shuts one gate, she usually sets open another; and this estate of yours, though it never so much broken, it will be soldered and made whole again. And many things may be revenged which are impossible to be remedied, whereas this hath a doubtful remedy, and a ready revenge.

Elicia. But by whom shall we mend ourselves? Of whom shall we be revenged, when as her death, and those that slew her, have brought all this affliction and anguish upon me? Nor doth the punishment of the delinquent less grieve me, than the error they committed. What would you have me to do, when as all the burden lies upon my shoulders? I would with all my heart that I were now with them, that I might not lie here, to lament and bewail them all as I do. And that which grieves me most is to see that for all this that villain Calisto, who hath no sense nor feeling of his servants' deaths, goes every night to see and visit his filth Melibea, feasting and solacing himself in her company, whilst she grows proud, glorying to see so much blood to be sacrificed to her service.

Areusa. If this be true, of whom can we revenge ourselves better? And therefore, he that hath eaten the meat, let him pay the shot.° Leave the matter to me, let me alone to deal with them. For, if I can but track them, or but once find the scent of their footing, or but have the least inkling in the world, when, how, where, and at what hour they visit one another, never hold me true daughter to that old pasty-wench whom you knew full well, if I do not give them sour sauce to their sweet meat, and make that their love distasteful, which now they swallow down with delight. And if I employ in this business that ruffian whom you found me railing against when you came into the house, if he prove not a worse executioner for Calisto than Sempronio was for Celestina never trust me more. Oh how quickly the villain would fat himself with joy, and how happy would he hold himself, if I would but implore any service upon him! For he went away from me very sad and heavy, to see how coarsely I used him: and should I but now send for him again, and speak kindly unto him, he would think himself taken up in some strange sweet rapture; so much will he be ravished with joy. And therefore tell me, cousin, how I may learn how this business goes, for I will set such a trap for them as if they be taken in it shall make Melibea weep as much as now she laugheth.

Elicia. Marry, I know, sweet cousin, another companion of Parmeno, Calisto's groom of the stable, whose name is Sosia, who accompanies him every night that he goes. I will see, what I can suck from him, and this (I suppose) will be a very good course for the matter you talk of.

Areusa. But hear you me, cousin, I pray do me the kindness, to send Sosia hither unto me, I will take him in hand a little, I will entertain talk with him; and one while I will so flatter him, another while make him such fair offers, that in the end, I will dive into him, and reach the very depth of his heart, and learn from him, as well what hath been already, as what is to be done hereafter; at least learn so much as we desire to know, or may serve our turn. And when I shall have effected this, I will make him and his master to vomit up all the pleasure they have eaten. And thou, Elicia, that art as dear to me as mine own soul, do not you vex yourself any more but bring your apparel and such implements as you have, and come and live with me. For where you are, you shall remain all alone: and sadness, you know, is a friend of solitariness. What, wench? A new love will make thee forget the old. One son that is born, will repair the love of three that be dead. With a new successor we receive anew the joyful memory and lost delights of forepassed times. If I have a loaf of bread, or a penny in my purse, thou shalt have half of it. And I have more compassion of thy sorrow than of those that did cause it. True it is, that the loss of that doth grieve a man more, which he already possesseth, than the hope of the like good can glad him, be it never so certain. You see, the matter is past all remedy, and dead men cannot be recalled. You know the old saying: Fie upon this weeping, let them die, and we live. As for the rest that remain behind, leave that to me; I will take order for Calisto and Melibea; I shall give them as bitter a potion to drink as they have given thee. Oh cousin, cousin, how witty am I when I am angry, to turn all these their plots upside down! And though I am but young, and a girl to speak of, to break the neck of these their devices, I shall overthrow them horse and foot.

Elicia. Bethink yourself well what you mean to do. For, I promise you, though I should do as you would have me, and should send Sosia unto you, yet can I not be persuaded that your desire will take effect. For the punishment of those who lately suffered for disclosing their secrets will make him seal up his lips, and look a little better to his life. Now for my coming to your house, and to dwell with you, as the offer is very kind, so I yield you the best kind of thanks I can render you. And Jove bless you for it,[504] and help you in your necessity; for therein dost thou well show that kindred and alliance serve not for shadows, but ought rather to be profitable and helpful in adversity. And therefore though I should be willing to do as you would have me, in regard of that desire which I have to enjoy your sweet company, yet can it not conveniently be done, in regard of that loss which would light upon me. For I know, it cannot but be greatly to my hindrance. The reason thereof I need not to tell you, because I speak to one that is intelligent, and understands my meaning. For there, cousin, where I am, I am well known. There am I well customed. That house will never lose the name of old Celestina. Thither continually resort your young wenches bordering thereabouts, loving creatures, willing worms, and such as are best known abroad, being half blood to those whom Celestina bred up, there they drive all their bargains, and there they make their matches, and do many other things besides (as you know well enough) whereby now and then I reap some profit. Besides, those new friends that I have, know not elsewhere to seek after me. Moreover, you are not ignorant how hard a matter it is to forgo that

---

[504] 'Dios te ampare', in the original (Lobera *et al.*, eds, 2000, p. 292).

which we have been used unto, and to alter custom is as distasteful as death. A rolling stone never gathers moss, and therefore I will abide where I am. And if for no other reason, yet will I stay there, because my house-rent is free, having a full year yet to come, and will not let it be lost, by lying idle and empty. So that though every particular reason may not take place, yet when I weigh them altogether, I hope I shall rest excused, and you contented. It is now high time for me to be gone; what we have talked of, I will take that charge upon me. And so farewell.

Actus XVI
The Argument

Pleberio and Alisa, thinking that their daughter Melibea had kept her virginity unspotted and untouched — which was as it seemed quite contrary — they fall in talk about marrying of Melibea; which discourse of theirs she so impatiently endured and was so grieved in hearing her father treat of it, that she sent in Lucrecia to interrupt them, that by her coming in she might occasion them to break off both their discourse and purpose.

INTERLOCUTORS
Melibea, Lucrecia, Pleberio, Alisa

Pleberio. My wife and friend Alisa, time, methinks, slips (as they say) from between our hands, and our days do glide away like water down a river. There is not anything that flies so swift as the life of man. Death still follows us, and hedges us in on every side; whereunto we ourselves now draw nigh. We are now, according to the course of nature, to be shortly under his banner. This we may plainly perceive if we will but behold our equals, our brethren and our kinsfolk about us. The grave hath devoured them all. They are all brought to their last home.[505]
10   And sithence we are uncertain when we shall be called hence, seeing such certain and infallible signs of our short abode, it behoveth us (as it is in the proverb) to lay our beard a soaking, when we see our neighbour's shaving off,[506] and to fear lest that which befell them yesterday may befall us tomorrow. Let

---

[505] These opening sentences are a free translation of Petrarch's *Familiares* I.i.1–7: 'Tempora, ut aiunt, inter digitos effluxerunt; spes nostre veteres cum amicis sepulte sunt [. . .] ego iam sarcinulas compono, et quod migraturi solent, quid mecum deferam [. . .] circumspicio [. . .] Quid enim, queso, fugacius vita est, quid morte sequacius?' (Lobera *et al.*, eds, 2000, p. 293, n. 7).

[506] Mabbe's literal translation of a common fifteenth-century Spanish proverb ('Cuando la barba de tu vecino vieres pelar, pon la tuya en remojo'), which still remains in current use (see Lobera *et al.*, eds, 2000, p. 293, n. 8 and their long note, p. 715). Rojas inserts this popular saying within a passage (ll. 11–19, 'And sithence we are uncertain [. . .] sudden and unprovided') which he has freely translated from Petrarch's *De remediis* II.117 (see Lobera *et al.*, eds, 2000, p. 294, n. 12).

us therefore prepare ourselves, and pack up our fardles[507] for to go this enforced journey which cannot be avoided. Let not that cruel and doleful-sounding trumpet of death summon us away on the sudden and unprovided. Let us prepare ourselves, and set them in order whilst we have time, for it is better to prevent than to be prevented. Let us confer our substance on our sweet successor. Let us couple our only daughter to a husband, such a one as may suit with our estate, that we may go quietly and contentedly out of this world. The which with much diligence and carefulness we ought from henceforth to endeavour and put in execution. And what we have at other times commenced in this matter, we ought now to consummate it. I would not by our negligence have our daugher in [a] guardian's hands. I like not she should be a ward. She is now fit for marriage, and therefore much better for her to be in a house of her own, than in ours: by which means we shall free her from the tongues of the vulgar. For there is no virtue so absolute and so perfect which hath not her detracting and foul-mouthed slanderers, neither is there anything whereby a virgin's good name is kept more pure and unspotted than by a mature and timely marriage. Who in all this city will refuse our alliance? Who will not be glad to enjoy such a jewel, in whom those four principal things concur, which are demanded and desired in marriage? The first, discretion, honesty and virginity. The second, beauty. The third, noble birth and parentage. The last, riches. With all these nature hath endowed her. Whatsoever they shall require of us, they shall find it to be full and perfect.

Alisa. My lord Pleberio, heaven bless her, and send her so to do, that we may see our desires accomplished in our lifetime. And I am rather of [the] opinion that we shall want one that is equal with our daughter, considering her virtue and nobleness of blood, than that there are over-many that are worthy to wear[508] her. But because this office more properly appertaineth to the father than the mother, as you shall dispose of her, so shall I rest contented and she remain obedient, as shall best beseem her chaste carriage, her honest life, and meek disposition.

---

[507] fardles] baggage.

[508] wear] to possess and enjoy as one's own, especially in reference to women as wives.

Lucrecia. (But if you knew as much as I do, your hearts would burst in sunder. Ay, ay, you mistake your mark: she is not the woman you wot of. The best is lost. An ill year is like to attend upon your old age. Calisto hath plucked that flower wherein you so much glory. There is not any that can now new film her, or repair her lost virginity. For Celestina is dead, the only curer of a cracked maidenhead. You have awaked somewhat of the latest; you should have risen a little earlier.) Hark, hark, good mistress Melibea! Hark, I say!

Melibea. (What does the fool there sneaking in the corner?)

Lucrecia. Come hither, Madam, and you shall hear how foward your father and mother are for to provide you a husband, you shall be married out of hand, out of hand, madam.

Melibea. For all love's sake speak softly, they will hear you by and by, let them talk on, they begin to dote. For this month they have had no other talk, their mind hath run on nothing else. It may be their heart tells them of the great love which I bear to Calisto, as also of that which for this month's space hath passed between us. I know not whether they have had an inkling of our meeting, or whether they have over-heard us, nor can I devise in the world what should be the reason why they should be so hot upon the matter, and more eager for the marrying of me now than ever heretofore. But they shall miss of their purpose, they shall labour it in vain. For to what use serves the clapper in the mill, if the miller be deaf?[509] Who is he that can remove me from my glory? Who can withdraw me from my pleasure? Calisto is my soul, my life, my lord, on whom I have set up my rest, and in whom I have placed all my hopes. I know that in him I cannot be deceived. And since that he loves me, with what other thing but love can I requite him? All the debts in the world receive their payment in a divers kind, but love admits no other payment, but love.[510] I glad

---

[509] The Spanish proverb in the original, as is frequently the case, appears truncated: 'por demás es la cítola en el molino' (Lobera *et al.*, eds, 2000, p. 296, i.e. 'Por demás es la cítola en el molino cuando el molinero es sordo'). 'Cítola' is the clapper, i.e. a wooden implement that kept noisily hitting the millstone as it moved: it was used to alert about the movement (or lack thereof) of the millstone (hence the refrain: it was useless for a deaf miller).

[510] The origin of this adage is Petrarch's *Rerum memorandum libri* III.lxxxii.3 (Lobera *et al.*, eds, 2000, p. 296, n.31).

myself in thinking on him. I delight myself in seeing him, and rejoice myself in hearing him. Let him do with me what he will, and dispose of me at his pleasure. If he will go to sea, I will go with him; if he will round the world, I will along with him; if he will sell me for a slave in the enemy's country, I will not resist his desire. Let my parents let me enjoy him, if they mean to enjoy me. Let them not settle their thoughts upon these vanities, nor think no more upon those their marriages. For, it is better to be well beloved, than ill married, and a good friend is better than a bad husband. Let them suffer me to enjoy the pleasure of my youth, if they mind to enjoy any quietness in their age; if not, they will but prepare destruction for me, and for themselves a sepulchre. I grieve for nothing more, than for the time that I have lost in not enjoying him any sooner, and that he did not know me, as soon as he was known unto me. I will [have] no husband. I will not sully the knots of matrimony, nor tread against the matrimonial steps of another man, nor walk in the way of wedlock with a stranger, as I find many have done, in those ancient books which I have read, which were far more discreet, and wiser than myself, and more noble in their estate and lineage, whereof some were held among the heathens for goddesses. As was Venus, the mother of Aeneas and of Cupid, the god of love, who being married, broke her plighted troth of wedlock. As likewise divers others, who were inflamed with a greater fire, and did commit most nefarious and incestuous errors: as Myrrha, with her father, Semiramis with her son, Canace with her brother.[511] Others also in a more cruel and beastly fashion, did transgress the law of Nature: as Pasiphae, the wife of King Minos, with a bull. And these were queens and great ladies, under whose faults (considering the foulness of them) mine may pass as reasonable, without note of shame or dishonesty. My love was grounded upon a good and just cause, and a far more lawful ground. I was wooed and sued unto, and captivated by Calisto's good deserts; being

---

[511] Semiramis was an Assyrian queen (Sammu-ramat), who according to a Greek legend abolished the laws against incest to consummate her passion for her own son. Canace was a character in Euripides's *Aeolus*. She became pregnant by her brother Macareus, and when the affair came to light, both lovers were led to commit suicide by their father, King Aeolus. On Pasiphae, see note to 1.207 above.

thereunto solicited by that subtle and cunning mistress in her art, dame Celestina, who adventured herself in many a dangerous visit, before that ever I would yield myself true prisoner to his love. And now for this month, and more (as you yourself have seen) he hath not failed, no, not so much as one night, but hath still scaled our garden walls, as if he had come to the scaling of a fort, and many times hath been repulsed, and assaulted it in vain, being driven to withdraw his siege. And yet for all this, he continued more constant and resolute still, and never would give over, as one that thought his labour to be well bestowed. For my sake, his servants have been slain; for my sake, he hath wasted and consumed his substance; for my sake, he hath feigned absence with all his friends in the city; and all day long he hath had the patience to remain close prisoner in his own house, and only upon hope (wherein he counted himself happy) to see me in the night. Far, far therefore from me be all ingratitude; far be all flattery and dissimulation towards so true and faithful a lover; for I regard (in my regard to him) neither husband, father, nor kindred. For in losing my Calisto, I lose my life, which life of mine doth therefore please me, because it pleaseth him; which I desire no longer to enjoy, than he shall joy in it.

Lucrecia. Peace, madam, hark, hark, they continue in their discourse.

Pleberio. Since, wife, methinks you seem to like well of this motion, it is not amiss, that we make it known to our daugher. We may do well to tell her how many do desire her, and what store of suitors would be willing to come unto her, to the end that she may the more willingly entertain our desire, and make choice of him whom she liketh best. For in this particular, the laws allow both men and women, though they be under paternal power, for to make their own choice.

Alisa. What do you mean, husband? Why do you talk and spend time in this? Who shall be the messenger to acquaint our daugher Melibea with this strange news, and shall not affright her therewith? Alas, do you think that she can tell what a man means, or what it is to marry, or be married? Or whether by the conjunction of man and woman, children are begot or no? Do you think that her simple and unspotted virginity, can suggest unto her any filthy desire, of that which as yet she neither knows, nor understandeth, nor cannot so much as conceive what it means? It is the least part of her thought. Believe it, my lord Pleberio, she doth not so much as dream on any such matter. And assure yourself, be he what he will be, either noble or base, fair or foul, we will make her to take whom it pleaseth us. Whom we like, him shall she like. She shall confirm her will to ours, and shall think that fit, which we think fit, and no further. For I know, I trow, how I have bred and brought up my daughter.

Melibea. Lucrecia, Lucrecia! Run! Hie thee quickly, and go in by the back door in the hall, and break off their discourse with some feigned errand or other, unless thou wouldst have me cry out, and take on like a bedlam,[512] so much am I out of patience with their misconceit of my ignorance.
Lucrecia. I go, madam.

---

[512] bedlam] a madwoman, originally an inmate of Bethlehem Hospital (also spelled Bedlam), London, or of a lunatic asylum, or one fit for such a place (*OED*).

Actus XVII
The Argument

Elicia wanting the chastity of Penelope,[513] determines to cast off the care and sorrow which she had conceived upon the deaths of those for whom she mourned, highly to this purpose commending Areusa's counsel. She gets her to Areusa's house, whither likewise comes Sosia, out of whom Areusa, by fair and flattering words, drew those matters of secrecy which passed betwixt Calisto and Melibea.

INTERLOCUTORS
Elicia, Areusa, Sosia

Elicia. I do myself wrong, to mourn thus. Few do visit my house, few do pass this way. I can hear no music nor stirring betimes in the morning. I have no amorous ditties sung by my lovers at my window. There are no frays nor quarrels before my door. They do not cut and slash one another anights for my sake, as they were wont to do. And that which most of all grieves me is that I see neither penny nor farthing, nor any other present to come within my doors. But for this, can I blame nobody but myself? Myself only is in fault, for had I followed the counsel of her who is my true and faithful sister, when as I brought her the other day the news of this sad and heavy accident which hath brought all this penury upon me, I had not lived alone mured up between two walls, nor others loathed to have come, and seen me. The devil, I think, makes me to mourn thus for him who, had I been dead, would scarce, perhaps, have shed one tear for me. Now I dare boldly say that Areusa told me truth. 'Sister', quoth she, 'never conceive, nor show more sorrow for the misfortune, or death of another, than he would have done for thee'. Sempronio, had I been dead, would have

---

[513] Unlike the young wench Elicia, Penelope remained adamant in her refusal to take another husband during Ulysses's long absence, and therefore became a symbol of steadfast marital fidelity. A rather ironic remark, penned by those printers or scholars who composed the arguments, the more so when read immediately after Melibea's list of great queens and goddesses, whom she has just mustered in the previous act to justify her affair with Calisto.

been never a whit the less merry, he would not have wronged his delights, nor abridged his pleasures. And why then like a fool should I grieve and vex myself for one that is dead and gone, and hath lost his head by order of law? And what can I tell, whether being a choleric and hasty hare-brained fellow as he was, he might have killed me too, as well as he did that old woman, whom I reckoned of as of mine own mother? I will therefore by all means follow Areusa's counsel, who knows more of the world than I do, and go now and then to visit her, that I may learn something from her how I may live another day. Oh what a sweet participation will this be! What a delightful conversation![514] I see it is not said in vaine that of more worth is one day of a wise man than the whole life of a fool. I will therefore put off my mourning weeds, lay aside my sorrow, dismiss my tears, which have hitherto been so ready to offer their service to my eyes. But sithence that it is the very first office that we do as soon as we are born, to come crying into the world, I nothing wonder that it is so easy to begin to cry and so hard to leave off. But this may teach one wit, by seeing the hurt it does to the eyes, by seeing that good clothes and neat dressings make a woman seem fair and handsome, though she be nothing so nor so, making her of old, young, and of young, younger, fair and handsome, though she be nothing so, nor so; making her of old, young; and of young, younger. Your coloured paintings and your ceruses° which give women such a pure white and red, what are they but a slimy clinging thing, a kind of birdlime, wherewith men are taken and ensnared? Come then thou my glass, come hither again unto me, and thou my antimonium,[515] for I have too much already wronged my eyes and almost marred my face, with my blubbering and weeping. I will on with my white veils, my wrought gorgets, my gay garments, my more pleasing attire, and such other apparel

---

[514] As was the case between Pleberio and Sempronio, the 'conversation', or mutually beneficial communion between servants and wenches creates society among them. This is the same discourse Celestina used to persuade Parmeno. The actual tragic results within the plot of the tragicomedy of these *societies* established for the pursuit of mutual self-interest implicitly undermine the humanist discourse that they were reproducing (see introduction).

[515] antimonium] antimony; *alcohol* in the Spanish original: i.e. the *al-koh'l* of the Arabs, used as make-up for the eyelids.

as shall speak pleasure. I will presently provide some lye for my hair, which now through neglect hath lost its bright burnished hue. And this being done, I will count my hens, I will make up my bed, for it glads a woman's heart to see things neat and handsome about her. I will have all well swept and made clean before my door, and the street that butts upon it sprinkled with water, as well to keep it cool as to lay the dust, to the end that they who pass by may plainly thereby perceive that I have banished all grief and shaken hands with sorrow. But first of all I will go and visit my cousin to know whether Sosia have been with her or no, and what good she hath done upon him. For I have not seen him since I told him that Areusa would fain speak with him. I pray Jove I may find her all alone, for she is seldom any more without gallants than a good tavern is without drunkards. The door is shut, there should be nobody within. I will knock and see. Tha, tha, tha.

Areusa. Who's at the door?

Elicia. I pray open it, it is Elicia.

Areusa. Come in, good cousin, heaven reward you for this kindness. Believe me, I think myself much beholding unto you, that would take the pains to come and visit me. Ay marry, wench, now it is as it should be, now thou pleasest me, thou canst not imagine what contentment my eye taketh, to see that habit of mourning and of sorrow to be changed into garments of joy, and of gladness. Now we will enjoy one another. We will laugh and be merry. Now I shall have some heart to come and visit thee, thou shalt come to my house, and I will come to thine. It may be that Celestina's death will turn to both our goods, for I find that it is better now with me than it was before. And therefore it is said, that the dead do open the eyes to the living, to some by wealth, to other some by liberty, as it is with thee.

Elicia. I hear somebody's at the door, we are too soon cut off from our discourse, for I was about to ask you, whether Sosia had been here or no?

Areusa. No, not yet. Stay, we will talk more anon. How loud he knocks! I will go down and see who it is. Sure, either he is a madman, or our familiar friend. Who is it that knocks there?

Sosia. Open the door, mistress. It is Sosia, servant to Calisto.

Areusa. (Now in good time. The wolf is in the fable.[516] Hide

---

[516] Mabbe's translation of 'el lobo es en la conseja'. Originally a Latin proverb

yourself, sister, behind these hangings, and you shall see how I will work him, and how I will puff him up with the wind of my fair and flattering words. And assure yourself that before we two part, I will make him wholly ours. He shall not go hence the same Sosia that he came, but with my smooth and enticing terms, my soft and gentle handling of him, I will quite unmaw[517] him, and draw from him all that he either knows concerning his master or anybody else, as he draws dust from his worses with his currycomb.)[518]

100 *Areusa.* What? My Sosia? My inward friend? Him whom I wish so well unto, though perhaps he knows not of it? Him, whom I have longed to know, led only by the fame and good report which I hear of him? What? He that is so faithful to his master? So good a friend to his acquaintance? I will embrace thee, my love, I will hug thee in mine armes. For now that I see thee, I see report comes short, and verily persuade myself, that there are more virtues in thee than I have been told of. Fame hath been too sparing of thy praise. Come, sweetheart, let us go in and sit down in my chamber, for it does me good to look upon
110 thee. Oh how dost thou resemble my unfortunate Parmeno! How lively doth thy person represent him unto me! This is it that makes this day to shine so clear, that thou art come to visit me. Tell me, gentle sir, did you ever know me before?
Sosia. The fame, gentlewoman, of your gentle and sweet disposition of your good graces, discretion and wisdom flies with so swift a wing and in so high a pitch through all this city, that you need not much to marvel if you be of more known than knowing. For there is not any man that speaks anything in praise of the fairest and beautifulest in this city, but that you
120 are ranked in the first place, and remembered as the prime and chiefest amongst them all.

('lupus in fabula', used by Terence, Plautus and Cicero), it also became common in Castilian (see Lobera *et al.*, eds, 2000, p. 301, n. 25, and their long note, p. 721); its significance here is equivalent to the English expression 'speak of the devil'.

[517] unmaw] to empty of knowledge, this is the only example in the *OED*.

[518] currycomb] a comb used to rub down or dress a horse, or any other beast of burden.

Elicia. (This poor silly fellow, this wretched son of a whore, to see how he exceeds himself, and speaks beyond the compass of his common wit! He doth not use to talk thus wisely. He that should see him go to water his horses riding on their bare ridge without a saddle and his naked legs hanging down beneath his canvas frock, cut out into four quarters, and should now see him thus handsome and well suited, both in his cloak and other his clothes, it would give a man wings and tongue, and make him crow, as this cockerel doth.)

Areusa. Your talk would make me blush and run away for shame were there anybody here to hear how you play upon me. But — as it is the fashion of all you men — you never go unprovided of such kind of phrases as these. These false and deceitful praises are too common amongst you; you have words moulded of purpose to serve your turn withal, and to suit yourselves as you see cause, to any woman whatsoever. Yet for all this, am I not afraid of you, neither will I start or budge from you. But I must tell you, Sosia, by the way, this praising of me thus is more than needs, for though thou shouldst not commend me, yet should I love thee. And that thereby thou shouldst think to gain my love is as needless, for thou hast gained it already. There are two things, which cause me, Sosia, for to send for thee, entreating thee to take the pains to come and see me, wherein if I find you to double or dissemble with me, I have done with you. What they are, I will leave them to yourself to relate, though I know it is for your own good, which makes me to do as I do.

Sosia. Heaven forbid that I should use any cogging° with you, or seek any subtlety to deceive you. I came hither upon the assurance that I had of the great favours which you intend, and now do me, holding myself not worthy to pull off your shoes. Do thou therefore direct my tongue, answer thou for me to thine own questions, for I shall ratify and confirm whatsoever thou shalt propound.

Areusa. My love, thou know'st how dearly I loved Parmeno. And as it is in the proverb, he that loves Beltram, loves anything that is his.[519] All his friends were always welcome unto me. His

---

[519] Mabbe's literal translation of a popular fifteenth- and sixteenth-century Spanish proverb, 'Quien bien quiere a Beltrán todas sus cosas ama' (Lobera *et al.*, eds, 2000, p. 303, n. 46, and their long note, p. 721).

good service to his master did as much please me, as it pleased himself. When he saw any harm towards Calisto, he did study to prevent it. Now as all this is true, so thought I it good to acquaint thee with it. First then did I send for thee, that I might give thee to understand how much I love thee, and how much I joy and ever shall, in this thy visiting me. Nor shalt thou lose anything by it, if I can help it, but rather turn to thy profit and benefit. Secondly, since that I have settled my eyes, my love and affection on thee, that I may advise thee to take heed how thou comest in danger, and besides, to admonish thee, that thou do not discover thy secrets to any. For you see what ill befell Parmeno and Sempronio, by imparting things of secrecy unto Celestina. For I would not willingly see thee die in such an ill fashion as your fellow and companion did. It is enough for me that I have bewailed one of you already, and therefore I would have you to know, that there came one unto me, and told me that you had discovered unto him the love that is betwixt Calisto and Melibea, and how he won her, and how you yourself night by night went along with him, and many other things which now I cannot call to mind. Take heed, friend, for not to keep a secret is proper only unto women, yet not unto all, but such as are fools and children. Take heed, I say, for here-hence great hurt may come unto you, and to this end did Nature give you two ears, and two eyes, and but one tongue, to the end that what you see and hear, should be double to that you speak. Take heed, and do not think your friend will keep your secret, when you yourself cannot keep it. When therefore thou art to go with thy master, Calisto, to that lady's house, make no noise, lest you be heard. For some have told me that every night you keep a coil,[520] and cannot contain yourselves, as men transported and overjoyed.

Sosia. Oh what busybodies, and what idle-headed persons be they who abuse your ears with such frivolous tales! Whosoever told you that he heard any such matter out of my mouth, he told you an untruth. And some others, perhaps, because they see me go a-nights when the moon shines to water my horses, whistling and singing, and such like kind of mirth to drive away care and to make me forget my toiling and my moiling,[521]

---

[520] coil] tumult, rattle.
[521] moiling] hard work, drudgery.

and all this before ten o'clock at night, conceive an evil suspicion, and of this suspicion make certainties and affirm that to be true which themselves do falsely surmise. And Calisto is not so mad or foolish that at such an hour as that he should go about a business of so great a consequence, but that he will first be sure that all abroad is quiet, and that every man reposes himself in the sweetness of his first sleep. And less are you to suppose that he should go every night unto her, for such a duty will not endure a daily visitation. And that you may, mistress, more manifestly see their falsehood — for, as the proverb is, a liar is sooner taken, than he that is lame[522] — we have not gone eight times a month. And yet these lying blabbers stick not to avouch we go night after night.

Areusa. If you love me, then, my dear lord, that I may accuse them to their faces and take them in the noose of their falsehood, acquaint me with those days you determine to go thither. And if then they shall err in their report, I shall thereby be assured of your secrecy and their roguery. For that being not true which they tell me, your person shall be secured from danger, and I freed from any sudden fear of your life, hoping long to enjoy you.

Sosia. Mistress, let us not stand any longer upon examination of witness. This very night, when the clock shall strike twelve, they have appointed to meet by the way of the garden. Tomorrow you may ask them what they know; whereof, if any man shall give you true notice, I will be content that he shall scotch and notch me for a fool.

Areusa. And on which side of the garden, my sweetheart, because I may contradict them the better, if I find them varying?

Sosia. By the street where the fat hostess dwells, just on the backside of her house.

Elicia. (No more, good man ragtail,[523] it is enough, we need no more. Cursed is he who makes such muleteers acquainted with his secrets. The blockhead hath swallowed the bait. He hath let her unhinge him).

---

[522] 'toman antes al mentiroso que al que coxquea' (Lobera *et al.*, eds, 2000, p. 304), Mabbe literally translates this Spanish proverb, still in common use, to express the idea that a liar is easily detected and exposed.

[523] ragtail] (ragge-tayle): disorganized; disreputable; untidy, shabby.

Areusa. Brother Sosia, this that thou hast said shall suffice to make known thy innocency and their wickedness. And so a good speed with thee: for I have some other business to dispatch, and I fear me I have spent too much time with you.
Elicia. (Oh wise wench! Oh what a proper dismission, well befitting such an ass, who hath so easily revealed his secrets!)
Sosia. Courteous sweet mistress, pardon me, if my long stay hath been troublesome unto you. And if it shall please you to accept of my service, you shall never light upon any that shall more willingly therein adventure his life. And so your own best wishes attend you.[524]
Areusa. And you too. (So, are you gone, muleteer? How proudly the villain goes his way! I have put a trick upon you, you rogue, I have bored you iwis, through the nose. Pardon me, if I turn my back to thee, and withdraw my favour from thee. I will have your coat soundly cudgelled for this gear.) But to whom do I speak? Sister, come forth, tell me what dost thou think of him whom I sent away? Have I not handsomely played my part with him? Thus know I how to handle such fellows. Thus do such asses go out of my hands, beaten and laden with blows. Thus your bashful fools. And no better do I use your discreeter men that are timorous, and your devout persons that are passionate, and your chaste men when they are once set on fire. Learn of me therefore, cousin. For this is another kind of art than that of Celestina. It is a trick beyond any that she had in her budget, though she took me for a fool because I was content to be so accounted at her hands. And sithence now that we have squeezed the orange, and wrung out of this fool as much as we desire to know, I think it not amiss that we go to seek out that dogs-face, at his house, whom on Thursday last I rated so bitterly out of mine. You shall make show as thou you were desirous to make us friends and that you had earnestly entreated me to come and see him.

---

[524] 'And so your own best wishes attend you' is Mabbe's translation of 'Queden los ángeles contigo', i.e. may the angels be with you (Lobera *et al.*, eds, 2000, p. 305). Mabbe translates Areusa's response, 'Dios te guíe' ('May God be your guide') as simply 'and you too'.

Actus XVIII
The Argument

Elicia, being resolved to make Areusa and Centurio friends, as Areusa had before instructed her, they go to Centurio's house; where they entreat him to revenge their friends' deaths upon Calisto and Melibea, which he promiseth them to do. And as it is the nature of such ruffians as he not to perform what they promise, he seeks to excuse himself, as you shall see in the sequel.

INTERLOCUTORS
Elicia, Centurio, Areusa

Elicia. Who's at home here?
Centurio. (Boy, run and see. Who dares presume to enter my house, and not first have the manners to knock at the door? Come, come back again, sirrah. I now see who it is). Do not cover your face, mistress, with your mantle, you cannot hide yourself from me. For when I saw Elicia come in before you, I knew she could not bring with her any bad company, nor any news that could offend me, but rather that should please and delight me.
Areusa. If you love me, sister, let us not in any further, for the villain stands upon his pantofles and begins to look big, thinking perhaps that I am come to cry him mercy. He had rather have such company as himself than ours. Come, let us go, for I am the worse to look upon him. I am ready to swound° with the very sight of such an ill-favoured face. Think you, sister, that you have used me well, to train me thus along to such as walk as this? It is a fit thing that we should come from good company and enter in here to see this villainous fellow, that flayeth off the skins from dead men's faces, that he may go disguised and unknown?
Elicia. If you love me, come back again. I pray you, do not you go, unless you mean to leave half your mantle behind you. I will hold you fast, indeed I will not let you go.
Centurio. Hold her, as you love me, hold her. Do not let her go.
Elicia. I wonder, cousin, what you mean by this? You seem to be wiser than I am. Tell me, what man is so foolish, or so void of reason, that is not glad to be visited, especially by women?

Come hither, Centurio. Now, trust me, I swear she shall embrace thee, whether she will or no. If she will be angry, let her, I will bear the blame of it.

Areusa. Embrace him? Marry gup with a murrain![525] I had rather see him under the power and rigour of the law, and had rather see him die by the hands of his enemies, than that I should do the slave such a kindness. No, no, I have done with him. I have nothing to say to him: as long as I live, he and I shall be two. And wherein, I pray, am I so beholding unto him, that I should embrace him? Nay, so much as once vouchsafe to look upon such a professed enemy as he? I did but entreat him the other day to have gone but a little way for me about a business that did as much concern me as my life, and do you think that I could get him to go? Speak him fair, entreat him, do what I could for my life, he still answered me, 'no'. And shall I embrace a villain, that regards me no more than so?

Centurio. Command me, mistress, in such things as I know. Exercise me in my art, and employ me in such offices as appertain to my profession, as to fight for you with three men at once. Or say they should be more: for your sake I would not refuse them, but challenge them the field. Command me to kill this or that man, to cut off a leg or an arm, to slash any woman over the face that shall stand in competition with thee, and deface her beauty. Such trifles as these shall be no sooner said than done. But do not, I prithee, entreat me to walk afoot nor to give thee any money, for thou know'st I have it not. Gold and silver will not tarry with me, they are flinchers, they will not abide with me. I may cut three capers and yet not shake one poor blank[526] out of my breeches. No man gives that which he has not. You can have no more of a cat than his skin. Heart and good will, but not a rag of money. I live here in a house as you see, wherein you may throw a bowl and meet with never a rub.[527] All the moveables that I have are not worth a button.

---

[525] marry gup with a murrain] an expression of derision and remonstrance; one of the examples provided by the *OED* (under 'gup') is an exact expression used by Mabbe in *The Rogue*.

[526] blank] Mabbe's translation of the original *blanca*, an early modern coin of very little value.

[527] The bowl (in the original a 'majadero', i.e. a pestle) will roll all over the house, and will find no obstacles, or anything to bump against, since all the rooms are empty.

My implements are such as you see here before me: an old jar with a broken brim, a rusty spit without a point ... The bed wherein I lie is bound about with hoops of bucklers; my sheets, shirts of torn mail; for my pillow I have a pouch filled with pebble-stones. And should I bestow a collation on you, I have nothing in the world that I can pawn save this poor ragged and threadbare cloak which I have on my back.

Elicia. So let me prosper as his words do exceedingly please me. Why, he is as obedient to you as a servant. He speaks to you like a suppliant, and he hath said nothing, but what is reason. What would you more of a man? I prithee, as thou lov'st me, speak unto him, and lay aside your displeasure. Suffer him not to live thus sad and melancholy, but speak kindly unto him, and put him out of his dumps, since he offers his person so willingly to your disposal.

Centurio. Offer myself, Elicia? I swear unto thee, by the Chriscross Row, by the whole alphabet and syllabication[528] of the letters,[529] that my arm trembles to think what I would execute for her sake. For it is and ever shall be my continual meditation to study how I may please her, but it is my unhappiness that it never hits right. The last night I was adreamed[530] that in her quarrel I challenged four men into the field, all of them well known unto her, if I should name them. And methought I slew one of them, and for the rest which fled, he that scaped best left his left arm at my foot. Much better should I have bestirred myself had it been day and that I had been awake, if the proudest of them should have once presumed but to have touched her shoe.

Areusa. I take thee at thy word; now we be friends; and in good time have we met. I here pardon what is past, but upon condition that you revenge me upon a gentleman, called Calisto, who hath wronged both me and my cousin.

Centurio. Oh how I turn *renegado*! How fain would I renew the condition! But tell me, has he made even with the world?[531]

---

[528] syllabication] syllabification; this is the earliest example in the *OED*.
[529] Mabbe's innocuous translation of Centurio's original 'yo te juro por el santo martirologio de pe a pa' (Lobera *et al.*, eds, 2000, p. 309), i.e. 'I swear by all the saints in the martyrology, from A to Z'.
[530] I was adreamed] I was visited by a dream
[531] *renegado*] translates '¡Oh, reniego de la condición!', a blasphemous expression. 'Made even with the world' is Mabbe's translation of 'Dime [. . .] si está

Areusa. All's one for that, take you no care.
Centurio. Well, seeing you will have it so, let us send him to dine in hell, without company.[532]
Areusa. But do you hear? Interrupt me not. Fail me not, I advise you: this night (if you will) you may take him napping.
Centurio. No more, I apprehend your meaning. I know the whole course of his love, how he carries himself in it, how such and such suffered in the business, as also where you two are galled. I know whither he goes, at what hour, and with whom. But tell me, how many accompany him?
Areusa. Only two, and those young fellows.
Centurio. This is too small a prey, too poor a pittance: my sword will have but a short supper. It would fare far better at some other time, than that which now you have concluded on.
Areusa. No, no. This is but to shift us off, and to excuse your not doing it. It will not serve your turn, you must give this bone to some other dog to pick.[533] I must not be fed with delays. I will see whether sayings and doings eat together at your table, whether deeds and words sit both at one board with you.
Centurio. If my sword could but tell you the deeds it hath done, it would want time to utter them. What does empeople° church-yards but it? Who makes surgeons rich but it? Who sets armourers a-work but it? Who hews and unrivets the finest mail but it? Who drives before him and shivers in pieces the bucklers of Barcelona, but it? Who slices the helmets of Calatayud but it? Who shreds the casks of Almazan as short as if they were made of pompions°, but it?[534] These twenty years hath it found me food; by means of it am I feared of men and beloved of women — only yourself excepted. For it the

---

confesado' (Lobera *et al.*, eds, 2000, p. 310), i.e. 'tell me [. . .] whether he has confessed', to which Areusa replies 'No seas tú cura de su ánima' (with a Spanish pun in *cura* as both 'cure' and 'priest'), i.e. 'Don't you care for his soul'. Mabbe eliminates the references to Calisto's soul and Centurio as the priest who must care for it.

[532] 'Mandémosle al infierno sin confesión', i.e. 'let's send him to hell without confession'.

[533] Mabbe's translation of 'A otro perro con ese hueso', a saying still in common use, that could be rephrased in this context as 'do not try to deceive me,' or 'do not try to make up deceitful excuses.'

[534] Barcelona, Calatayud and Almazan were all places where high-quality weapons were produced.

name of Centurio was given to my grandfather; for it, my father likewise was called Centurio, and so am I.

Elicia. But I pray, tell me, what did your sword, that your grandfather should gain his name by it? Was he by it made captain of a hundred men?

Centurio. No, he was made by it champion to a hundred women.[535]

Areusa. We will have nothing to do with your pedigree, nor famous acts of old. If you will do that I spake to you of, resolve suddenly, for we must be gone.

Centurio I long more for this night, wherein I may give you content, than you long to be revenged. And that everything may be done to your good liking, make your own choice what death you will have him die. For I can show you a bead-roll° (if you will see it) wherein there are set down some seven hundred and seventy several sorts of deaths, which when you have seen, you may choose that which likes you best.

Elicia. If you love me, Areusa, let not this matter be put into such a madman's hands. He is too bloody for the business. And it were better to let all alone, than that the city should receive such a scandal, so that our second harm shall be worse than the first.

Areusa. I pray content yourself, sister, hold your peace. Name that city unto us, if you can, which is not full or hurly-burlies and where some scandals do not arise.

Centurio. The affronts and disgraces which are now in request, and wherein I am most conversant, are banging a man over the shoulders with a sword having its scabbard on; dry-beatings, without drawing of blood; thumping him on the breast, or making his head ring noon with the pommel of my sword, or by falsifying of a thrust or blow to give him his payment where he least looks for it. Others I use like sieves, pricking them full of holes with my poniard. Some I cut in a large size, giving them a fearful *stocada*,[536] or mortal wound. And now and then I use my cudgel, or bastonado, that my sword may keep holiday, and rest itself from its labour.

Elicia For love's sake ha' done, tell us of no more. Bastonado him, I pray thee: for I would have him beaten, but not slain.

---

[535] Mabbe euphemistically translates 'rufián' (i.e. pimp) as 'champion'.
[536] stocada] i.e. 'estocada', in Spanish: a thrust of the sword.

160 *Centurio.* I swear by the whole generation of Turk and Termagant,[537] that it is as possible for this right arm of mine to bastonado a man, and not kill him, as it is for the sun to stand still in the firmament and never move.
Areusa. Sister, let not you and I sorrow for the matter. Why should we seem to pity him? Let him do with him what he will. Let him kill him as he finds himself humoured when he comes to do the business. Let Melibea weep as well as you have done before her. And so let us leave him. Centurio, see you give a good accompt[538] of that which is committed to your charge.
170 Take your own course, anyway, so as you revenge us on him, shall content us. But in any case take heed, that he do not escape without paying for his error.
Centurio. Oh heavens! He is going to Pluto I warrant you already. I will give him his passport, I warrant you, unless he betake him to his heels, and run away from me.[539] Dearest in my affection, it glads me to the heart that I have this occasion offered unto me —though it be but in a trifle and a matter scarce worth thanks — that you may know by this, how far I would (if occasion served) enforce myself for your sake.
180 *Areusa.* Mars direct thy hand aright.[540] And so farewell, for it is time for us to be gone.
Centurio. Well, adieu.

Centurio. (Go your ways, like a couple of headstrong and pertinacious whores as you be. Now will I bethink myself how I may excuse myself of my promise, and in such sort too that they may be persuaded that I used all possible diligence for to execute their desire, and that it was not of negligence, for the freeing of myself from danger. I will feign myself sick ... but
190 what will that profit me? For then they will be at me again

---

[537] Mabbe's translation of the somewhat absurd, but still irreverent, exclamation 'juro por el cuerpo santo de la letanía' (Lobera *et al.*, eds, 2000, p. 312), literally, 'I swear by the holy body of the litany'.
[538] accompt] account.
[539] 'Perdónele Dios si por pies no se me va' (*ibid.*), i.e. 'May God forgive him if he cannot flee from me'.
[540] 'Dios te dé buena manderecha' (*ibid.*), i.e. 'May God bring you good fortune'.

when I am well. Again, if I shall tell them that I have been there and that I forced them to fly they will ask me who they were, how many in number, and in what place I buckled with them, and what apparel they wore, and by what marks I knew them to be such and such . . . and the devil a whit shall I be able to tell them. And then all the fat is in the fire. What counsel then shall I take, that may comply with mine own safety and their desire? I will send for lame Thraso, and his companions, and tell them that because this night I shall be otherwise employed, they would go and make a clattering with their swords and bucklers in manner of a fray for to fear and affright certain young men whom they shall find in such a place, which service was faithfully recommended unto me to execute. This I know is a sure course, and no other hurt can follow thereupon, save to make them fly, and to get them home to bed.)

JOSÉ MARÍA PÉREZ FERNÁNDEZ

ACTUS XIX
THE ARGUMENT

Calisto, going with Sosia and Tristan to Pleberio's garden to visit Melibea — who stayed looking for him attended by Lucrecia — Sosia recounts unto Tristan all that which had passed betwixt him and Areusa, Calisto remaining in the garden with Melibea. Thraso and his companions come, sent thither by the appointment of Centurio for the fulfilling of that which he had promised to Areusa and Elicia, upon whom Sosia sallies forth. Now Calisto, hearing from the garden where he remained with Melibea the clashing and clattering which they made, would needs go forth amongst them. Which issuing forth was the cause that his days were finished: for this is the recompence which such lovers receive. Whence they may learn, that it is better for them not to love at all than so to love.

INTERLOCUTORS
Sosia, Tristan, Calisto, Melibea, Lucrecia

Sosia. Softly, that we may not be heard. As we go from hence to Pleberio's garden, I will tell thee all, brother Tristan, that passed this day betwixt Areusa and myself, taking myself now to be the happiest man in the world. Thou shalt understand then that upon the good report which she heard of me she fell extremely in love with me, and sent me word by Elicia that I would do her the kindness as to come and speak with her. But omitting many other speeches of good counsel, which then passed between us, she made present show unto me that she was now as much mine as ever she was Parmeno's. She requested me that I would continually come and visit her, and that she did not doubt but that she should long enjoy my love. And I swear to thee, brother, by that dangerous way wherein we walk, and as ever any good may hereafter befall me, that twice or thrice it was as much as ever I could do for my life, to forbear from boarding her. But that very shame did hinder me, seeing her so fair and so well clad, and myself in an old mouse-eaten cloak. Still as she moved and advanced herself, she did breath forth a most sweet and redolent odour of musk. And I never stirred or heaved my body but I sent forth a most rank scent of that horse-dung which had got within my shoes. She had a hand as white as snow, and ever and anon, as she pulled off her glove, thou wouldst have thought that she had scattered flowers of oranges about the room. So that as well in regard of this, as also because at that time she was somewhat busy, I was content to defer my boldness till another day, as likewise because all things at the first sight are not so tractable, for the more they are communicated, the better are they understood in their participation.

30 *Tristan.* Friend Sosia, another more ripe and mature brain, and better experimented in matters of the world than mine is, were very necessary to be your adviser in this business. Yet as far-forth as my tender age and the means of my natural parts and wit shall be able to reach unto, I will tell you what I think. This woman — as you told me yourself — is a known and a noted whore, and therefore whatsoever hath passed between you, flatter not yourself, but rather believe that her words do not want deceit. Her offers, I persuade me, were false — though I know not to what end she made them. If she love thee, because thou art a gentleman, how many better than thyself hath she rejected? If because thou art rich, she knows well enough that thou hast no other dust than that which clings to the curry-comb. If because thou art nobly descended and of high lineage, she knows thy name is Sosia, and so was thy father's', and that he was born and bred in a poor little hamlet, getting his living by following the plough-tail and breaking clods of earth, for which thyself art more fit than to make a lover. Be wise, Sosia, and consider with thyself if she do not go a-birding, to see if she would get out of thee the secrecy of this walk, whereby to work some heart-burning and breed no good blood betwixt Calisto and Pleberio, out of that envy which she bears to Melibea's pleasure. Beware, I say, for envy (I tell you) is an incurable infirmity when it is once settled: she is a guest that is always more troublesome than thankful for her lodging, and is never merry but at other folks' miseries, nor ever laughs but at a shrewd turn. Now then, if this be so: oh how this wicked woman will deceive thee with her smooth and subtle words, whereof such as she are never to seek, but have them still ready in the deck, and more perfect than their *Pater noster*? With this venomous vice she will not stick to damn her soul, so as she may please her appetite: she would fain turn all things

topsy-turvy and set men together by the ears, and only for to content her damnable desire. Oh ruffianly strumpet! Oh mankind quean! With what white bread hath she given thee crooked pins, to choke thee? She cares not how she sells and barters her body, so as she may truck and exchange it for strife and contention. Hear me, Sosia, and if thou doest as thou may'st presume upon it, that it is as I tell thee, deal (if thou wilt be advised by me) as double with her. For he that deceives the deceiver, you know what I mean . . . and if the fox be crafty, more crafty is he that catches him. I would have thee make a countermine against these her wicked and devilish imaginations. Set up scaling ladders to meet with her lewdness, and then cry quittance with her when she thinks herself most safe and secure. And laugh at her afterwards, when thou art by thyself all alone in thy stable: the bay horse thinks one thing, and he that saddles him, another.[541]

Sosia. Oh Tristan! Thou discreet young man, more hast thou spoken than could be expected from one of thy years. A shrewd suspicion hast thou raised in me, and I fear me too true. But because we are hard by the garden, and our master is close at our heels, let us break off this discourse, which is too large for the present, and defer it to some fitter opportunity.

Calisto. Do you hear there? Set up the ladder, and see you make no noise, for methinks I hear my mistress's tongue. Sure it is she, she is talking to somebody, whoever it be. I will get me up to the top of the wall, and there will I stand harking awhile, to see if I can hear from her any good token of her love to me, in this my absence.

Melibea. Sing on, Lucrecia, if thou lov'st me, I prithee sing on, for it does my heart good to hear thee. Sing on, I say, till my lord come. Be not too loud, and let us go aside into this green walk, that they that pass by may not hear us.

Lucrecia.   Oh that I kept the key,
    Which opes to these fair flowers,
    To pluck them day by day,
    When you do leave these bowers.
    The lillies and the roses,

---

[541] Mabbe's literal translation of yet another popular proverb ('Uno piensa el bayo, y otro el que lo ensilla', Lobera *et al.*, eds, 2000, p. 317, n. 30, and their long note, p. 727).

                Put on their newest colours,
                And when thy love reposes,
                They breath their freshest odours.
100 *Melibea.* Oh how sweet is thy music to mine ears! It makes my heart even to melt and dissolve for joy. I prithee give not over.
   Lucrecia.   Sweet is the fount, the place,
                I drank at, being dry;
                More sweet Calisto's face,
                In Melibea's eye.
                And though that it be night,
                His sight my heart will cheer,
                And when he down shall light,
                Oh how I'll clip my dear!
110   The wolf for joy doth leap
                To see the lambkins move,
                The kid joys in the teat,
                And thou joy'st in thy love.
                Never was loving wight,
                Of's friend desired so;
                Ne'r walks of more delight,
                Nor nights more free from woe.
   Melibea. Friend Lucrecia, methinks I see that which thou singest represented most lively unto me; methinks I see him as
120 perfectly with these mine eyes, as if he stood just before me. Go on, for thou dost exceeding well, and with an excellent air. I will bear a part with thee, and help thee as well as I can.
   Melibea and Lucrecia.
                Sweet trees, who shade this mold
                Of earth, your heads down bend,
                When thou those eyes behold
                Of my best-loved friend.
                Fair stars whose bright appear,
                Doth beautify the sky,
130   Why wake ye not my dear,
                If he asleeping lie?
   Melibea. Hear me now, I prithee. I will sing alone.
                You birds, whose warblings prove
                Aurora draweth near,
                Go fly, and tell my love,
                That I expect him here.
                The night doth posting move,

	Yet comes he not again;
	God grant some other love
140	Do not my love detain.

Calisto. The sweetness of thy voice hath ravished me. I cannot endure to let thee live any longer in a pained expectation. Oh my sweet mistress, and my life's happiness, what woman could ever be born into the world that should be able to deprive thee of thy great deservingness? Oh interrupted melody! Oh music suddenly broke off! Oh short-timed pleasure! Oh my dear heart, why didst thou not continue thy harmony, without interrupting thy joy, and complying with both our desires?

Melibea. Oh pleasing treason! Oh sweet sudden passion! What? My lord? My soul, is it he? I cannot believe it. Where hast thou been, thou bright shining sun? In what place hast thou hid thy brightness from me? Is it not a pretty while since that thou heard'st me? Why didst thou suffer me to send forth my words into the air, senseless and foolish as they were, and in this hoarse swannish voice of mine? Look on the moon, and see how bright she shines upon us; look on the clouds, and see how speedily they rack away; harken to the gurgling waters of this fountain, how sweet a murmure, and what a pretty kind of purling they make, rushing along these fresh herbs and pleasant flowers; harken to these high cypresses, how one bough makes peace with another by the intercession of a mild, gentle, and temperate wind, which moves them to and fro. Behold these silent and quiet shades, how dark they are, and how excellently well prepared for the covering and concealing of our sports. Lucrecia? Why, how now friend? What are you doing? Art thou turn'd mad with pleasure? Let me alone with my love, touch him not, I charge you. Do not you pluck and hale[542] him from me. Do not burden his body with your heavy arms. Let me enjoy what is mine, you shall not possess any part of my pleasure.

Calisto. Dear lady, and glory of my life, if you love me give not over your singing; let not my presence, which glads thee, be of a worse and more unfortunate condition than my absence which did grieve thee.

---

[542] hale] draw or pull away.

Melibea. Why, my love, would you have me sing? Or how can I sing? For my desire of thee was that which ruled my voice and made me to air my notes. But now that thou art come, that desire disappears, it is vanished, and the tone of my voice distempered, and out of tune. And because you, sir, are the pattern of courtesy and good behaviour, how can you in reason require my tongue to speak, when as you cannot rule your own hands, and keep them quiet? Why do not you forget these tricks, and learn to leave them? Lay your command upon them to be quiet, and will them to lay aside this offensive custom, and consider, my dearest, that as to see thee whilest thou carriest thyself quietly and civilly is the greatest happiness that either my heart or my eye can enjoy, so it is as displeasing unto me to see thee handle me so roughly. Thy honest sporting pleaseth me, but thy dishonest hands offend me, especially when they are too far out of reason. And, though love oftentimes forget reason, yet amongst your well-educated, and noble and generous spirits, kindness keeps a decorum, and revels not but with decency. Let such, sweetheart, be our embraces, such and so modest be our dalliance — my dearest Calisto, my love, my lord. And since I wholly subject myself to your pleasure, be it your pleasure, to take and make such worthy benefit of my affection, presence and service, as best beseems true lovers and is agreeable to both our high births and breeding. But alas silly woman, why should I direct you? No, I will not. Do, Calisto, do what you will, and say what you will, I am yours to use; please yourself, and you shall please me.[543]

---

[543] In the 1631 edition Mabbe alters the original meaning of the last few sentences, which is more explicit in the original: 'Deja estar mis ropas en su lugar, y si quieres ver si es el hábito de encima de seda o de paño, ¿para qué me tocas en la camisa, pues cierto es de lienzo? Holguemos y burlemos de otros mil modos que yo te mostraré; no me destroces ni maltrates como sueles. ¿Qué provecho te trae dañar mis vestiduras?' (Lobera *et al.*, eds, 2000, p. 321). The Alnwick manuscript is closer to the original here, and also in the following paragraphs: 'I praye lett my cloths alone; fye, what a-doe is heere? Good now, leave: o how you ruffle my clothes! You need not search so neere: I assure you my smocke is made of linnen; I praye doe not teare and rente it in peeces' (Martínez Lacalle, ed., pp. 257–58). Both the printed edition and the Alnwick manuscript fail to translate 'no me destroces ni maltrates como sueles', i.e. 'do not harm me, do not be rough with me, as is your wont', where Calisto comes across as a violent and unmannerly partner who is quite far from following the exquisite patterns of courtly love.

Calisto. Madam, fervency of love loves not to be idle. Pardon then, I pray you, if I have been too busy.[544]

Lucrecia. (Now never trust me again, if I harken to them any longer. Here's a life indeed! Oh how I feel myself melt within, like snow against the sun, and how squeamish my mistress seems, because, forsooth, she would fain be entreated! Assuredly, had I been in her case, and have lost so much time, I should think the worse of myself the longest day of my life.)[545]

210 *Melibea.* Sir, shall I send Lucrecia to fetch you some sweetmeats?

Calisto. No, lady; no other sweetmeats for me, save only to embrace this thy body, to fold it within mine arms and to have the possession of thy beauty. Everywhere a man may eat and drink for his money. That a man may have at any time, it is everywhere to be bought. But that which is not vendible, that which in all the world is not to be matched, and save only in this garden, not to be found again from one pole to the other, why wish you me not rather that I should not let slip the least

220 moment, in enjoying so sweet a treasure?

Lucrecia. (My head aches with hearing; and yet their tongue ache not with talking, nor their arms with colling,° nor their lips with kissing. Sure, they will make me gnaw the finger of my glove all to pieces.)[546]

---

[544] Calisto never apologizes in the original, where he responds with a sarcasm more faithfully rendered by Mabbe in the Alnwick manuscript: 'Señora, el que quiere comer el ave, quita primero las plumas' (Lobera *et al.*, eds, 2000, p. 321), 'Madam, he that will eate the birde must first plucke the feathers' (Martínez Lacalle, ed., p. 258).

[545] In the printed edition, Mabbe again omits certain explicit passages from the original, which were more closely rendered in the Alnwick Manuscript: 'Pero también me lo haría yo, si estos necios de sus criados me hablasen entre día; ¡pero esperan que los tengo de ir a buscar!' (Lobera *et al.*, eds, 2000, pp. 321–22), 'I would also haue taken part with them myselfe, and haue hazarded both peticote and smocke and bodie and all in the like bickerment, yf the fooles his men would haue askt but the Question' (Martínez Lacalle, ed., p. 258). Although the Alnwick manuscript runs closer to the original here, both versions slightly alter the dialogue. The printed version strives (albeit not too successfully) to conceal the more explicit tone of the original, in which the courtly scenes between the amorous Calisto and the coy Melibea have degenerated into a combination of voyeuristic comedy and rough sex, all of it a prelude to Calisto's imminent death.

[546] The Alnwick manuscript here expands the original, building on its explicit

Calisto. Oh my dear mistress! I would wish it would never be day, that I might still enjoy that sweet happiness, and fulness of content, which my senses receive in the noble conversing with this thy delicate and dainty sweet self.

Melibea. Sir, it is I that enjoy this happiness, this fulness of content. If anybody gain by it, it is I. And I must acknowledge myself most infinitely beholding unto you, that you would vouchsafe to vist me in so kind and loving a manner, as no thanks are able to requite so great a favour.

Sosia. Out, you ruffianly rascals! Come ye to fright those that fear you not? Had I been aware of your coming, or had you stayed any longer, I would have sent some of you packing, and have given you somewhat that should have stuck by you. Out, you rogues!

Calisto. Madame, this is Sosia's voice: suffer me to go and see, that they do not kill him, for there is nobody with him but a little page that came with me. Give me my cloak quickly, it lies under you.

Melibea. Oh unfortunate that I am! I pray do not go without your cuirasses. If you love me, come back. I will help to arm you myself.

Calisto. That, mistress, which a sword, a cloak and a good heart cannot do, can never be effected by cuirass, cask or cowardice.

Sosia. Yea? Are you come again? I shall be with you to bring by and by. You come for wool, do you?[547] But if you stay a little longer, I shall send you home without a fleece, I shall plume[548] you, I shall, you rascals!

---

contents (omitted in the printed edition): '¡Andar, ya callan! A tres me parece que va la vencida' (Lobera *et al.*, eds, 2000, p. 322), 'they are both as silente as yf they were in a trunce. Why, this battaile was ended at 3 blowes! Neuer sawe I quarrell more quickly fought. But I haue harde your *stoccado* fight is very quicke and desperate' (Martínez Lacalle, ed., p. 258).

[547] 'Quizás venís por lana' (Lobera *et al.*, eds, 2000, p. 323): a truncated proverbial expression, whose full version runs thus: 'ir a por lana y salir trasquilado', i.e. to go and try to gather wool, and end up fleeced instead.

[548] plume] pluck the feathers, rob, despoil.

Calisto. Lady, if you love me, let me go. The ladder stands ready for me.
Melibea. Oh miserable me! Why dost thou go so furiously, and so fast? And all disarmed as thou art, to hazard thy life amongst thou know'st not whom? Lucrecia, come hither quickly, for Calisto is gone to thrust himself into a quarrel. Let us take his cuirasses, and throw them over the wall, for he hath left them here behind him.

260 *Tristan.* Stay, sir, do not come down. They are gone. It is nobody but lame Thraso, and a company of other rogues with him, that made a noise as they passed by. And Sosia is come back again. Take heed, sir, hold fast by the ladder, for fear lest you fall.
Calisto. Oh, oh! Look upon me! Ay me! I am a dead man, oh![549]
Tristan. Come hither quickly, Sosia, for our unfortunate master is fallen from the ladder, and neither speaks nor wags.
Sosia. Master, master, do you hear, sir? Let us call a little at this other door. He hears on neither ear. He is as dead as a door-
210 nail. There is no more life in him than in my great-grandfather, who died some hundred years since. Oh foul mishap! What will become of us?
Lucrecia. Hark, hark, madam! What a great mischance is this?
Melibea. Oh wretch that I am! What do I hear?
Tristan. Oh my master, my master is dead! And with him all my happiness, all my good. He is fallen headlong down . . . He is dead! He is dead! And — which is a fearful thing — suddenly dead.[550] Oh pitiful, pitiful! Oh horrible sight! Help Sosia, help

---

[549] The original runs thus: '¡Oh válame Santa María, muerto soy! ¡Confesión!' (Lobera *et al.*, eds, 2000, p. 323), which the Alnwick manuscript renders as 'Saint Marie, haue mercie on my soule! I am slayne, I am slayne! *Confession, Confession*' (Martínez Lacalle, ed., p. 258). The first, sixteen-act version of *La Celestina* (i.e. the *Comedy*) was less merciful with Calisto, having him die an absurd death after a sexually explicit scene peppered with derisive asides from his own servants. Unlike the second version (i.e. the *Tragicomedy*), the *Comedy* does not afford Calisto the noble motivation of trying to succour his servants. Nor does Calisto beg for confession in the first version either (see Lobera *et al.*, eds, 2000, p. 323, n. 77, and their long note, pp. 731–32).

[550] '¡Oh triste muerte sin confesión!' in the original (Lobera *et al.*, eds, 2000, p. 324).

to gather up these brains that lie scattered here amongst the stones, and let us put them again into his head. Oh unfortunate master! Oh unlucky day! Oh sudden and unexpected end!

Melibea. Oh disconsolate woman that I am! What a thing is this? What vile mishap, that hath thus disturbed our quiet? What mischance can possibly prove so cruel, as that which I now hear? Help me, Lucrecia, to get up this wall, that I may see my sorrow, unless you will have me fill my father's house with cries and strikes. What? Is all my joy turned into smoke? Is all my pleasure lost? All my glory come to an end?

Lucrecia. Tristan, what's the matter, my love, why dost thou weep so bitterly? Why take you on so, beyond all measure and reason?

Tristan. I bewail my great misery. I bewail my many sorrows. My master Calisto hath fallen from the ladder, and is dead. His head is in three pieces, he died suddenly, and lamentably torn and dashed to pieces.[551] Bear this sad message to his new friend, that she must never more expect her pained lover. Sosia, do you take up his feet, and let us carry his body hence, that he may not in this place suffer dishonour, though he have suffered death. Let mourning go along with us! Let solitariness accompany us! Let discomfort wait upon us! Let sorrow apparel us! Let mourning weeds cover us, and let us put on sad habits!

Melibea. Ay me! Of all other the most miserable! So short a time to possess my pleasure! So soon to see my sorrows come upon me!

Lucrecia. Madam, tear not your face. Rend not your hair. What? But even now all pleasure, and now all sorrow? Out alas! That one and the selfsame planet should so suddenly afford an effect so contrary?[552] Where is your courage? Fie, what a faint heart

---

[551] The original insists on Calisto's death without confession: 'Sin confesión pereció' (Lobera *et al.*, eds, 2000, p. 324), which the printed edition again omits, whereas the Alnwick manuscript expands this into: 'He is fallen, he is fallen, dead, dead! And, which greives me most, without Confession. Had he bene absolued of his sinns, it had bene some comforte to his frendes; but to dye thus, to goe laden thus out of the world with his errours, o this is the greife, this is the *Hell* it selfe!' (Martínez Lacalle, ed., p. 258).

[552] planet] in the astrological sense, as an agent that exerts its influence upon human affairs.

have you? Pray you arise from the ground, let not your father find you in so suspicious a place, for if you continue thus you cannot choose but be heard. Why, madam, madam! I say, hear you me? Do you hear, lady? Of all loves, do not fall any more into these swounds°. Be as valiant and courageous in enduring your sorrow as you were hot and hardy in committing your errour.

Melibea. Hear you what moan these poor servants make? Hear you how woefully they lament his loss? Wailing, and weeping, praying, and answering each to other, they carry away from me all my good, all my happiness. My dead joy, my dearest love, they carry away from me! My time is come, I am but a dead woman, I can live no longer since I may no more enjoy the joy of my heart. Oh that I should let thee go! That I should hold that jewel no faster which I so lately held in my hands. Oh ungrateful mortals! Oh unthankful as we be, who never know our happiness until we want it!

Lucrecia. Up, up, madam, for it will be a greater dishonour unto you to be found thus here in the garden than either the pleasure you received by his coming, or the sorrow which you take for his death. Come, let us into your chamber. And go lay you down on your bed; and I will call your father. We will feign some other ill, since to hide this is impossible.

Actus XX
The Argument

Lucrecia comes to Pleberio's chamber, and knocks at the door. Pleberio asks her what's the matter. Lucrecia entreats him to come presently to see his daughter Melibea. Pleberio rises, and goes straight to Melibea's chamber. He comforts her, demanding what she aileth, and where was her grief. Melibea feigns her pain to be about her heart. Melibea sends her father forth for some musical instruments. She and Lucrecia get them, when he was gone, to the top of a tower. She sends away Lucrecia, and shuts the door after her. Her father comes to the foot of the tower. Melibea discovers unto him all the whole business of what had passed. That done, she throws herself down from the top of the tower.

INTERLOCUTORS
Pleberio, Lucrecia, Melibea

Pleberio. What would you, Lucrecia? What means this exceeding haste, and with so great importunity, and troubledness of mind? What ails my daughter? What sudden sickness hath seized on her, that I cannot have the leisure to put on my clothes? Nay scarce so much as time to rise?

Lucrecia. Sir, if you will see her alive, come quickly. What her grief is, I know not. Nay, scarce know I her, so disfigured is her face.

Pleberio. Come, let us go quickly. Lead the way: in afore. Lift up the hangings. Open this same window: set it wide open that I may have light enough to take full view of her.

Pleberio. Why, how now daughter? What's the matter? What is your pain? Where lies it? What a strange thing is this? What faintness do I see? What weakness and feebleness? Look upon me, daughter! I am thy father: speak unto me, for pity's sake, speak, and tell me the cause of your grief, that we may the sooner provide a remedy. Send not my grey hairs with sorrow to the grave: thou knowest I have no other good but thee, no

20 other worldly happiness. Open thy gladsome eyes, look cheerfully upon me.

Melibea. Ay me! What shall I do?

Pleberio. What woe can equal mine, to see thee in such woeful plight? Your mother, as soon as ever she but heard you were ill, fell presently into a swound,° and lies in that extremity, and in a manner senseless, that she is not able to come and see thee. Be of good cheer, pluck up thy heart, and so rise up thy spirits, that thou may'st rise and go along with me to visit her. Tell me, sweet soul, the cause of thy sorrow.

30 *Melibea.* My cure is remediless.

Pleberio. My dear daughter, the best beloved of thy aged father, for pity's sake, let not this thy cruel torment cause thee to despair of recovery, being carried away with the violence and infirmity of thy passion: for sorrow still assaulteth the weakest hearts, and conquers them most, that are most cowardly. If thou wilt but tell me thy grief, it shall presently be remedied. For neither physic, nor physicians, nor servants shall be wanting for the recovery of thy health, whether it consist in herbs, in stones, or in words, or remain more secret in the
40 bodies and bowels of beasts. Do not then vex me any more, torment me no longer, force me not out of my wits, make me not mad, but tell me, good daughter, what, and where is your pain.

Melibea. I feel a mortal wound, even in the very midst of my heart, the anguish whereof is so grievous unto me that it will scarce suffer me to fetch my breath, much less to speak. There is no malady like unto mine, it is of a different nature from all other diseases. And before you can come to cure it in my heart, you must first take out my heart; for it lies even in the hidden
50 and most secret place thereof.

Pleberio. Too soon hast thou received this feeling and sense of elder years. Youth should be a friend to pleasure and mirth, and an enemy unto care and sorrow. Rise then from hence, and let us go and take some fresher air along by the river side. Come, and make merry with your mother: you shall see that will ease and rid away your pain. Take heed what you do, do not wilfully cast away yourself, for if you fly and shun mirth, there is not anything in the world more contrary to your disease.

60 *Melibea.* Let us go whither you please. And if it stand with your

liking, sir, let us go up to the top of the leads,⁵⁵³ for from thence I may enjoy the pleasing sight of those ships that pass to and fro, and perhaps it may give some ease to my grief.

Pleberio. Come, let us go and take Lucrecia with us.

Melibea. With a very good will. I pray, father, will you cause some musical instrument to be sent unto me, that by playing thereon or singing thereunto I may see if I can drive away this grief? For though on the one side the force and violence thereof doth much torment me, yet on the other side I doubt not but those sweet sounding instruments and delightful harmony will much lessen and mitigate my sorrow.

Pleberio. This, daughter, shall presently be done. I will go myself and will it to be provided.

Melibea. Friend Lucrecia, this place, methinks, is too high. I am very loth to leave my father's company. I prithee make a step down unto him, and entreat him to come to the foot of this tower, for I have a word or two which I forgot to tell him, that he should deliver from me to my mother.

Lucrecia. I go, madam.

Melibea. They have all of them left me. I am now alone by my self, and nobody with me. The manner of my death falls fit and pat to my mind. It is some ease unto me that I and my beloved Calisto shall so soon meet again. I will shut and make fast the door that nobody may come up to hinder my death nor disturb my departure, nor to stop me in my journey wherein I purpose to post unto him, not doubting but to visit him as well this very day, as he did me this last night. All things fadge° aright and have fallen out as luckily as I would wish it. I shall now have time and leisure enough to recount to my father Pleberio the cause of this my short and sudden end. I confess, I shall much wrong his silver hairs, and offer much injury to his elder years. I shall work great woe unto him by this my error. I shall leave him in great heaviness and desolation all the days of his life.

---

⁵⁵³ leads] the terrace, the top of the house, from 'leads' (see 'lead' *n.* 17. *pl.* a, *OED*) as 'The sheets or strips of lead used to cover a roof; often *collect.* for a lead flat, a lead roof'.

But admit my death will be the death of my dearest parents, and put case that the shortening of my days will be the shortening of theirs: who doth not know, but that others have been more cruel to their parents than I am? Prusias, king of Bithynia, without any cause, not enduring that pain, which I do, slew his own father. Ptolomy, king of Egypt, slew both father and mother, and brother and wife, and all for the love of his mistress. Orestes killed his mother Clytemnestra, and that cruel emperor, Nero, only for the fulfilling of his pleasure, murdered his own mother. These, and such as they, are worthy of blame. These are true parricides: not I, who with mine own punishment and with mine own death purge away the guilt which otherwise they might more justly lay upon me for their deaths. There have been others far more cruel who have slain their own children and their own brothers, in comparison of whose errors mine is as nothing, at least nothing so great: Philip, king of Macedon; Herod, king of Jewry; Constantine, emperor of Rome; Laodice, queen of Cappadocia; and Medea the sorceress. All these slew their own sons and dearest children, and that without any reason or just cause, preserving their own persons still in safety. To conclude, that great cruelty of Phraates, king of the Parthians, occurs to my remembrance, who, because he would have no successor behind him, murdered Orodes, his aged father, as also his only son, besides some thirty more of his brethren.[554] These were delicts[555] worthy [of] blame indeed, because they keeping their own persons free from peril, butchered their ancestors, their successors, and their brethren. True it is, that though all this be so, yet are we not to imitate them in those things wherein they did amiss: but it is not in my power to do otherwise. And thou great governor of the heavens,[556] who art witness to my words, thou see'st the small power that I have over my passion, thou seest how my liberty is captivated and how my senses are taken with that powerful love of that late deceased gentleman who hath deprived me of that love which I bear to my living parents.

---

[554] All these *exempla* (lines 94–114) are translated in Rojas's original from a long passage in Petrarch's *De remediis* I.52 (see Lobera *et al.*, eds, 2000, p. 330, n. 21, and their long note, pp. 734–35).
[555] delicts] crimes, offences.
[556] 'Tú, Señor' in the original (Lobera *et al.*, eds, 2000, p. 331).

Pleberio. Daughter Melibea, what make you there alone? What is it you would have with me? Shall I come up to you?

Melibea. No, good father, content you where you are, trouble not yourself nor strive to come to me, you shall but disturb and interrupt that short speech which I am now to make unto you. Now, by and by shalt thou be suddenly wounded, thy heart shall presently be pricked with grief, and shall bleed abundantly, to see the death of thy only daughter. My end draws near, at hand is my rest and thy passion, my ease and thy pain, my hour of keeping company and thy time of solitariness. You shall not need, my most honoured father, to seek out any instruments of music to assuage my sorrow, nor use any other sound save the sound of bells for to ring my knell and bring my body to the grave. And, if thou canst harken unto me for tears, if thine eyes will give thine ears leave to hear, thou shalt hear the desperate cause of this my forced, yet joyful departure. See thou neither speak nor weep. Interrupt me not, either with tears or words, unless thou mean'st more hereafter to be tormented in not knowing why I do kill myself than thou art not sorrowful to see my death. Neither ask nor answer me anything, nor question me any further than what of mine own accord I shall willingly tell thee. For when the heart is surcharged with sorrow, the ear is deaf to good counsel; and at such a time, good and wholesome words rather incense than allay rage. Hear, my aged father, the last words that ever I shall speak unto you, and if you entertain them, as I hope you will, you will rather excuse than condemn my error. I am sure, you both well perceive and hear that most sad and doleful lamentation which is made throughout all this city. I am sure you hear this great noise and ringing of bells, the striking and crying out of all sorts of people, this howling, and barking of dogs, this noise and clattering of armour. Of all this have I been the cause. I, even this very day, have clothed the greater part of the knights and gentlemen of this city in mourning. I, even this very day, have left many servants orphaned and quite destitute of a master. I have been the cause that many a poor soul hath now lost its alms and relief. I have been the occasion that the dead should have the company of the most complete gentleman, for his good graces and qualities, that ever was born. I have been the occasion that the living have lost the only pattern and paragon of courtesy, of gallant inventions, of witty devices, of neatness and decency in his clothes, of speech, of gait, of kindness, and of virtue. I have been the occasion that the earth doth now enjoy the most noble body, and the freshest flower of youth, that ever was created in this age of ours. And because you may stand amazed and astonished at the sound of these my unusual and unaccustomed crimes, I will open the business, and make this matter appear more clear unto you.

It is now, dear father, many days since that a gentleman called Calisto, whom you knew well, as likewise his ancestors and noble lineage, did languish and pine away for my love. As for his virtues and goodness, they were generally known to the whole world. So great was his love-torment, and so little both place and opportunity to speak with me, that he was driven to discover his passion to a crafty and subtle woman, named Celestina. Which Celestina, coming as a suitor unto me in his behalf, drew my secret love from forth my bosom, and made me to manifest that unto her which I concealed from mine own mother. She found the means to win me to her will, she made the match between us, she plotted how his desire and mine should take effect. And if he dearly loved me, I was not therein deceived: she made up that sad conclusion of that sweet and unfortunate execution of his will. And thus being overcome with the love of Calisto, I gave him entrance into your garden, broke my chaste purpose by taking from me the flower of my virginity. And thus almost this month have we lived in this delightful error of love. And as he came this last night unto me, as he was wont to do, e'en just about the time that he should have returned home (as ill fortune would have it, who in the mutability of her nature ordereth and disposeth all things, according to her disordered custom) the walls being high, the night dark, the ladder light and weak, his servants that brought it unacquainted with that kind of service, he going down somewhat hastily to see a fray which he heard in the street between his servants and some others that then passed by, being in choler, making more haste than good speed, thinking he should never come soon enough, not eyeing well his steps, he let his foot quite besides the rounds and so fell down, and with that woeful and unfortunate fall, he pitched upon his head and had his brains beaten out and dashed in pieces against the stones and pavement of the street. Thus did the destinies cut off his thread, thus cut off his life without confession, cut off my hope, cut off my glory, cut off my company. Things therefore being thus: tell me, father, what cruelty were it in me, he dying disbrained, that I should live pained all the days of my life? His death inviteth mine ... Inviteth ...? Nay, enforced me, that it be speedily effected, and without delay; it teacheth me that I should also fall headlong down, that I may imitate him in all things. It shall not be said of me, that those that are dead and gone, are soon forgotten. And therefore I will seek to content him in my death, since I had not time to give him content in my life. Oh my love, and dear lord, Calisto, expect me, for now I come. But stay a little, though thou expect me, and be not angry, I prithee, that I delay thee, being that I am now paying my last debt, and giving it my final account to my aged father, to whom I owe much more. Oh my best beloved father, I beseech you, if ever you did love me in this painful forepassed life, that we may both be interred in one tomb, and both our obsequies be solemnized together. I would fain speak some words of comfort unto you, before this gladsome and well-pleasing end, gathered and collected out of those ancient books, which for the bettering of my wit and understanding, you willed me to read, were it not that my memory fails me, being troubled and disquieted with the loss and death of my love, as also because I see your ill-endured tears trickle so fast down your wrinkled cheeks. Recommend me to my most dear and best-beloved mother, and do you inform her at large of the doleful occasion of my death. I am glad with all my heart that she is not here present with you, for her sight would but increase my sorrow. Take, aged father, the gifts of old age, for in large days, large griefs are to be endured. Receive the pledge and earnest of thy reverend age, receive it at the hands of thy beloved daughter. I sorrow much for myself, more for you, but most for my aged mother: and so I recommend me to you both, and both of you unto your more happiness, to whom I offer up my soul,[557] leaving the care to you, to cover this body that is now coming down unto you.

---

[557] The original reads 'Dios quede contigo y con ella; a Él ofrezco mi alma' (Lobera *et al.*, eds, 2000, p. 335), i.e. 'May God be with you, and with her; to him I offer up my soul'. Mabbe has translated this reference to God as 'I recommend me [...] unto your more happiness'.

JOSÉ MARÍA PÉREZ FERNÁNDEZ

Actus XXI
The Argument

Pleberio, returning weeping to his chamber, his wife Alisa demands the cause of this so sudden an ill. He relates unto her the death of her daughter Melibea, showing unto her her bruised body. And so making lamentation for her, he gives a conclusion to this tragi-comedy.

INTERLOCUTORS
Alisa, Pleberio

Alisa. Why, Pleberio, my lord, what's the matter? Why do you weep and sob, and take on in such extreme and violent manner? I have lain ever since in a dead swound,° so was I overcome with grief when I heard that our daughter was so ill. And now hearing your pitiful lamentations, your loud crying, your unaccustomed complaints, your mourning and great anguish, they have so pierced my very bowels, made so quick a passage to my heart, and have so quickened and revived my troubled and benumbed senses, that I have now put away the grief which I entertained. Thus one grief drives out another; and sorrow expelleth sorrow. Tell me the cause of your complaint. Why do you curse your honorable old age? Why do you desire death? Why do you tear your milk-white hairs up by the roots? Why do you scratch and rend your reverend face? Is any ill befallen Melibea? For I pray you tell me, for if she be not well, I cannot live.

Pleberio. Out alas! Ay me! My most noble wife! Our solace is in the suds,° our joy is turned into annoy, all our conceived hopes are utterly lost, all our happiness is quite overthrown. Let us no longer desire to live. And because unexpected sorrows have a greater impression of grief, and because they may bring thee the sooner to thy grave, as also that I may not alone by myself bewail that heavy loss which belongs to us both, look out and behold her, whom thou broughtst forth, and I begot, dash't and broken all to pieces. The cause I understood from herself, but laid open more at large, by this her sad and sorrowful servant. Help to lament these our latter days, which are now growing to an end. Oh ye old people, who come to behold my sorrows, and you gentlemen, my loving friends, do you also assist to bewail my misery! Oh my daughter and my only good! It were cruelty in me that I should outlive thee. My threescore years were fitter for the grave than thy twenty, but the order of my dying was altered by that extremity of grief which did hasten thy end. Oh ye my hoary hairs, grown forth to no other end save sorrow, it would better have suited with you to have been buried in the earth than with these golden tresses which lie here before me. Too, too many are the days that I have yet to live. I will complain and cry out against death, I will accuse him of delay how long will he suffer me to remain here after thee! Let my life now leave me, since I must leave thy sweet company. Oh my dear wife, rise up from her, and if any life be left in thee, spend that little with me in tears and lamentations, in sobs and in sighs. But in case thy soul resteth now with hers, if out of very grief thou hast left this life, why wouldst thou lay this heavy burden on me? Why let me remain here alone, and have nobody to help me in the unsheathing of my sorrows? In this, yee women have a great advantage of us that are men, for some violent grief can make you go out of the world without any pain, or at least cast you into a swound,° which is some ease to your sorrows. Oh the hard heart of a father! Why dost thou not burst with grief? Why do not your heart-strings crack in sunder, to see thyself bereaved of thy beloved heir? For whom didst thou build these turrets? For whom got I honours? For whom planted trees? For whom built ships? Oh hard-hearted earth, why dost thou bear me any longer? Where shall my disconsolate old age find any resting place? Oh variable fortune, and full of change, thou ministress, and high steward-ness of all temporal happiness! Why didst thou not execute thy cruel anger upon me? Why didst thou not overwhelm him with thy mutable waves, who professes himself to be thy subject? Why didst thou not rob me of my patrimony? Why didst thou not set fire on my house? Why didst thou not lay waste mine inheritance? Why didst thou not strip me of my great revenues? What is it I would not thou shouldst have done, so as thou hadst left me that flourishing young plant over which thou ought'st not to have had such power? Thou might'st, oh fortune (fluctuant, and fluent as thou art) have given me a sorrowful youth and a mirthful age, neither have therein perverted order. Better could I have born thy blow, better endured thy persecutions, in that my more strong, and oaky age, than in this my weak and feeble declining. Oh life fulfilled with grief, and accompanied with nought but misery! Oh world, world! Much have men spoken of thee, much have men writ concerning thy deceits, and much have I heard myself. And mine own woeful experience is able to say something of thee, as one who have been in the unfortunate fair and have often bought and sold with thee, but never had anything that succeeded happily with me; as one who many a time heretofore, even to this present hour, have silenced thy false properties, and all because I would not purchase thy displeasure, and pull thy hatred upon me, and that thou shouldst not untimely pluck this flower from me, which this day thou hast cropt by the mightiness of thy power. And therefore now will I go without fear, like one that hath nothing to lose, or as one to whom thy company is now odious and troublesome, or like a poor traveller, who fearless of thieves, goes singing on his way. I thought in my more tender years that both thou and thy actions were governed by order, and ruled by reason. But now I see thou art pro and con, there is no certainty in thy calms, thou seemest now unto me to be a labyrinth of errors, a fearful wilderness, an habitation of wild beasts, a dance full of changes, a fen full or mire and dirt, a country full of thorns, a steep and craggy mountain, a field full of stones, a meadow full of snakes and serpents, a pleasant garden to look to but without any fruit, a fountain of cares, a river of tears, a sea of miseries, trouble without profit, a sweet poison, a vain hope, a false joy, and a true sorrow.[558] Oh thou false world! Thou dost cast before us the baits of thy best delights and when we have swallowed them, they seeming savoury unto us, then dost thou show us the hook that must choke us. Nor can we avoid it, because together with us, thou dost captivate our wills. Thou promisest mountains, but performest molehills; and then thou dost cast us off, that we may not put thee in mind of making good thy vain promises. We run through the spacious fields of

---

[558] This passage (from 'labyrinth of errors' to 'true sorrow', lines 90–97) was almost literally translated by Rojas from Petrarch's *Seniles* XI.xi (see Lobera *et al.* p. 340, n. 30, and their long note, pp. 741–42). As is the case with all the other passages inspired by Petrarch, or translated from him, it is taken from the 1496 Basel edition of his *Opera latina*.

thy rank vices recklessly and with a loose rein, and then doest thou discover thy ambushes unto us, when thou seest there is no way for us to retreat. Many have forsaken thee, fearing thy sudden forsaking of them. And well may they style themselves happy, when they shall see how well thou hast rewarded this poor heavy sorrowful old man for his long service. Thou dost put out our eyes, and then to make us amends, thou anointest the place with oil; thou breakest our head, and givest us a plaster; after thou hast done us a great deal of harm, thou givest us a poor cold comfort. Thou dost hurt unto all, that no man may boast that others have not their crosses as well as we, telling them that it is some ease to the miserable to have companions in their misery. But I alas, disconsolate old man stand all alone. I am singular in my sorrows. I am grieved, and have no equal companion of my grief. No man's misfortune is like unto mine; though I revolve in my troubled memory, persons both present and past, I cannot instance in the like. If I shall seek to comfort myself with the severity and patience of Paulus Aemilius, who having lost two sons in seven days, bore this brunt of fortune with so undaunted a courage, that the people of Rome had rather need to be comforted by him, than he by them. Yet cannot this satisfy me, for he had two more remaining that were his adopted sons. What companion then will they allot me of my misery? Pericles, that brave Athenian captain? Or valiant Xenophon?[559] Tush, they lost sons indeed, but their sons died out of their sight, having lost their lives abroad in foreign countries, far from home, so that it was not much for the one not to change countenance, but to take it cheerfully, nor for the other to answer the messenger who brought him the ill tidings of his sons' deaths that he should receive no punishment, because himself had received no grief; for all this is far differing from mine. Less canst thou say, thou world replenished with evil, that Anaxagoras and I were alike in our loss, that we were equal in our griefs, and that I should say of my dead daughter, as he did of his only son, when he said: 'being that I was mortal, I knew, that he whom I had

---

[559] The story of Paulus Emilius, and other sections in this passage — including the references to Pericles, Xenophon, and Anaxagoras — are all taken from two letters in Petrarch's *Familiares* (II.i and ii; see Lobera *et al.*, eds, 2000, pp. 342-43, notes 40-42 and 50).

begot was to die'. For my Melibea, willingly and out of her own election, killed herself before mine eyes, enforced thereunto through the extreme passion of her love, so great was her torment; whereas his son was slain in battle, in a just and lawful war. Oh incomparable loss! Oh most wretched and sorrowful old man that I am, who, the more I seek after comfort, the less reason do I find for my comfort, for much more miserable do I find my misfortune, and do not so much grieve at her death, as I do lament the manner of her death. Now shall I lose together with thee, most unhappy daughter, those fears which were daily wont to affright me. Only thy death is that which makes me secure of all suspicions and jealousies.[560] What shall I do, when I shall come into thy chamber, and thy withdrawing room, and shall find it solitary and empty? What shall I do, when as I shall call thee, and thou shalt not answer me? Who is he that can supply that want which thou hast caused? Who can stop up that great breach in my heart which thou hast made? Never any man did lose that which I have lost this day. Though in some sort, that great fortitude of Lambas de Auria, Duke of Genoa, seemeth to suit with my present estate and condition, who seeing his son was wounded to death, took him and threw him with his own arms forth of the ship into the sea.[561] But such kind of deaths as these, though they take away life, yet they give reputation. And many times men are enforced to undergo such actions, for to comply with their honour, and get themselves fame and renown. But what did enforce my daughter to die, but only the strong force of love? What remedy now (thou flattering world) wilt thou afford my wearisome age? How wouldst thou have me to rely upon thee, I knowing thy falsehoods, thy gins,° thy snares, and thy nets, wherein thou entrapst and takest our weak and feeble wills? Tell me, what hast thou done with my daughter? Where hast thou bestowed her? Who shall accompany my disaccompanied habitation? Who shall cherish me in mine old age? Who with gentle usage shall cocker my decaying years? Oh love, love, I did not think thou hadst had the power to kill thy subjects! I was wounded by thee in my youth. I did pass through the midst

---

[560] Petrarch, *De remediis* II.48 (Lobera *et al.*, eds, 2000, p. 343, n. 47, and their long note, p. 744).
[561] Another example extracted from Petrarch's *Familiares* (II.ii.7–9).

of thy flames. Why didst thou let me scape? Was it that thou might'st pay me home for my flying from thee then in mine old age? I had well thought, that I had been freed from thy snares, when I once began to grow towards forty, and when I rested contented with my wedded comfort, and when I saw I had that fruit, which this day thou hast cut down. I did not dream that thou would'st in the children have taken vengeance of the parents, and I know not whether thou woundest with the sword, or burnest with fire. Thou leavest our clothes whole, and yet most cruelly woundest our hearts. Thou makes that which is foul, to seem fair and beautiful unto us. Who gave thee so great a power? Who gave thee that name which so ill befitteth thee? If thou wert love, thou wouldst love thy servants; and if thou didst love them, thou wouldst not punish them as thou dost. If to be thy fellow were to live merrily, so many would not kill themselves, as my daughter now hath, and infinite of us. What end have thy servants and their ministers had? As also that false bawd, Celestina, who died by the hands of the faithfullest companions that ever she lighted upon in her life, for their true performance in this thy venomous and impoisoned service? They lost their heads. Calisto, he broke his neck, and my daughter, to imitate him, submitted herself to the selfsame death. And of all this thou wast the cause. They gave thee a sweet name, but thy deeds are exceeding sour: thou dost not give equal rewards, and that law is unjust, which is not equal alike unto all.[562] Thy voice promiseth pleasure, but thy actions proclaim pain. Happy are they who have not known thee, or knowing thee, have not cared for thee. Some, led with I know not what error have not sticked to call thee a god, but I would have such fools as these to consider with themselves, it savours not of a deity to murder or destroy those that serve and follow him. Oh thou enemy to all reason! To those that serve thee least thou givest thy greatest rewards, until thou hast

---

[562] The same community of interests that brought Celestina and the servants together also caused their downfall. And the sort of desire (self-interest, lust) that constituted the bedrock of this community of interests has eventually destroyed its agents too. The bonds of fidelity are broken (see introduction, and Pavel, 2005, pp. 93–95), and the love of the Neoplatonists, far from providing life with cohesion and continuity, is a cosmic legislator that does 'not give equal rewards'.

brought them at last into this thy troublesome dance. Thou art an enemy to thy friends, and a friend to thy enemies, and all this is because thou dost not govern thyself according to order and reason. They paint thee blind, poor, and young. They put a bow into thy hand, wherein thou drawest and shootest at random. But more blind are they that serve thee. For they never taste or see the unsavoury and distasteful recompense which they receive by thy service. Thy fire is of hot burning lightning, which scorches unto death, yet leaves no impression or print of any wound at all. The sticks which thy flames consume are the souls and lives of human creatures, which are so infinite and so numberless that it scarce occurreth unto me with whom I should first begin, not only of Christians, but of Gentiles and of Jews, and all forsooth in requital of their good services. What shall I speak of that Macias[563] of our times, and how by loving he came to his end, of whose sad and woeful death thou was the sole cause? What service did Paris do thee? What Helena? What Aegisthus? All the world knows how it went with them.[564] How well likewise didst thou requite Sappho, Ariadne, and Leander, and many other besides, whom I willingly silence because I have enough to do in the repetition of mine own misery?[565] I complain me of the world because I was bred up in it; for had not the world given me life, I had not therein begot Melibea; not being begot, she had not

---

[563] On Macias, see note to 2.85 above.

[564] On Paris and Helen, see note to 6.565 above. Aegisthus was part of a complex Homeric saga, then passed on to Greek tragedy, full of adultery, incest, and parricide. Aegisthus became Clytemnestra's lover while the latter's husband, Agamemnon, fought in Troy. After his return from war, the two lovers murdered Agamemnon. His death was in turn avenged by his son Orestes, who killed both Aegisthus and his lover, Orestes's own mother Clytemnestra.

[565] Sappho] the well-known seventh-century BC Greek poet, famous for her love lyrics. According to legend, she committed suicide after being rejected by a lover. Ariadne was the mythical daughter of King Minos and Pasiphae (see note to 1.207 above). Ariadne was abandoned by her lover Theseus, after she had helped him defeat the Minotaur. Leander was Hero's mythological lover, whose tragic story was immortalized in numerous poems, ancient and early modern. After Leander's death by drowning one stormy night after he had tried to swim across the Hellespont to meet Hero, she committed suicide by leaping from a tower. Mabbe has eliminated Rojas's reference to David, Solomon and Samson as victims of love.

been born; not being born, I had not loved her; and not loving her, I should not have mourned, as now I do, in this my latter and uncomfortable old age! Oh my good companion! Oh my bruised daughter, bruised even all to pieces! Why wouldst thou not suffer me to divert thy death? Why wouldst thou not take pity of thy kind and loving mother? Why didst thou show thyself so cruel against thy aged father? Why hast thou left me thus in sorrow? Why hast thou left me comfortless, and all alone, *in hac lacrimarum valle*, in this vale of tears, and shadow of death?[566]

FINIS

---

[566] The original ends with the Latin quotation, which Mabbe expands, as is his wont.

JOSÉ MARÍA PÉREZ FERNÁNDEZ

To the reader

Lo here thy Celestina, that wicked wight,
Who did her tricks upon poor lovers prove;
And in her company, the god of love.
Lo grace, beauty, desire, terror, hope, fright,
Faith, falsehood, hate, love, music, grief, delight,
Sighs, sobs, tears, cares, heats, colds, girdle, glove,
Paintings, Mercury sublimate, dung of dove.
Prison, force, fury, craft, scoffs, art, despight,
Bawds, ruffians, harlots, servants, false, untrue,
And all th'effects that follow on the same,
As war, strife, loss, death, infamy and shame.
All which and more, shall come unto thy view.
But if this book speak not his English plain,
Excuse him: for he lately came from Spain.

GLOSSARY

The glossary contains archaic, obsolete, or less common words found in the play. Unless otherwise indicated, synonyms and/or definitions are taken from the current online edition of the *OED*.

A

abortive	an aborted fetus; a stillborn child or animal
affiance	faith, trust
affront	a hostile encounter
ambidexter	double-dealer
ambuscado	ambush
anime	aromatic resin obtained from tropical trees

B

baggage	strumpet
bait	feed
bead-roll	catalogue
besom	broom
bluebottle	blue corn-flower (*Centaurea cyanus*)
botch	a tumour, or an ulcer
brangling	agitation

C

carbonade	slash, hack
causey	embankment, a raised footpath
ceruse	a pigment used to whiten the complexion
chaps	jaws
close / cloze	approach
cock	pipe, tap
cocker	indulge, pamper
coffin	a cone-shaped paper parcel, a cornet
cogging	cheating (*adj.*)
colling	embracing, hugging
company	to cohabit
constringe	to draw or squeeze together; to compress
controlment	restraint, check
court-jack	a kind of leathern bottle or jug

D

dish-clout   a dish-cloth, used to wipe the dirt off dishes

E

elder   a shrub, black-berried elder (*Sambucus nigra*)
empeople   to populate

F

fadge   to agree, fit in
farding   paint, or make up for the face
fay   faith
ferventness   eagerness
fistic   pistachio
flight   to avoid, shun
foisting   roguery
frankness   generosity

G

gadding   wandering
gin   craft, trap.
girt (gird, girth)   to bind (a horse) with a saddle-girth
gorbelly   a protuberant belly
gossipping   a christening or christening-feast
grey-falcon   the hen-harrier (*Circus cyaneus*)

H

handsmooth   downright
hie   to hasten, to make speed (*refl.*)
holm   the common holly
horn-fish   the garfish (*Belone vulgaris*)

I

impostume   a purulent swelling or cyst; an abscess
insult   attack, assault
intersert   interpolate
inwardness   intimacy, close friendship
iwis   certainly

GLOSSARY

J

jade	horse
jar	discord, disagreement
jump	to agree, coincide

L

labour	to urge, entreat
lapped	wrapped up, disguised
limbeck	alembic
lipsalve	salve or ointment for the lips

M

mother	uterus

N

nim	filch

O

occurrent	event, incident
offer	to attempt, to try, also dare
offerture	overture, proposal
overthwart	across

P

pie	magpie
pill	to pluck
pin	in archery, a peg fixed in the centre of a target
pompion	pumpkin
prove	to prosper, thrive
pullen	poultry, domestic fowls, chicks

Q

quean	a hussy; a prostitute
questionless	unquestionably, undoubtedly

R

recourse	a periodic return or recurrence
rent	to tear, pull apart
rosecakes	a cake of compressed rose petals
roll	a round cushion or pad in a woman's headdress
rundlet	a cask or vessel of varying capacity

S

shot	reckoning
sot	fool
soultage	coarse cloth or canvas used for packing or bags
spike	French lavender
starting	shock, surprise
storax	a fragrant gum-resin
sucker	a shoot thrown out from the base of a tree
suds	dregs, muck
sweet-water	a liquid perfume or scent
swound	swoon

T

tarriance	delay
ticklish	unstable, fickle
tind	ignite, kindle
train	trap
travel	labour, toil (as in *travail*)
trial	experience

U

unadvisedness	imprudence

V

violency	vehemence, passion

W

wag	a mischievous boy
wheel	plot, device, instrument, mechanism

GLOSSARY

white	archery, white target usually placed on the butt
winch	to start back or away, recoil, flinch; to wince
windlass	a circuitous course of action or crafty device
wretchless	heedless

BIBLIOGRAPHY

Modern editions of early modern texts appear between brackets, and are fully listed in the secondary bibliography under the names of their editors.

EDITIONS, TRANSLATIONS AND ADAPTATIONS OF *LA CELESTINA* CITED

Anonymous, trans., *Celestine in laquelle est traicte des deceptions des seruiteurs Enuers leurs maistres* [. . .] *trãslate dytaliê en frãcois* (Paris: Nicolas Cousteau pour Galliot du Pré, 1527) [Brault, ed. 1963]

Anonymous, trans., *Celestina: Ende is een Tragicomedie van Calisto ende Melibea* (Antwerpen: Hans de Laet, 1550) [Behiels, Lieve & Kathleen V. Kish, eds, 2005]

Barth, Kaspar, trans., *Pornoboscodidascalus Latinus. De lenonum, lenarum, conciliatricum, sevitiorum dolis, venefitiis, machinis plusquam diabolicis, de miseriis iuvenum incautorum qui florem aetatis amoribus inconcessis addicunt, de miserabili singulorum periculo et omnium interitu. Liber plane divinus lingua Hispanica ab incerto auctore instar ludi conscriptus Celestinae titulo, tot vitae instruendae sententiis, tot exemplis, figuris, monitis plenus ut par aliquid nulla fere lingua habeat. Caspar Barthius inter excercitia linguae Castellanae cuius fere princeps stilo et sapientia hic ludus habetur Latine transcribebat. Accedunt dissertatio eiusdem ad lectorem cum animadversionum commentariolo, inter Leandris eiusdem at Musaeus recensiti,* typis Wechelianis, apud Danielem et Davidem Aubrios et Clementem Schleichium, Francofurti, anno MDCXXIV. [Fernández, Enrique, ed., 2006]

Anonymous, trans., *La Celestina ov histoire tragicomiqve de Caliste et de Melibee* (Rouen: Charles Osmont, 1633)

Bush, Peter, trans., Fernando de Rojas, *La Celestina*. With an introduction by Juan Goytisolo (Harmondsworth: Penguin, 2009)

BIBLIOGRAPHY

Canet Vallés, José Luis, eds, *Comedia de Calisto y Melibea* (Valencia: Publicaciones de la Universidad de Valencia, 2011) [A recent edition of the 16-act version]

Clifford, John, trans. and adaptation, Fernando de Rojas, *La Celestina* (London: Nick Hern Books, 2004)

Cohen, J. M., *The Spanish Bawd. La Celestina. Being the Tragi-Comedy of Calisto and Melibea* (Harmondsworth: Penguin, 1964)

Hartnoll, Phyllis, *Fernando de Rojas. Celestina or the Tragicomedy of Calisto and Melibea* (London, 1959)

Lavardin, Jacques de, trans., *La Celestine fidellement repvrgee, et mise en meilleure forme* [. . .] (Paris: Nicolas Bonfons, 1578) [Drysdal, Denis L. ed. & introd., 1974]

Lobera, *et al.*, Fernando de Rojas (y 'Antiguo Autor'), *La Celestina. Tragicomedia de Calisto y Melibea*. Edición y estudio de Francisco J. Lobera y Guillermo Serés, Paloma Díaz-Mas, Carlos Mota e Iñigo Ruiz Arzálluz, y Francisco Rico (Barcelona: Crítica, 2000; 2nd edn Madrid: Real Academia Española, 2011)

Mabbe, James trans., *The Spanish bavvd, represented in Celestina: or, The tragicke-comedy of Calisto and Melibea: Wherein is contained, besides the pleasantnesse and sweetnesse of the stile, many philosophicall sentences, and profitable instructions necessary for the younger sort: shewing the deceits and subtilties housed in the bosomes of false seruants, and cunny-catching bawds* (London: Printed by I[ohn] B[eale] and are to be sold by Robert Allot at the signe of the Beare in Pauls Church-yard, 1631) STC (2nd ed.) 4911 [Fitzmaurice-Kelly, James ed. and introd., 1894; Allen, ed., 1908; Severin, ed., 1987]

Mabbe, James, trans., [Fernando de Rojas's] *Celestine or the Tragick-Comedie of Calisto and Melibea* [the Alnwick manuscript, Martínez Lacalle, ed., 1972]

Ordóñez, Alfonso, trad., *Tragicocomedia di Calisto e Melibea nouamente traducta de Spagnolo in Italiano idioma*. Roma:

Eucharium Silver *alias* Frank, 1506 [Kish, Kathleen B., ed., 1973]

Rojas, Fernando de, *La Celestina: Tragicomedia de Calisto y Melibea* (Salamanca: Matías Gast a costa de Simón Borgoñón, 1570) [Miguel, Emilio de, ed., 2006]

Rojas, Fernando de, *Celestina*, ed. with an introduction and notes by Dorothy Sherman Severin, with the translation of James Mabbe [1631] (Warminster: Aris & Phillips, 1987)

Simpson, L. B., *The Celestina: A Novel in Dialogue* [16-act version] (Berkeley-Los Angeles, 1955)

Singleton, M. H. *Celestina* (Madison: University of Wisconsin Press, 1958)

Wirsung, Christoph, trans., *Ain Hipsche Tragedia võ zwaien liebhabendn* [. . .] (Augsburg: Sigismund Grym & Marx Wirsung, 1520) [Kish, Kathleen B. & Ursula Ritzenhoff, eds, 1984]

OTHER PRIMARY SOURCES

Alemán, Mateo, *Primera Parte de Guzmán de Alfarache* (Madrid: Várez de Castro, 1599)

—, *Segunda parte de la vida de Guzmán de Alfarache, atalaya de la vida humana* (Lisboa: Pedro Crasbeeck, 1604)

Auctoritates Aristotelis et aliorum philosophorum maxime Senecae, Boethii, Platonis, Apuleii, Empedoclis, Porphyrii et G. Porretani [Lugduni: Joannes de Vingle, *c*. 1485]

Boccaccio, Giovanni, *La fiometa de Juan vocacio* [1st Castilian translation of *Fiammetta*, attributed to Pedro Roche], (Salamanca: [Workshop of Nebrija's *Gramática* (?)] 1497)

—, *Amorous Fiammetta* [trans. by Bartholomew Yong] (London: John Charlewood for Thomas Gubbin and Thomas Newman, 1587) [STC (2nd edn) 3179]

BIBLIOGRAPHY

Botero, Giovanni, *Obseruations vpon the liues of Alexander, Caesar, Scipio. Newly Englished* (London: Printed by A. Islip, for Iohn Iaggard, 1602) [STC (2nd edn) 3397]

Brinsley, John, *Ludus Literarius: or, The Grammar Schole* (London: Printed [by Humphrey Lownes] for Thomas Man, 1612) [STC (2nd edn) 3768]

Butler, Charles, *Ramae rhetoricae libri duo. In usum scholarum.* (Oxford: Joseph Barnes, 1597) [STC 4196.5]

—, *English grammar, or, The institution of letters, syllables, and words in the English tongue, whereunto is annexed an index of words like and unlike* (Oxford: Printed by William Turner, for the authour, 1633) [STC (2nd edn) 4190]

Cervantes, Miguel de, *The history of the valorovs and wittie Knight-Errant, Don-Quixote Of the Mancha. Translated out of the Spanish* [by Thomas Shelton] (London: Printed by William Stansby, for Ed. Blount and W. Barret, 1612) [STC (2nd edn) 4915]

—, *Novelas Ejemplares* (Madrid: Juan de la Cuesta, 1613)

—, *The second part of the history of the valorous and witty knight-errant, Don Quixote of the Mancha. Written in Spanish by Michael Ceruantes: and now translated into English* [by Thomas Shelton] (London: Printed [by Eliot's Court Press] for Edward Blount, 1620) [STC (2nd edn) 4917]

—, *The history and adventures of the renowned Don Quixote. Translated from the Spanish of Miguel de Cervantes Saavedra [. . .] by T. Smollett* (London: printed for A. Millar; T. Osborn, T. and T. Longman, C. Hitch and L. Hawes, J. Hodges, and J. and J. Rivington, 1755) [Smollett, trans., 2004]

Céspedes y Meneses, Gonzalo de. *Poema trágico del español Gerardo, y desengaño del amor lascivo* (Madrid: Luis Sánchez, 1615) [1st part, 2nd part, 1618]

—, *Gerardo the vnfortunate Spaniard. Or A patterne for lasciuious louers. Containing seuerall strange miseries of loose affection.*

Written by an ingenious Spanish gentleman, Don Gonzalo de Cespedes, and Meneses, in the time of his fiue yeeres imprisonment. Originally in Spanish, and made English by L.D. [Leonard Digges] (London: Printed [by George Purslowe] for Ed. Blount, 1622) [STC (2nd edn) 4919]

Correas, Gonzalo. *Vocabulario de refranes y frases proverbiales* [1627] [Combet, Louis, ed., 2000]

Corro, Antonio del, *Reglas gramaticales para aprender la lengua española y francesa, confiriendo la vna con la otra, segun el orden de las partes de la oration Latinas* (Impressas en Paris [i.e. Oxford]: [Ioseph Barnes], En el año de salud. 1586) [STC (2nd edn) 5789a]

—, *The Spanish grammer: with certeine rules teaching both the Spanish and French tongues. By which they that haue some knowledge in the French tongue, may the easier attaine to the Spanish; and the likewise they that haue the Spanish, with more facilitie learne the French: and they that are acquainted with neither of them, learne either or both. Made in Spanish, by M. Anthonie de Corro. With a dictionarie adioyned vnto it, of all the Spanish wordes cited in this booke: and other more wordes most necessarie for all such as desire the knowledge of the same tongue. By Iohn Thorius, graduate in Oxenford* (London: John Wolf, 1590) [STC (2nd edn) 5790]

Covarrubias Orozco, Sebastián de. *Tesoro de la lengua castellana o español* (Madrid: Luis Sánchez, 1611) [Maldonado & Camarero, eds, 1995]

Expositiones terminorum legum Anglorum. Exposiciones t[er]mino[rum] legu[m] anglo[rum]. Et natura breuiu[m] cu[m] diuersis casibus regulis [et] fundamentis legum tam de libris Magistri Litteltoni quam de aliis legum libris collectis [et] breuiter compilatis p[ro] iuuinib[us] valde necessariis. The exposicions of the termys of ye law of englond & the nature of the wryttys with dyuers rulys and pryncyples of ye law, aswell out of ye bokys of master lyttelton as of other bokys of the law gaderyd & breuely co[m]pilyd for yong men very necessary. ([Imprinted at Lo[n]do[n]: [By Johannes Rastell] i[n] chepe syde at powlys gate. cum priuilegio regali, [*c.* 1525]) [STC (2nd edn), 20702]

Fitzherbert, Anthony *La grande abbregement de la ley* (London: John Rastell, 1516)

Flores, Juan de. *Grimalte y Gradissa* [Lérida: Enrique Botel, *c.* 1495] [Parrilla, ed., 2008]

Florio, John, *Queen Anna's new world of words, or dictionarie of the Italian and English tongues, collected, and newly much augmented by Iohn Florio, reader of the Italian vnto the Soueraigne Maiestie of Anna, crowned Queene of England, Scotland, France and Ireland, &c. And one of the gentlemen of hir Royall Priuie Chamber. Whereunto are added certaine necessarie rules and short obseruations for the Italian tongue* (London: Printed by Melch. Bradwood [and William Stansby], for Edw. Blount and William Barret, Anno 1611) [STC (2nd edn) 11099]

Fonseca, Cristóbal de, *Discurso para Todos los Evangelios de la Cuaresma* (Madrid: En casa de Alonso Martín de Balboa a costa de Alonso Pérez, mercader de libros, 1614)

Gosson, Stephen, *Playes confuted in fiue actions: prouing that they are not to be suffred in a Christian common weale, by the waye both the cauils of Thomas Lodge, and the play of playes, written in their defence, and other obiections of players frendes, are truely set downe and directlye aunsweared. By Steph. Gosson, stud. Oxon.* (London: Imprinted for Thomas Gosson dwelling in Pater noster row at the signe of the Sunne, [1582]) [STC (2nd edn) 12095]

Gracián Dantisco, Lucas, *Galateo español* [*c.* 1582] ed. By Margherita Morreale (Madrid: Centro Superior de Investigaciones Científicas, 1968)

Guazzo, Stephano, *The ciuile conuersation of M. Stephen Guazzo, written first in Italian, diuided into foure bookes, the first three translated out of French by G. pettie. In the first is contained in generall, the fruits that may be reaped by conuersation [. . .] In the second, the manner of conuersation* [. . .] *In the third is perticularlie set forth the orders to be obserued in conuersation within doores, betweene the husband and the wife* [. . .] *In the fourth is set downe the forme of ciuile conuersation, by an example of a banquet, made in Cassale, betweene sixe lords and foure ladies. And now translated out of Italian into English by Barth. Young, of the middle Temple, Gent.* (Imprinted at London: By Thomas East, 1586) [STC (2nd edn) 12423]

Horace, *Satires, Epistles and Ars Poetica*, ed. & trans. by H. R. Fairclough (Cambridge, Mass. & London: Harvard University Press & William Heinemann Ltd., 1978)

Humphrey, Laurence, *Epistola de Graecis litteris et Homeri lectione et imitatione* (Basel: Oporinus, 1558)

—, *Interpretatio linguarum: seu de ratione convertendi et explicandi autores tam sacros quam prophanos* (Basel: Frobenius et Episcopius, 1559)

Jonson, Benjamin, *Bartholmew fayre: a comedie, acted in the yeare, 1614 by the Lady Elizabeths seruants, and then dedicated to King Iames, of most blessed memorie; The diuell is an asse: a comedie acted in the yeare, 1616, by His Maiesties seruants; The staple of newes: a comedie acted in the yeare, 1625, by His Maiesties seruants / by the author, Beniamin Iohnson* (London: Printed by I. B. [John Beale] for Robert Allot, and are to be sold at the signe of the Beare, in Pauls Church-yard, 1631) [STC (2nd edn) 14753.5]

—, *Timber, or Discoveries*. In *The workes of Benjamin Jonson. The second volume* (London: printed [by John Beale, John Dawson 2, Bernard Alsop, Thomas Harper, and Thomas Fawcet] for Richard Meighen [Thomas Walkley and Robert Allot], 1640 [i.e. 1641]) (STC 14754a) [Hutson, ed., 2012]

La Vida de Lazarillo de Tormes, y de sus fortunas y aduersidades (Medina del Campo: Mateo y Francisco del Canto, Alcalá de Henares: Atanasio de Salcedo, Burgos: Juan de Junta, and Antwerp: Martin Nutius, 1554) [Rico, ed., 2011]

Mabbe, James, trans., [of Mateo Alemán's *Guzmán de Alfarache*] *The rogue: or The life of Guzman de Alfarache. Written in*

Spanish by Matheo Aleman, seruant to his Catholike Maiestie, and borne in Seuill (London: Printed [by Eliot's Court Press and George Eld] for Edward Blount, 1622) [STC (2nd edn) 289]

—, trans., [of Cristóbal de Fonseca's *Discursos para todos los evangelios de la Cuaresma*] *Deuout contemplations expressed in two and fortie sermons vpon all ye quadragesimall Gospells written in Spanish by Fr. Ch. de Fonseca Englished by. I. M. of Magdalen Colledge in Oxford* (London: Printed by Adam Islip, anno Domini 1629) [STC (2nd edn) 11126]

—, trans., [of Juan de Santa María *República y policía cristiana*] *Policie unveiled: wherein may be learned, the order of true policie in kingdomes, and common-wealths: the matters of justice, and government; the addresses, maxims, and reasons of state: the science of governing well a people: and where the subject may learne true obedience unto their kings, princes, and soveraignes. Written in Spanish, and translated into English by I. M. of Magdalen Hall in Oxford* (London: Printed by Thomas Harper, for Richard Collins, and are to be sold at his shop in Pauls Church-yard, at the signe of the Three Kings, 1632) [STC (2nd edn) 14831a]

—, trans., [of Miguel de Cervantes's *Novelas ejemplares*] *Exemplarie nouells: in sixe books. The two damosels. The Ladie Cornelia. The liberall lover. The force of bloud. The Spanish ladie. The jealous husband. Full of various accidents both delightfull and profitable. By Miguel de Cervantes Saavedra; one of the prime wits of Spaine, for his rare fancies, and wittie inventions. Turned into English by Don Diego Puede-Ser* (London: Printed by Iohn Dawson, for R[alph] M[abbe] and are to be sold by Laurence Blaicklocke: at his shop at the Sugar-loafe next Temple Barre in Fleetstreet, 1640) [STC (2nd edn) 4914]

Mal Lara, Juan de. *La philosophia vulgar* (Sevilla: Hernando Díaz, 1568) [Bernal Rodríguez, ed., 1996]

Mena, Juan de, *Laberinto de Fortuna*, Salamanca [Workshop of Nebrija's *Introductiones latinae*, c. 1481–1487] [Cummings, ed., 2008]

Meres, Frances. *Palladis tamia. Wits treasury being the second part of Wits common wealth. By Francis Meres Maister of Artes of both Vniuersities* (At London: printed by P. Short, for Cuthbert Burbie, and are to be solde at his shop at the Royall Exchange, 1598)

Minsheu, John, *Pleasant Dialogues in Spanish* [published in 1599 with Percyvall's *Spanish Grammar*, and *A Dictionarie in Spanish and English*, see below] [STC (2nd edn) / 19622] [Cid, ed.]

Montaigne, Michel de, *Essays written in French by Michael Lord of Montaigne* [. . .] *done into English, according to the last French edition, by Iohn Florio* [. . .] (London: Printed by Melch. Bradvvood for Edvvard Blount and William Barret, 1613) [STC (2nd edn) 18042]

Montemayor, Jorge de, *Diana of George of Montemayor: translated out of Spanish into English by Bartholomew Yong of the Middle Temple Gentleman* (At London: Printed by Edm. Bollifant, impensis G[eorge] B[ishop], 1598) [STC (2nd edn) 18044]

Munday, Anthony & Salvian of Marseilles, *A Second and Third Blast of Retrait from Plaies and Theaters: the one whereof was sounded by a reuerend byshop dead long since; the other by a worshipful and zealous gentleman now aliue: one showing the filthines of plaies in times past; the other the abhomination of theaters in the time present: both expresly prouing that that common-weale is nigh vnto the cursse of God, wherein either plaiers be made of, or theaters maintained. Set forth by Anglophile Eutheo.* ([Imprinted at London: By Henrie Denham, dwelling in Pater noster Row, at the signe of the Starre, being the assigne of William Seres] Allowed by aucthoritie, 1580) [STC (2nd edn) 21677] [The 'second blast' is a translation of book 6 of *De gubernatione Dei* by Salvian of Marseilles; the third is sometimes attributed to Anthony Munday (i.e. Anglophile Eutheo?). The 'first blast' was *The schoole of abuse* by Stephen Gosson]

Nebrija, Antonio de, *Introductiones Latinae* (Salamanca: [Juan de Porras], 1481)

—, *Introduciones latinas contrapuesto el romance al latín* (Salamanca [Juan de Porras], 1488)

—, *Gramática sobre la lengua castellana* (Salamanca: [Juan de Porras], 1492) [Lozano, ed., 2011]

—, *A briefe introduction to syntax: Compendiously shewing the true vse, grounds, and reason of Latin construction. Collected for the most part out of Nabrissa his Spanish copie. With the concordance supplyed, by I. H. [John Hawkins] med. doct. Together with the more difficult assertions, proued by the vse of the learned languages* (London: Printed by Thomas Harper, for G. Edmondson, 1631) [STC (2nd edn) 688]

Núñez, Hernán, *Refranes o proverbios en romance que nueuamente colligió y glossó el Comendador Hernán Núñez* (Salamanca: Juan de Cánova, 1555)

Percyvall, Richard, *Bibliotheca Hispanica: Containing a grammar; with a dictionarie in Spanish, English, and Latine; gathered out of diuers good authors: very profitable for the studious of the Spanish toong. By Richard Percyuall Gent. The dictionarie being inlarged with the Latine, by the aduise and conference of Master Thomas Doyley Doctor in Physicke* (Imprinted at London: By Iohn Iackson, for Richard Watkins, 1591) [STC (2nd edn) 19619]

Percyvall, Richard, *A Spanish grammar, first collected and published by Richard Perciuale Gent. Now augmented and increased with the declining of all the irregular and hard verbes in that toong, with diuers other especiall rules and necessarie notes for all such as shall be desirous to attaine the perfection of the Spanish tongue. Done by Iohn Minsheu professor of languages in London. Hereunto for the yoong beginners learning and ease, are annexed speeches, phrases, and prouerbes, expouned out of diuers authors, setting downe the line and the leafe where in the same bookes they shall finde them, whereby they may not onely vnderstand them, but by them vnderstand others, and the rest as they shall meete with them* (Imprinted at London: By Edm. Bollifant, 1599) [STC (2nd edn) 19622]

Petrarca, Francesco, *Opera latina. (Bucolicum carmen. De vita solitaria. De remediis utriusque fortunae. Secretum de contemptu mundi. De vera sapientia. De rebus memorandis. Invectivae contra medicum obiurgantem. Epistolae familiares. Epistolae sine titulo. Epistola ad Carolum IV. regem Romanorum. Epistola de studiorum suorum successibus. Psalmi poenitentiales. De viris illustribus / cum supplemento Lombardi Serici). Benvenutus de Rambaldis: Libellus Augustalis. Annotatio principalium sententiarum ex libris F. Petrarcae collectarum* (Impressis Basileae: per magistrum Joannem de Amerbach, 1496)

Piccolomini, Aeneas Sylvius, *Historia de duobus amantibus* (Cologne: Ulrich Zell, 1470)

—, *Estoria muy verdadera de dos amantes* [Salamanca, workshop of Nebrija's *Gramática de la Lengua Castellana*, 1496(?)] [Ravasini, ed., 2003]

Pontano, Giovanni. *Pontani de Bello neapolitano et de sermone* (Neapoli: Pietro Summonte, 1509) [FRBNF31134834] [Bistagne, ed., 2008]

[Rastell, John?] *A new co[m]modye in englysh in maner of an enterlude ryght elygant [and] full of craft of rethoryk, wherein is shewd [and] dyscrybyd as well the bewte [and] good propertes of women, as theyr vycys [and] euyll co[n]dicio[n]s, with a morall co[n]clusion [and] exhortacyon to vertew* [[London]: Iohes rastell me imprimi fecit], [*c.* 1525] [STC (2nd edn) 20721] [The interlude of *Calisto and Melebea*] [López Santos & Tostado González, eds, 2001]

Reynolds, Henry. *Mythomystes wherein a short suruay is taken of the nature and value of true poesy and depth of the ancients above our moderne poets. To which is annexed the tale of Narcissus briefly mythologized* (London: Printed [by George Purslowe] for Henry Seyle, at the Tigers-head in St. Pauls Church-yard, [1632]) [STC (2nd edn) 20939] [Spingarn, ed., 1957]

Rowland, David, trans., *The pleasaunt historie of Lazarillo de Tormes a Spaniarde: wherein is conteined his marueilous deedes and life. With the straunge aduentures happened to him in the seruice of sundrie masters. Drawen out of Spanish by Dauid*

Rouland of Anglesey (Imprinted at London: By Abell Ieffes, dwelling in the fore streete without Crepell gate nere Groube streete at the signe of the Bell, 1586) [STC (2nd edn) 15336] [Whitlock, ed., 2003]

San Pedro, Diego de, *Cárcel de amor* (Sevilla: Cuatro compañeros alemanes [Pablo de Colonia, Juan Pegnitzer, Magno Herbst y Tomás Glockner] 1492) [Parrilla, ed., 1995]

—, *The pretie and wittie historie of Arnalt & Lucenda: with certen rules and dialogues set foorth for the learner of th'Italian tong: and dedicated vnto the Worshipfull, Sir Hierom Bowes Knight. By Claudius Hollyband scholemaster, teaching in Paules Churcheyarde by the sign of the Lucrece* (Imprinted at London: By Thomas Purfoote, 1575) [An Italian translation by Bartholomeo Maraffi, whose name appears on pi3v, *Tractado de amores de Arnalte y Lucenda* by Diego de San Pedro. With an English translation on facing pages, pronunciation guide, dialogues, and a short Italian grammar by Claudius Hollyband. Later, expanded and rearranged editions published as: *The Italian schoole-maister*] [STC (2nd edn) 6758]

Sanford, John, *Propylaion, or An entrance to the Spanish tongue.* (London: Printed by Thomas Haueland, for Nath. Butter and are to be sold at his shoppe at the Pide Bull vnder S. Austins gate in Paules Churchyeard, 1611)

Santa Maria, Juan de, *Tratado de republica y policia christiana para reyes y principes y para a los que en el gouierno tienen sus vezes* (Madrid: Imprenta Real, 1615)

Santillana, Marqués de (Íñigo López de Mendoza), *Proverbios con la glosa del autor y de Pedro Díaz de Toledo. Diego De Valera: Tratado de providencia contra fortuna* [Zaragoza: Juan Hurus, c.1488–90] [Gómez Moreno & Kerkhof, eds, 1988]

Seneca, Lucio Anneo, *Proverbia vel sententiae. Proverbios glosados por Pedro Díaz de Toledo* (Sevilla: Meinardo Ungut y Estanislao Polono, 1495)

Shakespeare, William, *Mr. William Shakespeares comedies, histories, & tragedies: Published according to the true originall copies* [The *First Folio*] (London: Printed by Isaac Iaggard, and Ed. Blount [at the charges of W. Iaggard, Ed. Blount, I. Smithweeke, and W. Aspley], 1623)

Smith, Sir Thomas, *De recta & emendata lingvæ Anglicæ scriptione, dialogus Thoma Smitho equestris ordinis Anglo authore* (Lutetiæ: ex officina Roberti Stephani typographi regij, M. D. LXVIII [1568]) [STC (2nd edn) 22856.5]

—, *A compendious or briefe examination of certayne ordinary complaints, of diuers of our country men in these our dayes: which although they are in some part vniust [and] friuolous, yet are they all by way of dialogues throughly debated [and] discussed. By W. S. Gentleman* [*A Discourse of the commonweal of this realm of England*] (Imprinted at London: In Fleetstreate, neere vnto Saincte Dunstones Church, by Thomas Marshe, 1581) [STC (2nd edn) 23134] [Dewar, ed., 1969]

Spenser, Edmund, *The Shepheardes Calender* (At London: Printed by Hugh Singleton, 1579) [STC (2nd edn) 23089]

Topsell, Edward, *Times Lamentation: or An exposition to the prophet Ioel, in sundry Sermons or Meditations* (At London: Printed by Edm. Bollifant, for George Potter, 1599) [STC (2nd edn) 24131]

Valdés, Juan de, *Diálogo de la lengua*, ed. by J. E. Laplana, Barcelona: Crítica, 2010)

Vega y Carpio, Lope de, *Rimas* [. . .] *ahora de nuevo añadidas: Con el nuevo arte de hazer comedidas deste tiempo* (Madrid: Alonso Martin. A costa de Miguel de Siles Librero, 1613)

Vives, Juan Luis, *De institutione foeminae christianae* (Antverpiae: apud Michaelem Hillenium Hoochstratanum, 1524)

—, *De institutione foeminae christianae* (Basileae: per Robertum Winter, 1538)

—, *Ioannis Lodouici Viuis Valentini De ratione dicendi libri tres: de consultatione* (Louanij: veñdant[ur] a Bartholomeo Grauio, sub sole aureo, 1533, pridie Idus septemb.(Louanij): ex officina Rutgeri Rescij) [Rodríguez Peregrina, ed., 2000]

—, [*A very fruitefull and pleasant booke called the instructio[n] of a Christen woma[n], made fyrst in Laten, and dedicated vnto the quenes good grace, by the right famous clerke mayster Lewes Vives, and turned out of Laten into Englysshe by Richard Hyrd. whiche boke who so redeth diligently shal haue knowlege of many thynges, wherein hew shal take great pleasure, and specially women shall take great co[m]modyte and frute towarde the[n]creace of vertue [and] good maners*] [Imprinted at London: In Fletestrete, in the house of Thomas Berthelet printer vnto the kynges mooste noble grace, at the signe of Lucrece, [*c.* 1529]] [STC (2nd edn) 24856] [Beauchamp *et al.*, eds, 2002]

SECONDARY SOURCES

A Catalogue of Hispanic Manuscripts and Books before 1700 from the Bodleian Library and Oxford College Libraries exhibited at the Taylor Institution 6–11 September [1962] (Oxford: Clarendon Press, 1962)

Allen, H. W., ed., *Celestina, or the Tragi-Comedy of Calisto and Melibea* (London: George Routledge and Sons, 1908)

Ardila, John G., 'Una traducción 'políticamente correcta': *Celestina* en la Inglaterra puritana' *Celestinesca*, 22 (1998), 33–48

Arellano, I. & J. M. Usunárriz, eds, *El mundo social y cultural de La Celestina* (Madrid & Frankfurt: Iberoamericana & Vervuert, 2003)

Baranda, Consolación, 'Cambio social en *La Celestina* y las ideas jurídico-políticas en la Universidad de Salamanca', in *El mundo social y cultural de 'La Celestina'*, ed. by I. Arellano & J. M. Usunárriz (Madrid & Frankfurt: Iberoamericana & Vervuert, 2003), pp. 9–25

Baranda, Consolación, *'La Celestina' y el mundo como conflicto* (Salamanca: Ediciones Universidad de Salamanca, 2004)

Baranda, Consolación & Ana María Vian Herrero, 'El nacimiento del "género" celestinesco: historia y perspectivas' in Orígenes de la novela, *Estudios*, dir. Raquel Gutiérrez Sebastián & Borja Rodríguez Gutiérrez (Santander: Servicio de Publicaciones de la Universidad de Cantabria & Sociedad Menéndez Pelayo, 2007), pp. 407–82

Beauchamp, V. W., E. H. Hageman & M. Mikesell, eds, Juan Luis Vives, *The Instruction of a Christen Woman* [*De institutione foeminae christianae*] trans. by Richard Hyrde [*c*. 1529]. (Urbana & Chicago: University of Illinois Press, 2002)

Behiels, Lieve & Kathleen V. Kish, eds, *Celestina: An annotated edition of the first Dutch translation (Antwerp, 1550)* (Louvain: Louvain University Press, 2005)

Bell, Aubrey F. G., *El renacimiento español*, trad. & introd. by Eduardo Julia Martínez (Málaga: Servicio de Publicaciones de la Universidad, 2004) [Facsimile of the edn published in Zaragoza by Ebro, in 1944]

Bennet, H. S., *English Books & Readers 1558–1603: Being a Study of the Book Trade in the Reign of Elizabeth I* (Cambridge: Cambridge University Press, 1965)

Bernal Rodríguez, Manuel, ed. Juan de Mal Lara. *Obras Completas*, 3 vols (Madrid: Fundación José Antonio de Castro, 1996)

Bistagne, Florence, ed & trad., Giovanni Giovano Pontano, *De Sermone. De la conversation* [1509] (Paris: Honoré Champion, 2008)

Boro, Joyce, 'Multilingualism, Romance, and Language Pedagogy; or Why Were So Many Sentimental Romances Printed as Polyglot Texts? in *Tudor Translation*, ed. by F. Schurink (London: Palgrave, 2011), pp. 18–38

Botta, Patrizia and Elizabetta Vaccaro, 'Un esemplare annotato della *Celestina* e la traduzione inglese di Mabbe', *Cultura Neolatina*, 52 (1992), 353–419

Bourland, C. B., 'Gabriel Harvey and the Modern Languages', *Huntington Library Quarterly* 4 (1940), 85–106

Brault, Gerard G., 'English Translations of *La Celestina* in the Sixteenth Century', *Hispanic Review* 28 (1960), 301–12

Brault, Gerard J., ed, *Celestine. A Critical Edition of the First French Translation (1527) of the Spanish Classic La Celestina with an introduction and notes by [. . .]* (Detroit, MI: Wayne State University Press, 1963)

Chevalier, Maxime, '*La Celestina* según sus lectores', in *Estudios sobre 'La Celestina'*, ed. by Santiago López Ríos (Madrid: Istmo, 2001), pp. 601–21

Combet, Louis, ed, Gonzalo Correas, *Vocabulario de refranes y frases proverbiales* (1627) (Bourdeaux: Institut d'Études Ibériques et Ibéro-Américaines de L'Université de Bordeaux, 1967; new rev. edn by Robert Jammes & Maïte Mir-Andreu, Madrid: Castalia, 2000)

Cook, Victor W., 'Charles Butler (*c.* 1560–1647)', in *Dictionary of Literary Biography*, vol 236, *British Rhetoricians and Logicians, 1500–1660*; First Series, ed. by Edward A. Malone (London: Buccoli Clark Layman, 2001), pp. 81–90

Cruz, Anne J., 'Sonnes of the Rogue: Picaresque relations in England and Spain', in *The Picaresque: Tradition and Displacement*, ed. by Giancarlo Mariorino (Minneapolis, MN: University of Minnesota Press, 1996), pp. 248–72

—, *Discourses of Poverty: Social Reform and the Picaresque Novel in Early Modern Spain* (Toronto: University of Toronto Press, 1999)

Cummings, John G., ed, Juan de Mena, *Laberinto de Fortuna* (Madrid: Cátedra, 6th edn 2008)

Dewar, Mary, ed, *A Discourse of the Commonweal of This Realm of England, attributed to Sir Thomas Smith* (Charlottesville: University of Virginia Press for the Folger Shakespeare Library, 1969)

Deyermond, A. D., *The Petrarchan Sources of 'La Celestina'* (Oxford: Clarendon Press, 1961)

—, 'La ficción sentimental: origen, desarrollo y pervivencia', in Diego de San Pedro, *Cárcel de amor*, ed. by Carmen Parrilla (Barcelona: Crítica, 1995), pp. ix-xxxiii

Di Camillo, Ottavio, 'When and where was the first act of *La Celestina* composed? A reconsideration' in *'De ninguna cosa es alegre posesión sin compañía'. Estudios celestinescos y medievales en honor del profesor Joseph Thomas Snow*, coord. D. Paolini (New York: Hispanic Seminar of Medieval Studies, 2010), pp. 91–157

Díez Borque, José María, *Sociedad y teatro en la España de Lope de Vega* (Barcelona: Bosch, 1978)

Drysdal, Denis L., ed & introd., *Fernando de Rojas's La Celestine*. In the French translation of 1578 by Jacques de Lavardin (London: Tamesis Books, 1974)

Fernández, Enrique, ed, *Pornoboscodidascalus Latinus (1624). Kaspar Barth's Neo-Latin Translation of 'Celestina'* (Chapel Hill: Department of Romance Languages, University of North Carolina, 2006)

Fitzmaurice-Kelly, James, ed and introd., James Mabbe, trans., *Celestina, or the Tragicke-Comedy of Calisto and Melibea. Englished from the Spanish of Fernando de Rojas by James Mabbe, anno. 1631* (London: David Nutt, 1894)

Fletcher, J. M., 'The Faculty of Arts', in *The History of the University of Oxford* (gen. ed, T. H. Aston), III, *The Collegiate University*, ed. by J. McConica (Oxford: Clarendon Press, 1986), pp. 157–98

Folena, Gianfranco. *Volgarizzare e tradurre* (Torino: Enaudi, 1991, first published in Trieste in 1973)

Fuchs, Barbara, 'Pirating Spain: Jonson's Commendatory Poetry and the Translation of Empire', *Modern Philology* 99 (2002), 341–56.

BIBLIOGRAPHY

García Santo-Tomás, Enrique, *Espacio urbano y creación literaria en el Madrid de Felipe IV* (Frankfurt & Madrid: Vervuet & Iberoamericana, 2004)

García Soriano, Justo, ed, *Diálogos de diferentes materias*. Colección de Escritores Castellanos Críticos, tomo 161 (Madrid: Imp. de G. Hernández y Galo Sáez, 1929)

García Valdecasas, José Guillermo, *La adulteración de 'La Celestina'* (Madrid: Castalia, 2000)

Gillespie, Stuart, *English Translation and Classical Reception: Towards a New Literary History* (Oxford: Wiley-Blackwell, 2011)

Gilman, Stephen, 'A generation of *conversos*', *Romance Philology*, 33 (1979), 87–101

Gómez Moreno, A. & M. P. A. M. Kerkhof, eds, Íñigo López de Mendoza, Márqués de Santillana, *Proverbios o Centiloquios*, en *Obras Completas* (Barcelona: Planeta, 1988)

González Echevarría, Roberto, *Celestina's Brood. Continuities of the Baroque in Spanish and Latin American Literature* (Durham and London: Duke University Press, 1993)

Goytisolo, Juan, 'Introduction' to Fernando de Rojas's *Celestina*, trans. by Peter Bush (Harmondsworth: Penguin, 2009), pp. vii-xvi

Hadfield, Andrew, *Shakespeare and Republicanism* (Cambridge, UK: Cambridge University Press, 2005)

Hamilton, Michelle M., 'Joseph ben Samuel Ṣarfati's 'Tratado de Melibea y Calisto': A Sephardic Jew's Reading of the *Celestina* in Light of the Medieval Judeo-Spanish Go-between Tradition', *Sefarad* 62 (2002), 329–47

Herriott, J. Homer, *Towards a Critical Edition of 'La Celestina'* (Madison, Wisconsin: University of Wisconsin Press, 1964)

Hotson, Leslie, *I, William Shakespeare Do Appoint Thomas Russell, Esquire. . . .* (London: Jonathan Cape, 1937).

—, 'The Library of Elizabeth's Embezzling Teller', *Studies in Bibliography* 2 (1949/1950), 49–61

Houck, Hellen Phips, 'Mabbe's Paganization of the *Celestina*' *PMLA* 54 (1939), 422–31

Hutson, Lorna, ed, Ben Jonson's *Discoveries*, in *The Cambridge Edition of the Works of Ben Jonson*, ed. by D. Bevington, M. Butler and I. Donaldson, VII, *1641. Bibliography* (Cambridge: Cambridge University Press, 2012), pp. 497–596

Iglesias, Yolanda, *Una nueva mirada a la parodia de la novela sentimental en 'La Celestina'* (Madrid & Frankfurt: Iberoamericana & Vervuert, 2009)

Infantes, Víctor, 'La prosa de ficción renacentista: Entre los géneros literarios y el género editorial', *Journal of Hispanic Philology* 13 (1989), 115–23

—, 'Los libros "traydos y viejos y algunos rotos" que tuvo el Bachiller Fernando de Rojas, nombrado autor de la obra llamada *Celestina*', *Bulletin Hispanique* 100 (1998), 7–51

Kish, Kathleen B., ed, *An Edition of the First Italian Translation of the 'Celestina'* (Chapel Hill: University of North Carolina Press, 1973)

Kish, Kathleen B. & Ursula Ritzenhoff, eds, *Die Celestina-Übersetzungen von Christof Wirsung. 'Ain Hipsche Tragedia' (Augsburg 1520). 'Ainn recht liepliches Buechlin (Augsburg 1534)* (Hildesheim, Zurich & New York: Georg Olms, 1984)

Ladero Quesada, Miguel Ángel, 'Aristócratas y marginales: aspectos de la sociedad castellana en La Celestina', *Espacio, Tiempo y Forma: Revista de la Facultad de Geografía e Historia*, 3 (1990), 95–120

Lida de Malkiel, María Rosa, *La originalidad artística de 'La Celestina'* (Buenos Aires: EUDEBA, 1962)

López Santos, Antonio & Rubén Tostado González, eds & trad., *Interludio de Calisto y Melibea* (Salamanca: Ediciones Universidad de Salamanca, 2001)

Lozano, Carmen, & Felipe González Vega, eds, Antonio de Nebrija. *Gramática sobre la lengua castellana. Paginae Nebrissenses* (Madrid: Real Academia Española 2011)

Maguire, Laurie, *Helen of Troy: From Homer to Hollywood* (London: Wiley-Blackwell, 2009)

Maldonado, Felipe C. R. & Manuel Camarero, eds, Sebastián de Covarrubias Orozco, *Tesoro de la lengua castellana o española*. [1611]. (Madrid: Castalia, 1995.)

Maravall, José Antonio, *El mundo social de La Celestina* (Madrid: Gredos, 1972)

Martín Abad, Julián, 'Noticia Bibliográfica', in Carmen Lozano & Felipe González Vega, eds, Antonio de Nebrija, *Gramática sobre la lengua castellana. Paginae Nebrissenses*. (Madrid: Real Academia Española 2011), pp. 453–470

Martínez Lacalle, Guadalupe, ed. and introd. James Mabbe, trans. [Fernando de Rojas's] *Celestine or the Tragick-Comedie of Calisto and Melibea* [the Alnwick manuscript] (London: Tamesis Books, 1972.)

McKeon, Michael. *The Origins of the English Novel. 1600 – 1740* (Baltimore & London: The Johns Hopkins University Press, 2002).

McLaren, A.N. *Political Culture in the Reign of Elizabeth I. Queen and Commonwealth 1558–1585* (Cambridge: Cambridge University Press, 1999)

McPheeters, D.W., 'Una traducción hebrea de *La Celestina* en el siglo XVI', in *Homenaje a Rodríguez-Moñino. Estudios de erudición que le ofrecen sus amigos o discípulos hispanistas norteamericanos* (Madrid: Castalia, 1966), I, pp. 399–411

Mencé-Caste, Corinne, 'Temporalité et éthique dans *La Celestine*'. *Celestinesca* 32 (2008), 209–229

Miguel, Emilio de, ed, Fernando de Rojas, *La Celestina: Tragicomedia de Calisto y Melibea* [Salamanca: Matías Gast a costa de Simón Borgoñón, 1570] (Madrid: Ediciones de la Fundación José Antonio de Castro, 2006)

Mondéjar Cumpián, José, *Castellano y Español. Dos nombres para una lengua, en su marco literario, ideológico y político.* (Granada: Universidad de Granada & Editorial Comares, 2002)

Olsen, Thomas G., ed, *The Commonplace Book of Sir John Strangways (1645–1666)* (Tempe, AZ: Arizona Center for Medieval and Renaissance Studies & Renaissance English Text Society, 2004)

Parrilla, Carmen, ed, Diego de San Pedro, *Cárcel de Amor*. Con la continuación de Nicolás Núñez. Estudio preliminar de Alan Deyermond (Barcelona: Crítica, 1995)

Parrilla, Carmen, ed, Juan de Flores, *Grimalte y Gradissa*. (Alcalá de Henares: Centro de Estudios Cervantinos, 2008)

Paterson, Alan, 'Translation in the formation of genre: Edmund Spenser and Gabriel Harvey testify', in *Remapping the Rise of the European Novel*, ed. Jenny Mander, *Studies on Voltaire and the Eighteenth Century* (Oxford: Voltaire Foundation, 2007), X, pp. 139–44

Pavel, Thomas, *Representar la existencia. El pensamiento de la novela* [*La pensée du roman*, 2003], trad. D. Roas Deus (Barcelona: Crítica, 2005)

Pérez Fernández, José María, 'Andrés Laguna: Translation and the Early Modern Idea of Europe', *Translation and Literature* 21 (2012), 299–318.

—, 'Translation, Diplomacy and Espionage: New Insights into James Mabbe's Career' (forthcoming in *Translation and Literature*)

Randall, Dale B. J., *The Golden Tapestry: A Critical Survey of Non-chivalric Fiction in English Translation* (Durham, NC: Duke University Press, 1963)

Ravasini, Ines, ed, Enea Silvio Piccolomini, *Estoria muy verdadera de dos amantes* (Roma: Bagatto Libri, 2003)

Rhodes, Neil, *Shakespeare and the Origins of English* (Oxford: Oxford University Press, 2004)

Rico, Francisco, *Nebrija frente a los bárbaros. El canon de gramáticos nefastos en las polémicas del humanismo.* (Salamanca: Universidad de Salamanca, 1978)

—, ed., *Lazarillo de Tormes* (Madrid: Real Academia Española, 2011)

Rodríguez, Juan Carlos, *La literatura del pobre* (Granada: Comares, 1994)

Rodríguez Peregrina, J .M., ed. & trad., Juan Luis Vives, *De ratione dicendi. Del arte de hablar* [1533] (Granada: Servicio de Publicaciones de la Universidad de Granada, 2000)

Rosenbach, Abraham S. Wolf, 'The Influence of *The Celestina* in the Early English Drama', *Jahrbuch der Deutschen Shakespeare-Gesellschaft* (1903), pp. 43–61

Round, Nicholas G., 'What made Mabbe so good?' *Bulletin of Hispanic Studies* 78 (2001), 145–66

Ruiz Arzallus, Íñigo. 'El mundo intelectual del 'antiguo autor': las *Auctoritates Aristotelis* en la *Celestina* primitiva', *Boletín de la Real Academia Española* 76 (1996), 265–84

Russell, P. E., 'A Stuart Hispanist: James Mabbe', *Bulletin of Hispanic Studies* 30 (1953), 75–84

Samson, Alexander, '1623 and the politics of translation'. In *The Spanish Match: Prince Charles's Journey to Madrid*, ed. by Alexander Samson (London: Ashgate, 2006), pp. 91–106

—, 'A Fine Romance': Anglo-Spanish Relations in the Sixteenth Century', *Journal of Medieval and Early Modern Studies* 39 (2009), 65–94

Scragg, Leah, 'Edward Blount and the History of Lylian Criticism', *Review of English Studies* 46 (1995)

—, 'Edward Blount and the Prefatory Material to the First Folio of Shakespeare', *Bulletin of the John Rylands University Library of Manchester* 79 (1997), 117–26

Secord, A.W., 'I. M. of the first folio Shakespeare and other Mabbe problems', *Journal of English and Germanic Philology*, 47 (1948), 374–81

Severin, Dorothy Sherman, *Tragicomedy and Novelistic Discourse in 'Celestina'* (Cambridge, UK: Cambridge University Press, 1989)

—, *Female Empowerment and Witchcraft in 'Celestina'* (London: Department of Hispanic Studies, Queen Mary and Westfield College, 1995)

—, 'Witchcraft in *Celestina*: A Bibliographical Update since 1995' *La Corónica* 36 (2007), 237–346

Smollett, Tobias, trans. Miguel de Cervantes. *The History and Adventures of the Renowned Don Quixote* [1755] Introd. by Carlos Fuentes, notes by Stephanie Kirk (New York: The Modern Library, 2004)

Snow, Joseph T, 'Hacia una historia de la recepción de *La Celestina*: 1499–1822', *Celestinesca* 21 (1997), 115–72

—, 'Historia de la recepción de *La Celestina*: 1499–1822, II.' *Celestinesca* 25 (2001), 199–282

—, 'Historia de la recepción de *La Celestina*: 1499–1822', III.' *Celestinesca* 26 (2002), 53–121

—, '*Celestina* en la corte de los Reyes Católicos', in *La literatura en la época de los Reyes Católicos*, eds Nicasio Salvador Miguel & Cristina Moya García (Madrid & Frankfurt: Iberoamericana, Vervuert, & Universidad de Navarra, 2008), pp. 293–303

Spingarn, J. E., ed, *Critical Essays of the Seventeenth Century, 1605–1650*, I (Oxford: Clarendon Press, 1908; Bloomington, IN: Indiana University Press, 1957)

Stern, Virginia F., *Gabriel Harvey: A Study of his Life, Marginalia, and Library* (Oxford: Oxford University Press, 1979)

Stoye, John W., *English Travellers Abroad, 1604–1667* (London: Jonathan Cape, 1952; rev. edn New Haven & London: Yale University Press, 1989)

Strype, John, *The Life of the Learned Sir Thomas Smith* (Oxford: Clarendon Press, 1820)

Taylor, Andrew W., 'Humanist Philology and Reformation Controversy: John Christopherson's Latin Translations of Philo Judaeus and Eusebius of Caesarea', in *Tudor Translation*, ed. by F. Schurink (London: Palgrave, 2011), pp. 79–100

Taylor, Gary, 'The cultural politics of Maybe', in *Lancastrian Shakespeare: Theatre and Religion*, eds R. Dutton, A. G. Findlay & R. Wilson (Manchester, UK: Manchester University Press, 2003), pp. 242–58

Trinkaus, Charles, *The Poet as Philosopher. Petrarch and the Formation of Renaissance Consciousness* (New Haven and London: Yale University Press, 1979)

Ungerer, Gustav, *Anglo-Spanish Relations in Tudor Literature* (Bern: Francke Verlag, 1956)

—, 'English Criminal Biography and Guzmán de Alfarache's Fall from Rogue to Highwayman, Pander and Astrologer', *Bulletin of Hispanic Studies* 76 (1999), 189–97

Whinnom, Keith, 'The problem of the 'best-seller' in Spanish Golden-Age Literature', *Bulletin of Hispanic Studies* 57 (1980), 189–198

Whitlock, K., ed, *The Life of Lazarillo de Tormes*, trans. by David Rowland (Warminster: Aris & Phillips, Ltd., 2003)

William, Gordon, *A Dictionary of Sexual Language and Imagery in Shakespearean and Stuart Literature*, 3 vols (London: The Athlone Press, 1994)

Yamamoto-Wilson, John R., 'James Mabbe's Achievement in his Translation of *Guzmán de Alfarache*', *Translation and Literature*, 8 (1999), 137–56

—, 'Mabbe's Maybes: A Stuart Hispanist in Context', *Translation and Literature*, 21 (2012), 319–42

ONLINE SOURCES

Cid, Jesús Antonio, ed. & introd. *Diálogos*. John Minsheu's [Online edition of the Spanish dialogues and a facsimile reproduction of the original edition]. *Pleasant Dialogues in* Spanish. <http://cvc.cervantes.es/literatura/clasicos/dialogos_minsheu/default.htm>

Mabbe, James, trans., *The Spanish Bawd* (London: John Beale, 1631). Literature Online (Chadwyck-Healey, 1997) has published an online transcription of the 1631 edition at <http://lion.chadwyck.co.uk/toc.do?offset=155063712&divLevel=3&action=expand&queryId=&area=Drama&mapping=tocMarc#scroll>

Pérez Fernández, José María, 'Introduction' to John Rastell, *A New Co[m]modye in Englysh in Maner of an Enterlude [. . .] wherein is Shewd [and] Dyscrybyd as Well the Bewte [and] Good Propertes of Women, as Theyr Vycys [and] Euyll Co[n]dicio[n]s* ([London] : Iohes Rastell me imprimi fecit, [c.1525]; *STC* 20721, Tract Supplement E4:2) [a translation of Fernando de Rojas's *La Celestina, Comedia o Tragecomedia de Calisto y Melibea*]. In the *EEBO* Introduction Series. General Editor Dr. Edward Wilson-Lee. <http://eebo.chadwyck.com/intros/htxview?template=basic.htx&content=calisto.htm>

—, 'Introduction' to *The Spanish Bawd, represented in Celestina: or, The tragicke-comedy of Calisto and Melibea* (London: printed by J. B. And are to be sold by Ralph Mab[be], 1631;

STC 4911 and 4911.2). In the *EEBO* Introduction Series, ed. by Edward Wilson-Lee. <http://eebo.chadwyck.com/intros/htxview?template=basic.htx&content=spanish_bawde.htm>

Vaccaro, Elizabetta, *Le traduzioni inglesi de 'La Celestina' ad opera di Mabbe. Accolta nell'edizione critica de La Celestina a cura di Patrizia Botta.* <http://rmcisadu.let.uniroma1.it/celestina/traduzioni_ing/mabbe/>

INDEX

A briefe introduction to syntax (see Hawkins, John)
Adagia (see Erasmus, Desiderius)
Aeneid (see Virgil)
Alemán, Mateo 5–6, 44, 8
  Guzmán de Alfarache 7, 8, 32, 33, 44, 288—n.448
Allot, Robert 1—n.3, 47, 68
Alnwick Manuscript 8—n.15, 13, 14, 15, 16, 17, 26—n.42, 34, 42, 54, 151—n.284, 155—n.291, 157—n.297, 213—n.375/378, 214—n.379, 228—n.402, 260—n.448, 343—n.543, 344, 346—n.549, 347—n.551
Antwerp 7, 15, 52, 63
Aristotle 33, 41, 58, 59, 60, 61, 77, 91, 92, 95—n.148, 118—n.213, 156—n.294, 160, n.305
  Auctoritates Aristotelis 41, 93—n.144, 95—n.148, 96—n.149/50, 115—n.209, 117—n.212, 119—n.215, 121—n.220, 127—n.227
  Ethics 41, 118—n.213
Ars Poetica (See Horace)
Arte nuevo de hacer comedias (See Vega y Carpio, Lope de)
Aspley, William 14, 15

Beale, John 47
Bibliotheca Hispanica (see Percyvall, Richard)
Bieito, Calixto 2, 3, 4
Blount, Edward 8, 9, 12, 32, 61
Boccaccio, Giovanni 23, 27—n.43, 41, 56, 91—n.140, 249—n.438

Fiammetta 23, 41, 42, 53, 56, 249—n.438
Borgoñón, Simón 3, 44, 45, 50
Boscán, Juan 44
Botero, Giovanni 13, 244—n.433
  Observations upon the liues of Alexander, Caesar, Scipio, Newly Englished 13
Brinsley, John/*Ludus Literarius* 10
Bucolicum Carmen: (see Petrarch, Francesco)
Bush, Peter 2, 29
Butler, Charles (and all texts) 9–10 passim

Calisto and Melebea, Interlude of 29, 45, 46, 47 (see also Rastell, John)
Cárcel de Amor 23, 24, 27—n.43 (See San Pedro, Diego de)
Cervantes, Miguel de 3, 6, 7, 27, 61
  Don Quijote 2, 3, 4, 8, 9, 28—n.43, 31, 32, 61
  Novelas ejemplares 7, 8
Céspedes y Meneses, Gonzalo de/*Poema tragico* 12
Christian Policie: or, The Christian Commonwealth 8
Cicero 24—n.41, 30, 37, 70, 118, 225, 304, 326
The Civile Conversation of M. Stephen Guazzo: (See Yong, Bartholomew, and Pettie, George)
Clifford, John 2, 29
Correas, Gonzalo/*Vocabulario de refranes y frases*

INDEX

proverbiales 111—n. 200, 135—n. 241, 140—n. 259, 286—n. 480 374, 385
Corro, Antonio del 54, 57
  Reglas Gramaticales 57
  Spanish Grammar 54, 57, 62, 63, 64 (See also Thorius, John)
Covarrubias, Sebastian de 69—n.103, 122—n.204
  Tesoro de la Lengua Castellana o Espanola 69—n.103, 126—n.227

De Institutione foeminae christianae: (See Vives, Juan Luis)
De Ratione dicendi (See Vives, Juan Luis)
De recta & emendata Linguae anglicae scriptione, dialogus: (See Smith, Sir Thomas)
De remediis: (See Petrarch, Francesco)
De republica anglorum (see Smith, Sir Thomas)
De sermone (see Pontano, Giovanni)
Dekker, Thomas 54
Devout Contemplations (see *Discurso para Todos los Evangelios de la Cuaresma*)
Diana (see Montemayor, Jorge de and Yong, Bartholomew)
Diaz de Toledo, Pedro, *Proverbios de Seneca* 41
Digby, Sir John 11,12, 13, 65
Digby, Sir Kenelm 64
Digges, Leonard 11, 12
  Gerardo the Vnfortunate Spaniard, Or a Patterne for lasciuious louers (see Céspedes y Meneses, Gonzalo de, *Poema tragico del español Gerardo, y desengaño del amor lascivo*)
Discourse of the commonweal: (see Smith, Sir Thomas)
Discoveries: (see Jonson, Ben)
Discurso para Todos los Evangelios de la Cuaresma (See Fonseca, Cristobal de)
Doctor Faustus (see Marlowe, Christopher)
Don Quijote (see Cervantes, Miguel de)
Doyley, Thomas 64, 65

Elegy of the Lady Fiammetta, The: (see Yong, Bartholomew)
English Grammar, or, The institution of letters, syllables, and words in the English tongue, whereunto is annexed an index of words like and unlike: (See Butler, Charles)
Epicurus 19
Epistles: (see Piccolomini, Aeneas Sylvius)
Epistola de Graecis litteris et Homeri lectione et imitatione: (See Humphrey, Laurence)
Erasmus 22, 30, 47, 59
  Adagia 47, 59
Estoria de dos amantes: (see Piccolomini, Aeneas Sylvius, *Historia de duobus amantibus*)
Eunuchus: (see Terence)
Exemplarie Novels; in Sixe Books (see Cervantes, Miguel de, *Novelas ejemplares*)
Expositione terminorum legum Anglorum (see Rastell, John)

Familiares (see Petrarch, Francesco)

Fiammetta (see Boccaccio, Giovanni)
Fitzherbert, Anthony/*La grande abbregement de la ley* 48
Flores, Juan de 23, 63
  Grimalte y Gradissa 23
Florio, John 8, 9, 51—n.77, 57, 105—n. 171, 188—n. 340, 192—n. 347.
  Queen Anna's New World of Words 8, 51—n. 77, 57, 192—n.347
Fonseca, Cristobal de/*Discurso para Todos los Evangelios de la Cuaresma* 8, 16—n. 33

Gerardo the Vnfortunate Spaniard, Or a Patterne for lasciuious louers (see Digges, Leonard)
Gosson, Stephen 50
Goytisolo, Juan 2, 29
Gramatica de la lengua castellana (see Nebrija, Elio Antonio de)
Greene, Robert 54, 74—n.115
Gresham, Sir Thomas 48, 53
Grimalte y Gradissa (see Flores, Juan de)
Guzman de Alfarache (see Aleman, Mateo)

Harvey, Gabriel 47, 54, 57, 78—n.120
Hawkins, John/*A briefe introduction to syntax* 64
Heraclitus 18, 19, 75
Historia de duobus amantibus: (See Piccolomini, Aeneas Sylvius)
Hollyband, Claudius 62
The Pretie and wittie Historie of Arnalt & Lucenda 63 (see also San Pedro, Diego de)

The Italian Schoole-Maister 63
Horace/*Ars Poetica* 38–39 passim
Humphrey, Laurence/*Epistola de Graecis*/*Interpretatio Linguarum* 11, 12

Index (to the *Opera Latina*): (see Petrarch, Francesco)

Jonson, Ben 9, 24, 30, 31—n.49, 38, 39, 47—n.69, 64, 75—n.116
  Discoveries 24—n.41, 38
  The Staple of News 47—n.69

Laberinto de Fortuna: (see Mena, Juan de)
La grande abbregement de la ley: (see Fitzherbert, Anthony)
Lavardin, Jacques de 2
Lazarillo de Tormes, 28—n. 44, 33—n.51, 48—n.72, 51, 52, 53, 54, 63
Lucretius 19
Ludus Literaruius: or, The Grammar Schole: (see Brinsley, John)

Machiavelli, Niccolo 50
Magdalen College, Oxford 9, 10—n.19, 11,12, 48, 65
Marlowe, Christopher/*Dr Faustus* 25
Mena, Juan de 21, 59, 304—n.497
  Laberinto de Fortuna 21, 304—n.497
Meres, Frances/*Palladis Tamia* 50
Minsheu, John 62, 63
  Pleasant and Delightful Dialogues in Spanish 62

INDEX

(see also Percyvall, Richard)
Montaigne, Michel de/*Essais* 9, 105
Montemayor, Jorge de 53, 63
  Diana 51, 52, 53, 63
More, Thomas 29—n.47, 46
Munday, Anthony 49, 50, 54
  Second and Third blast 49
Mythomystes: (see Reynolds, Henry)

Nashe, Thomas/*The Unfortunate Traveller* 54
Nebrija, Elio Antonio de 37, 38, 39—n.61, 45, 49, 56, 58, 59, 64, 65,
  Gramatica de la lengua castellana 37—n.56
  Introductiones Latinae 37, 64
  Vocabulario Espanol-Latino 56
Novelas ejemplares: (see Cervantes, Miguel de)
Núñez, Hernán 59, 111—n.200
  Refranes o proverbios en romance 59

Obseruations vpon the liues of Alexander, Caesar, Scipio, Newly Englished: (see Botero, Giovanni)
Opera Latina: (see Petrarch, Francesco)
Oratoriae libri duo: (see Butler, Charles)
Ordóñez, Alfonso 1, 2, 3, 17
Ovid 23, 27, 31, 225, 226

Percyvall, Richard 62, 64
  A Spanish grammar 62, 63, 64
  Bibliotheca Hispanica 64
Petrarch, Francesco 19, 30, 33, 46, *48*, 58, 304—n. 497
  Bucolicum Carmen 135—n.243, 175—n.323, 197—n.352, 222—n.390
  De Remediis 75—n.116/117, 77—n.118, 129—n.232, 156—n.294, 197—n.352, 198—n.355, 286—n.480, 317—n.506, 352—n.554, 360—n.560
  Familiaries 156—n.294, 303—n.496, 317—n.505, 359—n.559, 360—n.561
  Index (to the *Opera Latina*) 165—n.307, 166—n.308, 172—n.316, 174—n.322, 189—n.343, 197—n.352, 198—n.355, 221—n.388, 225—n.396/397, 230—n.408, 238—n.420, 250—n.439, 286—n.480
  Opera Latina 75—n.116, 96—n.150, 165—n.307, 174—n.322, 221—n.388, 358—n.558
  Rerum Memorandum Libri 186—n.336, 319—n.510
  Seniles 358—n. 558
Pettie, George/*Civile Conversation of M. Stephen Guazzo* 53
Philo Judaeus/*De Nobilitate* 11—n. 21
Picaresque 2, 7, 8—n.13, 25, 27, 28—n.44, 32, 33—n.51, 35—n.54, 41, 52, 54
Piccolomini, Aeneas Sylvius 24—n.41, 30, 41, 58
  Epistles 39, 47
  Historia de duobus amantibus 23, 39, 40—n.62, 41, 56, 204—n.366
Plautus 326—n.516
Playes Confuted in fiue Actions: (see Gosson, Stephen)

399

Pleasant and Delightful Dialogues in Spanish: (see Minsheu, John)
Poema tragico del español Gerardo: (see Cespedes y Meneses, Gonzalo de)
Ponsonby, William 9
Pontano, Giovanni 32, 38
   De Sermone 30, 31, 57
Pretie and wittie Historie of Arnalt & Lucenda 63 (see also San Pedro, Diego de)
Proaza, Alonso de 17, 45
Propylaion, or An entrance to the Spanish: (see Sanford, John)
Proverbios de Seneca: (see Diaz de Toledo, Pedro)
Proverbios o Centiloquios: (see Santillana, Marques de)

Queen Anna's New World of Words (See Florio, John)
Quintilian 24—n.41, 30, 37, 38, 39—n.61, 46, 49

Ramus, Petrus 10, 47
Rastell, John 29—n.47, 46, 47, 48
   Calisto and Melebea, Interlude of 29, 46, 47
   Expositione terminorum legum Anglorum 48
Refranes o proverbios en romance que nueuamenta colligió y glossó el Comendador Hernán Núñez: (see Núñez, Hernán)
Reglas gramaticales para aprender la lengua española y francesa: (see Corro, Antonio del)
República y policía cristiana para reyes y príncipes: (see Santa María, Juan de)

Rerum memorandum libri: (see Petrarch, Francesco)
Reynolds, Henry 51, 52
   Mythomystes 51
Rhetoricae libri duo (see Butler, Charles)
Richardson, Sir Thomas 55, 69
Rimas: (see Vega y Carpio, Lope de)
Rogue, The: (see *Guzmán de Alfarache*)
Rowland, David 48—n.72, 53

Sanford, John/*Propylaion, or An entrance to the Spanish tongue* 12
San Pedro, Diego de 23, 27—n.43, 62
   Cárcel de Amor 23, 24, 27—n.43.
   Tratado de Amores de Arnalte y Lucenda 62
Santa María, Juan de/*República y policía Cristiana para reyes y príncipes* 8
Santillana, Marqués de (Iñigo López de Mendoza) 59, 135—n. 241, 140—n.259
Second and Third Blast of Retrait from Plaies and Theaters (see Munday, Anthony)
Seneca, Lucius Annaeus 33, 41, 51, 58, 91, 92, 117, 118—n. 213, 198—n. 355 (see also Díaz de toledo, Pedro, *Proverbios de Seneca*)
   Proverbios o Centiloquios 135—n.241
Shakespeare, William 5, 8–9
   Shakespeare's First Folio 9—n.16
   Winter's Tale 106—n.181

INDEX

Shelton, Thomas 9, 32—n.50, 52, 61—n.94
Smith, Sir Thomas 11, 47, 48
   De Recta & emendata linguae anglicae scriptione, dialogues 48
   De Republica Anglorum 11
   Discourse of the commonweal 48
   Spanish Grammar: (see Corro, Antonio del)
   Staple of News, The: (see Jonson, Ben)
Strangways, Sir John 11, 13, 14

Talaeus, Audomarus 10
Terence 37, 134—n. 239, 326—n. 516
   Eunuchus 219—n.386
Tesoro de la Lengua Castellana o Española: (see Covarrubias Orozco, Sebastián de)
Thorius, John 54, 57
Times Lamentation: (see Topsell, Edward)
Topsell, Edward/*Times Lamentation: or An exposition to the prophet Joel, in sundry Sermons or Mediations* 50
Tratado de Amores de Arnalte y Lucenda (see San Pedro, Diego de)
Trenchard, Sir George 14

Unfortunate Traveller, The: (see Nashe, Thomas)

Valla, Lorenzo 37, 39—n.61, 56, 58
Vega, Garcilaso de la 44
Vega y Carpio, Lope de 11, 12, 50
   Arte nuevo de hacer comedias 12, 50
   Rimas 11, 12—n.22
Virgil 40, 92, 204
   Aeneid 186—n.336
Vives, Juan Luis 3, 22, 24—n.41, 29—n.47, 30, 38, 46, 47
   De institutione foeminae christianae 46
   De Ratione dicendi 31—n.49, 38—n.58
Vocabulario de refranes o frases proverbiales (see Correas, Gonzalo)
Vocabulario Español-Latino (see Nebrija, Elio Antonio de)

Winter's Tale (see Shakespeare, William)
Wirsung, Christopher von 6
Witchcraft 28, 41, 120—n.217, 203
Wolfe, John 52, 57, 64

Yong, Bartholomew 52, 53, 56, 249—n.438
   Diana 52, 53
   The Civile Conversation of M. Stephen Guazzo 53
   The Elegy of the Lady Fiammetta 53

www.ingramcontent.com/pod-product-compliance
Lightning Source LLC
Chambersburg PA
CBHW071437300426
44114CB00013B/1470